Lecture Notes
in Business Information Processing 48

Series Editors

Wil van der Aalst
  Eindhoven Technical University, The Netherlands
John Mylopoulos
  University of Trento, Italy
Michael Rosemann
  Queensland University of Technology, Brisbane, Qld, Australia
Michael J. Shaw
  University of Illinois, Urbana-Champaign, IL, USA
Clemens Szyperski
  Microsoft Research, Redmond, WA, USA

Alberto Sillitti   Angela Martin
Xiaofeng Wang   Elizabeth Whitworth (Eds.)

Agile Processes in Software Engineering and Extreme Programming

11th International Conference, XP 2010
Trondheim, Norway, June 1-4, 2010
Proceedings

 Springer

Volume Editors

Alberto Sillitti
Free University of Bolzano-Bozen
Center for Applied Software Engineering
39100 Bozen-Bolzano, Italy
E-mail: alberto.sillitti@unibz.it

Angela Martin
University of Waikato
Hamilton, 3216, New Zealand
E-mail: angela@cs.waikato.ac.nz

Xiaofeng Wang
University of Limerick
Lero - the Irish Software Engineering Research Centre
Limerick, Ireland
E-mail: xiaofeng.wang@lero.ie

Elizabeth Whitworth
Nokia gate5 GmbH
10115 Berlin, Germany
E-mail: elizabeth.whitworth@nokia.com

Library of Congress Control Number: 2010926588

ACM Computing Classification (1998): D.2, K.6

ISSN   1865-1348
ISBN-10   3-642-13053-4 Springer Berlin Heidelberg New York
ISBN-13   978-3-642-13053-3 Springer Berlin Heidelberg New York

springer.com

© Springer-Verlag Berlin Heidelberg 2010
Printed in Germany

Typesetting: Camera-ready by author, data conversion by Scientific Publishing Services, Chennai, India
Printed on acid-free paper   06/3180   5 4 3 2 1 0

Preface

Interest in agile development continues to grow: the number of practitioners adopting such methodologies is increasing as well as the number of researchers investigating the effectiveness of the different practices and proposing improvements. The XP conference series has actively participated in these processes and supported the evolution of Agile, promoting the conference as a place where practitioners and researchers meet to exchange ideas, experiences, and build connections.

XP 2010 continued in the tradition of this conference series and provided an interesting and varied program. As usual, we had a number of different kinds of activities in the conference program including: research papers, experience reports, tutorials, workshops, panels, lightning talks, and posters. These proceedings contain full research papers, short research papers, and experience reports. Moreover, we have also included in these proceedings the abstracts of the posters, the position papers of the PhD symposium, and the abstract of the panel.

This year we had two different program committees for evaluating research papers and experience reports. Each committee included experts in the specific area. This approach allowed us to better evaluate the quality of the papers and provide better suggestions to the authors to improve the quality of their contributions.

All of the submitted research papers went through a rigorous peer-review process using the mechanisms of double-blind reviewing to improve the overall quality of the reviews. Each paper was reviewed by at least three members of the program committee. Of the 39 papers submitted, only 11 were accepted as full papers (28%). All of the experience report papers also went through a rigorous selection process. A committee of experts evaluated each submission looking for new experiences that would be both interesting and beneficial to have published and accessible to the agile community. We received 50 submissions; only 15 papers were accepted (30%). Each of the accepted authors received the guidance of an experienced agile practitioner and author while writing their final paper.

We hope that the participants found XP 2010 useful for their professional and academic activities, and that they enjoyed the conference.

Finally, we would like to thank all the people who have contributed to XP 2010 including: the authors, the sponsors, the reviewers, the volunteers, and the chairs.

March 2010

Alberto Sillitti
Angela Martin
Xiaofeng Wang
Elizabeth Whitworth

Organization

Conference Chairs

General Chair

Hakan Erdogmus   Kalemun Research, Canada

Research Program Chairs

Kieran Conboy   University of Galway, Ireland
Tore Dybå   SINTEF, Norway

Industry Program Chairs

Rachel Davies   Agile Experience Ltd, UK
Lars Arne Skår   Miles, Norway

Organizing Chairs

Torgeir Dingsøyr   SINTEF, Norway
Nils Brede Moe   SINTEF, Norway

Research Paper Chairs

Alberto Sillitti   Free University of Bolzano, Italy
Xiaofeng Wang   LERO, Ireland

Short Paper Chair

Yael Dubinsky   IBM Haifa Research Lab, Israel

Poster Chairs

Minna Pikkarainen   VTT, Finland
Outi Salo   Nokia, Finland

Textbook on Agile Software Development Chairs

Torgeir Dingsøyr   SINTEF, Norway
Tore Dybå   SINTEF, Norway
Nils Brede Moe   SINTEF, Norway

PhD Symposium Chairs

Martin Høst   Lund University, Sweden
Per Runeson   Lund University, Sweden

Experience Report Chairs

Angela Martin   University of Waikato, New Zealand
Elizabeth Whitworth   Transporeon, Germany

Lightning Talk Chairs

Ola Ellnestam   Agical, Sweden
Aslak Hellesøy   Bekk, Norway

Workshop/Tutorial Chairs

Jessica Hildrum   Objectware, Norway
Lasse Koskela   Reaktor Innovation, Finland
Diana Larsen   FutureWorks Consulting, USA
Peter Axel Nielsen   Ålborg University, Denmark
Pär Ågerfalk   Uppsala University, Sweden

Open Space Chairs

Diana Larsen   FutureWorks Consulting, USA
Charlie Poole   Poole Consulting, USA

Electronic Art Chair

Letizia Jaccheri   Norwegian University of Science and
                       Technology, Norway

Sponsorship Chair

Jan-Erik Sandberg   DNV Software, Norway

Publicity Chairs

Steven Fraser   Cisco Research Center, USA
Anders Haugeto   Iterate, Norway

Official Photographer

Tom Poppendieck   Poppendieck LLC, USA

International Student Volunteer Chairs

Johanna Hunt   University of Sussex, UK
Mats Angermo Ringstad   NTNU, Norway

Research Program Committee

Chairs: Alberto Sillitti and Xiaofeng Wang

Pekka Abrahamsson   Karlheinz Kautz   Bala Ramesh
Par Agerfalk   Frank Keenan   Ramya Ravichandar
Nour Ali   Mikko Korkala   Hugh Robinson
Muhammad Ali Babar   Pasi Kuvaja   Barbara Russo
Robert Biddle   Kalle Lyytinenl   Helen Sharp
Stefan Biffl   José Carlos Maldonado   Carlos Solis
Ruth Breu   Michele Marchesi   Giancarlo Succi
David Bustard   Orla McHugh   Marco Torchiano
Gerardo Canfora   TheoDirk Meijler   Stefan VanBaelen
Ivica Crnkovic   Grigori Melnik   Aaron Visaggio
Massimiliano Di Penta Sandro Morasca   Barbara Weber
Steven Fraser   John Noll   Werner Wild
Alfredo Goldman   Witold Pedrycz   Claes Wohlin
Marjan Heričko   Adam Porter
Mike Holcombe   Rafael Prikladnicki

Industry Experience Reports Program Committee

Chairs: Angela Martin and Elizabeth Whitworth

Laurent Bossavit   Patrick Kua
Jutta Eckstein   Artem Marchenko
Michael Feathers

Table of Contents

Research Papers

Short Research Papers

Experience Reports

Posters

Ph.D. Symposium

Panel

Extending Refactoring Guidelines to Perform Client and Test Code Adaptation

Wafa Basit, Fakhar Lodhi, and Usman Bhatti

National University of Computer and Emerging Sciences, Lahore, Pakistan
{wafa.basit,fakhar.lodhi,usman.bhatti}@nu.edu.pk

Abstract. Refactoring is a disciplined process of applying structural transformations in the code such that the program is improved in terms of quality and its external behavior is preserved. Refactoring includes evaluation of its preconditions, execution of its mechanics and corrective actions required to retain the behavior of the program. These transformations affect various locations throughout a program which includes its clients and unit tests. Due to the complex dependencies involved within the program, preservation of program behavior often becomes nontrivial. The guidelines on refactoring by Fowler lack precision and leave opportunities for developers to err. In this paper, we analyze and present an exhaustive categorization of refactoring guidelines based on their impact on production and test code together. In addition, we present extended refactoring guidelines that adapt the clients and unit tests to keep it syntactically and semantically aligned with the refactored code.

Keywords: Refactoring guidelines, unit testing, production code, test code, adaptation.

1 Introduction

Refactorings are equivalence transformations that do not change the external behavior of the software system yet improve the internal structure of the code [1, 7]. Refactoring is a very strict and disciplined approach for code restructuring. Before the code transformation takes place, an early check is performed to evaluate certain prerequisites for the refactoring. If the required conditions are fulfilled refactoring is done, not otherwise. Next, the Refactoring mechanics are executed which include guidelines on restructuring and corrective transformations required to preserve the externally observable behavior of the program.

According to Opdyke [19] syntactic and semantic properties of programs can be easily violated if explicit checks are not evaluated before a program is refactored. Behavior preservation after refactoring is argued in terms of a set of properties of the program. These characteristics are related to inheritance, scoping, type compatibility and semantic equivalence. These properties ensure that the program before and after a refactoring must produce semantically equivalent references and operations. As presented by Opdyke in his thesis, the refactoring process can be labeled as complete if it checks its prerequisites and provide arguments that it is behavior preserving.

A. Sillitti et al. (Eds.): XP 2010, LNBIP 48, pp. 1–13, 2010.
© Springer-Verlag Berlin Heidelberg 2010

Refactoring involves restructuring the code segment that needs to be cleaned up. As a consequence, to preserve the program behavior, the client classes that use the functionality provided by the refactored code segment may also need to be updated. Fowler [1] provides guidelines for doing refactoring in a controlled and efficient manner. Unfortunately, we observe that, in many cases the mechanics given for refactoring are not precise and lack a consistent level of detail. In addition, in many cases, they are mute with reference to the changes required in the client code. Therefore, there is a need to extend these guidelines to minimize chances of breaking the code and fulfilling the condition for preserving the behavior of the entire program including the clients.

Proving that a refactoring is behavior preserving is non trivial and therefore reliance on test suite executions is generally considered the best choice as formal approaches are hard to employ. Therefore, unit tests are critical to the refactoring process because programmers rely on unit testing to determine whether a refactoring was applied correctly and the behavior of the production code is kept unchanged [1,7,10].

By production code we mean classes offering functionality in the system and their associated client classes. Test code in this context implies unit tests maintained by the developer as independent classes for testing.

Unit test cases can also be considered clients of the associated class and hence may also need to be updated as a result of refactoring. We observe that unit tests, being tightly coupled to the modules under test, may in certain cases require different transformational mechanics from that of ordinary clients. For example, in the case of *Move Method* refactoring, when a method is physically moved from the source class to the target class, the client classes need to invoke the method of the target class instead of the source class using the reference of the target class instead that of the source class. However, in the case of unit test, the code for testing that method itself has to be physically moved to the target's test class along with the method it is testing (See Section 5 for details). But the existing literature on refactoring does not differentiate between the unit test and ordinary clients (from now on simply referred to as clients).

Marick [15] is of the view that cost and effort involved in adapting unit tests to be consistent with the refactored code is huge. Particularly, when the tested scenarios are more complicated the adaptation gets even more complex and becomes a waste of time. Therefore new test cases should be developed. This approach sounds feasible when the adaptation is taking more time than the actual modifications to the system. The dual role of the developer (software and unit test development) is already an overhead; dealing with the adaptation and its effects makes it even worst. Even the utmost proponents of the test-driven development consider creation and maintenance of the unit tests a necessary evil [8]. However, unit tests represent a significant software effort and investment. Therefore, throwing them for the reason of inconsistency may sound imprudent. The guidelines provided by Fowler are once again mute as far as modifications to unit tests are required and are not sufficient to address the issues mentioned above. Therefore, there is need to devise patterns or guidelines to help the developer to modify the unit tests.

In short, refactoring guidelines as documented in [1] are not written in a consistent and precise manner and hence are difficult to use. In particular, many of these guidelines lack basic content required to adapt the client and test code accordingly.

Therefore, there is a need to augment these guidelines such that each refactoring is performed only if the target code and its clients qualify the conditions posed by it such that behavior is preserved.

This paper is organized as: Section 2 reports current literature on refactoring with respect to behavior preservation and unit testing. Later, in section 3 the characteristics of a unit test have been elaborated that differentiate it from an ordinary client. Next, we analyze and present an exhaustive categorization of existing refactoring guidelines [1] based on their impact on the program including its clients. In Section 5, we provide extended refactoring guidelines for one of the commonly used refactorings that adapt the client and test code to keep it syntactically and semantically aligned with refactored production code. In the end we draw our conclusions.

2 Related Work

2.1 Refactoring and Program Behavior Preservation

Transforming programs is easy. Preserving behavior is hard [20].

While refactoring a program, behavior preservation is always a major concern. Various researchers have extended the state of the art by providing studies that formally evaluate and analyze this phenomenon. Opdyke [19] broke the new grounds in this area, he in his PhD thesis presented twenty-three primitive refactorings and proved that if these refactorings fulfill certain preconditions, the given transformation preserves program behavior. Using the behavior preserving, primitive refactorings he built three composite refactorings. Since each primitive refactoring was behavior preserving, the composition necessarily preserved behavior.

Roberts in his dissertation [20] augmented the definition of the refactoring presented by Opdyke [19] by adding postcondition assertions. Based on the fact that Opdyke's primitive refactorings are too small to be performed in isolation, he claims that refactorings are mostly applied in sequences and their end result set up preconditions for later refactorings. This observation led to a new definition of refactoring that required refactorings to fulfill not only certain preconditions, but some postconditions as well. These postconditions appear because even if a refactoring qualifies its preconditions it may invalidate the program behavior on the way to restructuring. Therefore, he proved that in order to ensure the legality of a particular refactoring, it must meet its behavior preserving criteria which include both pre and post conditions.

Instead of taking a formal approach, Fowler [1] gave an extensive catalogue of refactoring guidelines in natural language. Because of its non-formal presentation, it has been widely adopted and used. Fowler's [1] catalogue has played a major role in bringing refactoring to the main stream development activity. Considering its wide range we only include Fowler's catalogue in our analysis. Nonetheless, our analysis shows that many of these guidelines lack basic content required for behavior preservation of a program as mentioned by the early pioneers of software refactoring. In such cases, these guidelines revolve around the piece of code that is refactored, but do not take care of effected elements outside this boundary. For example, Move Field refactoring can affect the source, target, clients and Unit test classes, but the existing guidelines do not provide details for the adaptation of all these artifacts.

2.2 Refactoring and Unit Tests Adaptation

As the refactorings change the internal structure of a program, they can also invalidate the associated unit test suites. Therefore, refactoring a program requires that the associated test suites should be adapted or extended to test the refactored code. The impact of refactoring on the test code has been reported by quite a number of researchers [2-6, 9, 17, 18].

Pipka in his work [17] focuses on the test-first practice of Extreme Programming (XP). He describes the adaptation of unit tests with respect to the target refactoring prior to the refactoring process called Test-first Refactoring (TFR). Initially, the tests fail as they are adapted to test the refactored code. Next, the code is refactored. Finally, the validity of refactoring is confirmed via modified test code. The process continues until all the tests pass. This work, however, lacks the presence of proper guidelines to adapt the test code according to the subsequent refactoring of the code. TFR fits well into the XP paradigm. However, in industry, people follow various norms and practices [11]. It is not always possible to test-first. We believe that their approach is not general enough to be used for adapting the test code at every step of refactoring, where required.

Test Driven Refactoring (TDR) is another name used for TFR in [12]. The core idea of this research is to automate the TDR, which requires that the developer finishes test adaptation before applying refactoring. The authors elicit the concept that to correctly extract the refactoring intents or opportunities, it is necessary to adapt test artifacts including unit tests. However, once again no general guidelines are provided for unit test adaptation.

Deursen et. al. explore the relationship between refactoring and unit testing [2]. They propose an extension to the refactoring guidelines to handle test code adaptation. Moreover, a test taxonomy is presented which categorizes refactorings based on their impact on test code [3]. A refactoring can be categorized as *compatible, backwards compatible, make backwards compatible,* and *incompatible*. We believe that the categorization is not accurate. For example, *Preserve Whole Object* and *Extract Class* [1] are refactorings that are listed as compatible i.e. they do not break the test code. But it can be easily demonstrated that these refactorings break the test code if proper adaptive actions are not taken. In addition, a refactoring can fall in one category or another depending upon certain developer's decision. Hence, the categorization presented by Deursen et al. is not accurate and requires further study and clarification.

Counsell et al. [4] have evaluated the testing taxonomy proposed by Deursen et al. [3] as mentioned above. They extend the latter by determining the inter-dependencies of the refactoring categories and a refactoring dependency graph is developed for Fowler's catalogue [1]. A shortened list of eight compatible refactorings is presented that excludes all the other refactorings that may use those refactorings that break unit tests. There are few problems in their approach. First, they suggest restricting refactoring exercise to those refactorings that do not break unit tests. Second, refactorings are wrongly categorized. Fowler's catalogue of refactorings includes many refactorings that may affect client and unit test but these are essential to improve program structure. The need is to extend the guidelines such that they describe ways to preserve the behavior of the impacted components.

The authors in [4] insist on avoiding *Incompatible Refactorings* since they destroy the original interface and therefore require large-scale modifications to the test code. Replace Constructor with Factory Method, Replace Type Code with State/Strategy, Replace Type Code with Subclasses are a few examples of the Incompatible refactorings. These and other refactorings of this category address most serious smells of the production code [1]. Avoidance is not the solution here. The need is to extend the guidelines such that they qualify the definition of refactoring. The authors extend this work by analyzing the different paths in the dependency graph and their effect on eradicating the bad smells from the code [5]. In [6], an empirical investigation has been done to understand the usage frequency of the chains. The key result determined was that refactorings producing longer chains had less utilization by developers than refactorings with shorter chains.

Fowler [1] is of the view that every class should have a main function that tests the class or separate test classes should be build that work in a framework to make testing easier. Which means that whatever is the physical location of test code be it the main method or some other class in a testing package, it cannot be separated from the production code. The claim is also supported by the fact that both production and the test code come under the owner ship of a developer and thus should be together. Therefore any process affecting the production code; should readily adapt the associated clients and the test code [2, 17].

3   Unit Test: A Specialized Client

Adaptation of the test code and the clients due to changes in the production code during refactoring can be defined as:

"The process of adaptation of unit test suites with the refactored code is defined such that there are no syntactic or semantic errors in the unit test suites and the test code's quality and capability to test remains equivalent to the state prior to refactoring production code".

Unit testing is a process of testing the methods contained in the classes (defined as units in object oriented paradigm). These tests are tightly coupled with the modules under test. Unit tests are very specific type of tests [14]. They test code at its lowest level of granularity. As they directly use the functionality provided by the classes they can safely be called clients to the programs under test. But this association can be characterized as an unusual client-server relationship.

Unit tests are directly affected due to any change in their respective modules either due to refactoring or any form of restructuring [13]. Many refactorings involve renaming of the entities in the production code like renaming packages, classes or methods which requires renaming of the respective test code entities. Removing and adding parameters often make test cases superfluous or require modification in the test fixture. Class extraction affects the test code in many ways, to preserve semantics many tests may have to be moved to the test class for the extracted class. The subclass extraction is followed by creation of a parallel hierarchy of test classes. On the contrary on in lining the class tests move in the opposite direction, sometimes the tests specifically related to the interaction of the two classes are eliminated. Refactorings that effect implementation inside a method have no impact on the test suites because unit tests are normally black-box tests [18].

Moving the method can have either of the effects: test cases are also moved to the target's test class or in case of delegation the test code might get duplicated. This is demonstrated in the example below (see figure 1 and 2). To keep the problem simple we demonstrate the case of move method refactoring in which the method is actually moved to the target class and not delegated.

A refactoring may affect the interface expected by the entities in the source, target, client or the test class (see figure 1). Existing mechanics for *Move Method* [1] include steps related to replacement of all the references in the production code. We propose extension of guidelines such that the mechanics for adapting test code are also included. By doing so, the mechanics help developers to eradicate a bad smell that could be introduced in the test code. The test method for the moved method *m1()* should be principally in the target's test class after refactoring as presented in figure 2. But the refactoring guidelines if followed as they are shall not preserve semantics of the test code and the method *m1()* shall remain in the source's test class (see figure 1).

This is because the current mechanics do not include any steps to fix the test code such that it is also semantically aligned with program under test. Therefore by ignoring the fact that unit tests have some unique characteristics which are not owned by usual clients, any restructuring of the code can invalidate the test code.

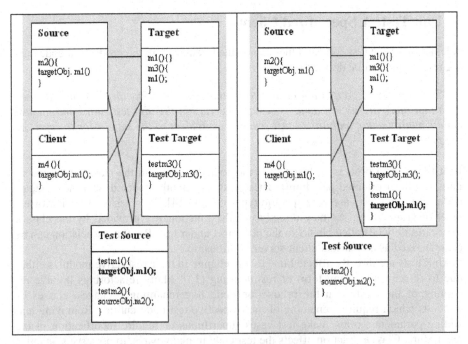

Fig. 1. Production and test code after m1() is moved from source to target class using move method refactoring

Fig. 2. Production and test code after m1() is moved from source to target class using move method refactoring including test code adaptation

Similar to the *Move Method* refactoring there are other refactorings that require different corrective actions from that of ordinary clients. For example, refactoring *Inline Method* [1] includes steps that update the clients by finding all calls to the method to be in lined and each call is replaced with the method body. But this doesn't apply to the unit test. The method call in the test method cannot be replaced by the method statements. The test method has to be eliminated because the method it is testing does not exist anymore.

The objective behind refactoring the production code is to improve the quality of the code. While refactoring production code, the focus should also be on improving test code quality. So the test code adaptation mechanism also includes identification and eradication of bad test smells generated due to any restructuring in the code [7, 14].

4   Impact of Refactorings on Production and Test Code

Refactoring is a systematic process of code transformation and restructuring such that externally observable behavior is not changed [1]. But in many cases due to obscure and imprecise guidelines production and/or test code do not preserve behavior. As the focus of this research is on identifying the loop holes in refactoring guidelines from clients and unit test's perspective, we have categorized these guidelines based on their impact on these components of a software system.

The purpose of this categorization is to target the potential problem areas in Fowler's catalog. It is merely a source of reducing our problem space. This classification is very much subject to change as we extend the guidelines to address client and test code adaptation. By the time we finish extending these guidelines, all of these shall belong to type I category and the other types shall be empty sets.

Refactoring guidelines can be broadly divided into three types with respect to their effect on production and test code together:

4.1   Type I: Refactoring Guidelines That Do Not Break the Production and/Or Test Code

Extract Method: The test taxonomy presented by Counsell *et al.* [4] labels this refactoring as 'backwards compatible'. They claim such refactorings require extension to the interface. But it is evident from the mechanics, there is no step that talks about exposing the extracted method to the clients, thus it does not become a part of public interface according to the guidelines laid down by Fowler [1]. This refactoring doesn't require change in the test code. Creating an independent test of the extracted method might be the developer's choice. But that does not come under the scope of the 'Extract Method'. The extracted method can be tested by the method invoking it.

4.2   Type II: Refactoring Guidelines That Correctly Refactor the Production Code but Break Or Require Extension to the Test Code

Preserve whole object: The refactoring as documented in [1] does not affect the setup fixture (initialization related test code) but does affect the test code related to test execution. The list of parameters expected by the method is replaced by the object owning those attributes. In the literature, this refactoring has been reported as 'compatible to the test code' [2] but it breaks the test code if the required corrective transformations are not performed.

4.3 Type III: Refactoring Guidelines That Are Insufficient for Restructuring Production and Test Code

Move field: It does the job of replacing all the references in the production and test code by the references to the target field. It does not take care of the constructors in the production code and nor of the setup fixture in the test code where the moved field is no more expected but required by the target and the client classes.

We categorize all 68 refactoring guidelines [1] into one of the three categories defined above (See Table 1).

Table 1. Refactoring Categorization based on their Impact on production and test code together

Type	Refactoring Names
Type I	Extract Method, Inline temp, Replace temp with query, Introduce Explaining variable, Split temporary variable, Remove assignment to parameters, Replace Method with method object, Substitute Algorithm, Self Encapsulate field, Decompose Conditionals, Remove Control Flag, Replace Nested Conditional with Guard Clauses, Introduce assertion, Consolidate Conditional Expression, Consolidate Duplicate Conditional Fragments, Hide Method, Replace Exception with test, Replace Delegation with inheritance (18)
Type II	Move Method, Inline Method, Introduce Foreign Method, Introduce local extension, Replace Data Value with Object, Change value with reference, Replace constructor with factory method, Replace Array with Object, Duplicate Observed Data, Change Unidirectional Association to Bidirectional, Change Bidirectional Association to Unidirectional, Replace magic Number with a symbolic constant, Encapsulate Field, Encapsulate Collection, Replace Type Code with class, Replace subclass with fields, Introduce Null object, Rename Method, Remove parameter, Separate query from the modifier, Parameterize Method, Replace parameter with Explicit Methods, Replace parameter with Method, Introduce Parameter Object, Remove Setting Method, Replace Error Code with Exception, Push down method, Change Reference to Value, Add Parameter, Extract Interface, Form Template Method , Extract subclass, Extract super , collapse hierarchy (33)
Type III	Move Field, Extract class, inline class, hide delegate, Remove Middle Man, Push down field, Pull up field, Replace Record with Data Class, Replace Type Code with subclasses , Replace Type Code with State/Strategy, Replace Conditional with Polymorphism, Preserve whole object, Encapsulate Downcast, pull up method, pull up constructor body, Replace Inheritance with Delegation (17)

This classification is based on the pattern of testing that says [16]:

"Test the interface not the implementation".

The implementation or private methods in the class are not tested because these are tested by the other methods that invoke them to implement their functionality. In the existing categorization of refactorings, one of the mostly commonly used refactoring named *Extract Method* [1] is categorized as the one that extends the interface and requires addition of new test code. However, the mechanics of the refactoring suggest otherwise because there is no such step which talks about exposing the extracted method to the clients. Hence, following the testing principle mentioned above there is no need to test the new extracted method independently as it is invoked inside other methods. The extraction can be followed by making the method public but it is not the effect of the refactoring but only the developer's decision. Every refactoring is performed against a formally defined code smell and it eradicates the code smell, keeping the external behavior intact. Predicting the actions of a developer before or after a refactoring can be helpful in many contexts but these predictions should not be considered as the impact of refactoring mechanics.

In the existing test taxonomy by Deursen et. al. [2] later appraised in [4] and empirically evaluated in [5-6], the authors present details of the dependency graph of refactorings that portray the interdependence of different refactorings. They state that there are 126 chains out of 282 chains induced by the 72 refactorings [1] in which *Extract Method* appears. Now they categorize it as the one that extends test code so all refactorings using *Extract Method* are considered to add to the test code. Moreover, we do not consider wrapping up the entities to make the test code backwards compatible instead we believe that there is a need to provide patterns and guidelines to remove the bad smells from the roots of the production code.

As clear from the definitions in the text above, Type I refactorings would not require any change in the refactoring guidelines from the perspective of production and test code adaptation. But clearly we can see that most of the refactorings listed in type I do not actually require change in clients and unit tests. Because their mechanics involve transformation at the implementation level and do not break the interface.

Type II refactoring guidelines should be extended so that they also include steps on test code adaptation. Now Type III refactorings pose a serious problem because the refactoring guidelines are not written at the level of detail as the other refactoring guidelines: these not only break the test code but also miss critical steps to refactor the production code.

We do not take account of the *big refactorings* [1] in this analysis because these are composed of smaller refactorings that are listed in Table I. The big refactorings include *Convert Procedural Design to Objects, Separate Domain from Presentation, Tease Apart Inheritance, and Extract Hierarchy*. The impact of these refactorings on test and production code can be evaluated by combining the effect of series of other small refactorings used by them.

5 Extending Refactoring Guidelines

There are various tools available in the market that support automated refactorings, but not all refactorings are provided by these tools. There is a need for proper guidelines and patterns to refactor the code, such that all the preconditions are evaluated and the required corrective actions are performed prior to the refactoring process. Fowler has done a significant job by providing a catalogue of refactoring guidelines. But there is a need to strive for more complete, precise and unambiguous refactoring "recipes". The new improved guidelines would not only help manual refactoring but shall also aid refactoring automation.

The current literature based on Deursen et. al. [2] test taxonomy emphasizes on prevention by avoiding the refactorings that eventually break the test code. After analyzing the list of refactorings, it is observed that there are only 18 refactorings that do not require corrective transformation in the test code to run safely (see Type I refactorings in Table 1). Therefore, if the approach suggested in [4] is followed, many refactorings listed under Type II and Type III may become obsolete.

The proposed solution discussed in this paper addresses this issue and also the problems discussed earlier. We propose extension of the existing refactoring guidelines [1] to cover both aspects of software development, which is programming as

Table 2. Extended Refactoring Guidelines For Move Field Refactoring

Fowler's Guideline	Extended Guideline for Production Code	Extended Guideline for production and test code
Determine how to reference the target object from the source,	Determine how to reference the target object from the source and the clients	Determine how to reference the target object from the source, the clients and test classes.
o An existing field or method may give you the target. If not, see whether you can easily create a method that will do so. Failing that, you need to create a new field in the source that can store the target. This may be a permanent change, but you can also do it temporarily until you have refactored enough to remove it.	o An existing field or method may give you the target. If not, see whether you can easily create a method that will do so. Failing that, you need to create a new field in the source that can store the target. This may be a permanent change, but you can also do it temporarily until you have refactored enough to remove it.	o An existing field or method may give you the target. If not, see whether you can easily create a method that will do so. Failing that, you need to create a new field in the source that can store the target. This may be a permanent change, but you can also do it temporarily until you have refactored enough to remove it.
Remove the field on the source class.	Remove the field on the source class.	Remove the field on the source class.
	Remove the assignments to the field from the constructors in the source class.	Remove the assignments to the field from the constructors in the source class.
	Update the constructors of the target class to assign the value to the moved field.	Update the constructors of the target class to assign the value to the moved field.

Table 2. (*Continued*)

		Determine the way to get the value of removed field from the setup fixture in the test code of source class to update the initialization code in unit test for the target object.
	Use the value of moved field in the initialization code of the source class to update the initialization code for the target class's object in the client classes.	Use the value of moved field in the initialization code of the source class to update the initialization code for the target class's object in the client and test classes.
Replace all references to the source field with references to the appropriate method on the target	Replace all references to the source field with references to the appropriate method on the target in production code.	Replace all references to the source field with references to the appropriate method on the target both in production and test code.
o For accesses to the variable, replace the reference with a call to the target object's getting method; for assignments, replace the reference with a call to the setting method. o If the field is not private, look in all the subclasses of the source for references.	o For accesses to the variable, replace the reference with a call to the target object's getting method; for assignments, replace the reference with a call to the setting method. o If the field is not private, look in all the subclasses of the source for references.	o For accesses to the variable, replace the reference with a call to the target object's getting method; for assignments, replace the reference with a call to the setting method. o If the field is not private, look in all the subclasses of the source and their associated test classes for references.
Compile and test	Compile and test	Compile and test

well as unit testing. We present detailed guidelines for 'Move Field' refactoring, which is commonly used and simple to understand. Table 2 has been divided into three columns: In column1 we present original Fowler's guidelines. In the next column we extend the guidelines for production code adaptation. The last column exhibits the final version of the guidelines covering both, the production code and test code. In the example illustrated above we can clearly see that in the original guidelines the mechanics related to constructor definitions, object initialization and value assignments are missing. The extended guidelines cover the missing parts by considering all the entities effected due to the refactoring process. This one example cannot demonstrate all possible scenarios. However, it can give readers an idea on how these guidelines can be improved.

6 Conclusions

Refactoring is supposed to be a disciplined process of restructuring the code. But the refactoring catalogue documented by Fowler [1] in many cases lacks precision and leaves opportunities for developers to do mistakes in terms of breaking the production and test code. Most of the existing guidelines for refactoring do not provide mechanics for adapting the clients and unit tests. The behavior of a system cannot be preserved if its clients do not function properly. Secondly, the behavior cannot be tested if the test code is invalidated. Therefore, we propose extension of guidelines to cover both perspectives.

Refactoring guidelines [1] are hard to follow manually because most critical of them are not written at the required and a consistent level of detail. This is the reason most of the critical refactorings are not automated and thus are not provided by the refactoring tools. Following the similar approach as presented in this paper we intend to provide a theoretical foundation in terms of extended guidelines for all refactorings to ease manual as well as automated refactoring.

In order to locate the problem areas in refactoring catalogue [1], we created an exhaustive classification of the 68 refactorings. We have come up with three broad categories of refactoring guidelines. Type I, do not break the test code (18 in number). Type II, break the test code but are adequate for refactoring production code (33 in number); than Type III refactoring mechanics, that are insufficient both for production code refactoring and test code adaptation (17 in numbers).

There is very limited work done on analyzing the impact of refactoring guidelines on the production and test code. Quite a number of researcher report the need for test code adaptation but we do not find proper guidelines for refactorings that can cater problems mentioned above. In this paper we present extended mechanics for 'Move Field' refactoring belonging to type III. We demonstrate that by adding mechanics related to test code and client adaptation behavior of a program can be preserved.

This research in its current form might raise questions in reader's mind about the implications of its usage in the practical world. But being part of the software research and development community, we often come across situations where rolling back the effects of refactoring becomes a night mare. The purpose of this paper is to make the problems pertaining refactoring evident. The next step on our agenda is to rectify these problems by providing a more formal and an authentic solution.

References

[1] Fowler, M.: Refactoring: Improving the Design of Existing Code. Addison-Wesley, Reading (1999)
[2] Deursen, A.V., Moonen, L.: The video store revisited—thoughts on refactoring and testing. In: Proceedings of the 3rd International Conference on Extreme Programming and Flexible Processes in Software Engineering (2002)
[3] Deursen, A.V., Moonen, L., Bergh, A.V.D., Kok, G.: Refactoring test code. In: Proceedings of the 2nd International Conference on Extreme Programming and Flexible Processes in Software Engineering (2001)

[4] Counsell, S., Hierons, R.M., Najjar, R., Loizou, G., Hassoun, Y.: The Effectiveness of Refactoring Based on a Compatibility Testing Taxonomy and a Dependency Graph. In: Proceedings of Testing: Academic and Industrial Conference (2006)

[5] Counsell, S., Swift, S., Hierons, R.M.: A Test Taxonomy Applied to the Mechanics of Java Refactorings. In: SCSS (1), pp. 497–502 (2007)

[6] Counsell, S.: Is the need to follow chains a possible deterrent to certain refactorings and an inducement to others? In: Proceedings of second International Conference on Research Challenges in Information Science (2008)

[7] Bannwart, F., Müller, P.: Changing Programs Correctly: Refactoring with Specifications. In: Proceedings of FM, pp. 492–507 (2007)

[8] Beck, K.: Test Driven Development: By Example. Addison-Wesley, Reading (2002)

[9] Walter, B., Pietrzak, B.: Automated Generation of Unit Tests for Refactoring. In: Eckstein, J., Baumeister, H. (eds.) XP 2004. LNCS, vol. 3092, pp. 211–214. Springer, Heidelberg (2004)

[10] Guerra, E.M., Fernandes, C.T.: Refactoring Test Code Safely. In: Proceedings of the International Conference on Software Engineering Advances (2007)

[11] George, B., William, L.: An Initial Investigation of Test Driven Development in Industry. In: Matsui, M., Zuccherato, R.J. (eds.) SAC 2003. LNCS, vol. 3006, Springer, Heidelberg (2003)

[12] Jiau, H.C., Chen, J.C.: Test code differencing for test-driven refactoring automation. ACM SIGSOFT Software Engineering Notes 34(1) (January 2009)

[13] Schwaiger, W., Kropp, M.: A Tool for integrated Test Driven Development – iTDD. In: TAIC PART Conference, Fast Abstract Proceedings (2008)

[14] Meszaros, G., Fowler, M.: xUnit Patterns: Refactoring Test Code. Addison-Wesley, Reading (2007)

[15] Marick, B.: Testing for Programmers, Lecture Notes available at,
     http://www.exampler.com/testing-com/writings/
     half-day-programmer.pdf

[16] Demeyer, S., Ducasse, S., Nierstrasz, O.M.: Object –oriented reengineering patterns. Morgan Kaufmann, San Francisco (2003)

[17] Pipka, J.U.: Refactoring in a "test first"-world. In: Proceedings of 3rd Int'l. Conference on eXtreme Programming and Flexible Processes in Software Engineering (2002)

[18] Link, J., Frohlich, P.: Unit Testing in Java: How Tests Drive The Code. View Larger Image. Morgan Kaufmann, San Francisco (2003)

[19] Opdyke, W.F.: Refactoring object-oriented frameworks. PhD thesis, University of Illinois (1992)

[20] Roberts, D.B.: Practical Analysis for Refactoring. PhD thesis, University of Illinois (1999)

Security Testing in Agile Web Application Development - A Case Study Using the EAST Methodology

Gencer Erdogan[1], Per Håkon Meland[2], and Derek Mathieson[1]

[1] CERN - The European Organization for Nuclear Research
CH-1211 Genève 23, Switzerland
{Gencer.Erdogan,Derek.Mathieson}@cern.ch
[2] SINTEF ICT, System development and security
NO-7465 Trondheim, Norway
Per.H.Meland@sintef.no

Abstract. There is a need for improved security testing methodologies specialized for Web applications and their agile development environment. The number of web application vulnerabilities is drastically increasing, while security testing tends to be given a low priority. In this paper, we analyze and compare Agile Security Testing with two other common methodologies for Web application security testing, and then present an extension of this methodology. We present a case study showing how our Extended Agile Security Testing (EAST) performs compared to a more ad hoc approach used within an organization. Our working hypothesis is that the detection of vulnerabilities in Web applications will be significantly more efficient when using a structured security testing methodology specialized for Web applications, compared to existing ad hoc ways of performing security tests. Our results show a clear indication that our hypothesis is on the right track.

Keywords: Security testing, Web applications, Scrum.

1 Introduction

Using agile methodologies for Web application development is a growing trend [1] and there is evidence that confirms that this is a good fit [2]. Web applications are routinely exposed to malicious attacks, and in order to mitigate the security risks, several ways of integrating security into agile development methodologies [3,4,5,6,7,8] have been suggested. Most security methodologies are built on traditional development methodologies, which are qualitatively and quantitatively different from agile development methodologies [5]. Furthermore, the traditional security methodologies are often sequential rather than iterative. This often leads to a "big design up front" in order to assess the security of a system [3], which is considered as an anti-pattern in the Agile Manifesto [9].

The number of web application vulnerabilities is drastically increasing. In their Global Internet Security Threat Report, Symantec reports that they detected 499,811 new malicious code threats during the second half of 2007, which

A. Sillitti et al. (Eds.): XP 2010, LNBIP 48, pp. 14–27, 2010.

is a 571% increase over the second half of 2006 [13]. These numbers indicate that security tends to be overlooked [14]. Particularly, the provision of sufficient security testing of Web applications is often neglected because of their short time-to-market, and the difficulty of proving a significant payoff for the effort [10,11,12].

In this paper, we analyze and compare Agile Security Testing (as defined by Tappenden et al. [15]) with two other common methodologies for Web application security testing. We then present an extension of this methodology, named EAST, which has been specialized for Web applications development in combination with Scrum. Furthermore, we present a case study showing how EAST performs compared to a more ad hoc approach used within an organization, before we discuss our results and conclude the paper.

2   Agile Security Testing for Web Based Applications

The use of agile development methodologies is a growing trend for Web application development. This has further lead to the idea of agile security engineering, which adopts the same philosophy as agile software engineering in order to mitigate security risks in software [15]. It is a highly iterative process for delivering the security solution and translating security objectives (requirements) into automated security test cases. In addition, it promotes the idea of creating security test cases before the system exists, i.e., test driven development (TDD).

2.1   Agile Security Testing

The Agile Security Testing methodology, suggested by Tappenden et al. [15], consists of three main steps. **Step 1**, the modeling of security requirements, is executed by creating abuser stories [16,17] and/or misuse cases [18,19] in order to elicit security requirements. These are then used as reference points when testing for security in order to verify or falsify a given security requirement. **Step 2**, a highly testable architecture, is achieved by adding a test layer on top of each of the three layers that Web applications typically consist of, i.e., presentation layer, business service layer and data service layer. The resulting architecture is very well suited to agile development methodologies because of its many test layers. Additionally, it is useful for security testing because the architecture makes it possible to employ various security testing techniques within any number of the test layers. **Step 3**, running automated security tests, which is necessary in order to fully benefit from Agile Security Testing.

2.2   Penetration Testing

Penetration Testing is the most commonly applied security testing methodology, but it is also the most commonly misapplied security testing methodology [20]. It is misapplied firstly, by being carried out at the end of the development life cycle and secondly, by being performed in a "time boxed" manner where a small and predefined portion of time and resources is given to the effort. In order to prevent the misapplication of penetration testing, Thompson [21] suggests a structured penetration testing methodology. Although this methodology is more formal than Agile Security Testing, it is applicable to Web application development and consists of five main steps. **Step 1** is to create a threat model in order to get a detailed, written description of the risks that threatens the application. The goal is to get an overview of the various conditions (vulnerabilities) that have to be present in order to realize a given threat. **Step 2** is to build a test plan. The test plan acts as a road map for the total security testing effort. It is created to get a high-level overview of the security test cases, an overview of how exploratory testing (i.e., simultaneous learning, test design, and test execution) will be conducted, and to get an overview of the components that will be tested. **Step 3** is to execute the security tests. These are divided into four main groups; dependency testing, user interface testing, design testing and implementation testing. **Step 4** is to create a report of the findings from the security testing process. The report must at least cover reproduction steps, severity and exploit scenarios. **Step 5** is to execute a postmortem evaluation. A postmortem evaluation is basically a meeting held by the security test team where the focus should be on why vulnerabilities (bugs or flaws) were missed during development, and how to improve the process to prevent or isolate such security issues in the future.

2.3   The Open Web Application Security Project (OWASP) Testing Framework

The OWASP Testing Framework is not developed for a specific development process, but is rather a comprehensive generic development model that contains the necessary activities needed for systematic security testing of Web applications. This framework consists of five main phases [22] where each phase has its associated activities. **Phase 1** (before development begins): Review policies and standards, and develop measurement and metrics criteria (ensure traceability). **Phase 2** (during definition and design): Review security requirements, review design and architecture, create and review UML models, and create and review threat models. **Phase 3** (during development): Code walkthroughs and code reviews. **Phase 4** (during deployment): Application penetration testing and configuration management testing. **Phase 5** (maintenance and operations): Conduct operational reviews, conduct periodic checks and ensure change verification.

2.4   Comparison of Methods

The Penetration Testing Approach and the OWASP Testing Framework are applicable in Web application development, but they are not very suitable in an agile setting without customization. They were not developed with the Agile Manifesto in mind. E.g., step 2 and step 4 in the Penetration Testing Approach are heavily dependent on documentation. This also applies for phase 2 in the OWASP Testing Framework. Furthermore, as mentioned in Section 2.3, the OWASP Testing Framework is created for a general software life cycle, which makes it possible to pick and choose the necessary phases. However, the activities are sometimes closely coupled. E.g., in phase 3; to only carry out a code walkthrough without carrying out a code review afterwards would not be of any particular benefit.

The Agile Security Testing methodology has a rather low complexity compared to the other two methodologies. There are three main steps that needs to be carried out compared to five and thirteen steps in the Penetration Testing Approach and the OWASP Testing Framework respectively. These three main steps require little intervention by security experts (but does not eliminate the need completely). All methodologies work with threats and/or security requirements, which can reduce the scope of the testing and helps to decrease the knowledge gap between security experts and software developers. None of the methodologies have any step or activity for mitigating false positives, which is one of the great real-life challenges. In Agile Security Testing we also miss steps for postmortem evaluations and describing security decisions, which are found in at least one of the others.

3 Extending Agile Security Testing and Integrating It into Scrum

As shown in the previous section, there are gaps between Agile Security Testing and methodologies more specific to Web application development (but which are not typically agile). We have therefore defined our own variant named *Extended Agile Security Testing* (EAST) (see Figure 1), which seeks to close these gaps by including three new complementary activities:

Penetration testing and mitigating false positives: False positives (nonexistent bugs that are reported as detected by a testing tool) and false negatives (i.e., existing bugs that are not detected by a testing tool) are known to be a problem in automated software security testing. A high rate of false positives creates high workload and makes it difficult to find and fix the actual bugs in the software. We therefore integrate a false positive mitigation process with the penetration testing process. The penetration testing process is regarded as a part of step 3 in Agile Security Testing. The false positive mitigation process is to be carried out in the following way:

  1. The penetration testing tool is used to perform a penetration test.
  2. After a penetration test, the result is reviewed and the false positives are marked so that they will not be registered as bugs next time the tool performs a penetration test. Each marked false positive vulnerability is associated with its respective Web site.

However, this approach is dependent on either: (1) the penetration testing tool having the ability to mark and remember specific false positives or, (2) the penetration testing tool having the ability to import a false positive repository (e.g., false positive database, XML file, etc.).

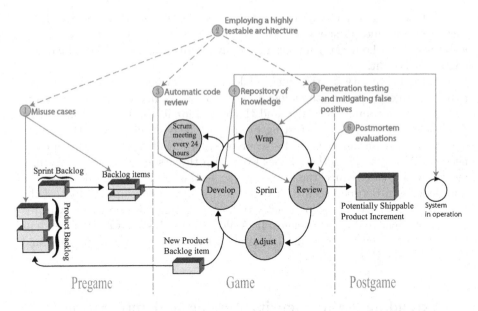

Fig. 1. The EAST steps integrated in the appropriate phases of Scrum

Postmortem evaluations: In order to continuously harden the security testing process, a postmortem phase needs to be in place at the end of the security testing process. It is realized by executing the following steps:

1. Provide answers to why certain vulnerabilities were missed during development.
2. Improve the issued development process in order to mitigate or isolate the underlying vulnerabilities.
3. Create, or find, or improve a security testing activity in order to detect the underlying vulnerabilities.

Repository of knowledge: According to Rus et al. [23], a software organization's main asset is its intellectual capital. One obvious problem in this respect is that intellectual capital lies within the minds of the employees. As experienced people leave the organization, so does the knowledge with them. In order to keep the knowledge alive within the organization, knowledge management must be present in the organization. Knowledge management is beyond the scope of this paper, but by adding a phase in Agile Security Testing that triggers the security testing participants (e.g., developers, QA people, decision makers etc.) to document and archive why certain security decision were made, security specific knowledge can be kept in repositories, and thereby kept alive within the organization. This is realized by executing it during the development and the review phase of the development life cycle. Additionally, it is important to maintain the repository for the underlying system while it is in operation.

As shown in Figure 1, EAST has been integrated into Scrum. Scrum was selected mainly because of its general popularity, according to a survey carried out by Davidson [24], the most widely used agile development methodology is Scrum, followed by eXtreme Programming. Scrum was also the prevalent methodology in our case study organization. The following points describe *how* and *why* the six EAST steps are integrated in Scrum as indicated in Figure 1:

EAST Step 1 (Misuse cases): – *How*: The pregame phase in Scrum consists of planning and system architecture/high level design, which is carried out by creating product backlog items that are further refined into sprint backlog items. The creation of misuse cases are therefore executed in two steps in the pregame phase, in which step 1 is optional and step 2 is mandatory:

1. During the creation of product backlog items, high level misuse cases (i.e., misuse cases that contain high level specifications of the system) are created for each product backlog item. Since the level of system specifications in a product backlog item is at a high level (not refined), the resulting misuse cases will also contain high level specifications. This step can be skipped if the product backlog item does not contain enough details in order to create misuse cases (e.g., missing details about the system architecture and design).

2. When a sprint backlog item is refined into several backlog items (indicated in the pregame phase in Figure 1), the system specifications are well defined and set up for development. The same transformation is to be applied on the misuse cases created in step 1 in order to create detailed misuse cases. If no misuse cases were created in step 1, they must be created containing detailed specifications of the system in this step. Finally, security requirements are to be derived using the resulting misuse cases.

– *Why*: First, misuse cases let developers to think like an attacker (malicious user) and thereby enables them to get an overview of potential threats and vulnerabilities the evolving system may possess. Second, by using the misuse cases as a starting point the developers can create security requirements. The security requirements are then used to verify whether the system fulfils the required level of security (during the security testing process). Third, the creative process of creating misuse cases let developers gain security specific knowledge. Last but not least, discovering vulnerabilities and creating countermeasures during definition, high level design, and low level design are the three most cost efficient ways of mitigating vulnerabilities [25].

EAST Step 2 (Employing a highly testable architecture): – *How*: Unit security testing is achieved by performing automatic code review during the development phase (EAST step 3). System security testing is achieved by performing penetration testing after the creation of an executable version of the part or parts of the system during the wrap phase (EAST step 5). Security acceptance testing is achieved by using the security requirements (EAST step 1) as reference points to verify or falsify the required level of security. Furthermore, EAST step 3 can be regarded as development testing, EAST step 5 can be regarded as system testing, and EAST step 1 can be regarded as basis for acceptance testing.

- *Why*: A highly testable architecture is both useful for agile development methodologies and security testing. The highly testable architecture introduces test layers on top of the Web application layers as explained in Section 2. It is therefore an architecture that suits agile development methodologies very well. Furthermore, it makes it possible to apply various security testing techniques within any number of the test layers (automatic code reviewing, penetration testing, etc.).

EAST Step 3 (Automatic code review): – *How*: The development phase in Scrum consists of the following activities: Domain analysis, design, development, implementation, testing and documentation. Since testing is one of the activities, automatic code review is to be carried out in this phase while source code is being developed. I.e., for each unit (e.g., a class) the developer finishes, he or she must perform automatic code analysis on that particular unit. This is to be carried out using a static analysis tool.

- *Why*: By integrating automatic code review in the development phase, developers are able to correct the existing bugs at an early stage. Furthermore, this process continuously hardens the source code against security bugs. However, in order for this activity to be of maximum benefit, the developers need to have experience using the underlying static analysis tool and have security specific knowledge [37].

EAST Step 4 (Repository of knowledge): – *How*: Every security decision that has been made during the development phase and the review phase must be documented. More specifically, this has to be done during the documentation activity in the development phase and while reviewing potential risks in the review phase. The goal is to justify and document why certain security specific decisions were made. Additionally, the repository needs to be updated whenever a vulnerability is discovered while the system is in operation (illustrated by the arrow going from EAST step 4 to the "System in operation" loop in Figure 1). The level of detail on the justification may vary, but it must at least contain the following points:

- **Application:** The name of the application that the security decision applies for.
- **Decision ID:** An ID for the given security decision.
- **What:** A short explanation of what the security decision is.
- **Where:** The name of the affected part(s) of the application(s) due to the security decision (class(es), module(s), etc.).
- **How:** A short explanation of how the security decision is realized.
- **Why:** A short explanation of why the given security decision was made.

- *Why*: By documenting security specific decisions that has been made during development it is possible to keep the decisions in a repository, and thereby possible to keep security specific knowledge alive within the organization. E.g., for training purposes and for tracing earlier security specific decisions in order to understand why certain things are done the way they are. At first glance, this step may be regarded as a contradiction to one of the key thoughts in agile development, which is to document as little as possible [9]. However, there is a knowledge gap between security experts and software developers [26]. Additionally, there is a risk of losing years of knowledge when people quit their position. We have therefore added this step in the EAST methodology in order to mitigate the knowledge gap and to mitigate the loss of security specific knowledge within the organization. Furthermore, the documentation of such security specific decisions are not comprehensive, but rather a brief summary and justification of the underlying security decision.

EAST Step 5 (Penetration testing and mitigating false positives)

- *How*: After an executable part or parts of a system is created in the wrap phase, a penetration test using a Web Vulnerability Scanner has to be carried out on the executable part(s). The penetration testing results are then to be analyzed and the false positives are to be marked. The false positives are to be marked as explained earlier in this section.

- *Why*: By performing penetration tests in the wrap phase makes it possible to discover vulnerabilities in the application during a sprint (continuously). This creates a base for the review phase in which, among other things, risks are discussed, countermeasures are created and EAST Step 6 (Postmortem evaluations) is carried out. Furthermore, by continuously marking false positives, the testing tools' knowledge base is improved to better understand the application under test, and consequently report fewer false positives in subsequent iterations.

EAST Step 6 (Postmortem evaluations): – *How*: During the review phase there has to be a postmortem evaluation meeting session. The postmortem evaluation is to be carried out after the wrap phase and EAST Step 5. Furthermore, it is to be carried out as explained earlier in this section.

- *Why*: This step enables the security testing participants to reflect over the vulnerabilities, the development process and the security testing process. This is important in order to continuously improve the security testing process.

4   Case Study

Our case study was carried out in the Administrative Information Services (AIS) group at CERN - The European Organization for Nuclear Research. The AIS group has the responsibility for all administrative applications and corporate data at CERN, and has currently six main applications in operation for users inside and outside CERN. One of the six applications is the Electronic Document Handling (EDH), which has approximately 14 000 users worldwide and is CERN's largest administrative Web application. The services that are provided by EDH are called EDH documents, which are basically Web forms. The security tests in our case study were applied to EDH, but since EDH is very large and complex, only two of the most frequently used EDH Web forms were considered in our experiment; Internal Purchase Request (DAI) and Material Request (MAG). Three developers volunteered to participate in the case study, with *Acunetix WVS* [35] and *PMD* [34] as the main testing tools, and *SeaMonster* [36] for security modelling. The case study consisted of two parts:

The first part was to execute the security testing in four iterations; two iterations using the security testing methodology normally applied by the AIS group (which is an ad hoc way of performing security tests), and two iterations using the EAST methodology. Furthermore, the testing iterations were executed in the following chronological order: *The AIS group's methodology → EAST → the AIS group's methodology → EAST*. The security testing methodology that is applied by the AIS group is carried out in two main steps:

1. A penetration testing is carried out in the postgame phase. Web Vulnerability Scanners are not used. Instead, guidelines are used by the testing participants to manually perform penetration tests.
2. The participants creates a report of the findings after the penetration testing. The report is used as a basis to create countermeasures for the vulnerabilities. Then, the countermeasures are added in the product backlog. Finally, the vulnerability is mitigated for the next product increment by performing the Scrum phases on the particular backlog item containing the vulnerability countermeasures.

Additionally, the penetration tests are often carried out in an ad hoc fashion, i.e., they are not always carried out before each and every "Potentially Shippable Product Increment" step (see Figure 1).

The second part was to evaluate EAST based on the results from the security testing iterations.

Automated security tests can last for hours given the limitless supply of Web application vulnerabilities [27,28,29], and the vast array of automated vulnerability tests a Web Vulnerability Scanner can perform. We therefore used the OWASP top 10 vulnerabilities [30] as a starting point and decided to test for the following vulnerabilities:

V.01 Reflected Cross Site Scripting
V.02 Stored Cross Site Scripting
V.03 SQL Injection
V.04 Malicious File Execution
V.05 Insecure Direct Object Reference
V.06 Cross Site Request Forgery (CSRF)
V.07 Information Leakage and Improper Error Handling
V.08 Broken Authentication and Session Management
V.09 Failure to Restrict URL Access

The top two vulnerability classes defined by OWASP are Cross Site Scripting (XSS) and Injection Flaws. Each of these vulnerability classes consists of four and eight vulnerability "types" respectively. E.g., Cross Site Scripting consists of: Reflected XSS, stored XSS, DOM XSS and Cross Site Flashing. V.01 was tested because Reflected XSS is known to be the most frequent type of XSS attack [31]. V.02 was tested because Stored XSS is known to be the most dangerous type of XSS attacks [32]. V.03 was tested because SQL injection is one of the most frequently applied attack type [33]. Insecure Cryptographic Storage and Insecure Communications from the OWASP top 10 list were not tested. The former is not possible to test using automated security scanning tools, and the latter was not tested because EDH uses Hypertext Transfer Protocol Secure (HTTPS) during all communication it has with a client.

5   Results and Discussion

There are three factors that were used as basis to compare the efficiency of the security testing methodology applied by the AIS group and the EAST methodology, respectively:

1. The amount of time spent on the security testing process.
2. The amount of vulnerabilities found during the security testing process.
3. The ability to mitigate false positives during the security testing process.

Figure 2 shows an overview the test results obtained from each test iteration. By studying the results, we discovered the following:

– By comparing the average time spent on testing both DAI and MAG using the security testing methodology applied by the AIS group, versus the

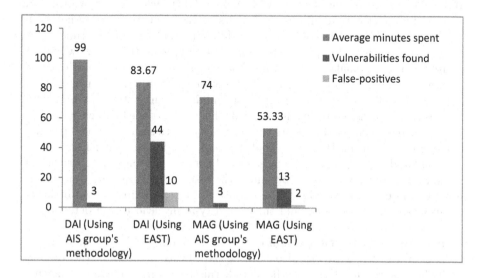

Fig. 2. Comparison of the test results

average time spent on testing both DAI and MAG using the EAST methodology, we discovered that the EAST methodology is in average 21% more effective.

- The number of vulnerabilities found by testing DAI and MAG using the security testing methodology applied by the AIS group is 3, while the number of vulnerabilities found by testing DAI and MAG using the EAST methodology is 56. In this respect, the EAST methodology is approximately 95% more effective. However, the three vulnerabilities that were found by using the security testing methodology applied by the AIS group were not found when using the EAST methodology. This indicates that human intervention is necessary in circumstances where tools have limited capabilities.
- By testing DAI and MAG using the EAST methodology, there were found 12 false positives. The false positives were marked via Acunetix WVS and thereby added to a false positive repository. Next time DAI and MAG were scanned, the marked false positives were regarded as false positives and not as vulnerabilities. In turn, this mitigates false positives during the security testing process. The security testing methodology applied by the AIS group does not have an activity in place that mitigates false positives. Hence, only the EAST methodology mitigates false positives during the security testing process. However, this approach to false positive mitigation is dependent on either: (1) the penetration testing tool (that is being used in the EAST methodology) must have the ability to mark and remember specific false positives or, (2) the penetration testing tool must have the ability to import a false positive repository (e.g., false positive database, XML file).

The following points describe the threats to the generalizability of the test results:

Tools: The usage of one specific Web Vulnerability Scanner is obviously an important factor that affects the results of the security tests. Other Web Vulnerability Scanners could produce different results regarding time spent and vulnerabilities found. Furthermore, it was decided that *PMD* would be used as the automatic code scanner tool. This was due to the participants' previous experience in using PMD. A better starting point in this respect would be to find a tool that produces the minimum amount of false positives. This risk is mitigated by leaning towards the findings done by Baca et al. [37], i.e., the best security testers are those who have both security experience and experience in using the static analyzer tool. Finally, the participants used an unfamiliar tool to model misuse case diagrams. The lack of experience in using this tool would inevitably affect the test results regarding time spent.

Security specific knowledge: The majority of the participants had little security specific knowledge, and this would typically lead to the detection of less vulnerabilities.

Security testing experience: All of the participants had little experience in security testing. This can also be used as a basis to question the validity of the test results. On the other hand, this is another indication showing that structured security testing is still not widely applied in organizations.

This risk can only be mitigated by continuously applying structured security testing using, e.g., the EAST methodology.

Testing thoroughness: The thoroughness of the participants' test execution was not measured. This risk is mitigated (or believed to be mitigated) by the fact that the participants actively volunteered.

Psychological effects, and the number of participants: As explained in Section 4, the test iterations were carried out sequentially. This will have a learning effect on the participants, i.e., for each iteration, the participants would gain more security specific knowledge and more experience in performing the tests. Obviously, this would be to the benefit of the participants, which would further produce better results. In this context, better results means spending less time to complete a test iteration and/or to find more vulnerabilities. Although the participants knew that the purpose of the testing process was to observe the testing methodologies, they may have been more effective while performing the security tests and thereby improving the results, as a response to the fact that they were the ones that produced the results that were taken into consideration. Thus, the participants may have considered themselves as a part of the "object" being observed and thereby improved the test results. This form of reactivity is referred to as the Hawthorne effect. Figure 2 shows that the average time spent on the test iterations decreases for each test iteration. This indicates that there has indeed been a learning effect on the participants during the testing process. Furthermore, the number of participants is another factor that could be used to question the validity of the test results. However, this was a side effect of the limited time and resources at our disposal.

6   Conclusion and Further Work

There is a need for security testing methodologies specialized for Web applications and their agile development environment. The EAST methodology is mainly based on Agile Security Testing, but is more tailored for Web development in combination with Scrum. A case study evaluation performed in an organization showed that compared to the current more ad hoc way of doing security testing, the EAST methodology is approximately 21% more effective in average regarding time spent, approximately 95% more effective regarding the amount of vulnerabilities found, and has the ability to mitigate false positives.

Future evaluations of the EAST methodology should be focused on mitigating the threats to the validity of the results presented in Section 5. They should also address the question of how efficient EAST is compared to extensive security testing methodologies applied on Web applications. These extensive security testing methodologies would naturally require more time and thereby be less efficient regarding time spent. However, what would be interesting to discover, is whether the EAST methodology lacks activities that are vital for the overall security testing process, compared to the traditional security testing methodologies.

References

1. Jazayeri, M.: Some trends in Web application development. In: International Conference on Software Engineering, pp. 199–213. IEEE Computer Society, Washington (2007)
2. McDonald, A., Welland, R.: Agile web engineering (AWE) process. Technical report, Department of Computer Science, University of Glasgow, UK (December 2001)
3. Kongsli, V.: Towards agile security in web applications. In: Companion to the 21st ACM SIGPLAN symposium on Object-oriented programming systems, languages, and applications (2006)
4. Ge, X., Paige, R.F., Polack, F.A.C., Chivers, H., Brooke, P.J.: Agile development of secure web applications. In: Proceedings of the 6th international conference on Web engineering. ACM, New York (2006)
5. Chivers, H., Paige, R.F., Ge, X.: Agile security using an incremental security architecture. In: Baumeister, H., Marchesi, M., Holcombe, M. (eds.) XP 2005. LNCS, vol. 3556, pp. 57–65. Springer, Heidelberg (2005)
6. Siponen, M., Baskerville, R., Kuivalainen, T.: Integrating security into agile development methods. In: Proceedings of the 38th Annual Hawaii International Conference on System Sciences, vol. 7, p. 185a (2005)
7. Wayrynen, J., Bodén, M., Bostrom, G.: Security Engineering and eXtreme Programming: An Impossible Marriage? In: Zannier, C., Erdogmus, H., Lindstrom, L. (eds.) XP/Agile Universe 2004. LNCS, vol. 3134, pp. 117–128. Springer, Heidelberg (2004)
8. Beznosov, K.: Extreme Security Engineering: On Employing XP Practices to Achieve "Good Enough Security" without Defining It. In: First ACM Workshop on Business Driven Security Engineering (BizSec), Fairfax, VA (2003)
9. Agile Manifesto, http://agilemanifesto.org/ (Last date accessed 2009-12-10)
10. Hieatt, E., Mee, R.: Going Faster: Testing The Web Application. IEEE Software 19, 60–65 (2002)
11. Di Lucca, G.A., Fasolino, A.R., Faralli, F., De Carlini, U.: Testing Web applications. In: Proceedings of International Conference on Software Maintenance, pp. 310–319 (2002)
12. Di Lucca, G.A., Fasolino, A.R.: Testing Web-based applications: The state of the art and future trends. Information and Software Technology 48, 1172–1186 (2006)
13. Turner, D., Fossi, M., Johnson, E., Mack, T., Blackbird, J., Entwisle, S., Low, M.K., McKinney, D., Wueest, C.: Symantec Internet Security Threat Report: Trends for July-December 2007. Technical report, Symantec Corporation, Vol. XIII (2008)
14. Thompson, H.H.: Why Security Testing Is Hard. IEEE Security & Privacy 1, 83–86 (2003)
15. Tappenden, A., Beatty, P., Miller, J., Geras, A., Smith, M.: Agile security testing of Web-based systems via HTTP Unit. In: Proceedings of Agile Conference, pp. 29–38 (2005)
16. Peeters, J.: Agile Security Requirements Engineering. In: Symposium on Requirements Engineering for Information Security (2005)
17. McGraw, G.: Software Security: Building Security. Addison-Wesley, Reading (2006)
18. Sindre, G., Opdahl, A.L.: Eliciting security requirements with misuse cases. Requirements Engineering 10, 34–44 (2005)
19. Røstad, L.: An extended misuse case notation: Including vulnerabilities and the insider threat. In: The Twelfth Working Conference on Requirements Engineering: Foundation for Software Quality (2006)

20. Arkin, B., Stender, S., McGraw, G.: Software penetration testing. IEEE Security & Privacy 3, 84–87 (2005)
21. Thompson, H.H.: Application penetration testing. IEEE Security & Privacy 3, 66–69 (2005)
22. The Open Web Application Security Project. OWASP Testing Guide V3.0, http://www.owasp.org/index.php/Category:OWASP_Testing_Project (Last date accessed 2009-11-13)
23. Rus, I., Lindvall, M.: Knowledge management in software engineering. IEEE Software 19, 26–38 (2002)
24. Davidson, M.: Survey: Agile interest high, but waterfall still used by many. Agile Trends Survey (2008), http://searchsoftwarequality.techtarget.com/news/article/0,289142,sid92_gci1318992,00.html (Last date accessed 2009-11-26)
25. Wysopal, C., Nelson, L., Dustin, E., Nelson, L., Zovi, D.D.: The Art of Software Security Testing. Addison-Wesley, Reading (2006)
26. Erdogan, G., Baadshaug, E.T.: Extending SeaMonster to support vulnerability inspection modeling. Technical report, NTNU, Department of computer and information science (2008)
27. BugTraq mailing list, http://www.securityfocus.com/archive/1 (Last date accessed 2009-11-13)
28. Common Vulnerabilities and Exposures, http://cve.mitre.org/ (Last date accessed 2009-11-13)
29. Computer Emergency Readiness Team (CERT), http://www.cert.org/ (Last date accessed 2009-11-13)
30. OWASP Top 10 vulnerabilities, http://www.owasp.org/index.php/Top_10_2007 (Last date accessed 2009-11-13)
31. Hope, P., Walther, B.: Web Security Testing Cookbook. O'Reilly, Sebastopol (2008)
32. The Open Web Application Security Project. OWASP Testing Guide V3.0, http://www.owasp.org/index.php/Category:OWASP_Testing_Project (Last date accessed 2009-12-02)
33. Andrews, M.: Guest Editor's Introduction: The State of Web Security. IEEE Security and Privacy 4, 14–15 (2006)
34. PMD - Java source code scanner (Static Analysis Tool), http://pmd.sourceforge.net/ (Last date accessed 2009-11-14)
35. Acunetix Web Vulnerability Scanner, http://www.acunetix.com/ (Last date accessed 2009-11-14)
36. SeaMonster V3.0, http://sourceforge.net/projects/seamonster/ (Last date accessed 2009-11-14)
37. Baca, D., Petersen, K., Carlsson, B., Lundberg, L.: Static Code Analysis to Detect Software Security Vulnerabilities - Does Experience Matter? In: IEEE International Conference on Availability, Reliability and Security, pp. 804–810 (2009)

Adoption of Team Estimation in a Specialist Organizational Environment

Tor Erlend Fægri

SINTEF ICT, NO-7465 Trondheim, Norway
Tor.E.Fegri@sintef.no

Abstract. Specialist organizational environments and lack of redundant knowledge reduce flexibility and therefore inhibits transition to agile development. This action research reports from the adoption of team estimation as a vehicle to increase redundant knowledge within a group of specialists. The group suffered from low levels of group learning legitimized by high work pressure and a specialist organizational environment. This resulted in poor planning and optimistic task estimates which contributed to increase the work pressure even higher. I framed the research as double-loop learning; I illustrate how different barriers to team estimation arose from conflicts with existing efficiency norms and then how benefits from team estimation created sufficient momentum to change practice. The results are obtained from qualitative analysis of empirical data gathered during one year of collaboration with the group. The article contributes to understanding of barriers to group learning and agile adoption in software organizations[1].

1 Introduction

A seemingly inherent trend in society is specialization. As our technological systems become larger and increasingly more complex there is significant motivation for people to focus their attention towards particular areas of the problem domain. The focusing implies that the individual gains more experience and hence obtain a higher level of proficiency within this particular area and often receives personal benefits such as status and influence in decision-making [21]. Many organizations adopt a bureaucratic structure and encourage specialization for improved efficiency. Specialization is seen in formalization of roles and fixed allocation of people to problem domains. In this manner the organization can gain higher efficiency for predictable work.

However, developing software systems can hardly be classified as predictable. Rapid changes in influential technologies, difficulty of settling requirements up-front and software's inherent flexibility creates a highly turbulent environment for many software organizations [17]. Efficiency in such environments depends upon flexibility. An important prerequisite for flexibility is redundancy. For example, if a group of people have overlapping skills then the group can deal with unforeseen changes in

[1] The work described was supported by the Research Council of Norway through the project EVidence based Improvement of SOFTware engineering (EVISOFT). I am grateful for the constructive comments from anonymous reviewers.

A. Sillitti et al. (Eds.): XP 2010, LNBIP 48, pp. 28–42, 2010.

task demands by dynamically re-allocating. Furthermore, redundant knowledge improves efficiency of communication. Without a shared understanding of fundamental concepts, coordinated and collaborative teamwork becomes difficult.

Agile software development is a software process paradigm rooted among software practitioners that has promised to flexibility and learning capability [17, 28]. Since its inception, agile software development has gained significant industrial momentum. However, researchers have identified numerous challenges with the transition to agile methods [4, 27]. One of these challenges is the transition to self-organizing teams in which members must have overlapping skills and accept interchangeable roles.

On November 13, 2007 I participated in a meeting with IT-Corp where we discussed the potential for research collaboration. I learned that a product group within IT-Corp called CardPay had recently started a transition to agile software development using Scrum [29]. However, there was a perception that the transition was only skin deep – a range of fundamental problems were still present. One of CardPay's representatives believed that a high degree of specialist knowledge made the transition difficult. This last comment triggered my interest so I agreed to a new meeting with CardPay to discuss a potential collaboration. We had two more meetings and by the end of November 2007 the collaboration was formally established.

2 Theoretical Background

The overall objective with this research was to investigate barriers to successful transition from plan-based to agile development methods. The two approaches have significant differences and the shift involves complex organizational change [8, 27]. Organizational change requires the questioning and productive inquiry into existing practices. This can be highly problematic as it may entail questioning and adjusting governing values and norms that are deeply embodied in the organization [1, 14].

Redundant knowledge is a requisite for flexibility and efficient teamwork and hence becomes important for agile development [24, 28]. Excessive specialization among individuals and specialist organizational culture inhibits team collaboration and constitute barriers to self-managing teams and agile development [23, 25]. A systematic review covering empirical studies up to and including 2005 found 7 studies giving evidence regarding introduction and adoption of agile methods [11]. Of these, three investigated the introduction and adoption process [2, 18, 30]. Bahli and Zeid [2] found adoption of XP to be eased by a high level of knowledge creation stemming from the numerous coordination events prescribed by XP. Hilkka et al. [18] found that practices similar to XP already had been evolving in the two case organizations' teams; the practices supported tight collaboration and extensive sharing of domain knowledge. Svensson and Höst [30] investigated adoption of agile methods in a large organization and found that a culture of redundant knowledge were already present as all developers were encouraged to work on the same code. More recent research has also investigated challenges regarding introduction and adoption of agile methods [7, 12, 19] but did not discuss lack of redundant knowledge as a barrier.

There are many practices that can be used to increase redundant knowledge. Agile development processes suggest practices such as collective code ownership and pair programming. Other practices include communities of practice [6] and job rotation.

Within the agile development community a practice called Planning Poker has been established as a light-weight, work estimation practice for teams that can improve accuracy of estimates and reduce occurrences of optimistic estimates [16, 26]. Contributing to these effects is that participants must justify estimates which again promote discussions and identification of lack of information [5]. Planning Poker is thus a vehicle to build shared understanding of tasks within teams [15]. A benefit with this practice is that it can integrate knowledge between different roles, not just developers [22]. However, barriers to adoption have not been empirically investigated.

Because the building of redundant knowledge may easily create conflicts with bureaucratic efficiency values and norms [13], it might be difficult to introduce such practices into an organization. This leads to the research question: *What barriers can be met when introducing practices to increase redundant knowledge in software organizations and how can benefits of redundant knowledge overcome these barriers?* My collaboration with IT-Corp and CardPay was a suitable context for addressing the question; the transition to agile development was apparently hindered by insufficient levels of redundant knowledge and the collaboration enabled a longitudinal, in-depth investigation. I will now describe the research approach.

3 Research Approach

Action research (AR) was used for this investigation. AR is a research approach that guides the production of scientific knowledge from organizational change [14]. Altering software development practices to improve alignment with agile principles has the potential to provide both relevant and credible knowledge for the software community. Further, the ambition with the investigation was to understand key premises for learning in software organizations, to which AR's strong roots in organizational learning were valuable [1, 3].

AR is collaborative. In seeking to stimulate organizational change from critical inquiry of established practices, the action researcher collaborates with practitioners to build theoretically-informed and theoretically-informing cycles of learning. In this particular project, I wanted to understand and improve upon the situation in CardPay with respect to the specialist knowledge emphasis inhibiting agile development. To achieve this, the key idea was to introduce a practice for building redundant knowledge and observe the group's acceptance and adoption of the practice. Hence, AR was a particularly useful research approach in this investigation.

In order to ensure credibility and relevance in the research, I adopted the five principles of Canonical AR (CAR) [10]. Table 1 explains how each principle is addressed.

I followed the CardPay product group from December 2007 to December 2008 with the highest intensity of collaboration in the period January – June 2008. The collaborative nature of AR demands clarity in the role of the researcher as it can easily become that of a consultant. Prior to this particular engagement, IT-Corp had accepted the role as an industrial partner in a large AR program in which I was already associated. The research program agreement contained the juridical sections necessary to allow me participation solely with the intention to conduct research. Nevertheless, I used the last meeting in November 2007 to present the AR model for CardPay to ensure that we had a mutual understanding of the collaboration and of my role.

Table 1. Implementation of CAR principles

1. Researcher-client agreement. There is a long history of research collaboration with IT-Corp focusing on software process improvement. The study presented here was conducted as part of an on-going AR program in which IT-Corp and researchers cooperate with a number of other software organizations.
2. Cyclical process model. I adopted the five-stage, cyclical process model: Diagnosing, action planning, action taking, evaluating and specifying learning. One full cycle was completed after which CardPay had institutionalized team estimation.
3. Theory principle. The main theoretical ambition was to expand current understanding regarding the barriers to redundant knowledge in software organizations.
4. Change through action. I collaborated with CardPay during the whole investigation. Nevertheless, my engagement should be classified as moderate as I did not take on any direct responsibility for CardPay development activities. My role was similar to the facilitative, participative researcher [3].
5. Learning through reflection. Numerous gatherings with CardPay members in between observations enabled collective discussions and reflections. I initiated formal group meeting when in need for group commitment and broader reflection. I participated in IT-Corp's Scrum forum meetings to exchange experience with other Scrum projects in IT-Corp. My collaboration with IT-Corp included 53 named individuals that contributed information to the research and enabled a deeper understanding of IT-Corp's organizational constraints and idiosyncrasies.

In order to understand barriers to building redundant knowledge and how these barriers could be overcome I decided to base data collection in observations, retrospectives and a combination of individual and group meetings. This provided understanding of actual practice and frequent comparisons with opinions expressed in meetings. Gaps between practice and espoused theory is a central element of understanding organizational change [1]. Furthermore, I wanted to understand the longitudinal properties of the change. Hence, I decided that CardPay's biweekly Sprint planning meetings were the right choice for regular observations over a reasonable time span. Scrum prescribes these planning meetings to coordinate the work to be done in the coming iteration and involve all the people with contributing roles in the iteration. The Scrum Master would normally allocate 3 hours for these meetings, but the meetings could occasionally be longer.

Starting in December 2007, I participated as observer in CardPay's Sprint planning meetings. During the observations I did not participate in any discussions and I made my role as an observer clearer by pulling my chair close to a corner of the meeting room. Initially my presence was awkward for some group members; they would often seek to get eye contact and occasionally tried to engage me in their discussions. However, I refrained from such participation. After a few observations people got used to my role and seemed to ignore my presence.

I did engage in conversations before and after observations, as well as during the breaks however. People showed interest in reflection – quite often I ended up having 'debriefing' meetings with 2-5 group members. These meetings contributed to build trust and confidence in my intention of wanting to assist in improving the situation.

A gradually more confident and open dialogue with CardPay group members was very valuable and supported the emergent process of understanding the change process [20]. It also allowed me to freely question and confront difficult situations [1]. I also participated in Scrum forum meetings at the corporate level where we exchanged experience with Scrum in different IT-Corp projects. On two occasions I was also directly approached by senior IT-Corp executives that wanted to understand more about my research and my findings. We had informative, albeit rather brief meetings. However, they gave me useful insights into the organizational context surrounding CardPay.

Additionally, I also spent some time working from at desk in the CardPay group's office area. I was sitting in close proximity to the group members but I did not obtain particularly interesting or useful data. People were focusing on their own work; although interrupted by occasional phone calls or requests from colleagues. Table 2 shows a summary of the data collected throughout the collaboration.

After each day at Corp-IT I added new notes and reflections. I used a tool for qualitative data analysis to support the coding of the data. Analysis was fundamentally driven by critical interpretivism [20]. The longitudinal nature of the collaboration, the numerous informants that introduced me to Corp-IT and CardPay's organizational context and the flexibility of the tool to support gradually emerging coding hierarchies and conceptualizations greatly supported this.

Table 2. Data collected throughout the collaboration

What	Explanation
Participatory observations	Field notes from observation of 16 Sprint planning meetings, 1 daily standup meeting and 1 Sprint review meeting.
Direct involvement	I was directly involved in planning, preparing and guiding the adoption of team estimation using specifically designated meetings. I made meeting notes and collected meeting documentation such as presentations.
Coordination with IT-Corp	I participated in 3 Scrum forum meetings exchanging experiences with other Scrum projects in IT-Corp. I made meeting notes and collected meeting documentation such as presentations.
Informal meetings	During the collaboration I participated in numerous informal meetings with a range of people at Corp-IT. This also included coffee-breaks and lunches. I made meeting notes.
Documentation	I had access to documents regarding CardPay's activities occurring outside the periods I was present.

4 Action Research in CardPay

4.1 Diagnosing

IT-Corp is a large and complex organization with a long history of mergers and acquisitions. In 2008 IT-Corp employed more than 5,000 people in Europe and India.

One of four business areas is ICT solutions for banking and finance which is characterized by a substantial body of formalized rules and procedures. The vast amount of domain knowledge is reflected by the complexity of the software systems and is a strong driver for specialist knowledge [21]. I was told that new employees to the business area normally spent 1-2 years before reaching a level of proficient performance. Furthermore, the bureaucratization of the business area mirrored the pre-determined structure of tasks and knowledge. Nevertheless, legislative bodies such as the Payment Card Industry and EU/SEPA impose periodically updated requirements to which solutions must conform.

CardPay is both a product group and a product that belongs to the banking and finance business area within IT-Corp. The CardPay product group had 13 core members working in various roles such as product configuration, development, product management, systems management, database specialist, and testing. Additionally, there were numerous people with other roles that had significant interaction and interest in the CardPay product, such as department management, customer project management and IT management. The wide repertoire of roles is a strong indicator of specialist organizational culture.

The CardPay product provides functionality for processing transactions from payment cards. A major restructuring of the product started autumn 2007. The work was mainly funded by a large customer project with tight deadlines. The restructuring involved replacing key business logic with a 3rd party software module delivered by a European company here named EuroPay. An important part of the development work was adapting and rewriting existing application interfaces, as well as reports and miscellaneous utilities, to support the customer in a smooth migration to the new CardPay system. Combining customer project funding and integration with a hitherto unknown software module incurred significant complexity and risk; many of my contacts noted that the ambition level was high compared with the uncertainty and complexity of the undertaking. Furthermore, many of the customer's requirements were not fully understood and the contract promised the customer significant benefits from being the sponsor of the transition to the new technology. CardPay members complained that the CardPay product had been promised ready far too early. To make matters even more complicated, CardPay management signed another contract for migration of a second customer to the new CardPay product. The CardPay group would now have two streams of customer requirements.

Hence, the CardPay group faced an extremely turbulent environment. Challenges with competing customer requirements and a significant number of quality issues with the EuroPay module created an atmosphere near chaos. Soon, the CardPay group struggled with considerable overtime and even people having to work during the night and through weekends to respond to quality issues. And the CardPay product manager, IS, was responsible for aligning long-term product plans with the more pressing customer requirements. More often than not, he was deeply concerned that the high attention to customers' feature requests jeopardized ambitions to build a solid, high-quality product. It seemed clear that management's customer-driven product development strategy created friction with existing culture within the group.

The CardPay product group introduced Scrum in October 2007 to coincide with the restructuring of the product. Prior to this, the group followed IT-Corp's established ISO-certified processes for software development which were largely document-driven and adhered to waterfall principles. Introduction and adoption of Scrum happened from initiative by department management as part of a process improvement program led by IT-Corp staff. At the time of adoption only 3-4 projects were using Scrum within IT-Corp but several new projects were in the pipeline. A key motivation was to improve productivity and the ability to deal with changes.

From the initiation meetings I learned that the CardPay group considered the transition to Scrum problematic already from the beginning. There were complaints about lacking Scrum discipline and a seemingly insurmountable stream of enquiries from the two customers that made planning difficult. This surprised me; I came with the presupposition that agile development would be most suitable in turbulent environments. Gradually however, I concluded that the problems were likely to be even more challenging without iterative planning. Probably, agile development brought the turbulence more into light.

Flexibility from overlapping skills might have helped the CardPay group to deal with such turbulence but seemed like luxury. In the Sprint planning meetings key members were repeatedly pushed from one crisis to the next while others went about their tasks as normal. Building flexibility from redundant knowledge in such circumstances is difficult; there seemed to be no buffer capacity. Additionally, decision-making in the group was highly centralized. ARS, the most senior member of the group, showed an impressive proficiency in the whole range of challenges facing the project. He had extensive contact with various people within IT-Corp and within customers' organizations. In fact, ARS seemed to master everything, and worked immense amounts of overtime in order to meet demands from customers. But as a result he also brought significant authority in all decision-making. It was difficult for less tenured members of the group to stand up to him. Discussions were often concluded after strong arguments from ARS.

A lack of redundant knowledge was an identified, general problem within Corp-IT, confirmed by numerous of my Corp-IT informants. The problem was so eminent that it had its own name (SPoK, Single Point of Knowledge) to signal vulnerability in the face of unpredictable events. Also, in a workshop the CardPay group acknowledged that a specialist culture inhibited team commitment to Sprints. Instead, it was individuals such as ARS who committed themselves to the product.

From my observations of Sprint planning meetings the specialist culture was manifested also in the allocation of tasks. During diagnosing I made notes from 109 tasks being planned but only 7 included discussions of alternatives for task allocation. In the vast majority of cases, the tasks were either pre-allocated or allocated without questions. The language used emphasized the specialist culture. Expressions such as "this is a Joe task" and "I've already talked with Peter about this task" confirmed how the content of the task determines who was supposed to do it.

More importantly, there were very few occasions of tasks being openly discussed. I recorded no instances of task estimates being questioned by more than 2 people. The typical scenario was that the person allocated to the task updated the Scrum Master on the task estimates. Generally, task estimates were far too optimistic and resulting in Sprint burndowns that were nowhere near completion at the Sprints' end. However, the Scrum Master had literally no technical competence and he had limited inclination to question the estimates. Contributing to this was ARS's authority in the group.

In summary, both CardPay's turbulent environment and the strong specialist culture created a barrier to redundant knowledge. And the CardPay group seemed unable to cross the barrier on their own.

4.2 Action Planning

Early March 2008 a fellow researcher and I facilitated a project retrospective for the CardPay group. We had nine participants that reflected collectively upon improvement actions. A large number of proposals were generated, grouped and ranked according to importance by voting. In order of descending votes the topics were: method, architecture, competence, task planning, miscellaneous and discipline.

In a follow-up meeting five days later we discussed how the topics could be addressed. We focused on the method topic since it had received the highest number of votes. The proposals allocated to this topic centered on three core issues: a) discipline in the use of ScrumWorks[2], b) the need for an improved tool that would integrate multiple process tools and c) an improved estimating method. With respect to a), the main problem was that tasks were too vaguely specified in ScrumWorks, if at all. It was difficult for others in the group to understand what the task was about. With respect to b) the meeting could only make recommendations to IT-Corp. With respect to c) I argued that a team estimation process could help in resolving multiple issues simultaneously: 1) it had the potential to improve participation and involvement in the group which could bring substantial benefits in improving team culture and team commitment, 2) it had the potential to ensure that vaguely specified tasks in Scrum-Works would be spotted and revised online, 3) it had the potential to build competence within the group and also improve task planning by producing more accurate estimates. Hence, addressing concerns raised by 1st, 3rd and 4th priority topics. The meeting concluded that team estimation should be introduced as from the beginning of April 2008 with a trial of four planning meetings.

To improve the likelihood of successful adoption, I arranged for a new CardPay group briefing in the end of March whereby I sought to actively involve the members in the change process [1, 14]. In this meeting I presented a summary of my observations and the retrospective meeting. I also presented a model of double-loop learning that illustrated how I believed that the group had to 'take a step back' and critically review existing practice in order to improve the situation [1]. I argued that team estimation was a realistic practice that could help. At the end I presented the Planning Poker practice [15] as an example, light-weight practice. The participants appeared enthusiastic about trying the practice.

After the group briefing 4-5 group members remained in the room. They expressed concerns that CardPay was an atypical software organization: "You know, developing software is only a part of what we do. We have a lot of other specialist functions here as well such as product configuration, report generation, product testing, transaction monitoring and transaction correction." I recognized this concern and explained that team estimation was a generic practice that addressed the need to improve coordination and group-learning; contrary to pair-programming and collective code ownership the practice of team estimation does not require actual programming work to give

---

[2] The tool used by CardPay for recording and organizing Scrum iterations.

benefits. The product manager said: "Well, this is something that we have to try." The others agreed.

4.3 Action Taking

At the beginning of the first Sprint planning meeting of April 2008 I did a repeated introduction of the Planning Poker practice (see textbox "Planning Poker in Card-Pay"). From an AR point of view the practice has several benefits. First, it is very simple. It takes only minutes to explain and requires no tools except the estimation cards. I handed out stacks of estimation cards[3] to each group member prior to the introduction. There were occasional laughs – from the idea of playing cards at work.

Secondly, the practice prescribed that the Product Owner should present the tasks and hence encouraged him to take more ownership of the task definitions.

Because the practice is simple, engaging and entertaining people quickly got the hang of it. After 3-4 estimation sessions in the first Sprint meeting I noticed how the group established new, collective action [9]. Group members' attention shifted from the practice itself towards the challenge of understanding the task and estimating the work effort associated with it.

Planning Poker in CardPay:
- Each task to be estimated is presented by the Product Owner. The Product Owner does not estimate.
- The group members ask for any clarifications they feel necessary in order to estimate the task effort. Normally this triggers a group-wide discussion.
- Upon notification from the Scrum Master each member presents the card showing the estimate believed to best approximate the task effort.
- If the estimates are roughly similar the Scrum Master uses the most frequent estimate as the task estimate.
- If there is wide disagreement in the estimates the task is discussed again and the group members present updated estimates.

Team estimation required significantly more time than previous estimation practice. And already at the end of the first Sprint planning session there were signs of defensive behavior that threatened the new practice. The Scrum Master expressed concerns that they were running out of time. But several other group members protested and commented that it was useful nevertheless and that it was valuable discussions and also that it was alright to spend more time on estimation in the beginning.

During a break I repeated that this was in fact the fundamental problem we were trying to solve and that a certain degree of patience was required. The Product Owner agreed. The Sprint planning meeting continued with using Planning Poker. It was also decided that a follow-up meeting the next morning would estimate the few remaining tasks. I spent time after the meeting for de-briefing with the Scrum Master. He was largely happy with the practice but said that he had felt a pressure to stay with the

---

[3] The estimation cards resemble normal playing cards but carries effort estimates as the card value. The effort estimate values are '?', 0, 1/2, 1, 2, 3, 5, 8, 13, 20, 40, 100 and 'infinity'.

original time schedule for the meeting. While we were talking the department manager appeared, joined the conversation and gave further support to the continued use of Planning Poker. However, in the following Sprint planning meeting there were still several examples of defensive behavior. The Scrum Master simply short-circuited the estimation process by inserting seemingly arbitrary estimates on the tasks and stating that "we don't have time for such detailed discussions now." I could hear sighs and comments from group members that wanted to stick with the practice.

During de-briefing after the next Sprint planning meeting I was somewhat surprised when the Scrum Master exclaimed: "I would like to use Planning poker from now on in all the Sprint planning meetings." It was in striking contrast to his behavior in the Sprint planning meeting. I concluded that he wanted to continue the practice but that other factors forced him to stop. He explained: "I get really tired of these long planning meetings. Besides, new issues appear continuously that require me to think over things again and coordinate further." He had already thought out an alternative: "I think we will divide the planning session into two separate events, in this way I've got the time to prepare better for the last round."

Thus, a variant of the practice was invented; a pre-planning session preceded the real Sprint planning session. In the former, only a subset of the group was present together with the customer project mangers and no explicit estimation of effort was done, it was solely meant clarify content of tasks to be resolved by the group. In the proper Sprint planning session Planning Poker was used, although, only for roughly two thirds of the tasks. From now on the practice was institutionalized.

4.4 Evaluating

Team estimation was institutionalized in CardPay and I consider this as an indication of successful double-loop learning. Table 3 below summarizes practice adoption by contrasting distribution of different estimation event types before (pre) and after (post) introducing Planning Poker. Most importantly, the data show that Planning Poker was used for 27 of the 40 recorded estimation events in the post-action phase (13 + 27). In my last meeting with the Scrum Master in December 2008 he confirmed that Planning Poker was now used in all Sprint planning meetings. The practice was established and used in the group despite my absence.

We now return to the research question in order to evaluate the action research: *What barriers can be met when introducing practices to increase redundant knowledge in software organizations and how can benefits of redundant knowledge overcome these barriers?*

4.4.1 Barriers to Team Estimation
When identifying barriers to team estimation I carefully analyzed the 30 tasks estimated by individuals or for which no estimation process was recorded (13 + 17). During my observations the Scrum Master decided for which tasks Planning Poker was used. However, he never appeared as an individualistic leader. Rather, he constantly sought legitimacy from the other group members. This was not surprising given his lack of actual experience with the CardPay product (cf. section 4.1). Occasionally he was even encouraged by others in the group to 'step up' and make clear decisions. From this I concluded that group members' opinion of the team estimation practice strongly influenced its continued use.

Table 3. Summary of task discussion events and estimation practice used

	Pre-action phase	Post-action phase
Estimates by individuals	43	13
Estimates by team	0	27
Unknown, N/A[4]	66	17
Sum	109	57

Team estimation was quickly associated with detailed and thorough discussions on which ground it was abandoned on at least three occasions. The Scrum Master explained it by saying: "We don't have time for such detailed discussion now." Hence, he revealed a conflict between group discussions and efficiency ideals. On other occasions, team estimation was abandoned because precise estimates were not considered necessary for small tasks (less than 2-3 hours). The fact that detailed group discussions were not considered rational for all tasks illuminates that there was a perceived threshold of necessity for group clarification of tasks. Diversity in task types also contributes to explain the abandonment of team estimation for certain tasks.

Another strong barrier for team estimation was lack of information. Planning Poker brought out viewpoints from all group members and this contributed to expose areas of vagueness in the task understanding. In such situations, final estimation of the task was postponed until more information was made available. Further, on four occasions the lack of information was attributed to "the most knowledgeable person is not present" which is itself symptomatic of a lack of redundant knowledge and is an example of the 'Single Point of Knowledge' problem found during diagnosis (cf. section 4.1). There was not enough redundant knowledge to sustain a realistic estimate in the absence of certain persons.

Somewhat related to lack of information was a barrier created by size of tasks. If tasks were too big, the discussions did not bring sufficient clarity to the problem-solving strategy. The group could not reach agreement on organization of the work. Hence, Planning Poker exposed the need to divide tasks into smaller, more manageable tasks. I noted that for tasks believed to constitute more than 100 hours of work they were broken down into smaller units. For example, the habit of more participation and more information becoming communicated would contribute to the acknowledgement of conflicts between the two funding customer projects which introduced additional complexity into the task.

---

[4] The high number of task discussions in the pre-action phase for which I recorded no estimation practice (66) is due to the fact that the task estimates were often set without talking or mention. Some tasks were also not estimated because they were already completed, there was lack of information within the group or a decision was made to split the task into subtasks. Further, the number of task discussions in the post-action phase for which I recorded no estimation practice (17) is subject to reduced accuracy. The intensity of discussions in the post-action phase was so high that I occasionally failed to capture discussions and decisions.

4.4.2 Benefits of Team Estimation

As group members tried to understand the individual tasks there were many interesting situations. Most importantly, it was evident that very few group members understood individual tasks. The lack of redundant knowledge was exposed by group member's eager attempts to ask for clarifications. And for a number of tasks it became clear that no-one in the meeting had enough information to explain the work. These tasks were tagged appropriately and then skipped for the next Sprint planning meeting.

Participation in the discussions increased radically. Prior to team estimation the task discussions were mostly status updates communicated directly to the Scrum Master. In the post-action phase, most, if not all, group members tried to contribute and understand the tasks. One result I found very intriguing was that participation seemed higher for all tasks, even for those not being subjected to the final card game. The reason for this was that the group members developed a habit of more active participation and that the Scrum Master rarely made the decision to abandon team estimation before a certain period of discussion had been going on.

Further, the team estimation discussions contributed strongly to actual problem-solving. Most frequently, estimates were higher in the second round of estimation – i.e. new information brought into the discussion contributed to appreciation of greater task complexity and size. Discussions were normally centered on problem-solving and often included contributions by group members with experience from similar tasks. However, there were also a few occasions where these contributions resulted in better problem-solving strategies that reduced the initial task estimates.

One CardPay group member named TAM had previously skipped all prior Sprint planning meetings started showing up. He illustrated another benefit of team estimation; the estimation discussion had become a collective arena for demonstration of competence. I had many times requested the Scrum Master to put stronger force onto involving TAM into the Sprint planning meetings but without success. TAM was working on the same tasks as ARS and was normally given tasks by ARS directly. Apparently, TAM was the quiet type that wanted clear directions in his work. But during team estimation sessions he showed great enthusiasm and contributed greatly to clarification and problem-solving.

4.5 Specifying Learning

The combination of both group observations and individual meetings and debriefing gives the possibility to compare what people do in the group learning situation and what they uphold as espoused theory [1]. One key to double-loop learning is for the researcher to initiate critical inquiry of established practices and illustrating models of new, productive learning while avoiding that practitioners 'loose their face' in the process. Introducing team estimation seemed to achieve exactly this. Although there were clear signs of defensive behavior as existing values and norms of efficiency were being confronted (cf. section 4.3), I noticed no occurrences of embarrassment. Rather, Planning Poker contributed almost instantly to seemingly more realistic estimates of tasks while achieving dramatic increases in group member participation and subsequent improvement of redundant knowledge. Also, team estimation exposed occasions when not enough information was available. I believe this is an important factor that explains the group's continued use of Planning Poker. Although it may take a long time to build the culture of trust and respect that facilitates pluralist decision-making [27] team estimation created the environment in which the CardPay group could adjust fundamental efficiency values and engage in double-loop learning [1].

By institutionalizing Planning Poker the CardPay group they established a new practice for group learning that was productive in building redundant knowledge. Team estimation shifted more of the problem-solving into the Sprint planning meeting. As group members actively sought to contribute with their own knowledge problem-solving now became a group activity where group members narrated shared stories to explain viable problem-solving strategies [6]. Hence, the CardPay group was able to 'talk solutions into existence' [22] and exploit the collective strength of the group's practice-based knowing in completing the CardPay product [9]. The improvement in redundant knowledge was not reflected in markedly higher flexibility of task allocation however. This will take more time. Task allocation discussions increased by 5 % in the post-action phase and the share of task allocations done without discussing alternatives dropped by 6 % in the post-action phase.

Although team estimation gives such benefits it is also understandable that Card-Pay didn't want to use team estimation for every task in the Sprints. There are overheads with it that must be weighed against the benefits. The CardPay group used Planning Poker for 27 of the 40 estimated tasks in the post-action phase (see table 3).

Furthermore, specialist knowledge is still required in CardPay. It would certainly not be efficient for all group members to have the exact same skills. By allocating group learning to a rather confined venue such as Sprint planning the group was able to improve redundant knowledge without overdoing it.

4.6 Limitations

Interpretation of the results should be subjected to validity and generalizeability considerations. Generalizations from such single-case studies depends on rich and relevant context descriptions and theoretically-informed interpretation of outcomes [3] as well as application of established AR guidelines, such as CAR [10]. Much attention in the article is therefore given to this. The triangulation between multiple data sources can also improve validity. However, validity of AR resides primarily in the workability of the action [14] in which respect this research was successful.

A limitation of the investigation is lack of data to enable analysis of the team estimation accuracy. However, these effects of Planning Poker have been reported elsewhere [16, 26]. During my observations in the post-action phase I did notice significantly better Scrum burndowns. The Scrum Master confirmed this at my last meeting with him. Another limitation of the investigation is its duration. A longer duration of investigation would be necessary to confirm effects on task allocation flexibility.

5 Conclusions

Despite the barriers created by turbulence and specialist organizational environment this action research successfully altered CardPay's practice towards increased collaborative problem-solving and building of redundant group knowledge. By working as a group, CardPay was able to benefit from individual members' skills and experience. Arguably, this capability will improve the CardPay group's software development capability in an increasingly fierce and turbulent market.

I see four important factors that contributed to the success of this action research: 1) The need for change was based in extensive diagnosing and had wide commitment within the group. 2) The change itself was simple and thus easy to describe and implement. 3) The change created immediate and visible benefits. 4) The practice could be easily adapted to the group's context. These factors should be kept in mind by other organizations struggling with achieving group learning in a turbulent, specialist organizational environment.

However, it takes time and commitment to change peoples' practices. Thus, changing practice can be difficult for groups deeply concerned with pressing tasks. Creating the momentum for change might therefore depend on collaboration with outsiders.

References

1. Argyris, C., Schön, D.A.: Organizational learning II: Theory, method, and practice. Addison-Wesley, Reading (1996)
2. Bahli, B., Zeid, E.S.A.: The role of knowledge creation in adopting extreme programming model: an empirical study. In: ITI 3rd International Conference on Information and Communications Technology: Enabling Technologies for the New Knowledge Society (2005)
3. Baskerville, R., Wood-Harper, T.A.: Diversity in information systems action research. European Journal of Information Systems 7(2), 90–107 (1998)
4. Boehm, B., Turner, R.: Management challenges to implementing agile processes in traditional development organizations. IEEE Software 22(5), 30–39 (2005)
5. Brenner, L.A., Koehler, D.J., Tversky, A.: On the evaluation of one-sided evidence. Journal of Behavioral Decision Making 9(1), 59–70 (1996)
6. Brown, J.S., Duguid, P.: Organizational learning and communities-of-practice: Toward a unified view of working, learning, and innovation. Organization Science 2(1), 40–57 (1991)
7. Börjesson, A., Martinsson, F., Timmerås, M.: Agile improvement practices in software organizations. European Journal of Information Systems 15, 169–182 (2006)
8. Cohn, M., Ford, D.: Introducing an agile process to an organization. IEEE computer 36(6), 74–78 (2003)
9. Cook, S.D.N., Brown, J.S.: Bridging epistemologies: The generative dance between organizational knowledge and organizational knowing. Organization Science 10(4), 381–400 (1999)
10. Davison, R.M., Martinsons, M.G., Kock, N.: Principles of canonical action research. Information Systems Journal 14(1), 65–86 (2004)
11. Dybå, T., Dingsøyr, T.: Empirical studies of agile software development: a systematic review. Information and Software Technology 50(9-10), 833–859 (2008)
12. Fitzgerald, B., Hartnett, G., Conboy, K.: Customising agile methods to software practices at Intel Shannon. European Journal of Information Systems 15, 200–213 (2006)
13. Fægri, T.E.: Building General Knowledge in Agile Software Organizations: Experiences with job rotation in customer support. In: Dubinsky, Y., Dybå, T., Kruchten, P. (eds.) Agile 2009, pp. 46–54. IEEE Computer Society, Chicago (2009)
14. Greenwood, D.J., Levin, M.: Introduction to action research: Social research for social change. SAGE Publications, Thousand Oaks (2007)

15. Grenning, J.: Planning poker (2002), `http://renaissancesoftware.net/papers/14-papers/44-planing-poker.html`
16. Haugen, N.C.: An empirical study of using planning poker for user story estimation. In: Proceedings of the AGILE 2006 conference (AGILE 2006). IEEE Computer Society, Los Alamitos (2006)
17. Highsmith, J., Cockburn, A.: Agile software development: The business of innovation. IEEE computer 34(9), 120–127 (2001)
18. Hilkka, M.-R., Tuure, T., Matti, R.: Is extreme programming just old wine in new bottles: A comparison of two cases. Journal of Database Management 16(4), 41–61 (2005)
19. Karlström, D., Runeson, P.: Integrating agile software development into stage-gate managed product development. Empirical Software Engineering 11(2), 203–225 (2006)
20. Klein, H.K., Myers, M.D.: A set of principles for conducting and evaluating interpretive field studies in information systems. MIS Quarterly 23(1), 67–94 (1999)
21. Kolb, D.A.: Experiential learning: Experience as the source of learning and development. Prentice-Hall, New Jersey (1984)
22. Mackenzie, A., Monk, S.: From cards to code: How extreme programming re-embodies programming as a collective practice. Computer Supported Cooperative Work 13(1), 91–117 (2004)
23. Marchenko, A., Abrahamsson, P.: Scrum in a multiproject environment: An ethnographically-inspired case study on the adoption challenges. In: Agile 2008, Toronto, Canada (2008)
24. Maruping, L.M., Zhang, X.J., Venkatesh, V.: Role of collective ownership and coding standards in coordinating expertise in software project teams. European Journal of Information Systems 18(4), 355–371 (2009)
25. Moe, N.B., Dingsøyr, T., Dybå, T.: Overcoming barriers to self-management in software teams. IEEE Software 26(6), 20–26 (2009)
26. Moløkken-Østvold, K., Haugen, N.C.: Combining estimates with Planning Poker - An empirical study. In: Proceedings of the 2007 Australian Software Engineering Conference (ASWEC 2007), pp. 349–358. IEEE Computer Society, Los Alamitos (2007)
27. Nerur, S., Mahapatra, R., Mangalaraj, G.: Challenges of migrating to agile methodologies. Communications of the ACM 48(5), 72–78 (2005)
28. Nerur, S., Balijepally, V.: Theoretical reflections on agile development methodologies: The traditional goal of optimization and control is making way for learning and innovation. Communications of the ACM 50(3), 79–83 (2007)
29. Schwaber, K., Beedle, M.: Agile software development with Scrum. Prentice Hall, New Jersey (2002)
30. Svensson, H., Höst, M.: Introducing agile process in a software maintenance and evolution organization. In: Ninth European Conference on Software Maintenance, CSMR 2005 (2005)

Extreme Product Line Engineering –
Refactoring for Variability: A Test-Driven Approach

Yaser Ghanam and Frank Maurer

Department of Computer Science
2500 University Dr. NW, Calgary
Alberta, Canada T2N 1N4
{yghanam,fmaurer}@ucalgary.ca

Abstract. Software product lines - families of similar but not identical software products - need to address the issue of feature variability. That is, a single feature might require various implementations for different customers. Also, features might need optional extensions that are needed by some but not all products. Software product line engineering manages variability by conducting a thorough domain analysis upfront during the planning phases. However, upfront, heavyweight planning approaches are not well-aligned with the values of minimalistic practices like XP where bottom-up, incremental development is common. In this paper, we introduce a bottom-up, test-driven approach to introduce variability to systems by reactively refactoring existing code. We support our approach with an eclipse plug-in to automate the refactoring process. We evaluate our approach by a case study to determine the feasibility and practicality of the approach.

Keywords: variability, software product lines, agile methods, refactoring.

1 Introduction

1.1 Software Product Line Engineering

Software product line (SPL) engineering enables organizations to manage families of products that are similar but not identical [1]. The idea is to target a certain market domain, but be able to satisfy the various requirements of different market sectors (i.e. customers) in that domain. This is achieved by developing a common platform from which different instances of the system are derived. Being able to customize the products during the instantiation process is due to the concept of variability [2].

Variability refers to the notion that the components that constitute the system may exist or behave differently in different instances of that system. Moreover, some components may be optional and, hence, may not exist in every instance of the system. Every product line has a variability profile that encompasses a number of variation points and a set of variants for each variation point. A variation point is an aspect in a certain requirement that can have multiple states of existence in the system. Each state of existence is called a variant.

A. Sillitti et al. (Eds.): XP 2010, LNBIP 48, pp. 43–57, 2010.

Consider the example in Figure 1a. The weather module has two variation points. The first is of type "option" – the weather trend analyzer. Options are either selected (variant 1) or discarded (variant 2). That is, the weather trend analyzer is optional depending on whether the customer would like to have it or not. The second variation point is of type "alternatives" – the weather UI panel. Alternatives are mutually exclusive – if one is selected, the other alternatives cannot be selected. That is, the weather UI panel can have one of two different formats depending on whether the application is to run on a handheld device (variant 1) or a normal PC (variant 2).

When the customer purchases a smart home system with the weather module, a decision has to be made on what variants should be selected for every variation point in the system. Based on these decisions, different instances can be produced such as the ones shown in Figure 1b. Decision making is usually governed by the wants and needs of the customer, as well as any technical or business constraints.

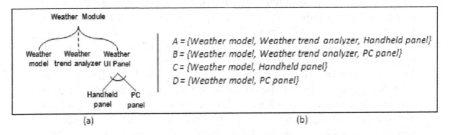

Fig. 1. Example of variability in a module

Organizations that use product line practices to manage their software production have a competitive advantage. Some organizations reported reductions in the number of defects in their products and cuts in costs and time-to-market by a factor of 10 or more [3]. This is because dealing with a single configurable entity that is considered the base for all products in a given category provides for many benefits such as:

a. Software Reuse: Reuse of the same source code to produce a number of systems provides an economic advantage.

b. Increased software stability: Reused components can be better tested as the effort amortizes over a larger number of software systems.

c. Mass customization: Mass customization means that a wider range of customers can be satisfied even though their needs might be different.

d. Reduced maintenance effort: Maintaining a single base is more efficient than maintaining separate products. For example, if a bug needs to be fixed, the change should only happen within the single base, and the change will take effect in all individual products as soon as they are re-instantiated.

1.2 Software Product Lines and Agility

In the previous section, we explained what a SPL is and why it is a useful practice. This section discusses SPLs in the context of agile software development.

Traditionally, SPL engineering favors upfront, proactive approaches. Planning for variability is done during the domain engineering phase in order to determine what may vary and how. The variability profile is then taken into account to build a flexible reference architecture for all the instances to be built in the future. During the next phase, namely application engineering, customized instances of the system are derived and delivered to the customers.

For agile organizations, adopting a SPL approach in its traditional form is challenging. This is due to the common values and principles [4] in the agile culture that can be seen as being in direct conflict with essential aspects of SPL engineering. For one, agile methods encourage working on what is currently needed and asked for rather than what might be needed in the future. Therefore, dedicating an entire domain analysis phase to make predictions about variability might be a risky option. Furthermore, in the agile culture, it is deemed important to deliver working software on a regular basis – which in a SPL context is too difficult to achieve especially in the early phases.

In this paper, we argue that for agile organizations to adopt a SPL practice, a reactive – as opposed to proactive – approach is more befitting. We focus on the notion of variability considering that it is one of the most important aspects of SPLs. We describe a bottom-up, reactive approach to gradually construct variability profiles for existing systems. The approach relies on common agile practices such as refactoring and test-driven development to introduce variability into systems only when it is needed. The approach can provide the reuse and maintainability benefits of SPLs while keeping the delivery-focused approach coming from agile methods.

The next section describes the proposed approach in detail. In Section 3, we present an evaluation of the approach followed by a discussion of limitations. Section 4 discusses relevant literature and underscores our distinct contribution.

2 The Extreme Software Product Line Approach

2.1 Overview

The fundamental verdict of our approach to variability in the agile context is that variability should be handled on-demand. That is, unless requirements about variations in the system are available upfront, the agile organization should not proactively invest into predicting what might vary in the system. Rather, the normal course of development should take place to satisfy the current needs of the customers. Later on, should a need to introduce a variation point arise – whether during development or after delivery – agile teams shall have the tools to embrace this variability reactively. When a product line practice is not adopted, embracing variability is usually done by: a) clone-and-own techniques where the base code is copied and then customized to satisfy the new variation, or b) ad-hoc refactoring, where it is left up to the developer to refactor existing code to satisfy both the new as well as the existing variation. In the first case, the organization will have to maintain and support more than one base code, which is highly inefficient and error prone. In the second case, there is neither a systematic way to refactor the code nor a way to convey knowledge about the existence of variation points – which may cause variability in the system to become too cumbersome and expensive to maintain, and may render the instantiation process vague.

The approach we propose here is different in that it enforces systematic and test-driven practices to deal with variability in order to ensure consistency and efficiency.

2.2 The Role of Tests

In agile approaches like Extreme Programming [5], automated tests are deemed essential. There usually exist two types of tests: unit tests and acceptance tests. Our approach makes use of both types; however, this paper focuses on the use of unit tests only. A unit is defined as the smallest testable part of a system. A unit test verifies the correctness of the behavior of an individual unit, or the interaction between units. In test-driven development, unit tests are written before writing production code. Tests are automated to be executed frequently and help in refactoring of the code base.

In our approach, unit tests are relevant in three different ways:

1. Unit tests are used as a starting point to drive the variability introduction process. This point will be discussed further in the upcoming sections.
2. When a variation point is introduced along with its variants, unit tests ought to exhaust all the different variants, and therefore they are part of the variability introduction process.
3. Unit tests serve as a safety net to make sure the variability introduction process did not have any destructive side effects.

2.3 The Variability Introduction Process

To illustrate the proposed approach, we use a very simple example. Say, within a smart home security system, we have an electronic lock feature on every port (door or window). The diagram in Figure 2 illustrates the current state of the system. The Lock class is tested by the LockTest class. Arrows show the call hierarchy. E.g. Lock-Test.testSetPassword() calls the public method Lock.setPassword(), which in turn calls the private method Lock.isValidPassword(String).

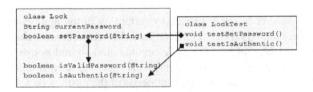

Fig. 2. Current state of the Lock feature

Currently, the system allows the user to set a 4-character password for the locks. The password criteria are checked in the Lock.isValidPassword() method below. Say we need to introduce a variation point to the lock feature to allow customers to choose the desired security level needed on the locks before they purchase the system. Variants include a 4-char lock (the original lock), an 8-char lock (a new alternative), or a non-trivial 8-char lock (another new alternative - characters cannot be all the same and cannot be consecutive).

```
class Lock {
      String currentPassword="";

      public boolean setPassword(String password) {
              if(isValidPassword(password)) {
                      this.currentPassword = password;
                      return true;
              }
              return false;
      }

      boolean isValidPassword(String password) {
              if (password.length()==4) return true;
              return false;
      }


      public boolean isAuthentic(String password) {
              if(password == currentPassword) return true;
              return false;
      }
}
```

One way[1] to design this is to use an abstract factory pattern [6] to reach the configuration shown in Figure 3. We can abstract the method that is responsible for password validation (i.e. Lock.isValidPassword(String)) and provide three different implementations for it.

Our tool supports this refactoring process: when a developer wants to introduce a variation, the tool helps in the required refactoring of the code base. It creates an abstract factory, corresponding concrete classes, and the required test classes.

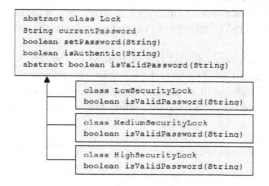

Fig. 3. The new state of the Lock feature

---

[1] There are other techniques and patterns to realize variability. Choosing the appropriate technique for each case is beyond the scope of this paper. Our approach, however, should work fine with any code-based variability implementation technique.

Refactoring the code to reach the configuration in Figure 3 has consequences. First of all, we need to write unit tests that reflect the new changes. Also, we need to change all instantiations of the old Lock class to use the new factory instead. And we need to determine which implementation we want before every instantiation of the Lock class. For this to work, we also need to provide an implementation selector class to return the proper implementation.

To take care of the refactoring process and all its consequences, we take advantage of the existing traceability between unit tests and production code. We provide a formalization of the variability introduction process in order to automate it:

There exists in the system a set of unit test classes C_u. Each testing class c_{ui} has a set of testing methods.

$$C_u = \{c_{u1}, c_{u2}, c_{u3}, \dots, c_{ui}\}$$
$$c_{ui} = \{m_{ui1}, m_{ui2}, m_{ui3}, \dots, m_{uij}\}$$

Each testing method m_{uij} may instantiate or use a number of classes in the system - set C. Each class c_k consists of a set of methods.

$$C = \{c_1, c_2, c_3, \dots, c_k\}$$
$$c_k = \{m_{ck1}, m_{ck2}, m_{ck3}, \dots, m_{ckn}\}$$

Each method in c_k may instantiate or use a number of other classes in the system.

Over the previous sets, we define a process to introduce a variation point to the system. The process consists of the following functions:

1. A Variation Initialization function to determine:

    a. The unit test of interest as a starting point $m_{uij} \in c_{ui}$. This feeds into the next step.
    b. One of two variation types: *alternatives*, or *options*. This determines the kind of refactoring needed to embrace the variation point.

These two attributes should be determined by the developer. The developer chooses the unit test that tests the scenario where variability needs to exist. In the example above, it is the LockTest.testSetPassword() method shown below[2], because this is where we mainly test for the setting password part of the feature.

```
public void testSetPassword() {
    Lock lock = new Lock();
    Assert.assertFalse(lock.setPassword(""));
    Assert.assertFalse(lock.setPassword("Hello"));
    Assert.assertTrue(lock.setPassword("Helo"));
}
```

---

[2] This unit test is for illustration only. It is understood that in real life best practices like one-assert per test should be observed.

Then the developer decides whether the new variability is due to the need to provide alternative implementations or to add options to the feature at hand. In the example, we choose alternatives.

1. A Call Hierarchy function to determine the transitive closure of the unit test m_{uij} selected in step 1. This includes all methods in the system that are invoked due to the invocation of m_{uij}.

    In the example above, the call hierarchy of LockTest.testSetPassword() includes the methods: Lock.setPassword(String) and Lock.isValid Password(String).

    At this stage, developer's input is needed to identify where in the call hierarchy the variation point should exist. This determines the method that is causing the variation to happen. For example, because the variation point we need to inject is pertaining to the validation of the password criteria, we choose Lock.isValidPassword(String).

2. A Variability Trace function that – given the method m_{ckn} chosen in 2 – determines all the classes and methods that can potentially be affected by introducing the variation point.

    In the example above, say there is a class Port that instantiates the Lock class. This instantiation needs to be updated to use the new factory.

3. A Refactoring and Code Generation function to perform the code manipulations needed to introduce the variation point and the variants based on the variation type determined in 1b. Given the method $m_{ckn} \in c_k$ from the previous step, the following code manipulations will take place:

    a. Refactoring c_k so that m_{ckn} is abstracted as a variation point.

```
abstract class Lock {
      String currentPassword="";
      public boolean setPassword(String password) {
            if(isValidPassword(password)) {
                  this.currentPassword = password;
                  return true;
            }
            return false;
      }
      abstract boolean isValidPassword(String password);
      public boolean isAuthentic(String password) {
            if(password == currentPassword) return true;
            return false;
      }
}
```

    b. Generating implementations for the variants:

```
class LowLock extends Lock {
    boolean isValidPassword(String password) {
        if (password.length() == 4)
                return true;
        return false;
    }
}
class MediumLock extends Lock {
    boolean isValidPassword(String password) {
        // TODO Auto-generated method stub
        return false;
    }
}
class HighLock extends Lock {
    boolean isValidPassword(String password) {
        // TODO Auto-generated method stub
        return false;
    }
}
```

c. Declaring a new enumeration to explicate the variation point and its variants:

```
public enum VP_SECURITY_LEVEL { V_LOW, V_MEDIUM, V_HIGH }
```

d. Creating/updating a configurator class:

```
public class VariantConfiguration {
    public static VP_SECURITY_LEVEL securityLevel =
                                    VP_SECURITY_LEVEL.V_LOW;
}
```

The configurator serves two purposes. For one, it enables easy configuration and instantiation of products. Every variable in this class represents a variation point. The value assigned to each variable represents the variant we need to choose. Secondly, the configurator helps explicate the variability profile of the system so that it is visible to the stakeholders (later, we plan to link this profile to feature modeling tools to provide a better visualization).

e. Generating an implementation selector:

```
public class LockFactory {
    public static Lock createLock() {
        if (VariantConfiguration.securityLevel ==
VP_SECURITY_LEVEL.V_LOW) return new LowLock();
        if (VariantConfiguration.securityLevel ==
VP_SECURITY_LEVEL.V_MEDIUM) return new MediumLock();
        if (VariantConfiguration.securityLevel ==
VP_SECURITY_LEVEL.V_HIGH)     return new HighLock();
        else return null;
    }
}
```

f. Updating affected code segments found in step3 to use the new factory:

```
Lock lock = LockFactory.createLock();
```

4. A Test Update function to update affected unit tests and generate unit tests for the new variants. This not only makes sure the new changes did not have a destructive effect on the original system, but also encourages test-driven development because it generates failing tests for developers to write before writing the logic for the new variants.

In the example above, the LockTest.testSetPassword() method is refactored to LockTest.testSetPassword_Low() as a test for the first (original) variant. Two more tests are added to test the other two variants. In each test, the first statement selects the variant to be tested. In the case of *options*, we generate tests for all combinations of options. This of course has to go through a validation engine to filter invalid combinations but this is yet to be implemented in the tool. Generated tests initially have the same body of the original test (where the process started) as a template for the developer to change as required. However, these tests initially are forced to fail to remind the developer to edit the test and its corresponding production code.

```
@Test
public void testSetPassword_Low() {
        VariantConfiguration.securityLevel =
                            VP_SECURITY_LEVEL.V_LOW;
        Lock lock = LockFactory.createLock();
        Assert.assertFalse(lock.setPassword(""));
        Assert.assertFalse(lock.setPassword("Hello"));
        Assert.assertTrue(lock.setPassword("Helo"));
}
@Test
public void testSetPassword_Medium() {
        // TODO Auto-generated method stub
        VariantConfiguration.securityLevel =
                            VP_SECURITY_LEVEL.V_MEDIUM;
        Lock lock = LockFactory.createLock();
        Assert.assertFalse(lock.setPassword(""));
        Assert.assertFalse(lock.setPassword("Hello"));
        Assert.assertTrue(lock.setPassword("Helo"));
        org.junit.Assert.fail();
}
@Test
public void testSetPassword_High() {
        // TODO Auto-generated method stub
        VariantConfiguration.securityLevel =
                            VP_SECURITY_LEVEL.V_HIGH;
        Lock lock = LockFactory.createLock();
        Assert.assertFalse(lock.setPassword(""));
        Assert.assertFalse(lock.setPassword("Hello"));
        Assert.assertTrue(lock.setPassword("Helo"));
        org.junit.Assert.fail();
}
```

2.4 Automation

The abovementioned process to introduce a variation point in a system entails a number of steps that can be error prone and time consuming. We built an eclipse plug-in that automates the whole process assisted by input from the developer. The tool is open source and is available online [7]. When a variation point is to be refactored into the system:

1. The developer navigates to the unit test corresponding to the aspect of the feature where the variation point should be added.
2. The developer chooses to add a variation point of a certain type.
3. The tool finds the transitive closure of all objects and methods used in the chosen unit test. The developer selects the method that is considered the source of variation.
4. The developer specifies a name for the new variation point, and specifies names for all different variants. Figure 4 shows a snapshot of a expected input.

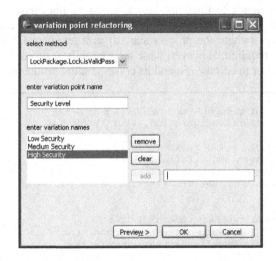

Fig. 4. Expected input from the developer

5. The tool will do the proper refactoring and code generation as described in the previous section. In fact, all the refactored and generated code we provided at each step in the previous section was the output of our eclipse plug-in. Namely, the tool will:

- Abstract out the source of variation.
- Provide an implementation class for each variant.
- Provide a factory to select the proper implementation.
- Define an enumeration to enable easy configuration of the system at instantiation time. All variation points will be packaged nicely in a configuration file to convey knowledge about variability in the system and the decisions that need to be made.

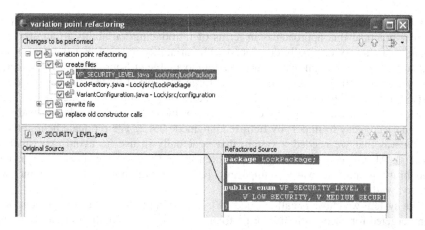

Fig. 5. The developer is made aware of the refactoring steps

As shown in Figure 5, before any refactoring takes place, the developer is made aware of all the changes.

6. The tool will update all references of the old class to the correct object instantiation technique.
7. The tool will provide unit tests for every variant. In case of options, unit tests will be provided to test all possible combinations of extensions.

3   Evaluation

So far in this paper, we described a bottom-up, test-driven approach to construct variability profiles for software systems. The previous sections provided an overview of what the variability introduction process entails and how to formalize it for automation purposes. We also presented an eclipse plug-in that we built as an enabling tool for developers to automate the process.

3.1   Goals and Setting

The goal of the evaluation was to check whether the proposed approach is feasible and practical with the help of the plug-in we developed. We conducted a limited case study to investigate these two issues.

To check for feasibility, we used the simple example we presented earlier in this paper as a starting point. Then, we extended the example in a number of ways, namely: adding more classes, adding more unit tests, applying various object-oriented techniques like subclasses and interfaces, and using different types of constructors like parameterless constructors, parameterized constructors and super constructors. After each extension to the mockup system, we tried to apply a number of operations such as adding variation points of different types, and adding variants. The main aim was to find how feasible it is to inject variability into a system through systematic refactoring given all the complications of object-oriented design.

On the other hand, the aim of the practicality check was to elicit an initial insight on how practical this approach is in terms of introducing variability to an arbitrary system that was not originally developed with variability in mind. For this part of the evaluation, we used a real open source system available at SourceForge. We selected this system by listing all projects in sourceforge.net, sorted by the number of downloads in a descending order, and with a Java as a programming language filter. Then we examined the projects one by one looking for those projects that already had unit tests and were easy to import by Eclipse Ganymede 3.4.2. The rationale behind these criteria was that we needed a system that is actually in use (to avoid experimental projects). Also, because our plug-in is written for Eclipse, it only supports Java. The availability of unit tests was also important, because we did not want to write our own tests to avoid any biases.

The system we chose is called Buddi [8]. It is a simple financial management program targeted for users with little or no financial background. It allows users to set up accounts, create spending and income categories, record transactions, and check spending habits. Up till the end of November, Buddi has been downloaded 647,354 times. It has about 24,775 lines and 227 classes.

Buddi was originally intended for personal use. In order to introduce variability to Buddi, we asked the question: what do we have to do to make Buddi suitable for small businesses? We developed a number of scenarios such as:

1. Buddi usually accepts credit payments (transactions). To use this feature to support store-credit, we need to provide the possibility of assessing risks. This yields the first variation point *Risk Assessment* with the variants (alternatives): *None*, *Flexible* and *Strict*. The *None* variant represents the original implementation of Buddi that did not have the notion of risk assessment. The *Flexible* variant puts some restrictions on the credited amount, and checks balance status for the past few months. The *Strict* variant adds more restrictions on any store-credit such as considerations of when the account was opened.

2. Buddi updates the balance of a customer after each transaction. For fraud-detection, we might need to take some security measures. This yields the second variation point *Security Measures* with the variants (options): *Log Balance Updates*, and *Send SMS to Customer*.

Following a product line approach, we can honor these requests without having to maintain a personal version as well as business version of Buddi. In our evaluation, the goal is to see how practical it is to use our approach to inject this variability using the Eclipse plug-in.

3.2 Results and Limitations

The feasibility evaluation enabled us to refine our approach in an iterative manner before we use our plug-in on a real system. We found some issues that we managed to fix such as dealing with instantiations where parameterized constructors are used, resolving call hierarchies and refactoring instantiations where there already is a design pattern in use, and dealing with classes that already are abstract. We also faced complications that are yet to be resolved such as handling inheritance. For example, if the original code was: Lock c = new SubLock() where Lock is not necessarily abstract, it is not possible for the static code analyzer we are using to detect at compile time which subclass is being used (if there is more than one). After a number of rounds, we came to the conclusion that the approach is indeed feasible, but more experiments need to be set in order to detect cases where systematic refactoring is tricky.

Checking for practicality, we used our plug-in to refactor the code systematically as per the proposed approach. The plug-in was in fact able to handle both types of variations (i.e. alternatives and options) without any human interference – except for input from the developer wherever it was prescribed in the approach. The output of using the approach for each variation was as expected. That is, relevant code was re-factored and new code was generated as prescribed. The process did not create any compilation errors or cause a test to fail.

However, we noticed that the Call Hierarchy function caused a noticeable delay of about 9 seconds on average. Although this delay might not limit the usefulness of the tool, it might, for larger projects with millions of lines of codes, limit its practicality. We intend to investigate this issue further to find more efficient ways to obtain only relevant units rather than the whole hierarchy. Also, we realized that the transitive closure for some tests might be too large to navigate. This is a tool specific issue that we hope to deal with in the future where we can visualize the call hierarchy in a better fashion. A real limitation to the practicality of the current implementation of our plug-in was the inability to combine variation points in a hierarchical manner. For example, currently we do not support scenarios where a variation point of type alternatives need to be defined, and one or more of these alternatives have a number of options to select from. Nonetheless, we believe that this issue can be resolved with more sophisticated code analysis and refactoring.

Currently, the tool does not support dependencies between variation points and variants. For example, multiplicity constraints between alternatives and options are not taken into account. We are at this time working on extending the tool to handle constrains and support more complex variation scenarios.

3.3 Threats to Validity

The cases we chose to test in our feasibility evaluation might be subjective. Although we tried to cover a wide range of object-oriented configurations, we understand that our evaluation for feasibility did not exhaust all possible cases, which made it hard to claim that the approach is completely feasible for any project and under any circumstances. Moreover, the practicality evaluation is limited to one project only, which might threaten the validity of the generalization that the tool is practical for other projects. Also, the scenarios we generated might be subjective which might have biased the results.

Another obvious threat to validity is that we ourselves conducted the evaluation. Confirmation bias might exist. And the sample size is too small to even consider statistical validity.

We intend to collect a larger sample of projects of different scales and architectural styles in order to evaluate our approach more thoroughly. Furthermore, we think a controlled experiment will be useful to evaluate the approach from a developer's perspective.

4   Related Work

There is a large body of research on SPL engineering. Main topics of interest in this domain include scoping, domain engineering, reuse, and variability management. In our work, we deal with variability management, but we also focus on incremental introduction of product line practices to software organizations. Similar efforts in the literature include Kruger's work [9] on easing the transition to software mass customization. Kruger built a tool that utilizes the concept of separation of concerns to manage variability in software systems. Moreover, Clegg et al. [10] proposed a method to incrementally build a SPL architecture in an object-orientated environment. The method does not discuss how to extract and communicate variability from the requirement engineering phase to the realization phase. O Brien et al. [11] discussed the introduction of SPLs in big organizations based on a top-down mining approach for core assets. They assume the organization has already developed many applications in the domain. None of these approaches follows test-driven practices.

Agility in product lines is a fairly new area. Carbon et al. [12] proposed the use of a reuse-centric application engineering process to combine agile methods and SPLs. The approach suggests that agile methods take the role in tailoring products for specific customers (during application engineering). The approach does not discuss the role of agile methods in the domain engineering phase. Hanssen et al. [13] described how SPL techniques can be used at the strategic level of the organization, while agile software development is used at the medium-term project level. While these efforts are interesting attempts to combine concepts from agile software development and SPL engineering, their focus is different from the focus of our research. They suggest using agile approaches in the application engineering/product instantiation phase but assume upfront domain engineering. Our work is focused on a lightweight, bottom up approach to start product lines in a non-disruptive manner using agile methods. To the best of our knowledge, this research focus is original and has not been previously discussed in the literature. The use of a test-driven approach for incremental SPLs was initially proposed in one of our earlier works [14].

5   Conclusion

SPL engineering provides organizations with a significant economic advantage due to reuse and mass customization opportunities. For agile organizations, there is a considerable adoption barrier because of the upfront, heavyweight nature of SPL practices. In this paper, we contribute a novel approach to introduce variability to existing systems on-demand. We propose a test-driven, bottom-up approach to create variability profiles for software systems. Systematic refactoring is used in order to inject variation points and variants in the system, whenever needed. We also contribute an Eclipse plug-in to automate this process.

A limited evaluation of the feasibility and practicality of the approach was presented. The approach, supported by the plug-in, was found to be feasible and practical, but suffered some limitations that we are currently trying to address.

Our next research goal is to find out how acceptance tests can play an effective role in this process. Since acceptance tests are usually used at the feature level, we hope to be able to use them as anchor points for variability in a given system.

Acknowledgment

This work is partially funded by iCore (Alberta Ingenuity Fund). Also, we would like to thank Steffen Salbinger for his great contribution to the development of the tool.

References

1. Clements, P., Northrop, L.: Software Product Lines: Practice and Patterns. Addison-Wesley, Reading (2001)
2. Gurp, J., Bosch, J., Svahnberg, M.: On the Notion of Variability in Software Product Lines. In: Working IEEE/IFIP Conference on Software Architecture, WISCA 2001 (2001)
3. Schmid, K., Verlage, M.: The Economic Impact of Product Line Adoption and Evolution. IEEE Software 19(4), 50–57 (2002)
4. Manifesto for Agile Software Development,
   http://agilemanifesto.org/principles.html
5. Beck, K., Andres, C.: Extreme Programming Explained: Embrace Change, 2nd edn. Addison-Wesley Professional, Reading (2004)
6. Gamma, E., Helm, R., Johnson, R., Vlissides, J.: Design Patters: Elements of Reusable Object-Oriented Software. Addison-Wesley, Reading (1995)
7. https://fitclipse.svn.sourceforge.net/svnroot/fitclipse/trunk/ProductLineDesigner
8. SourceForge, http://sourceforge.net/projects/buddi
9. Kruger, C.: Easing the Transition to Software Mass Customization. In: Proceedings of the 4th International Workshop on Product Family Engineering, Germany (2002)
10. Clegg, K., Kelly, T., McDermid, J.: Incremental Product-Line Development. In: International Workshop on Product Line Engineering, Seattle (2002)
11. OBrien, L., Smith, D.: MAP and OAR Methods: Techniques for Developing Core Assets for Software Product Lines from Existing Assets, CMU/SEI-2002-TN-007 (2002)
12. Carbon, R., Lindvall, M., Muthig, D., Costa, P.: Integrating PL Engineering and Agile Methods: Flexible Design Up-front vs. Incremental Design. In: 1st International Workshop on Agile Product Line Engineering (2006)
13. Hanssen, G., Fægri, T.: Process Fusion: An Industrial Case Study on Agile Software Product Line Engineering. Journal of Systems and Software (2008)
14. Ghanam, Y., Park, S., Maurer, F.: A Test-Driven Approach to Establishing & Managing Agile Product Lines. In: Proceedings of the 5th Software Product Line Testing Workshop (SPLiT 2008) in conjunction with SPLC 2008, Limerick, Ireland (2008)

Introducing Agile Methods in a Large Software Development Team: The Impact on the Code

Mary Giblin[1], Padraig Brennan[2], and Chris Exton[3]

[1] Athlone Institute of Technology, Dublin Road, Athlone, Co. Westmeath, Ireland
mgiblin@ait.ie
[2] Ericsson Software Campus, Cornamaddy, Athlone, Co. Westmeath, Ireland
padraig.brennan@ericsson.com
[3] University of Limerick, Plassey, Limerick, Co. Limerick, Ireland
chris.exton@ul.ie

Abstract. The adoption of agile methods of software development has gained momentum within the software industry. NW Soft Solutions Ltd. (a pseudonym) is a large software development unit that develops large-scale network centric software solutions. NW Soft Solutions Ltd decided to adopt an agile development methodology. In this case study, we use object-oriented metrics to evaluate and characterise the source code of an application produced by a team using agile methods. We compare the results obtained from the source code produced using agile methods with the results for source code produced for a similar type of application by the same team using a more traditional methodology. The contrast is stark. This case study shows that agile methods have guided the developers to produce code that manifests better quality and maintainability characteristics.

Keywords: agile, methods, code quality, large organization, developers, maintainability, OO metrics.

1 Introduction

Since the earliest days of software development, Software Process Improvement has been an ongoing research topic resulting from the need of organisations to constantly yield productivity and quality improvements. To be able to respond rapidly to changing customer requirements in a timely and cost effective manner, many organizations worldwide in different market segments are using Agile Methods in preference to some of the more traditional methods such as Waterfall [1], Spiral [2] and RUP [3]. Methods that fall under the agile umbrella are Scrum [4], XP [5], Crystal [6] and Lean [7].

Agile methods are based on a set of principles and practices that value the interactions among people working together to produce high-quality software that creates business value on a frequent basis [8]. Because software maintainability and software re-usability are key concerns, in this paper the authors set out to answer the question "What impact does the introduction of an agile methodology have on the code?" *"The total cost of maintaining a widely used program is typically 40 percent or more of the*

A. Sillitti et al. (Eds.): XP 2010, LNBIP 48, pp. 58–72, 2010.

cost of developing it." according to Fred Brooks [9]. Other more recent work concurs with this, particularly for large organizations and systems [10].

The remainder of this paper is organized as follows. In Section 2, we review some related work. In Section 3, we describe the model used to evaluate the code and our data collection techniques. Section 4 describes some background information on NW Soft Solutions Ltd and its agile adoption strategy. Section 5 contains our findings and Section 6 describes team factors that could have influenced the findings. The final summary and conclusion is contained in Section 7.

2 Related Work

Studies exist that propose different metric suites to assess an Object Oriented Design. Sato, Goldman and Kon, [11] analyze and evaluate OO metrics from seven projects with different approaches of agile adoption. Their findings showed that a project with less agile practices presented higher complexity and coupling measures. Concas et al. [12] have similar findings, where an improvement in quality metrics was correlated to the use of agile practices by skilled developers. Moser et al. [13] propose a method for assessing the evolution of maintainability during software development called the Maintainability Trend (MT). However they could not conclude "in absolute terms" that XP results in more maintainable code since the metrics were not run on code produced using more traditional methodologies.

Marchenko and Abrahamsson have investigated the use of static analysis tools to predict software defects [14].

A number of studies focus on the practice of Test Driven Development (TDD) and more over its effect on defect density. Nagappan et al. [15] report on four products where the defect density decreased between 40% and 90% relative to similar projects that did not use TDD. Maximillien and Williams [16] found that the application of TDD reduced the defect rate by 50%.

3 Software Metrics and Data Collection

3.1 The Overview Pyramid

Quality metrics for OO Design has been the subject of many studies. With regard to maintenance effort, the Chidamber and Kemerer (CK) suite of quality metrics [17] has been used and validated in the literature. Li and Henry studied the link between CK metrics and the maintenance effort [18]. Basili et al. found that some of the CK metrics were associated with fault-proneness of classes [19]. The Overview Pyramid introduced by Lanza and Marinescu [20] is a simple way to characterize a design based on some well-known metrics, such as, the Cyclomatic Number defined by McCabe [21] and the CK metric Weighted Method Count (WMC) [17]. Because the Overview Pyramid is grounded in proven metrics and also has a visual aspect to it, we felt it would be suitable for our task of comparing the characteristics of two software designs. The Overview Pyramid shows key metrics for the source code along with

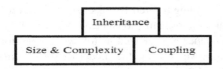

Fig. 1. The major structural aspects of a system quantified by the Overview Pyramid

comparisons to industry-standard ranges for those metrics. As shown in Figure 1, the Pyramid uses complexity, coupling and usage of inheritance to evaluate the structure of an object-oriented system.

Size and Complexity: The following direct metrics are used for the Size and Complexity part of the pyramid.

- o **NOP – Number of Packages**
- o **NOC- Number of Classes** (not counting library classes)
- o **NOM – Number of Methods**
- o **LOC – Lines of Code**
- o **CYCLO – Cyclomatic Number**

The direct metrics above are then used to compute the following proportions, which are independent of product size and can easily be used for comparisons.

- o **High-level Structuring (NOC/Package).** This provides the high level structuring policy of the system.
- o **Class Structuring (NOM/Class).** This reveals how methods are distributed among classes.
- o **Method Structuring (LOC/Method).** This is an indication of how well the code is distributed among methods.
- o **Intrinsic Method Complexity (CYCLO/Code Lines).** This ratio characterizes how much conditional complexity we are to expect in methods (e.g. 0.2 means that a new branch is added every five lines)

Figure 2 shows an example of the size and complexity characterization from the Overview Pyramid.

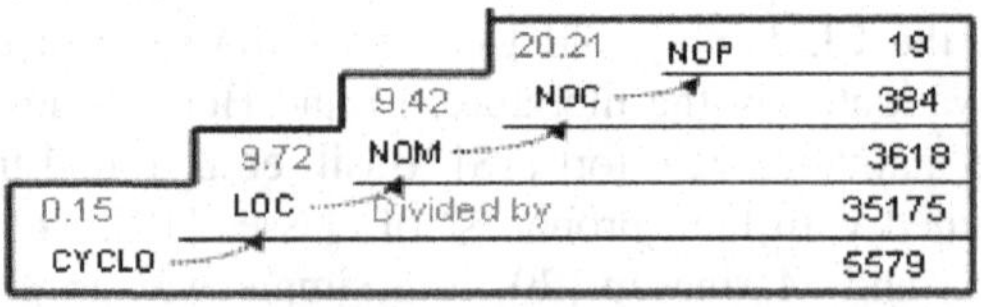

20.21	NOP	19
9.42	NOC	384
9.72	NOM	3618
0.15	LOC Divided by	35175
CYCLO		5579

Fig. 2. Example of size and complexity characterization

System Coupling: The following direct metrics are used for the System Coupling part of the pyramid.

- ○ **CALLS – Number of Method Calls:** This metric counts the total number of distinct method calls (invocations) in the code, by summing the number of methods called by all the user-defined methods.
- ○ **FANOUT – Number of Called Classes** (Sum of the FANOUT as defined in [22]

Based on the direct metrics, the following proportions result:

- ○ **Coupling intensity (CALLS/Method)**
- ○ **Coupling dispersion (FANOUT/Method Call)**

Figure 3 shows an example of the system coupling characterization from the Overview Pyramid.

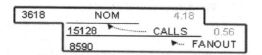

Fig. 3. Example of characterizing a system's coupling

Inheritance: We did not use the Inheritance part of the pyramid in our evaluation.

3.2 Detection Strategies

Because metrics alone cannot answer all the questions about a system, Lanza and Marinescu [20] also propose a number of detection strategies to detect design problems. The detection strategies are based on the work of Fowler et al. [23], Martin [24] and Riel [25]. In section 5 we compare the code produced using agile methodologies with the code produced using traditional methods. The four design disharmonies referred to in section 5 are described below.

God Class
A God Class performs too much work on its own. This has a negative impact on the reusability and the understandability of that part of the system. This design problem is comparable to Fowler's "Large Class" bad smell [23]. Taking the "God Class" [25] design flaw, its properties are class complexity, class cohesion and access of foreign data, therefore Lanza and Marinescu chose the following metrics to detect a God class.

- ○ **WMC – Weighted Method Count**
- ○ **TCC – Tight Class Cohesion**
- ○ **ATFD- Access to Foreign Data**

Figure 4 shows the graphical representation of the "God class" detection strategy. Lanza and Marinescu derived the limits used for comparison based on data from eighty industrial and open source projects.

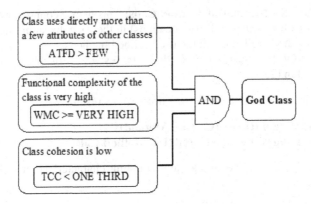

Fig. 4. Detection of a God Class

Brain Method

A Brain Method tends to centralize the functionality of a class, in the same way as a God Class centralizes the functionality of an entire subsystem or system. A Brain Method will be hard to understand and debug and practically impossible to reuse. This design problem is based on three simple code smells (*long methods*, *excessive branching* and *many variables used*) described by Fowler [23]. Lanza and Marinescu use the following metrics to detect a Brain Method.

o   **LOC – Lines Of Code**
o   **CYCLO – Cyclomatic Number**
o   **MAXNESTING – Maximum Nesting Level**
o   **NOAV – Number Of Accessed Variables**

Figure 5 shows the graphical representation of the "Brain Method" detection strategy.

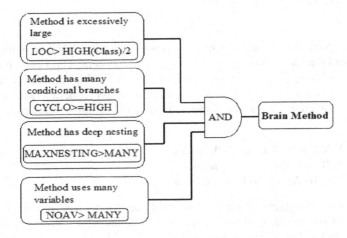

Fig. 5. Detection of a Brain Method

Brain Class

The primary characteristic of a Brain Class is that is contains a Brain Method. Figure 6 shows the graphical representation of the "Brain Class" detection strategy.

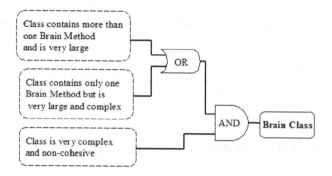

Fig. 6. Detection of a Brain Class

Data Class

A Data Class is a data holder on which other classes strongly rely. Detection of a Data Class is a sign of a design that lacks encapsulation and has poor data-functionality proximity. The **WOC – Weight Of Class** metric is used in the detection strategy. Figure 7 shows the graphical representation of the "Data Class" detection strategy.

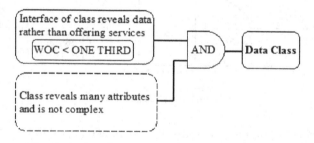

Fig. 7. Detection of a Data Class

3.3 Data Collection

iPlasma (integrated **Pl**Atform for **S**oftware **M**odelling and **A**nalysis) is a software tool used to generate the overview pyramid, class blueprints and detect design flaws ([26] and [27]).

Because of the nature of the applications developed by NW Soft Solutions Ltd., we were able to take the code developed by a team using traditional methods and take code for a very similar type of application developed by the same team using agile methods.

As part of an audit into the level of adoption of agile practices we conducted a group interview with four members of the development team that produced the code. The objective of the interview was:

o To obtain information about the level of adoption of various agile practices such as pair programming, test driven development, stand-up meetings etc. within the team.

o To assess if the developers preferred the agile way of working to the traditional approach

o To assess if more organizational support was needed to continue with the agile way of working.

The interview was semi-structured using a guideline questionnaire and afterwards the interview was transcribed and Qualitative Data Analysis Software (Weft QDA) was used to analyze the interview. We use data from the interview to place the metrics based analysis of the code in context.

4   Overview of Organization and Adoption Process

NW Soft Solutions Ltd. is responsible for the design, development and maintenance of Network Management solutions for the Wireless Access and Core Network. It employs in excess of 300 software developers, testers and systems engineers in this development unit and is part of a large multi-national organization. The product being developed consists of a number of sub-applications or features so the developers tend to be grouped into feature teams with separate "siloed" functional units as shown in Figure 8.

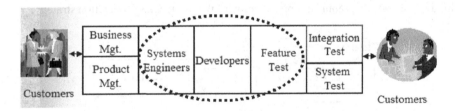

Fig. 8. Functional Units

In introducing agile ways of working, the organization opted to keep the systems, developers, and feature test as separate entities or functions, but having a close co-operation between the units. A systems engineer would act as product owner [4] for a feature and work closely with developers formulating user stories [5] etc. One or more testers would move in to work with the feature team developers writing and running acceptance tests.

NW Soft Solutions Ltd. embarked on a change program that included the adoption of a mixture of XP practices (User Stories, Pair Programming, Test Driven Development, Continuous Integration, Cross-Functional Teams) and Scrum (Sprints, Product Backlog, Estimating Effort, Product Owner, Scrum Masters, Daily Stand Up Meetings).

5   Results and Findings

In 5.1, 5.2 and 5.3 we compare a metrics based analysis of a software module developed by a team using traditional methods with the metrics for a software module that contains similar functionality and developed by the same team using an agile methodology.

5.1 Size and Complexity

From the direct metrics listed in Table 1, we notice that when the agile methods were employed, the Cyclomatic number has decreased from 803 to 593. The number of lines of code has almost halved from 8516 to 3495 and the total number of classes increased from 10 to 42.

Table 2 shows the computed proportions. Unlike the direct metrics, which are absolute values, the computed proportions allow easy comparison of projects independent of their size. The L, A, H signify if the value is Low, Average or High respectively according to the thresholds used in iPlasma. The thresholds set in iPlasma are based on an analysis of 45 Java and 37 C++ open source and commercial systems. CYCLO/LOC characterizes how much conditional complexity exists in the code. The value increased when using agile methods, but it is still lower than average and its increase is attributed to the large decrease in Lines Of Code. The LOC/NOM is an indication of how well the code is distributed among methods and this value has decreased from what was classed as a very high value to an average value. NOM/NOC reflects the quality of class design because it shows how methods are distributed among classes. Again there is a big improvement here where the value has decreased from 23 to 10.11. NOM/NOC is still higher than the average threshold, which is 7. NOC/NOP did not vary much and is still below the average value, which is 17.

Table 1. Size and Complexity Comparison – Direct Metrics

Metric	Traditional Methods	Agile Methods
NOP	1	4
NOC	10	42
NOM	233	425
LOC	8516	3495
CYCLO	803	593

Table 2. Size and Complexity Comparison – Computed Proportions

Metric	Traditional Methods	Agile Methods
NOC/NOP	10 (L)	10.5 (L)
NOM/NOC	23 (H)	10.11 (H)
LOC/NOM	36.54 (H)	8.45 (A)
CYCLO/LOC	0.09 (L)	0.16 (L)

5.2 System Coupling

Table 3 contains the direct metrics for the System Coupling characteristic. The computed metrics contained in Table 4 better characterize the coupling of the system. CALLS/NOM decreased from a value of 4.96 (classified as high) to 2.6, which is in the average band. CALLS/NOM denotes on average how many other methods are called from each method. Very high values would indicate excessive coupling. The FANOUT/CALLS value was low to start with and didn't change significantly. The FANOUT/CALLS is an indication of how much the coupling involves many classes (A value of 0.5 means that every second method call involve another class).

Table 3. System Coupling Comparison – Direct Metrics

Metric	Traditional Methods	Agile Methods
CALLS	1156	1109
FANOUT	693	606

Table 4. System Coupling Comparison – Computed Proportions

Metric	Traditional Methods	Agile Methods
CALLS/NOM	4.96 (H)	2.6 (A)
FANOUT/CALLS	0.59 (L)	0.54 (L)

5.3 Design Flaws

Table 5 shows that the number of design flaws detected by iPlasma reduced dramatically in the code that was designed using an agile methodology.

Table 5. Design Flaws Detected

Design Flaw	Traditional Methods	Agile Methods
Brain Class	2	0
Brain Method	28	0
God Class	2	1
Data class	5	1

5.4 Re-structuring of a God Class

We now look at a class that was detected as a God class (called *AdjustSoftwareTask*) in the code designed using traditional methods. In the code designed using agile methods there is a class (*AdjustTask*) that has a similar purpose, but it is no longer classified by iPlasma as a God class. This code is part of a Network Management Application and in general terms both classes would: -

- o   Communicate with a Network Element (NE)
- o   Read an inventory of software from the NE in XML format
- o   Parse the XML information that is returned from the NE
- o   Store the information returned from the NE in a database

The classes also have to handle any error conditions that occur (for example an error when connecting to the database). The basic difference between the two classes is that they deal with different Network Elements. On examining the classes we saw that in the *AdjustSoftwareTask* class, it was handling everything to do with all the points listed above by itself, but in the package structure containing the *AdjustTask* class, new packages had been added to the structure. The new packages handled the connection to the database, error cases when connecting, writing to the database and the xml parsing. This meant that *AdjustTask* was more of a coordinator and it was much simpler. There was less coupling and a greater possibility that code could be re-used in the future. If for example the format of the xml file changed in the future, then the change would be easier to accommodate because the xml parsing was placed in a separate package.

First we ran iPlasma on the individual classes *AdjustSoftwareTask and AdjustTask* and examined the results.

Table 6. Size and Complexity Comparison – Direct Metrics

Metric	AdjustSoftwareTask (Trad.)	AdjustTask (Agile)
NOC	1	1
NOM	54	15
LOC	1095	188
CYCLO	146	54

Table 6 shows that the Cyclomatic number has significantly decreased from 146 to 54.

Table 7. Size and Complexity Comparison – Computed Proportions

Metric	AdjustSoftwareTask (Trad.)	AdjustTask (Agile)
NOM/NOC	54 (H)	15 (H)
LOC/NOM	20.27 (H)	12.53 (H)
CYCLO/LOC	0.13 (L)	0.12 (L)

From Table 7 we can see that while the cyclomatic number per line of code hasn't changed that much, the lines of code per method has decreased, even though AdjustTask still has a value that is slightly higher than the average value defined by Lanza and Marinescu [20].

Table 8. Design Flaws Detected

Design Flaw	AdjustSoftwareTask (Trad.)	AdjustTask (Agile)
Brain Method	4	0
God Class	2	0
Data Class	4	0

Table 8 shows that the class developed using the agile methodology has no design flaws whereas the class developed using traditional methods had ten design flaws. *AdjustSoftwareTask* has a number of nested classes, which caused some of the problems. The God classes are *AdjustSoftwareTask* itself and its nested class called *XmlSoftwareParser*. The separation of the XML parsing functionality into another package has eliminated this problem for *AdjustTask* . The Data Classes are again nested classes called XmlNodeItem, XmlSoftwareModel, XmlSwItem and XmlUpItem. Again these classes were used to process the Xml data and certainly the choice to move the processing of the xml data to a separate package was the correct thing to do.

Another observation made from studying the code was that the tendency to unnecessarily duplicate code no longer existed in the code produced using agile methods. Here we see a code example from the AdjustSoftwareTask where there is a tendency to duplicate code.

```
catch (final CppCsNodeNotConnectedException e) {
    failed = true;
    LOGGER.warning("Exception caught: "
    +SmUtil.getMessage(e))
    failureMessage = SmUtil.getMessage(e);
    reportMessage(SmUtil.getMessage(e));
    retryableReported = true;
    operationFinished(false);
    SM_LOGGER.error(SmErrorTypes.EXCEPTION,
    SmSeverityEnum.MINOR, "USER=" + userId + ";
    NE="+ neName+ "; MSG=startOperation(): Exception
    caught:" + SmUtil.getMessage(e));}

  catch (final CppCsException e) {
    failed = true;
    LOGGER.warning("Exception caught: " +
    SmUtil.getMessage(e));
    failureMessage = SmUtil.getMessage(e);
    reportMessage(e);
    operationFinished(false);
    SM_LOGGER.error(SmErrorTypes.EXCEPTION,
    SmSeverityEnum.MINOR, "USER=" + userId + ";
    NE=" +neName + "; MSG=startOperation():Exception
    caught:" + SmUtil.getMessage(e));

    ....
```

A similar case in the code produced using agile methods is shown below:

```
catch (final NodeIoException exception) {
    retryableReported = true;
    handleException(adjustFailed, exception); }
catch (final NetConfException exception) {
    retryableReported = true;
    handleException(adjustFailed, exception);

    ....

private void handleException(final String message,
final Exception exception){
    failed = true;
    logger.warning("Exception caught:" +
    SmUtil.getMessage(exception));
    failureMessage = message + ": " +
    SmUtil.getMessage(exception);
    reportMessage(message, exception);
    operationFinished(false);
```

```
smLogger.error(SmErrorTypes.EXCEPTION,
SmSeverityEnum.MAJOR, "USER="+ userId + ";
NE=" + neName+ ";
MSG=startOperation(): Exception caught:"
+ SmUtil.getMessage(exception));}
```

6 Team Factors

Section 5 shows that in this case study the code produced with an agile methodology as analyzed using iPlasma was significantly better than similar code produced by the same team using more traditional methods.

As part of an audit on the agile practices, the team that developed the code was interviewed. A systems engineer, two developers and a tester represented the team. The interview was semi-structured where questions regarding the level of adoption of the various agile practices, benefits of the practices and benefits or drawbacks of agile etc. were asked. We analyzed the interview transcript looking for factors such as developer attitudes, agile practices, level of agile adoption to which the findings could possibility be attributed and to put the findings in context. We felt the factors listed below are relevant. We include a small number of example quotations in each section. The time of quotation during the interview is used as a reference. For example [00:09:36] means 9 minutes and 36 seconds into the interview.

1. Overall the team was new to agile methods, but they had one developer that has previous experience with agile methods. The team felt that this was very helpful.
"We had Matthias, yeah we had quite good I mean Matthias was very experienced from XP practices I think " [00:15:23]

2. The team members very motivated and eager to learn about agile methods.
"For me I browsed a few books, read on the internet and practised some and looked at some more books ..." [00:20:41]
"It is very motivating to have people around you that are interested – everyone is interested in what they are doing" [01:12:30]

3. Pair programming was happening quite naturally within the team and to a large extent.
"I think everybody worked with everybody. In the beginning we had quite static pairs but then we tried to change each day." [00:24:11]
"We tried to do everything in pairs." [00:24:37]

4. The team implemented test driven development. They felt that they mastered test driven development. They had a high level of code coverage in unit test. Having a person with previous experience in XP practices and test driven development, in particular, was seen to be beneficial and the team saw the benefits of test driven development.
"For unit tests we had quite high coverage so... approximately 95% of the code we wrote" [00:30:27]

"That is, in general, or whatever tip I can give is to have one good really experienced guy in the team that has worked with TDD before. Otherwise you will take short cuts probably." [00:37:00]

"I think it was one of the crucial parts of our success actually for this project really, TDD, this way of working" [00:38:08]

"and I know from those other guys that have not worked with TDD before, now they see the benefit of it" [00:38:37]

5. The number of bug reports received on the code was very low and the team felt that the test driven development had a positive impact on quality.

"The initial design might have been slower but I think we got that back when we didn't have to fix a lot of TRs (bug reports)" [01:08:36]

But I mean quality look at I mean we delivered over 2 thousand IP (Implementation Proposal) *hours and we have 3 or 4 TRs* (bug reports) *and 3 of them are not even at code level"* [01:12:53]

6. The team were unanimous in their endorsement of agile methods and were keen to continue in that way of working and continuously improve their practices.

7 Summary and Conclusions

Our study shows that in this case study, the code as analyzed using iPlasma was significantly better than code produced by the same team using more traditional methods. There have been improvements in terms of:

- o   Overall Complexity
- o   High Level Structuring
- o   Method Structuring
- o   Number of Design Flaws

The team being studied was overall an inexperienced agile team, but they had at least one developer with previous experience of XP practices. The team had a very positive experience in the adoption of agile methods. For a team that was new to agile, they adopted pair programming and test driven development to a high degree. As well as an improved code structure, only a few bugs were found during the test phases. So the improvement evident in the metrics based static analysis of the code did actually manifest itself as a real quality improvement. The team themselves felt that the test driven development played a large part in the quality improvement experienced. They felt that the test driven development was critical to their success.

Our results concur with the findings of Sato, Goldman and Kon, [11] and Concas et al. [12]. Our research also shows that in this case the improvements in metrics resulted in a tangible result in terms of much fewer bugs being reported. We also found iPlasma to be a useful tool for this type of analysis and the High, Average and Low thresholds used in iPlasma were a useful benchmark.

In further work, we plan to analyze code from teams that have had different experiences with agile adoption.

References

1. Royce, W.: Managing the Development of Large Software Systems. In: Proceedings of IEEE WESCON 1970 (1970)
2. Boehm, B.W.: A Spiral Model of Software Development and enhancement. IEEE Computer (1988)
3. http://www-01.ibm.com/software/awdtools/rup/ (Last accessed November 22, 2009)
4. Schwaber, K., Beedle, M.: Agile Software Development with SCRUM. Prentice Hall, Englewood Cliffs (2002)
5. Beck, K.: Extreme Programming Explained-Embrace Change. Addison-Wesley, Reading (2004)
6. Cockburn, A.: Agile Software Development. Addison-Wesley, Reading (2002)
7. Poppendiek, M., Poppendiek, T.: Lean Software Development: An Agile Toolkit. Addison-Wesley, Reading (2003)
8. Beck, K., et al.: Manifesto for agile software development (February 2001), http://agilemanfesto.org (Last access, November 2009)
9. Brooks, F.: The Mythical Man-Month. Addison-Wesley, Reading (1975)
10. Coleman, D., Lowther, B., Oman, P.: The Application of software Maintainability Models in Industrial Software Systems. Journal of Software Systems 29(1), 3–16 (1995)
11. Sato, D., Goldman, A., Kon, F.: Tracking the Evolution of Object-Oriented Quality Metrics on Agile Projects. In: Concas, G., Damiani, E., Scotto, M., Succi, G. (eds.) XP 2007. LNCS, vol. 4536, pp. 84–92. Springer, Heidelberg (2007)
12. Concas, G., Di Francesco, M., Marchesi, M., Quaresima, R., Pinna, S.: An Agile Development Process and Its Assessment Using Quantitative Object-Oriented Metrics. In: Proceedings of 9th International Conference XP 2008 (2008)
13. Moser, R., Scotto, M., Sillitti, A., Succi, G.: Does XP Deliver Quality and Maintainable Code? In: Concas, G., Damiani, E., Scotto, M., Succi, G. (eds.) XP 2007. LNCS, vol. 4536, pp. 105–114. Springer, Heidelberg (2007)
14. Marchenko, A., Abrahamsson, P.: Predicting Software Defect Density: A Case Study on Automated Static code Analysis. In: Concas, G., Damiani, E., Scotto, M., Succi, G. (eds.) XP 2007. LNCS, vol. 4536, pp. 137–140. Springer, Heidelberg (2007)
15. Nagappan, N., Maximillien, E., Bhat, T., Williams, L.: Realizing quality improvements through test driven development: results and experiences of four industrial teams. Empirical Software Engineering 13, 289–302 (2008)
16. Maximillienm, E., Williams, L.: Assessing test driven development at IBM. In: Proceedings of 25th International Conference of Software Engineering, pp. 564–569 (2003)
17. Chidamber, S., Kemerer, C.: A metrics suite for object-oriented design. IEEE Trans. Software Eng. 20, 476–493 (1994)
18. Li, W., Henry, S.: Object oriented metrics that predict maintainability. J. Systems and Software 23, 111–122 (1993)
19. Basili, V., Melo, L.B.: A validation of object oriented design metrics as quality indicators. IEEE Transactions on Software Engineering 22, 751–761 (1996)
20. Lanza, M., Marinescu, R.: Object–Oriented Metrics in Practice Using software Metrics to Characterize, Evaluate, and Improve the Design of Object-Oriented Systems. Springer, Heidelberg (2006)
21. McCabe, T.J.: A measure of complexity. IEEE Transactions on Software Engineering 2(4), 308–320 (1876)

22. Lorenz, M., Kidd, J.: Object-Oriented software metrics: A Practical Guide. Prentice-Hall, Englewood Cliffs (1994)
23. Fowler, M., Beck, K., Brant, J., Opdyke, W., Roberts, D.: Refactoring: Improving the Design of Existing Code. Addison-Wesley, Reading (1999)
24. Martin, M. C.: Agile Software Development. Principles, Patterns and Practices. Prentice-Hall 2002
25. Riel, A.: Object Oriented Design Heuristics. Addison-Wesley, Boston (1996)
26. iPlasma, http://loose.upt.ro/iplasma/ (Last accessed, November 2009)
27. Marinescu, C., Marinescu, R., Mihancea, P., Ratiu, D., Wettel, R.: iPlasma: An integrated Platform for Quality Assessment of Object-Oriented Design. In: Proceedings of the 21st IEEE International Conference on Software Maintenance (ICSM 2005), pp. 77–80 (2005)

Agile Undercover: When Customers Don't Collaborate

Rashina Hoda, James Noble, and Stuart Marshall

Victoria University of Wellington,
New Zealand
{rashina,kjx,stuart}@ecs.vuw.ac.nz
http://www.ecs.vuw.ac.nz

Abstract. Customer collaboration is vital to Agile projects. Through a Grounded Theory study of New Zealand and Indian Agile teams we discovered that lack of customer involvement was causing problems in gathering and clarifying requirements, loss of productivity, and business loss. "Agile Undercover" allows development teams to practice Agile despite insufficient or ineffective customer involvement. We present the causes and consequences of lack of customer involvement on Agile projects and describe the Agile Undercover strategies used to overcome them.

Keywords: Agile Software Development, Customer Involvement, Agile Undercover, Grounded Theory.

1 Introduction

Customer involvement in traditional software development projects is typically limited to providing the requirements in the beginning and feedback towards the end, with limited regular interactions between the customer and the development team [15,16,20,27]. In contrast, customer collaboration is a vital feature and an important success factor in Agile software development [5,8,17,18,25,26,27]. Agile methods expand the customer role within the entire development process by involving them in writing user stories, discussing product features, prioritizing the feature lists, and providing rapid feedback to the development team on a regular basis [9,15,25,27].

In this paper, we present the results of a Grounded Theory study, involving 30 Agile practitioners from 16 different software development organizations in New Zealand and India. Our study revealed that *Lack of Customer Involvement* was one of the biggest challenges they faced. We analyze the causes and consequences of lack of customer involvement and present *Agile Undercover* — a set of strategies used by Agile practitioners to overcome the lack of customer involvement on Agile projects [19]. The rest of the paper is structured as follows: section 2 describes our research method followed by the results of the study in sections 3 to 9. Section 10 is discussion of our findings in light of related works. Section 11 describes limitations of our study followed by the conclusion in section 12.

2 Research Method

Grounded Theory (GT) is the systematic generation of theory from data analyzed by a rigorous research method [12,13]. GT was developed by sociologists Glaser and Strauss

A. Sillitti et al. (Eds.): XP 2010, LNBIP 48, pp. 73–87, 2010.
© Springer-Verlag Berlin Heidelberg 2010

[14]. We chose GT as our research method for several reasons. Firstly, Agile methods focus on people and interactions and GT, used as a qualitative research method, allows us to study social interactions and behaviour. Secondly, GT is most suited to areas of research which have not been explored in great detail before, and the research literature on Agile team-customer relationships is scarce [15]. Finally, GT is being increasingly used to study Agile teams [6,7,25,31]. Following Glaser's guidelines, we started out with a general area of interest — Agile project management — rather than beginning with a specific research problem [7].

2.1   Data Collection

We collected data by conducting face-to-face, semi-structured interviews with Agile practitioners using open-ended questions. The interviews were approximately an hour long and focused on the participants' experiences of working with Agile methods, in particular the challenges faced in Agile projects and the strategies used to overcome them. We also observed several Agile practices such as daily stand-up meetings (co-located and distributed), release planning, iteration planning, and demonstrations. In order to get a rounded perspective, we interviewed practitioners in various roles: Developers, Agile Coach (Scrum Master and XP Coach), Agile Trainer, Customer, Business Analyst, Tester, and Senior Management. Data collection and analysis were iterative so that constant comparison of data helped guide future interviews and the analysis of interviews and observations fed back into the emerging results.

2.2   Data Analysis

We used open coding to analyze the interview transcripts in detail [10,12]. We began by collating key points from each interview transcript [10]. Then we assigned a *code* — a phrase that summaries the key point in 2 or 3 words— to each key point [10]. The codes arising out of each interview were constantly compared against the codes from the same interview, and those from other interviews and observations. This is GT's *constant comparison method* [11,14] which was used again to group these codes to produce a higher level of abstraction, called *concepts* in GT.

The constant comparison method was repeated on the concepts to produce another level of abstraction called a *category*. As a result of this analysis, the concepts *Skepticism and Hype, Distance Factor, Lack of Time Commitment, Dealing with Large Customers*, and *Ineffective Customer Representative* gave rise to the category *Lack of Customer Involvement*. These concepts help describe the category *Lack of Customer Involvement* and are referred to as its *properties* [11].

Another set of concepts uncovered from the analysis include *Changing Priority, Risk Assessment Up-Front, Story Owners, Customer Proxy, Just Demos, E-collaboration* and *Extreme Undercover*. These concepts led to the emergence of the category *Agile Undercover*.

Fig 1.a shows the levels of data abstraction using GT and Fig 1.b illustrates how the category *Lack of Customer Involvement* emerged from underlying concepts.

We analyzed the observations and compared them to the concepts derived from the interviews. We found our observations did not contradict but rather supported the data

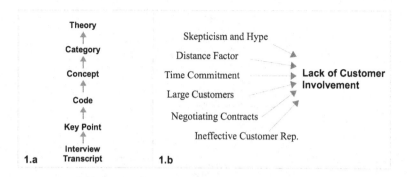

Fig. 1. a: Levels of data abstraction in GT b: Emergence of category *Lack of Customer Involvement* from concepts

provided in interviews, thereby strengthening the interview data. The use of *memoing* — theorizing write-up of ideas about codes and their relationships — was vital in recording the relationships between codes [12]. The conceptual *sorting* of memos was done to derive an outline of the emergent theory, showing relationships between concepts.

2.3   Generating a Theory

The final step of GT is generating a theory, also known as *theoretical coding*. Theoretical coding involves conceptualizing how the categories (and their properties) relate to each other as a hypotheses to be integrated into a theory [12]. Following Glaser's recommendation, we employed theoretical coding at the later stages of analysis [11], rather than being enforced as a coding paradigm from the beginning as advocated by Strauss [30].

Glaser lists several common structures of theories known as *theoretical coding families* [12,13]. By comparing our data with the theoretical coding families, it emerged that the coding family best 'fit' for our data was the *Six C's* coding family [12,13,21]: Contexts, Conditions, Causes, Consequences, Contingencies, and Covariances. Using the Six C's theoretical model we describe (1) Contexts: the ambiance (Agile development teams in NZ and India) (2) Conditions: factors that are prerequisites for the category, *Lack of customer involvement*, to manifest (3) Causes: reasons that cause lack of customer involvement (4) Consequences: outcomes or results of lack of customer involvement (5) Contingencies: moderating factors between causes and consequences (*Agile Undercover* strategies) (6) Covariances: correlations between different categories (*Agile Undercover* strategies change when factors that cause *Lack of Customer Involvement* change).

3   Results

In the following sections we present our theory. We have adapted Glaser's Six C's model diagram [12] to illustrate our theory of lack of customer involvement (Figure 2). The category *Lack of Customer Involvement* is at the center of the diagram. Each of the

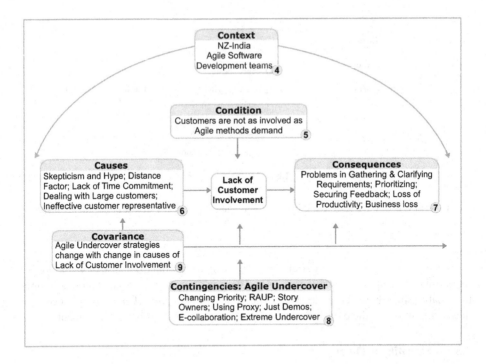

Fig. 2. Six C's as properties of category *Lack of Customer Involvement*

Six C's are represented in the other rectangles in relation to the central category, with corresponding section numbers (in circles) where we describe them.

In the following sections, we have selected quotations drawn from our interviews that shed particular light on the concepts. Due to space reasons we cannot describe *all* the underlying key points, codes, and concepts from our interviews and observation that further ground the discussion.

4   Context

We interviewed 30 Agile practitioners from 16 different software development organizations over 2 years, half of whom were from New Zealand and half from India. Figure 3 shows the participants and project details. In order to respect their confidentiality, we refer to the participants by numbers P1 to P30. All the teams were using Agile methods, primarily combinations of Scrum and eXtreme Programming (XP) — two of the most popular Agile methods today [3,28,29]. The teams practiced Agile practices such as iterative development, daily stand-ups, release and iteration planning, test driven-development (TDD), continuous integration and others. Participants' organizations offered products and services such as web-based applications, front and back-office applications, and local and off-shored software development services.

The level of Agile experience varied across the different teams. While some teams had under a year of experience, others had been practicing Agile for over 5 years. The

Partipants	Agile Position	Agile Method	Org. Size	Country	Domain	Team Size	Project Duration	Iteration
P1	SM	Scrum & XP	S	NZ	E-commerce	4	2	4
P2-P4	Dev × 3	Scrum & XP	S	NZ	Environment	4 to 6	12	1
P5	AC	Scrum & XP	L	NZ	Social Services	4 to 10	3 to 12	2
P6	Cust Rep	Scrum	XS	NZ	Entertainment	6 to 8	9	4
P7-P12	AC, BA, Tester, Dev × 2, Cust Rep	Scrum	M	NZ	Health	7	9	2
P13	AC	Scrum & XP	XL	NZ	Telecom & Transportation	6 to 15	12	4
P14	AC	Scrum & XP	S	NZ	Government Education	4 to 9	4	2
P15	Dev	Scrum & XP	XS	NZ	Software Development	7	6	2
P16-P20	Dev × 3, SM × 2	Scrum & XP	S	India	Software Development & Consultancy	5	6	2
P21	AC	Scrum & XP	L	India	Telecom	8 to 15	3	4
P22-P25	AC × 4	Scrum & XP	M	India	Software Development	7 to 8	3 to 6	2
P26	AC	Scrum & XP	S	India	IT & Agile Training	7 to 8	48	3
P27	Designer	Scrum & XP	S	India	Web-based services	5	1	2
P28	AC	Scrum & XP	M	India	Financial Services	8 to 11	36	2
P29	AT	Scrum	XS	India	Agile Training	7	8	3
P30	BA	Scrum & XP	M	India	Software Development	15	12	1

Fig. 3. Participant and Project Contexts. (Agile Position: Agile Coach (AC), Developer (Dev), Customer Rep (Cust Rep), Business Analyst (BA), Senior Management (SM), Agile Trainer (AT); Organizational Size: XS < 50, S < 500, M < 5000, L < 50,000, XL > 100,000 employees; Project duration is in months & iterations are in weeks.).

Indian teams were mostly catering to off-shored customers in Europe and USA and most of the NZ teams were catering to in-house customers, some of whom were located in separate cities. We include more details of the context in sections below as necessary.

5   Condition

Most participants did not receive the level of customer involvement that Agile methods demand (P1-P12, P14-P19, P21-P23, P25, P26, P28-P30). Lack of customer involved was seen as *"the most difficult part of Agile"* and *"the biggest problem"* because *"Agile [requires] fairly strong customer involvement"* (P4, P17, P30).

6   Causes

6.1   Skepticism and Hype

Customers harbour skepticism about Agile methods and pose resistance to involvement. They don't readily understand Agile practices such as 'fail fast' and its intended benefits

— that minimum time and effort may be wasted on a project that's bound to fail — and become prejudiced:

> *"Agile terms...say option to fail early - believe me customers don't want to hear it. Customers don't want to admit that there could be some problem with the nice idea they put on paper. Forget about fail early, we dont want to fail at all!"*
> — P19, Senior Management, India

On the other extreme, with the increasing popularity of Agile methods, some customers treat Agile as a buzzword and are eager to reap the benefits of Agile projects without fully understanding their own responsibilities of collaboration and involvement:

> *"I mostly work [with] Indian companies with client in US...they see is client can make changes all the time and they think wow that sounds great!...They don't understand the counter-balancing discipline...customer involvement."* — P29, Agile Trainer, India

Agile practitioners mentioned both skepticism and hype as a major cause for lack of customer involvement (P5, P11, P14, P16, P17, P19, P22, P26, P29).

6.2   The Distance Factor

The majority of the Indian participants were catering to off-shored customers in Europe and USA which made customer collaboration challenging for them due to geographic and time-zone differences.

> *"Customer involvement is poor, very adversarial relationship. Basically the customers big fear is being cheated — because they are far away, they don't know the team — every mistake seems like an indication of incompetence or vendors trying to deceive [them]."* — P29, Agile Trainer, India

The effect of distance was apparent on a NZ team whose local customer was actively involved while their distanced customer was unwilling to participate.

> *"Relationship with [distanced customer] is very different from one in [same city]. We can call at short notice...and can we borrow somebody for half a day, they are willing to do it."* — P9, Tester, NZ

Distance between the team and their customers promoted misunderstandings (P11) and caused lack of customer involvement due to problems of communicating and co-ordinating over distances (P8-P12, P17, P29).

6.3   Lack of Time Commitment

Teams complain of not receiving enough collaboration time from their customer reps:

> *"[Customers say] 'I want to have Taj Mahal' but of granite or marble? They don't even have time to talk about that!"* — P25, Agile Coach, India.

At the same time, they realize that the customer rep's operational job may sometimes take precedence over their involvement on Agile projects because the rep has"*got a full-time job...and is quite busy, trying to fit us in.*" (P7). Development teams find the ability of the customer rep to devote time for collaboration is dependent on the customer (boss).

> "*I've never worked on [a project] where customer representative was given enough time to really be able to do the amount that they should.*" — P2, Developer, NZ

Eliciting adequate time from customers was challenging for the Agile teams and a cause for lack of customer involvement (P2, P4, P5, P7, P15, P19, P25, P26).

6.4 Dealing with Large Customers

Large customers and customers with larger projects showed a preference for traditional ways of working and were unwilling to collaborate as Agile customers.

> "*Larger the organization, they are a bit less flexible towards trying out new things.*" — P16, Developer, India

Large customers were often not bothered about the internal development-level practices of smaller Agile vendor companies, and tried to assert their traditional style of working on the team:

> "*Because of their size they were running hundreds of projects, they didn't want to care that this small organization was talking about, they just wanted to have things done in their own way.*" — P17, Developer, India

We found evidence of this only in India (P16, P17) and not in New Zealand.

6.5 Ineffective Customer Representative

While Indian Agile teams had limited face-to-face interactions with their customers, some NZ teams had a customer employee assigned to the project as a *customer rep.* An effective customer rep was described as "*someone who understands the implications of that system...where it fits into the business process*" and at the very least "*someone who knows how to use a computer!*" (P5, P9). Some NZ practitioners found their respective customer reps to be ineffective in providing timely requirements and feedback, while others found them lacking in proper understanding of Agile practices.

> "*Unfortunately the person who is [the customer rep] has an I.Q. of literally 25...doesn't really know how the current system works, doesn't know much about the business process, is petrified of the project sponsor, and is basically budget-driven. So she doesn't really care if it's not going to work in a way that the end users like.*" (undisclosed) Developer

Several NZ participants expressed their frustration over not being able to choose the customer reps (P2, P7, P8, P9). It is not enough to have a customer rep for the project, it is also important for that rep to be effective in providing requirements and feedback to the team. An ineffective customer rep was a contributing factor to the Agile teams wanting more or better customer collaboration.

7   Consequences

7.1   Problems in Gathering and Clarifying Requirements

Agile teams found gathering requirements from customers as *"one of the worst things"* and *"biggest frustration"* on the projects (P8,P10). Getting customer reps to clarify requirements are also a problem because of their unavailability:

> *"Things [awaiting clarification] would queue up for them and then they'd just answer the whole queue at once...then as soon as they got busy again it would start to get a bit harder."* — P2, Developer, NZ

As a result of insufficient or ineffective customer involvement, the development teams were unable to gather requirements and to get customer reps to clarify them in time for development to commence.

7.2   Problems in Prioritizing Requirements

Providing and clarifying requirements is not enough, the customers are also required to prioritize them in order of business value. Understanding and using the concept of prioritization doesn't always come naturally to customers:

> *"We're meant to have one list of product backlog and it's supposed to be prioritized but when the client says 'Oh that's all priority' we have to go back and say 'which?! what do you mean?!...you can't have all priority!'"*. — P11, Developer, NZ

> *"Customer needs to tell his priorities that this is the first thing we want."* — P16, Developer, India

Teams faced difficulties in getting customer reps to prioritize the requirements and as such they were unsure about what features to develop and deliver first. (P7, P16)

7.3   Problems in Securing Feedback

Customer feedback is of vital importance in ensuring the desired product is being developed and delivered incrementally. As a senior developer pointed out *"the whole point of the two week iterations was so that the end users could know if we were on the right track"* (P15) and required customer reps providing feedback on developed features.

> *"If [the customer reps] didn't respond you just didn't care about their opinion...and at the end of the project...the business units that didn't give much feedback, when it went to a user, started complaining. And it's like well if we didn't get any critique it's not really our fault!"* — P2, Developer, NZ

In absence of customer feedback, teams were unable to assess how well the features met the requirements.

7.4 Loss of Productivity

Inability to gather requirements in time for the iterations could result in "*the project get[ting] stalled*" (P5) or loss of productivity:

> "*The team has the capacity...[but] with Agile if you don't have the requirement you can't do anything...because you are supposed to be in-line with business.*"
> — P10, Developer, NZ

Without clear requirements and feedback, the teams were forced to "*make more business decisions than [the team] would like*" (P15) and as a result would get "*misaligned from the desired business drivers*" (P5) consequently requiring costly rework (P2, P4, P15). Rework is taxing for developers because they have to revisit stories developed several iterations ago due to delay in customer feedback:

> "*Yes [we had to rework] but it's not the re-work, it's re-worked easily as long as it's near the time you did it. So having to go back and augment what you did three weeks ago was [hard].*" — P2, Developer, NZ

7.5 Business Loss

The most extreme consequence of lack of customer involvement was business loss that the vendor organization suffered because there was "*no match between what Agile says and the way [the customers] wanted.*" (P17). Some customers were explicitly opposed to Agile practices and did not want to be involved in an Agile project. Some Agile vendor organizations, in such cases, decided to suffer business loss over working on an Agile project with no customer involvement.

> "*We've lost business multiple times...We try to find out early on if [Agile is] gonna be a problem and if it is, we say 'Okay, lets go our separate ways.'*" —
> P1, Senior Management, NZ

8 Contingencies: Agile Undercover

8.1 Changing Priority

In an effort to maintain the iterative and incremental nature of their Agile projects, teams were forced to change priority of user stories that were awaiting customer requirements, clarification, or prioritization. Such stories were usually demoted in priority and pushed further down into the product backlog until the required customer response was secured and development on those stories could re-commence. Agile teams confessed to that they changed the priority of the story in absence of enough, clear, and prompt requirements (P2, P8, P14, P26).

> "*[If] we know exactly what business want or we know eighty percent of what they want, we include that story in the sprint; otherwise if we have something that's a little bit unsure, we don't include that in the sprint.*" — P10, Developer, NZ

A similar strategy, called *definition of ready* [2] was adopted by an Indian team:

> *"We have recently started using...the definition of ready.....product owner will not take something that is not 'done' and similarly developers are not going to take something that's not 'ready'."* — P18, Developer, India

A user story was considered *ready* when the customers had provided the business goals and expected outcome associated with the story and implementation details necessary to estimate the story had been discussed. A story that was not *ready* was not able to achieve priority in the product backlog.

8.2   Risk Assessment Up Front

One of the participants mentioned using an Agile risk assessment questionnaire as a basis to gauge the level of customer involvement on the project up front. The questionnaire included questions such as 'what is the commitment of the customer rep in terms of time?' and had multi-choice answers:

> *"'They're either assigned to this project or available as a first priority' [is] the best situation and the worst situation [is] 'Just as time allows'"* — P14, Senior Agile Coach, NZ

Performing risk assessment upfront before the start of the project allows the team to discover if the indicated level of customer involvement is a potential risk to the Agile project. Usually the reason behind limited involvement is lack of funding or unavailability of the customer rep. The approach taken to overcome this problem was to negotiate with the customer for freeing up the customer rep's time by providing funding from the project. The aim was to *"allow [the rep] to become a project team member, in a more permanent way for the duration of the project"* (P14) which is the ideal level of customer collaboration on Agile projects [3,8,29]

8.3   Story Owners

The practice of assigning story owners was an adaptation to the Scrum practice of allocating a product owner [29]. Story owners were responsible for particular stories (less than a week long), instead of *all* the stories in the product backlog: *"every story had to have an owner to get into prioritisation."* (P14) Assigning story owners served a threefold purpose. Firstly, having multiple story owners instead of a single customer rep for entire project meant no one person from the customer's organization was expected to be continuously available.

> *"We didn't need that story owner for the duration of the project, we normally only need them for part of an iteration."* – P14, Senior Agile Coach, NZ

Secondly, it allowed the team to plan out stories for development in synchronization with the corresponding story-owner's availability. Thirdly, it encouraged a sense of ownership among customer reps as they were encouraged to present their own stories to peers at end of iteration reviews.

"We get the [story owners] to demonstrate those stories to their peers at the end of the iteration review, this concept is something we've evolved over the project." — P14, Senior Agile Coach, NZ

After one such presentation a particularly skeptical customer rep was *"quite chuffed [pleased], and at the [next] iteration planning meeting, that person was all go! Instead of sitting back with their arms folded, they had their elbows on the table, leaning forward, and were driving the story detailing conversations we were having."* (P14)

8.4   Customer Proxy

Some Agile teams used a customer proxy — a member of the development team co-ordinating with the customers — to secure requirements and feedback. The use of proxy was visible in Indian teams where the customers were physically distant (P16, P19, P23, P28).

"Using Client proxy, so we assign a customer representative who interacts with the team much often but then passes on the feedback from the customer to the team and vice versa." — P28, Agile Coach, India

The use of proxy to co-ordinate between the customers and the team was also observed in New Zealand, where a Business Analyst and couple of developers on different teams served as the proxies because of their communication skills (P2, P4, P8).

"We've got two people [playing proxy]...[due to] their ability to communicate ideas; they're well-spoken and able to get those ideas across...which is great for developers!" — P3, Developer, NZ

8.5   Just Demos

Despite their reluctance or inability to attend other meetings, almost all customers were interested enough to attend demonstrations (demos) as it gave them an opportunity to see new functionalities of their software (P7, P11, P17). Demos were often the *only* regular collaboration that these Agile teams received from the customer reps and they used this opportunity to discuss features and receive feedback. As the local and involved customer rep of a NZ team disclosed:

"Just the sprint demos...and [we see] three pieces of functionality and it's all done in fifteen minutes, we take the full hour to discuss the other things...the demos were fun. I don't know if that's their intent, but they were!" — P12, Customer Rep, NZ

8.6   E-Collaboration

Electronic collaboration (e-collaboration) was a popular means of regularly communicating with customers using video/voice conferencing, phone, email and chat. For Indian teams with off-shored customers, e-collaboration was a practical work-around:

"Video conferencing becomes very important. Its all about collaboration [when] time difference is a problem...with Europe [there is a] 4 hours overlap." — P17, Developer, India

Teams used web-conferencing and chats to conduct stand-up meetings and demos over the web (P13). New Zealand teams were also observed using phone conferencing with shared documents and emails using online forums called webEx (P9) and Skype, which *"doesn't cost that much to use; Skype [costs] literally zero."* (P10) E-collaboration was particularly important for our Agile teams because (a) Agile requires *regular* customer involvement (b) several teams had physically distant customers making face-to-face collaboration difficult and (c) e-collaboration was a convenient and inexpensive.

8.7   Extreme Undercover

In an effort to avoid extreme consequences of lack of customer involvement such as business loss, Agile teams chose to follow Agile practices internally at the team level while keeping the customer unaware:

"In none of the [three] cases the customer was aware of Agile, they didn't really want to do Agile...but what we had done was...taken charge of the projects [and] we had made it Agile - internally following Agile." — P17, Developer, India

Other practitioners confessed that they *"don't mention the 'A' word"* to customers who were explicitly opposed to Agile despite all the team's efforts to convince them (P28). Over the span of the research study, however, we have observed a decrease in the use of this particular practice due to increasing popularity of Agile methods among customers.

9   Covariance

Covariance occurs when one category changes with the changes in another category [12,21]. We found that *Agile Undercover* strategies vary with the factors that cause *Lack of Customer Involvement*. For example, *Customer Proxy, Just Demos* and/or *Changing Mindset*[1] were found in practice where participants faced *Ineffective Customer Reps*. Figure 4 presents the covariance relationships between *Agile Undercover* strategies being used and the factors that cause *Lack of Customer Involvement*.

10   Discussion and Related Work

While some *Agile Undercover* strategies such as *Changing Priority, Risk Assessment Up-front, Story Owners* and *Extreme Undercover* adapted existing practices, others such as using *Customer Proxy, Just Demos* and *E-collaboration* were existing Agile practices used specifically to overcome lack of customer involvement. Following classic GT, we

---

[1] An *Agile Undercover* strategy used to convince customers by highlighting benefits of Agile methods — described earlier [18] and not reiterated here for space reasons.

	Changing Priority	RAUP	Story Owners	Customer Proxy	Just Demos	E-Collab	Extreme Undercover	Changing Mindset[1]
Skepticism & Hype			√		√		√	√
Distance Factor				√	√	√		
Time Commitment	√	√	√		√			
Large Customers							√	√
Ineffective Customer Rep				√	√			

Fig. 4. Covariance between Agile Undercover and Lack of Customer Involvement. RAUP is Risk Assessment Up-Front.

discuss implications of *Agile Undercover* in light of existing literature after presenting the our research results [14].

Using the *definition of ready* for user stories [2] forced customers to provide detailed requirements with clear business drivers. The *definition of ready* complemented the existing Scrum definition of done [29]. The practice of assigning *Story Owners* was an adaptation of the existing product owner practice. Unlike the product owner [8,29], the story owner was only responsible for one story at a time. This was an effective way of overcoming the limited availability of customer reps. Story owners also provide an alternative to the practice of on-site customer which has been found to be effective but burdening and unsustainable for long-term use [8,15,22,25].

A *Customer Proxy* is known to be used in situations were customer involvement is not ideal [20,23,24]. Participants agreed that being a proxy was demanding yet useful in co-ordinating with distant customers (P10, P11, P16, P28). Face-to-face communication is considered "*the most efficient and effective method of conveying information to and within a development*" [20,17], followed by video-conferencing, telephone, and email [22]. Our participant used *E-collaboration* extensively but noted that "*it does not take the place of having somebody sitting beside you*" (P9). Other limitations were imposed by the tool itself, such as Skype not supporting three or more people through video chatting (P10). Although demos are a regular Agile feature, they were often the only face-to-face collaboration time our participants received from their customers and they used *Just Demos* to discuss features and receive clarifications in addition to feedback.

The customer rep is ideally an individual who has both thorough understanding of and ability to express the project requirements and the authority to take strategic decisions [9,15,27]. Boehm advocates dedicated and co-located CRACK (Collaborative, Responsible, Authorized, Committed, Knowledgeable) customers for Agile projects [4]. In addition, our participants suggested that customers should choose reps that understand Agile practices and their own responsibilities in the process of Agile software development (P5, P12, P29).

Extreme Undercover was used by Indian teams as a last resort, specially when facing business loss. While one NZ team disclosed facing business loss, they chose to bear it. Over the research period (2 years) we found that the use of *Extreme Undercover* diminished with the increase in popularity of Agile methods. Participants found that *Agile*

Undercover strategies were effective in ensuring the success of their projects despite insufficient or ineffective customer involvement.

11   Limitations

Since the codes, concepts, and category emerged directly from the data, which in turn was collected directly from real world, the results are grounded in the context of the data [1]. We do not claim the results to be universally applicable: rather, they accurately characterize the context studied [1]. Our choice of research destinations and participants were limited in some ways by our access to them.

12   Conclusion

We conducted a GT study, involving 30 Agile practitioners from 16 different software development organizations in New Zealand and India, over a period of 2 years. The results reveal that customers are not as involved on these Agile projects as Agile methods demand. In this paper, we have described (a) the causes of lack of customer involvement (b) its the adverse consequences on Agile projects and (c) *Agile Undercover* strategies used by our participants to practice Agile despite insufficient or ineffective customer involvement. Some *Agile Undercover* strategies were adapted practices while others were close to existing Agile practices. Although we do not prescribe *Agile Undercover* strategies as replacement for real and valuable customer involvement, they may assist Agile teams facing similar lack of customer involvement. Participants found the *Agile Undercover* strategies to be largely useful and effective in their own contexts. Future studies could explore the viability and success of these strategies in different contexts such as in other countries and cultures.

Acknowledgments. Our thanks to all the participants. This research is generously supported by an Agile Alliance academic grant and a NZ BuildIT PhD scholarship.

References

1. Adolph, S., et al.: A Methodological Leg to Stand on. In: CASCON. ACM, USA (2008)
2. Beaumont, S.: The Definition of READY. Xebia blogs,
   http://blog.xebia.com/2009/06/19/the-definition-of-ready
   (December 4, 2009)
3. Beck, K.: Extreme Programming Explained, 2nd edn. Addison-Wesley, Reading (2004)
4. Boehm, B., Turner, R.: Rebalancing Your Organization's Agility and Discipline. In: Marchesi, M., Succi, G. (eds.) XP 2003. LNCS, vol. 2675, Springer, Heidelberg (2003)
5. Chow, T., Cao, D.: A survey study of critical success factors in agile software projects. J. Syst. Softw., pp. 961–971 (2008)
6. Cockburn, A.: People and Methodologies in Software Development. PhD thesis, University of Oslo, Norway (2003)
7. Coleman, G., et al.: Using GT to Understand Software Process Improvement: A Study of Irish Software Product Companies. J. Inf. Softw. Technol. 49(6), 654–667 (2007)

8. Dybå, T., Dingsoyr, T.: Empirical Studies of Agile Software Development: A Systematic Review. J. Inf. Softw. Technol. 50(9-10), 833–859 (2008)
9. Fraser, S., et al.: The Role of the Customer in Software Development: the XP Customer - Fad or Fashion? In: OOPSLA, pp. 148–150. ACM, USA (2004)
10. Georgieva, S., Allan, G.: Best Practices in Project Management Through a Grounded Theory Lens. E. J. Business Research Methods (2008)
11. Glaser, B.: Basics of Grounded Theory Analysis: Emergence vs. Forcing, CA (1992)
12. Glaser, B.: Theoretical Sensitivity. Sociology Press, Mill Valley (1978)
13. Glaser, B.: The Grounded Theory Perspective III: Theoretical Coding. Sociology Press, Mill Valley (2005)
14. Glaser, B., Strauss, A.L.: The Discovery of Grounded Theory. Aldine, Chicago (1967)
15. Grisham, P.S., Perry, D.E.: Customer relationships and Extreme Programming. In: HSSE 2005. ACM, USA (2005)
16. Hanssen, G.K., Fgri, T.E.: Agile Customer Engagement: A Longitudinal Qualitative Case Study. In: ISESE, Brazil, pp. 164–173 (2006)
17. Highsmith, J., Fowler, M.: The Agile Manifesto. Software Development Magazine (2001)
18. Hoda, R., Noble, J., Marshall, S.: Negotiating Contracts for Agile Projects: A Practical Perspective. In: XP 2009, Italy (2009)
19. Hoda, R., Noble, J., Marshall, S.: Agile Undercover. In: Agile 2009 RiP, Chicago (2009)
20. Judy, K.H., Krumins-Beens, I.: Great Scrums Need Great Product Owners: Unbounded Collaboration and Collective Product Ownership. In: HICSS, Hawai, pp. 462–462 (2008)
21. Kan, M.M., Parry, K.W.: Identifying Paradox: A grounded theory of leadership in overcoming resistance to change. The Leadership Quaterly, 467–491 (2004)
22. Korkala, M., Abrahamsson, P., Kyllonen, P.: A Case Study on the Impact of Customer Communication on Defects in Agile Software Development. In: AGILE 2006, USA (2006)
23. Lowery, M., Evans, M.: Scaling Product Ownership. In: Agile 2007, USA (2007)
24. Mann, C., Maurer, F.: A Case Study on the Impact of Scrum on Overtime and Customer Satisfaction. In: ADC, pp. 70–79. IEEE Computer Society, USA (2005)
25. Martin, A., et al.: The XP customer role in practice: Three studies. In: ADC 2004, pp. 42–54. IEEE Computer Society, Washington (2004)
26. Misra, S.C., et al.: Identifying some important success factors in adopting agile software development practices. J. Syst. Softw. 82(11), 1869–1890 (2009)
27. Nerur, S., et al.: Challenges of migrating to agile methodologies. Com. ACM, 72–78 (2005)
28. Pikkarainen, M., et al.: The impact of agile practices on communication in software development. J. Empirical Softw. Engg., 303–337 (2008)
29. Schwaber, K., Beedle, M.: Agile Software Development with Scrum. Prentice-Hall, Englewood Cliffs (2001)
30. Strauss, A., Corbin, J.: Basics of Qualitative Research. Sage, Newbury Park (1990)
31. Whitworth, E., Biddle, R.: The Social Nature of Agile Teams. In: Agile 2007, pp. 26–36. IEEE Computer Society, USA (2007)

Exploring Defect Data, Quality and Engagement during Agile Transformation at a Large Multisite Organization

Kirsi Korhonen

Nokia Siemens Networks
Hatanpään valtatie 30
33100 Tampere, Finland
kirsi.korhonen@nsn.com

Abstract. Agile methods promise improvements in code quality, but getting the full benefits is claimed to take years. A lack of visibility to improvements in the early stages of agile transformation can result in motivation decrease among the people in the organization, and thus slow down the agile transformation progress. In this study we analyzed defect data in a large multisite organization during the first six months of agile transformation. Defect data was compared to the results of a survey on agile transformation experiences and perceptions, which was conducted in the organization six months after starting the agile transformation. According to the results, improvements were visible in the defect data, but less than 25% of the people in the organization felt that quality had improved. Further study revealed that a realistic perception of the positive changes in the defect data coincided with positive emotional engagement in agile transformation.

Keywords: defect management, agile adoption, distributed development, software quality, agile transformation, emotional engagement.

1 Introduction

Empirical research results [20, 14] suggest that agile methods help to improve product quality and reduce the number of faults. This has encouraged organizations to take agile practices into use, and a number of guidelines are available for successful agile transformation [21, 18].

Since an agile transformation does not take place overnight [2, 22], lacking visibility to gradual improvements can cause frustration and motivation decrease, which in turn may delay the agile adoption process within the organization [2]. This is problematic especially in large multisite organizations, where known communication problems [16, 8] may further hamper the dissemination of information about improvements made. Our hypothesis is that in this kind of environment potential motivational problems are largely induced by the fact that people are unaware of improvement data.

Previous studies have used various methods to show that quality has improved with agile practices. These methods include analyses of the number of defects [20, 15], formal code reviews [1] and surveys exploring the perception of quality that people in

A. Sillitti et al. (Eds.): XP 2010, LNBIP 48, pp. 88–102, 2010.

the organization have [1, 2, 22]. However, these studies do not discuss the impact of the changes on the individuals' engagement level to agile transformation.

In this research we studied a large, globally distributed telecommunications software development organization migrating from traditional (waterfall) development to agile methods. The goals of this study were to identify whether there had been a change in software quality already during the first six months after the agile transformation started, if this change was visible to people in the organization, and if this visibility (or the lack of it) had any impact on the individuals' engagement in agile transformation. The data was collected by analyzing and comparing defect statistics from one software development project before the transformation with two consecutive projects after the transformation had started. Further, a survey on individuals' agile experiences and opinions was conducted in the organization half a year after starting the migration.

The analysis results showed a clear change in defect data already in the early stage of the agile transformation. But according to the survey results, this change was seen only by 24.4% of the respondents. Further study revealed that a realistic perception of the positive changes in the defect data coincided with positive emotional engagement to agile transformation. Based on the results it is proposed that the organization should consider making the communication of changes in defect data into an integrated part of their agile transformation process from the beginning on, so that the impact of agile methods becomes visible to everyone involved in the transformation. This can contribute to strengthening individual engagement in agile adoption, thus making the agile transformation process smoother in the organization.

This paper is organized as follows: the next section provides background information about the expected challenges and impacts of the agile transformation. In section 3 the research design is defined together with the methods and the context. Section 4 describes the empirical results, which are discussed in section 5. Conclusions and final remarks are presented in section 6.

2 Background

Agile transformation is a challenge to any organization [11, 5, 14]. Initial experiences with agile practices can be tough, as problems become painfully visible and changes are required in the working habits and mindsets of individuals, teams and organizations alike. It is tempting to blame the agile methodology for all and any problems [4] and even abandon new practices that challenge the team most [2]. Especially in a large multisite organization there can be additional challenges caused by dependencies between teams on different sites [16], problems with communication [16, 8] or unclarity on defect management practices [9], just to mention a few issues. Despite the known problems, the success stories of agile methods [20, 14, 13, 15, 12] report a reduced number of defects and improvement in quality, which have encouraged other organizations to start the journey towards agile way of working.

In the following sections we discuss in more detail the changes expected to happen with agile transformation in defect management and in perceptions of quality, as well as some agile transformation challenges.

2.1 Less Defects in Agile Development

In lean software development [19], defects are considered waste, and the way to reduce the impact of defects is to find them as soon as they occur. The Agile engineering practices, such as continuous integration [23] and test driven development (TDD) [23] support this goal. Fixing the found faults has higher priority than developing new content, thus at the end of each sprint the software should be in shippable condition [23, 17, 19].

Based on the success stories of agile adoption, it would seem realistic to expect that there would be fewer defects to manage after adopting agile methods [e.g. 1, 12, 15, 20]. Agile engineering practices will help teams fix their faults early; on the other hand, inside co-located agile teams there is no need to report defects with separate problem reporting tools [9], since defects are handled on flipcharts or with post-it notes. But in a large, distributed organization there are dependencies between teams on different sites, which make the use of fault reporting tools more important as a communication channel and as a way to share information [9].

2.2 Improved Code Quality in Agile Development

There are studies which indicate that after adopting agile methods, software quality has improved. For example, it is reported at Primavera [20] that agile adoption increased their product quality by 30%. This figure was based on the number of customer-reported defects per KLOC in the first nine months following the release. After 7 sprints of implementing TDD, the number of defects was reduced by 10% per team, which meant over 75% improvement in defect rates compared to the previous release.

At Cisco [13], members of the 10-person pilot team adopting agile practices felt that product quality was higher, and they were consistently delivering at the end of each iteration.

At Yahoo! [2], feedback on agile transformation was collected from the teams, and 54% of the respondents felt that agile practices improved the overall quality and "rightness" of what the team produced.

2.3 Challenges in Agile Transformation

All these good results cannot be expected to become visible immediately. A three-month long agile pilot project at Ericsson [1] resulted in a 5.5% decrease in defects, but formal code review revealed that the quality of the code was the same as previously.

A recent survey made at Nokia Siemens Networks [22] concludes that several agile engineering practices as well as a sustainable pace need to be in place before significant improvements on code quality can be reached. In this study, "basic" agile practices included short time-boxed iterations [24], product backlog [24], continuous integration [23], retrospectives [24] and self-organizing teams [19]. "Intermediate" agile practices add to basic practices refactoring [23], TDD, or acceptance test driven development (ATDD) [23], or tests written at the same time as code. More practices than that would be equated to a "fully agile" organization. In large organizations, getting to the fully agile level can take a few years [22, 2], and patience is required.

Team capability, including expertise and motivation, is proposed to be one of the main success factors in agile software development [3]. In an agile pilot at Ericsson [1], team members found practices like pair programming as highly motivating, and as they enjoyed the challenge of new things and learning, there was little resistance to agile transformation.

One of the building blocks of motivation in agile transformation is a sense of progress [19]. Visibility into progress reinforces motivation, and is one way to empower the team [19]. But it can be difficult to measure your success against a predetermined plan because in agile development the plan can change in every sprint [24]. To address this problem at Primavera [20], the impact of scrum practices was measured by product quality and time to market instead of comparing to the original plan.

Working software itself is the primary measure of progress [17]. Software defects are failures in the required behavior of the software system [6], therefore it is natural to use defects to measure the progress. There are defect-related quality metrics introduced in agile studies; for example, the number of customer-reported defects in a specified time following the release [20], the number of defects by iteration [12, 15], enhancements made per defects reported [19], effort spent on bug fixing [15] and defects carried over to the next iteration [7].

One simple way to provide feedback on agile transformation progress is to compare defect metrics before and after agile transformation [15]. Also guidelines have been designed for appropriate agile measurement [7]. However, these examples do not discuss the impact of defect data metrics on the perception of quality or on individual engagement in agile transformation.

3   Research Setup

This section gives an overview of the organization, projects, research methods and the data collection process used in this study.

3.1   Research Context

The organization in the study is large, and project personnel in the studied projects comprised more than 150 experts working on several different locations globally. Their software development projects produced new versions of an existing product in the telecommunications domain. Altogether 78 responses to the survey were gathered.

During the study period there were three consecutive projects, one project before the agile transformation (project 1), one project right after the transformation started (project 2), and a third project starting while the agile transformation had been ongoing for a few months (project 3). The agile transformation was started gradually in the teams in this study (later referred as "Organization"), and figure 1 presents the agile experience of the personnel in the projects of the organization measured by months. The gradual start of the agile transformation can be seen in figure 1, as there were people who had had less than 3 months of experience, or who felt they did not have any experience yet. On the other hand, there were more experienced people involved as well with over six months' experience, having worked in agile projects before.

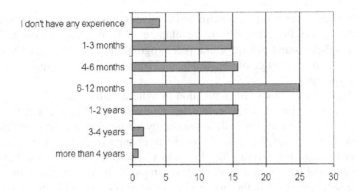

Fig. 1. Agile experience of the scrum team members based on Agile transformation feedback survey responses conducted in the organization half a year after transformation start

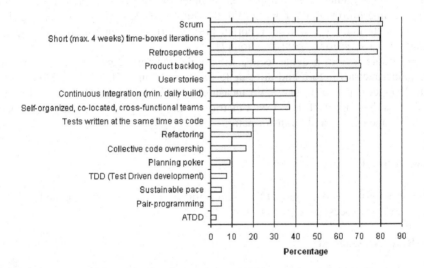

Fig. 2. Agile practices in use in the scrum teams after half a year of starting the agile transformation based on the responses on Agile transformation feedback survey

The basic level agile methods [22] were used in projects 2 and 3 after the start of the agile transformation. These basic methods included e.g. retrospectives (reported to be in use by 78.2% of the respondents) short time-boxed iterations (79%) and scrum (80.8%) (Figure 2). More advanced practices, such as TDD and pair-programming, were not yet so widely in use (less than 10%).

This indicates a very early phase of agile adoption, with the scrum process in place, but not yet many of the other known practices being used. Another aspect is that the teams in this study consisted of both development and system level testing scrum teams, and the practices which were mainly meant to support code development, were not used in system level testing scrum teams as such. System level testing scrums concentrated on non-functional testing after the different components of the software had been integrated together.

3.2   Research Methods and Data Collection

The primary goal of this study was to provide answers to two questions: 1) is there a change in defect data due to agile adoption during the first six months of transformation and 2) is this change visible to project personnel in the organization. At the same time, the organization wanted to collect feedback on the agile transformation, and both defect and agile transformation related questions were combined into one survey. During the analysis of the results two additional research questions emerged: 3) does a realistic perception of the changes in the defect data have a corresponding impact on the perception of code quality, and 4) does a positive perception of changes in turn make people more engaged in the agile transformation. The data analysis was extended to cover these questions as well.

Defect data records were collected once a week from the defect reporting tool in each project. The defect data was analyzed first by creating and comparing three metrics: the number of open defects, defect lifetime and defect finding profile. These metrics were chosen based on an earlier case study where the metrics were shown to support quality objectives in a large distributed organization [10].

There were certain assumptions of the behavior of these three metrics in an agile transformation. First, the number of open defects should decrease [20, 15]. Second, there should not be any major peaks in defect reporting over time, since according to agile principles, new content is being developed and defects reported steadily in every sprint [19]. Third, defect lifetime should not be longer than one sprint in agile projects, as the goal is to fix defects as soon as they are found [19, 23], and therefore most defects should be found and fixed during each development sprints. It was assumed that by analyzing defect data and by using these three simple metrics, it will be possible to find evidence on the progress of the agile transformation.

The survey on the progress was conducted six months after starting the agile transformation. The survey consisted of closed questions offering a number of defined response choices. By the time the survey was conducted, project 2 had already released the software, and project 3 was still ongoing. The respondents were divided into four groups according to their perception of the change in the code quality. Statistical analysis was conducted to explore whether there were significant differences between the groups, and where these differences lay.

4   Empirical Results

In this section the impact of agile transformation measured by the change in defect data is presented together with the survey results on participants' perception of quality and their engagement in the agile transformation process.

4.1   Defect Data

The changes in the defect data during agile transformation were analyzed with three metrics: the number of open defects, defect lifetime and defect finding profile.

Number of Open Defects. This metric measures the number of open defects at a given point of time. An open defect is a problem which has been found in the software but not yet corrected, or the correction has not yet been verified. In this study the number of open defects was recorded once a week for each project and the number was compared to the maximum number of open defects measured during project 1. The results are presented in Figure 3 by comparing the projects' daily number of open defects several sprints before until a few sprints after the system was integrated for non-functionality testing on system level.

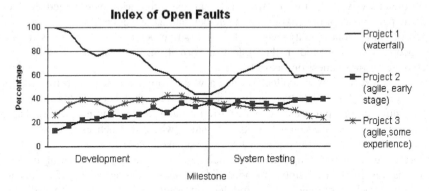

Fig. 3. Open defects index by project during development and system testing phases

Based on figure 3, agile adoption has had an impact on the defect count. The number of open defects was lower, and the trend line was steadier in projects 2 and 3 than in project 1. An interesting detail in the figure is the small variance between the three projects at the milestone before the system testing start (indicated by the vertical Milestone line).

Defect Lifetime. Defect lifetime is measured from the date when the defect was found and reported in the defect reporting tool until the date when the correction has been verified for the reported problem. The dates were collected from the fault reporting tool, and defect lifetimes were compared to sprint length.

The Mann-Whitney U test, a non-parametric alternative to t-test of independent variables, was conducted to compare the defect lifetimes between projects 1, 2 and 3. Due to confidentiality of the defect data, only p and r values are presented here. There was no significant difference (p=.393) between the agile projects 3 and 2. But a statistically significant difference was found when comparing these projects to the non-agile project 1. The median defect lifetime was improved in projects 2 and 3, both being 12.5% shorter than the median in project 1. The magnitude of the differences in the medians was small both in project 2 ($p<.01$, $r=0.09$) and in project 3 ($p<.01$, $r=0.09$). More defects were corrected and verified in time equal to sprint length (or faster) in agile projects 2 (75.4%) and 3 (77.7%) than in the non-agile project 1 (68.4%).

Defect Finding Profile. The defect finding profile indicates at which phase of the project defects are found. Most of the defects should be found and fixed during the development sprints, and only a limited number of defects should be reported during later phases, such as system testing. Table 1 presents the defect finding profile of projects 1, 2 and 3.

Table 1. Percentage of defects found in development sprints versus system testing

	Project 1	Project 2	Project 3
Development	58.9%	44.9%	70.4%
System testing	41.1%	55.1%	29.6%

In project 2 there were fewer defects reported during the development phase than in project 1. This was not an expected result. One explanation can be that during project 2 the defect reporting practices were not clear, and plenty of defects were not entered into the fault reporting tool. Guidelines were specified in more detail for project 3, so that for example faults which were not fixed during one sprint should be reported into the tool. In project 3 the change can be seen clearly: over 70% of the defects were reported during development, and less than 30% were found during system testing. Compared to project 1, this change is now as expected, and it is in line with the assumptions made about the changes due to agile adoption.

4.2 Perceptions of Code Quality

The respondents of the survey were asked to evaluate the impact of the agile transformation on code quality by using the ratings 'Much Improved'(5), 'Somewhat improved'(4), 'No Impact'(3), 'Somewhat worse'(2), 'Much worse'(1) or 'I do not know'(0). Based on their perception of code quality, four equal-sized groups of respondents emerged from the data (table 2).

Table 2. Groups based on perception on code quality

Grp1: Improved	Grp2: No Impact	Grp3: Gotten Worse	Grp4: I Do Not Know
24.4.%	25.6%	23.1%	26.9%

The impact of individuals' agile experience and the practices in use were further analyzed for these groups. There were no significant differences between the four groups in length of experience according to Kruskall-Wallis Test (p=.058).

No differences were recorded in the number of agile practices in use either between the groups Grp1:Improved (Md=6), Grp2:No Impact (Md =6) and Grp3:Gotten Worse (Md =7.5) (table 3). This might be related to the early stage of agile adoption, with only few agile practices being in use in general. The only statistically significant difference (Bonferroni corrected) was found with group Grp4: I do not know (Md=4). Compared to the other groups, fewer agile practices were in use in Grp4: I do not know, which might explain why they felt that they could not evaluate the change in code quality.

This grouping based on the perception of change in the code quality was later on used for finding out if there were differences between the groups as to 1) their perception of changes in the defect data due to agile practices and 2) their engagement in agile transformation. Special focus was put to analyzing groups Grp1 and Grp3 because their opinions were opposite. These results are discussed in next sections.

Table 3. Mann-Whitney U test results on the number of agile practices in use between the groups

Comparison	U	z	p
Grp1-Grp2	180	-.286	.775
Grp3-Grp1	161	-.307	.759
Grp3-Grp2	159	-.606	.553
Grp4-Grp3	96	-2.831	.005
Grp4-Grp2	135	-1.983	.047
Grp4-Grp1	96	-2.831	.005

4.3 Perception of Change in Defect Data

The respondents were asked to rate the impact of agile transformation on four defect management practices: Q1: Early detection of defects, Q2: Number of open defects at milestones, Q3: Defect lifetime and Q4: Number of serious defects reported. The Kruskal-Wallis test, a non-parametric one-way between-groups analysis of variances, was conducted on the answers, and there was a statistically significant difference across the four groups. The results between groups 1 and 3 are presented in table 4.

Table 4. Kruskall-Wallis test results on defect questions between groups Grp1:Improved and Grp3:Gotten worse

	df	n	χ^2	p
Q1: Early detection of defects	3	37	12.02	0.007
Q2: Open faults at milestones	3	37	14.612	0.002
Q3: Defect Lifetime	3	36	9.306	0.025
Q4: Number of serious bugs reported	3	37	19.587	0.000

The differences between groups Grp1:Improved and Grp3:Gotten worse were further analyzed with the Mann-Whitney U test (table 5) and the test confirmed significant difference between these two groups in all four defect questions. Those who felt that the code quality had improved (Grp1: Improved) also saw that defect management had improved (Q1 Md= 4, Q2 Md=3, Q3 Md=4, Q4 Md=4). On the other hand, in Grp3: Gotten worse, code quality and defect management in agile were consistently seen as more negative (Q1 Md= 3, Q2 Md=2, Q3 Md=3, Q4 Md=2).

Table 5. Mann-Whitney U test results for defect questions between groups Grp1:Improved and Grp3:Gotten worse

	U	Z	p	r
Q1: Early detection of defects	76.5	-3.083	.002	0.507
Q2: Open faults at milestones	94.5	-2.404	.016	0.395
Q3: Defect Lifetime	93	-2.386	.017	0.398
Q4: Number of serious bugs reported	45	-3.981	.000	0.654

The Mann-Whitney U test between groups Grp1:Improved and Grp2:No Impact (table 6) revealed a significant difference between these two groups in defect questions as well except for Q3:Defect lifetime.

Table 6. Mann-Whitney U test results for defect questions between groups Grp1:Improved and Grp2:No impact

	U	Z	p
Q1: Early detection of defects	141	-1.320	.187
Q2: Open faults at milestones	154.5	-.811	.418
Q3: Defect Lifetime	146	-.525	.600
Q4: Number of serious bugs reported	97.5	-2.628	.009

A statistical difference was recorded also when comparing Grp2:No Impact to Grp3: Gotten worse (table 7) with two questions, Q1 and Q4. With questions Q2 and Q3 there was no statistical difference found.

Table 7. Mann-Whitney U test results for defect questions between groups Grp3:Gotten Worse and Grp2:No impact

	U	Z	p
Q1: Early detection of defects	107.5	-2.102	.036
Q2: Open faults at milestones	110	-1.931	.053
Q3: Defect Lifetime	109	-1.823	.067
Q4: Number of serious bugs reported	103	-2.213	.027

Based on the analysis, those who felt that there had been no change in code quality, saw the changes in defect management a bit more positive than people in Grp3:Gotten Worse, but more negative than people in Grp1: Improved.

4.4 Engagement in Agile Transformation

In this section it is first discussed what engagement means in this study, and after that, the survey results related to engagement in agile transformation are presented.

Defining Personal Engagement. According to a literature review on employee engagement [26], there is no universal definition for personal engagement, and several ways are introduced in literature for measuring engagement. According to Kahn [25], engagement is a combination of a persons's physical, cognitive and emotional expression. The physical aspect is about the physical energies utilised by the person. Cognitive aspect concerns the individual's beliefs about the organization, its leaders and working conditions. Emotional aspect describes the individuals feeling about those three.

In this study the definition by Kahn [25] was adapted for agile aspects. It was assumed that in order to be fully engaged in the agile transformation in the organization, a person needs to 1) have rational understanding of the agile transformation, 2) be motivated to utilize agile practices, and 3) have an emotional attachment to the transformation.

Rational engagement is related to understanding the reasons behind the change, and believing in the goals of the agile transformation. The rationally engaged person supports agile practices.

Motivational engagement comes from being able to apply individual skills and abilities in the scrum team by using the agile methods. A motivationally engaged person wants to help the others in the scrum team to be successful with using agile practices.

Emotional engagement is based on feelings. Emotionally engaged person is proud to tell others about using agile in his work, and feels good about what they do in the scrum team by being agile. This person would recommend agile practices to others, and he feels that agile practices inspire him to do his best work.

Results. Each one of the engagement types; rational, motivational and emotional, studied with several questions to form an overall view. The Kruskal-Wallis test revealed no significant difference in the responses to rational and motivational questions between the four groups. But with the emotional questions (presented in Appendix A), a statistical difference was found ($\chi2(3, n=76)=10.279, p=.016$). The questions on emotional engagement were grouped together to form one scale. Engagement on an emotional scale has a good internal consistency with Cronbach's alpha coefficient .802. The Mann-Whitney U test was conducted to analyze emotional engagement between the groups Grp1: Improved, Grp2: No Impact and Grp:Gotten worse.

In the Grp2: No Impact the emotional engagement results were erratic, and there was no significant difference compared to Grp1: Improved (p=.15) and Grp3:Gotten worse(p=.057).

But the test revealed a significant statistical difference (Bonferroni corrected) between the groups Grp1:Improved (Md=3.75, n=18) and Grp3:Gotten worse (Md =3.125, n=18), U = 81.5, z=-2.56, p=.01, r=.43. People in group Grp1:Improved were more emotionally engaged in agile transformation than people in group Grp3:Gotten worse.

5 Discussion

The defect data analysis revealed that a positive change was visible already during the first six months after the agile transformation had started. The results were in line with the assumptions based on literature study: the total number of defects declined [20, 15], the defects were found steadily over time [19, 23], and there was an improvement in defect closing time [19].

Even though there was this positive development in the defect data, the survey results revealed that not everybody was aware of the positive change (table 2). Only 24.4% of the respondents felt that quality had improved, 25.6% saw no impact, and 23.1% felt that quality had gotten worse. 26.9% of the respondents replied that they could not say what the impact had been propably because the agile transformation had been going on for such a short time.

The organization's progress in the adoption of agile practices was explored to find out if there were any differences between the groups to explain why the improvement on defect data was not visible throughout the organization. An analysis of survey results revealed that the length of agile experience, or the number of agile practices in use did not have impact on the perception on the quality in this organization. This might be due to an early stage of agile transformation in the organization – majority of the respondents had less than a year of experience in agile development (Figure 1). The organization in this study had just incorporated some basic level agile practices (on the scale basic - intermediate - fully agile [22]) and those practices have been utilized for six months. This result is in line with a previous study which suggested that the code quality improvement is related to how mature the organization is with their agile practices [22]. For this organization there were many more agile practices to be taken into use to improve code quality.

In the further analysis it was found that there was a statistically significant difference among the groups in the perception of change in defect data and the perception of improvement in code quality. If a person felt that the agile transformation impact on defect data had been positive, he also saw the impact on code quality as positive. The changes were seen positive in the early detection of defects, in defect lifetime and in the number of serious defects reported, which all had improved based on the defect data. The number of open faults at milestones did not differ that much according to defect data analysis, and the perception of improvement in this area was a bit lower as well. Overall, the perception of the positive change was quite realistic when compared to the defect data analysis results.

As there was a clear statistical difference between groups on how people perceived change in the defect data and improvements in code quality, personal engagement in agile transformation was analyzed from rational, motivational and emotional viewpoints to see if there were any differences in engagement levels of the groups. It was found that rational understanding of the agile transformation and motivation to use effort on agile practices did not have a link with the perception of code quality. However, people who saw that code quality had improved were more emotionally engaged in agile transformation than those who had perceived the changes in code quality as negative.

The result is perhaps not surprising: when one has a positive attitude towards the agile transformation, one easily interprets all changes as positive. It could also be interpreted that if a person had detected a positive impact on defects, he would more easily develop a positive attitude towards the agile transformation than someone who did not see a similar positive impact. However, it is very interesting that all these three aspects – perceived changes in defect data, perception of quality, and emotional engagement in the agile transformation, are tightly connected with each other. Therefore if you change one, it would seem reasonable to expect a similar change in the other two. For example, if people feel more engaged, the quality is perceived improved as well, or improvement in defect data metrics could improve the engagement. This is an important finding, as according to previous studies, highly engaged teams will outperform teams with lower employee engagement levels and the organization can only reach its full potential through emotionally engaged employees [27, 28]. So if there is even a slight change that positive feedback on progress would improve emotional engagement, organization should pursue his possibility.

As an outcome of this study it is proposed that an organization should utilize simple defect data metrics comparisons before and during the agile transformation to follow up the progress of the change. Providing visibility to the progress and communicating the changes in defect data consistently and continuously throughout the organization can help in making corrective actions in time. On the other hand, the positive feedback on progress can support people in their agile transformation and thus help the organization to proceed with the agile transformation more smoothly and increase organizational performance.

6   Conclusions

In this research we studied defect data and conducted a survey during the agile transformation of a large multisite organization to see whether the visibility of real change in defect data has an impact on the perception of code quality and on individual engagement in agile transformation. The results gave evidence that defect data visibility has no major impact on rational or motivational engagement in agile transformation. However, it was found that defect data visibility has a clear link with emotional engagement.

Based on the results it is proposed that the organization should consider making the analysis and communication of defect data into an integrated part of their agile transformation process. Analysis could be carried out by comparing those defect data metrics where agile practices are expected to make a difference before and after the agile transformation. This would help the organization to follow up the progress already at a very early stage of the transformation. Positive feedback via communication of changes might also have an impact on individual engagement in agile adoption. thus making the agile transformation smoother in the organization. Analysis and communication could be carried out in many ways, for example by integrating a defect data visualization tool in the development environment to provide online data on defect metrics and trendlines, or by publishing defect data regularly in retrospective meetings.

In future, this study will be continued with research into defect data development as the agile transformation proceeded, and most people in the organization had gained at least one year's experience in agile and more agile practices had been taken into use. The goal is to study if defect data visibility and more experience on agile practices influenced participants' perceptions of changes in quality and defect data as well as if the different aspects of engagement changed accordingly.

Acknowledgements. The author thanks Kai Koskimies, Hannu Korhonen, Erik Hiltunen, Steve Kan and Maria Lahti for their comments and insights.

References

1. Auvinen, J., Back, R., Heidenberg, J., Hirkman, P., Milovanov, L.: Improving the engineering process area at Ericsson with Agile practices. A Case Study. TUCS Technical report No 716 (October 2005)
2. Benefield, G.: Rolling out Agile in a Large Enterprise. In: Proceedings of the 41st Annual Hawaii International Conference on System Sciences, p. 462 (2008)
3. Chow, T., Cao, D.-B.: A Survey study on critical success factors in agile software projects. Journal of Systems and Software 81(6), 961–971 (2008)

4. Cloke, G.: Get your agile freak on! Agile adoption at Yahoo!Music. In: Agile '07: Proceedings of the AGILE 2007, pp. 240–248. IEEE Computer Society, Los Alamitos (2007)
5. Cohn, M., Ford, D.: Introducing an Agile Process to an Organization. Computer 36(6), 74–78 (2003)
6. Fenton, N., Pfleeger, S.: Software Metrics: A rigorous and practical approach, 2nd edn. PWS Publishing Company (1991)
7. Hartmann, D., Dymond, R.: Appropriate Agile Measurement: Using Metrics and Diagnostics to Deliver Business Value. In: Proceedings of Agile 2006, pp. 128–134 (2006)
8. Herbsleb, J.D., Mockus, A., Finholt, T.A., Grinter, R.E.: Distance, dependencies, and delay in a global collaboration. In: Proceedings of the ACM Conference on Computer Supported Cooperative Work, pp. 319–328. ACM Press, New York (2000)
9. Korhonen, K.: Migrating Defect Management from Waterfall to Agile Software Development in a Large-Scale Multi-Site Organization: a Case Study. In: Proceedings of XP 2009, Italy, pp. 73–82 (2009)
10. Korhonen, K., Salo, O.: Exploring Quality Metrics to support Defect Management Process in Multi Site Organization – a Case Study. In: Proceedings of ISSRE (2008)
11. Lawrence, R., Yslas, B.: Three-way cultural change: Introducing agile with two non-agile companies and a non-agile methodology. In: Proceedings of AGILE Conference (2006)
12. Laymann, L., Williams, L., Cunningham, L.: Exploring extreme programming in context: an industrial case study. In: Agile Development Conference (2004)
13. Lifshitz, G., Kroskin, A., Dubinsky, Y.: The story of transition to agile sw development. In: Proceedings of XP 2008, Ireland, pp. 212–214 (2008)
14. Lindvall, M., Muthig, D., Dagnino, A., Wallin, C., Stupperich, M., Kiefer, D., May, J., Kahkonen, T.: Agile software development in large organizations. Computer 37(12), 26–34 (2004)
15. Ileva, S., Ivanov, P., Stefanova, E.: Analyses of an agile methodology implementation. In: Proceedings of Euromicro Conference, pp. 393–407. IEEE Computer Society Press, Los Alamitos (2004)
16. Mahanti, A.: Challenges in Enterprise Adoption of Agile Methods – A Survey. Journal of Computing and Information Technology CIT 14(3), 197–206 (2006)
17. Agile manifesto at, http://www.agilemanifesto.org/
18. Misra, S., Kumar, U., Kumar, V., Grant, G.: The organizational changes required and the challenges involved in adopting agile methodologies in traditional software development organizations. In: Digital Information Management, pp. 25–28 (2006)
19. Poppendieck, M., Poppendieck, T.: Lean Software development. Addison-Wesley, Reading (2007)
20. Schatz, B., Abdelshafi, I.: Primavera Gets Agile: A Successful Transition to Agile Development. Software 22, 36–42 (2005)
21. Sidky, A., Arthur, J.: A disciplined approach to adopting agile practices: the agile adoption framework. In: Innovations in Systems and Software Engineering, pp. 203–216. Springer, Heidelberg (2007)
22. Vilkki, K.: Impacts of Agile Transformation. Flexi Newsletter (January 2009)
23. Crispin, L., Gregory, J.: Agile testing. A Practical guide for testers and agile teams. Addison-Wesley, Reading (2009)
24. Schwaber, K., Beedle, M.: Agile software development with Scrum. Prentice Hall, Englewood Cliffs (2002)
25. Kahn, W.A.: Psychological conditions of personal engagement and disengagement at work. Academy of Management Journal 33, 692–724 (1990)

26. Kular, S., Gatenby, M., Rees, C., Soane, E., Truss, K.: Employee Engagement: A Literature Review. (Working Paper) Kingston upon Thames, U.K. Kingston Business School, Kingston University, 28 p (2008), http://eprints.kingston.ac.uk/4192/
27. ISR, International Survey Research (2004), http://www.isrsurveys.com
28. Johnson, M.: Gallup study reveals workplace disengagement in Thailand. The Gallup Management Journal (May 12, 2004),
http://gmj.gallup.com/content/16306/3/
Gallup-Study-Reveals-Workplace-Disengagementin.aspx

Appendix A: Emotional Engagement Survey Questions

On a scale from 1 to 5, describe how do you see the agile practices in your work:
1= Strongly disagree, 2=Disagree, 3=Not agree nor disagree, 4= Agree, 5= Fully Agree, 0=I do not know.

1. I am proud to tell others I am using agile practices in my work.
2. I am passionate about what we do in our scrum team by using the agile methods.
3. I would recommend taking agile practices into use in other teams.
4. Agile practices inspire me to do my best work.

Auto-tagging Emails with User Stories Using Project Context

S.M. Sohan, Michael M. Richter, and Frank Maurer

Department of Computer Science
University of Calgary
2500 University Drive NW Calgary
AB, Canada, T2N 1N4
{smsohan,mrichter,frank.maurer}@ucalgary.ca

Abstract. In distributed agile teams, people often use email as a knowledge sharing tool to clarify the project requirements (aka user stories). Knowledge about the project included in these emails is easily lost when recipients leave the project or delete emails for various reasons. However, the knowledge contained in the emails may be needed for useful purposes such as re-engineering software, changing vendor and so on. But, it is difficult to relate texts such as emails to certain topics because the relation is not explicit. In this paper, we present and evaluate a technique for automatically relating emails with user stories based on their text and context similarity. Agile project management tools can use this technique to automatically build a knowledge base that is otherwise costly to produce and maintain.

Keywords: Distributed Agile, Collaboration, Software Documentation, Agile Tool.

1   Introduction

In agile projects, requirements are commonly expressed using "user stories" in everyday language. These stories are not formalized and the meaning cannot be formally extracted. An example user story is as follows:

As a shopper, I want to pay online to checkout my shopping cart using Master-Card, Visa or Amex credit card from a secured web page only.

However, as the developers start developing the stories, they often consult with customers and other teammates to further clarify such user stories. Face-to-face communication is used as the principal communication medium between customers and developers in agile processes [1] [2] [3] [5]. In distributed teams, people often use emails where face-to-face communication is not an option [7]. For an example, the developer may send the following email to the customer to further clarify the example user story.

Subject: Clarification required on online credit card payment

Hi Bob

Please clarify if the shoppers need to provide the security code of the credit card while doing checkout.

A. Sillitti et al. (Eds.): XP 2010, LNBIP 48, pp. 103–116, 2010.

But, as someone leaves the team, it becomes hard to access that knowledge when needed later down the road. This paper presents and evaluates a solution that addresses this issue.

In this paper, we present a machine learning technique, Case Based Reasoning, to automatically relate emails with specific user stories. We do it by looking at the text, people and temporal similarity between emails and user stories. The results show that a well trained software can auto-tag emails with user stories. Also, we found that combining context with text similarity helps to find the related user stories with higher accuracy than using just text match alone.

We discuss the following topics in the next sections: Section 2 contains the problem statement and Section 3 contains related works in this area. Next, Section 4 presents our solution details and Section 5 illustrates the solution with an example. We discuss the results and evaluation of our solution in Section 6 and finally, we summarize the paper at the Conclusion.

2   The Problem

In collocated agile teams people mostly use face-to-face communication to share project related knowledge. But, in distributed agile teams, especially in hugely different time zones, people often use emails or text based communication for this purpose. As a side effect, distribution is beneficial for capturing knowledge for long term use in agile teams. However, even people in collocated teams often use emails to communicate with their customers and other stakeholders that are not located in the same office.

In software development projects, developers sometimes leave the team for various reasons. As said before, in distributed agile projects, important knowledge is often shared by emails. To transfer this knowledge for future use, one first needs to find the project related emails. Secondly, to build a usable knowledge-base, these emails should be related to specific user stories. If this is done, then another developer of the team will be able to easily find the necessary information when required.

From an end users' point of view, manually finding and relating the emails with user stories is a time-consuming and costly process. So, if a software can do this, then it may work as a knowledge-base even after someone leaves the team.

The core technical challenge in devising such a software solution is understanding the emails and relating them to specific user stories. The relation between an email and a user story is not explicit. The idea of using story ids or some kind of explicit markers in the emails also imposes the fact that one needs to look up the id in advance. Other approaches like modified email clients also imposes a behavioral change or a learning curve, which is often difficult for the people at the business end. We propose the auto-tagging to be a minimal change solution of the existing email process.

To find out the implicit relation between a free-format email and a use story, a software needs to handle similarity between two texts, which is a standard problem. However, pure text retrieval limits how accurate the assignment of email and user stories can be. Using context information has the potential to increase this accuracy. So, a software needs to be able to combine both the text and context similarity for auto-tagging emails with user stories.

3   Related Work

From the agile software development perspective, customer collaboration and interaction among individuals are valued over following a strict plan or process [1]. El-Shinnawy et al. found that face-to-face communication is the richest form of communication [6]. But, globally distributed teams need to use asynchronous communication tools to make up for time zone differences and schedule conflicts. Layman et al. suggests that email offers a useful and prompt solution in such needs [7].

Distributed agile projects often use globally-available project management tools to facilitate awareness on everyday activities [7]. There are commercial and free web-based agile project management tools like VersionOne[8], ScrumPad [9], XPlanner [10] etc. Some of these tools offer message threads and project wiki for knowledge sharing. The use of wiki was also advised by Chau et al. [11] and Auer et al [12]. However, in a case study based on suggestions from [7], Korkala et al. found email to be the preferred medium for sharing knowledge in asynchronous communication [13]. But, none of the available tools can intelligently grab and auto-tag the emails with specific project artifacts. So, people are either forced to use the tool features (e.g. message threads or wiki) or the knowledge is no longer available in a single shared place.

Previous works explored mining emails and software repositories. Cubranic et al. explored mining information from public forums with software artifacts and code repositories in their "Hipikat" project [14]. Before this, Berlin et al. implemented a group memory system called Teaminfo [15] that collected all emails from a given mail address and categorized the mails depending on predefined patterns. Our project follows the same approach for collecting the collaboration with the exception that we make use of the context information of an agile user story to auto-tag the emails. This context is formed by the developer, customer and iteration time frame of the user stories which are matched against the email meta-data. Using our solution, one can see all emails associated with a user story based on their text and context similarity.

However, for understanding emails and tagging with specific user stories a software has to deal with document indexing and retrieval. One approach to the retrieval process takes a purely document oriented view where one does not get information about the content of a document but rather about its existence. This is however of little interest for this paper. The second approach is of central interest for this paper, where one studies the content of a document using statistical methods. In the center of interest was the study of co-occurrence and its second order extensions. This goes back to H. Schuetze [18] and has been extended in various ways. All these extensions require a large amount of documents that are not typically available as user stories in software projects. However, the problem addressed by this paper needs to utilize a domain specific similarity that combines both text matching and context matching.

4   Our Approach

4.1   Assumptions

Our solution is based on the following assumptions for auto-tagging emails with user stories.:

1. An email is potentially related to a user story when:
   - it is sent during the iteration time frame of the user story and
   - it is among people that are customers and/or developers of the user story and
   - there is a minimum degree of free text similarity between the two.
2. A web-based project management software is used to manage the distributed agile project.
3. The software knows about a project's team, user stories, iteration dates and scopes.
4. Each project in the project management software has its own email address.

4.2   The Project Context

The Project Context of an agile user story is defined by the following attributes:

1. **Temporal context.** User stories are developed in *iterations* defined by specific start and end dates. We define these time-boxes as the temporal context of the user stories.

2. **People context.** User stories are assigned to *team members* and owned by *customers*. We define these as the people context of the user stories.

We use this context information in combination with the text similarity to guess if an email is related to a user story.

4.3   Similarity Measure

Based on the above assumptions, we used Case Based Reasoning (CBR) to find the nearest user story of an email. In CBR, each case of the case-base is described using attribute-value pairs where attributes have defined types. For example, integer, symbol, free text, etc. According to local-global principle, CBR uses two kinds of similarity measures: **i) local similarity** and **ii) global similarity** [16]. Local similarities between an example and a case are measured for each attribute individually. On the other hand, global similarity combines the local similarities.

In our solution, the case-base of the CBR system contained the user stories from multiple projects. An email was treated as a new example and the target was to find the most related cases (user stories) from the case-base. So, we transformed the email attributes to map with the user story attributes as shown in Table 1.

Table 1. Mapping Between Email and User Story Attributes

Email	User Story	Type
Sender	Developer or Customer	Symbol
Recipient	Developer or Customer	Symbol
Email date	Iteration time frame	Date
Email text (subject + body)	Description	Free text

Source: *primary*

Using this mapping, we computed three local similarities between an email and a user story for three attributes. For the local similarity computation we used the following formulae:

$$S_{Date} = \begin{cases} 1 & \text{iteration start} \leq \text{email date} \leq \text{iteration end} \\ 0 & \text{if email date is within the buffer of the story's iteration} \\ -1 & \text{else} \end{cases} \quad (1)$$

$$S_{People} = \begin{cases} 1 & \text{both the developer and customer are present in email} \\ 0.5 & \text{either developer or customer is present in the email} \\ 0 & \text{else} \end{cases} \quad (2)$$

$$S_{Text} = [0,1], \text{ Free text similarity score (See below)} \quad (3)$$

Here, computing text similarity is technically the most challenging part and a software needs to pay special attention to understand and find relevance between two texts. We used a statistical approach called OKAPI BM25 [19] text ranking formula for this purpose. This formula uses bag-of-words retrieval function and ranks the documents based on the frequency of query terms appearing in the documents. This formula and some of its newer variants are being used in document retrieval such as web-search engines.

Next, we computed the global similarity between an email and a user story using a weighted sum of the three local similarities as follows:

$$S_{Global} = (W_{Date}*S_{Date} + W_{People}*S_{People} + W_{Text}*S_{Text})/(W_{Date} + W_{People} + W_{Text}) \quad (4)$$

where,

$$W_{Date} = \text{relative weight of date similarity} \quad (5)$$

$$W_{People} = \text{relative weight of people similarity} \quad (6)$$

$$W_{Text} = \text{relative weight of text similarity} \quad (7)$$

4.4   The Architecture

Next, we present the block diagram of the system in Figure 1. As shown in the figure, the core work is done by a web-based project management tool. This tool already knows about the user stories, their developers, customers and also iteration schedule. The following list explains the architecture as a workflow:

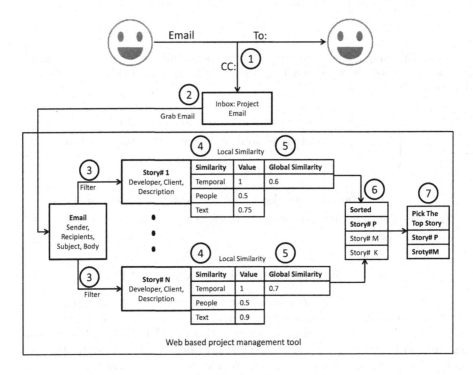

Fig. 1. The solution workflow steps

1. **Copy emails to project mail address.** Whenever an email is sent to someone about a project, the "project email" is added in the CC. This is the only change in the business process that needs to be implemented by the distributed team.
2. **Grab email.** The web-based project management software grabs all incoming emails at the project's email inbox using POP or IMAP.
3. **Filter.** Next, the search space is reduced by filtering out the user stories from far past or future compared to the email sent date.
4. **Compute local similarity.** The program computes three local similarity measures between the email and existing user stories using the equations (1), (2) and (3).
5. **Compute global similarity.** Next, the program computes the global similarity measures using equation (4).

6. **Sort.** After this, user stories are sorted according to the global similarity measures in descending order.

7. **Pick.** Finally, we pick the user stories having global similarity scores above a predefined threshold. As a result, the project management software can suggest multiple user stories that are possibly discussed in a single email and make it available as a knowledge-base.

4.5   Learning Weights

To compute the global similarity between email and user stories using equation (4), our software learned the relative weights using a simple Reinforcement Learning [17] technique. The learning data was from four real world software projects as outlined in the data collection section later. First, we tagged emails with user stories exclusively for each attribute: data, people and text. The number of correct tagging using an attribute was normalized and used as the initial weight for that attribute. Next, the following algorithm was used to learn the relative weights:

```
date_weight     = initial_date_weigth
people_weight   = initial_people_weight
text_weight     = initial_text_weight

for all_training_emails do |email|
   result = find_most_similar_user_story(email)
   is_correct = result.guessed_story == email.actual_story
   is_date_similar = result.date_weight > date_threshold

   if (is_correct and is_date_similar) or
      (!is_correct and !is_date_similar) then
    date_weight = reward(date_weight)
   else
    date_weight = punish(date_weight)
   end
   #do the same for people and text similarity
   end
end
```

We used this algorithm to tune the relative weights following a simple reward-punishment approach. The weight of an attribute is rewarded with additional value if: i) the attribute was similar and the email was related to the user story or, ii) the attribute was not similar and the email was not related to the user story. Otherwise, the weight for that attribute was punished with a decrease in value. This training helped with finding the relative importance for the attributes based on our training data.

4.6   CBR Implementation

We looked into several off-the-shelf tools for implementing the CBR system. But some tools that were capable of handling both text and non-text attributes were too complex to modify for our solution. On the other hand, the simpler ones lacked the support for free text attributes. So, we developed a simple CBR system from scratch.

We used Ruby programming language (v. 1.8.6) on Rails Framework (v. 2.3) to develop the CBR. We could also use an existing agile project management tool, but a custom-built one was easier for this experiment. The front-end was a web-based user interface for defining projects, teams, iterations and user stories. Once the data was provided to the system, it automatically guessed the potentially relevant user stories for an email.

The back-end of the CBR was implemented using a Microsoft SQL Server 2008 database. It was populated with the case-base. The similarity measures, as shown in equations (1-4), were then computed using custom Transact-SQL functions. For the free-text similarity, we used the built-in FREETEXTTABLE function of Microsoft SQL Server 2008 Advanced Services. This function ranks texts using the OKAPI BM25 formula.

The front-end ruby code used the back-end database functions to get the similarity measures. Then it guessed the relevant user stories for an email if the similarity score was above a threshold. However, if the guess was incorrect, the user interface provided an option to manually override the relation to a correct one. Having this overriding capability ensures the final verdict can always come from actual people using the system to rectify the mistakes in the automated guessing.

4.7   Evaluation Data

The sizes and compositions of the data are summarized in Table 2.

The data for learning the weights and evaluating the implementation was obtained from four projects that used the agile project management tool called

Table 2. Training and evaluation Data

Project Name	Description	Users	Itera-tions	It. Len. (days)	User Stories	Emails
BI for Car Dealers	A decision support tool for vehicle dealers	7	11	14	70	213
ManyWheels	A web application for transporters and shippers	5	12	14	97	158
VarsityDays	A social networking application for school sports teams	5	15	14	88	46
MindAndMarket	A project collaboration tool	3	6	7	28	40
Total					283	457

Source: *www.ScrumPad.com*

ScrumPad [9]. ScrumPad offers a forum for each project where people can collaborate using message threads on specific user stories. These linked messages helped us in both training and evaluating our implementation.

Three of the four projects, BI for Car Dealers, ManyWheels and VarsityDays, were developed by Code71, Inc. (www.Code71.com) and developers were from Bangladesh and USA on the same teams. On the other project, MindAndMarket, the team had 1 person from Bangladesh and 2 from Belgium and worked for a Belgian company called Belighted (www.Belighted.be).

The techniques presented in this paper can be applied to any data set that has similar characteristics. ScrumPad helped us to evaluate the technique using real industry data collected over a few years across different projects. But other than this, our solution is independent of ScrumPad.

5   An Example

The following example illustrates the step-by-step email auto-tagging process. Here is a small list of four user stories from a project:

While working on the project, developer D1 sent the following email to C1:

Now for this email, the similarity computation with the user stories yields the following results as shown in Table 4: Here, the similarity scores are computed based on Equations 1-4 of Section 4.3. From the above table we see that Story #1 is the most similar story to the given email with a similarity score of 0.72. This is greater than the threshold of 0.58 (details discussed in the Evaluation section

Table 3. User Stories

#	Iteration	Cust-omer	Deve-sloper	Description
1	#1, Dec 14-25, 2008	C1	D1	As a/an 'VM User' I want to add/edit/view dealer account profile so that VM can earn revenue from charging a monthly subscription fee. Dealers will have three contacts: Billing, General Manager and Owner. Also, there will be a primary and secondary contact. More information is attached.
2	#1, Dec 14-25, 2008	C1	D2	As a/an 'VM Admin' I want to add/edit/view VM users. Administrator must be able to see username but not password VM Users will be one of inside rep and outside rep. Required fields and more information are attached...
3	#2, Dec 28, 2008-Jan 08, 2009	C1	D1	As a/an 'VM user' I want to load DMV data from Experian from a CSV/Excel file into VM database. Sample data attached.
4	Not As-signed	C1	D1	As a/an 'VM User' I want to activate and deactivate a dealer

Source: *www.ScrumPad.com*

To: C1
From: D1
Date: Dec 14, 2008
Subject: Initial Questions on **Dealer setup**
Body:
Please clarify the following questions regarding dealer setup data-
1. Is it ok to assume that the billing, GM and Owner contacts of a dealer will also contain username/passwords. Note that, the main and secondary contacts as well as the Used car manager contact contain user name/passwords.
2. What data should we collect for Physical Address and Mailing Address of a dealer? Is it free text? Or collected as fields street1, street2, city, state, zip, country?
3. Is it possible that for a dealer both an inside and outside salesman is assigned?
4. Apart from the name and pricing, is there any other field associated with the "program" main/platinum information?
5. What is meant by the "Location" field of the outside VM Rep?
6. Is it possible to provide us with a sample input data that will be used to set up an inside/outside VM user's commission? Please provide examples of default, bonus, retension and special commissions.
7. What are the required fields of all the dealer setup fields?
8. The Business Address is mentioned twice under the 5.6.1.5 - do we need to capture two business addresses?

Fig. 2. An example email

Table 4. Similarity Scores

Story#	Date Similarity	Date Weight	People Similarity	People Weight	Text Similarity	Text Weight	Global Similarity
1	1	33	1	28	0.29	39	**0.72**
2	1	33	0.5	28	0.26	39	0.57
3	0	33	1	28	0.08	39	0.31
4	-1	33	1	28	0.25	39	0.05

Source: *Primary*

below) and thus the system auto-tags the email with Story #1. However, the other stories are not considered as related as those failed to reach the threshold similarity score. We ran the auto-tagging solution on the evaluation data in the same way as illustrated in this example and found the following results.

6   Results

The evaluation results showed that after some training, the system could correctly auto-tag 70% of the emails. We present our findings in detail in the next subsections.

6.1   Evaluation

We learned the relative weights by training the system with real life data from four distributed agile projects. For training and evaluation purposes, we partitioned this data into two parts: i) training data and ii) evaluation data. A total of 150 user stories and 250 emails from the four projects were used as training data. Also, we changed the training and evaluation data sets to reduce the impact of special cases. Table 5 shows the relative weights after training:

Table 5. Relative weights before and after training

Relative weights	Initial	After training
Date weight	34	33
People weight	16	28
Text weight	50	39

Source: *primary*

After learning these weights, we added the rest of the user stories into the case-base. Then, we presented the rest 207 unseen emails (from four projects) to the system in random order without specifying their relations with user stories and found the following results:

Table 6. Evaluation Results

1. Total number of evaluation emails: 207
2. Number of emails actually related to user stories: 200
3. Guesses using text and context similarity: 90% (187 out of 207)
4. Correct guesses using text and context similarity: 70% (144 out of 207)
5. Correct guesses using only text match: 47% (97 out of 207)

For the evaluation, we had 200 out of a total 207 emails that were actually related to specific user stories. The remaining 7 emails were related to their respective projects but not to any particular user story. Such emails usually talked about general project related matters such as architectural decision, milestones, etc. The auto-tagging system was judged wrong if it tagged any such generic project related emails to a user story. Here is an example in Figure 3.

We set a **minimum threshold similarity score of 0.58** for making a guess. This cut-off point was found through trial and error. Using this cut-off the system made guesses for 90% or 187 out of 207 evaluation emails. A value above or below this threshold resulted in lower guesses or higher mistakes respectively. With this cut-off value, the system didn't make any guess for 10% of the emails because the most similar user story for the emails had a similarity score less than 0.58. In effect, this minimum threshold value was the optimum one for the given training data.

Subject: FTP Folder Convention
Hi All:
At FTP we have the following folders:-
1. Experian - Only DMV data files should be dropped here.
2. Deploy - All Deployment related files should be dropped here.
The rest of the folders are for data sources as indicated in the names. Please make sure
the folders are used correctly. It will be easy to manage in future.

Fig. 3. An example email that is not related to any specific user story

Out of the 187 guesses, the software rightly guessed the related user stories for 77% or 144 emails. Considering the total evaluation input of 207 emails, this is a 70% accuracy. It should be noted that the presence of the free text component leads to a fuzzy match and a 100% accuracy may not be achieved as a result of this.

However, using only text matching, the system could correctly guess the user stories for 47% or 97 out of 207 emails. This is 23% lower compared to the case when both text and context similarities were used. So, we found that Case Based Reasoning helped in improving the accuracy of the system. Some of the user stories of a project often shared a common vocabulary. As a result, when comparing with emails, the text similarity score of a user story from far past or future may be higher than the score of a user story in the same time context. Also, people assigned to the user stories as developers or customers are more likely to send emails on the stories compared to other individuals. So, adding temporal and people similarity scores helped in eliminating some of the outliers in terms of text matching alone.

6.2 Limitations

We recognize a few limitations of our solution as follows:

1. **Human subject study.** Although our results show that the email auto-tagging accuracy improves using a project context, we do not know if this actually makes a difference in distributed agile teams. A human subject study may investigate this question.
2. **Possible bias in data.** Our implementation is trained and evaluated using data from multiple projects. But all this data is collected from a single source (www.ScrumPad.com) and hence there might be an unintentional bias in the data. This limitation may be overcome by evaluating the system using data from various other sources.
3. **Size of data.** We recognize the fact that the evaluation results could be statistically more significant with a larger size of data.

6.3 Future Work

The following is a list of potential future extensions of our current implementation:-

1. **Evaluation with distributed agile teams.** An actual evaluation with a distributed agile team is required to see the effectiveness of our email auto-tagging solution.
2. **Use of algorithms.** In future, we would like to try using other algorithms for learning relative weights and finding text similarity. The choice of other algorithms may produce better accuracy than the current results.
3. **Inclusion of more attributes.** It might be possible to improve the accuracy of the solution by adding more attributes. For example, an email might contain useful knowledge in the attachments. Also, the subject line of an email may carry more specific knowledge than the body. In the present solution both are treated as email text and no distinction is made in terms of importance. Adding such changes to the existing solution may produce better results.

7 Conclusions

In related work, we found that a significant portion of knowledge in distributed agile software development is actually shared through emails. In this paper, we described a solution to capture this information for reuse when people leave a project. The result indicates that it is possible to automatically build a reusable knowledge base from the emails.

Our implementation combined both text and context similarity. We discovered that this combination produced better results than using only free text matching. However, we anticipate that it is possible to extend this solution with using better algorithms and adding new features. Our ongoing work will focus on improving the accuracy of this solution by adding several candidate extensions.

References

1. Manifesto for Agile Software Development, http://agilemanifesto.org
2. Beck, K.: Extreme Programming Explained: Embrace Change. Addison-Wesley Professional, Reading (2000)
3. Beedle, M., Schwaber, K.: Agile Software Development with SCRUM. Prentice Hall, Englewood Cliffs (2001)
4. Cockburn, A.: Agile Software Development. Addison-Wesley, Reading (2002)
5. Ambler, S., Jeffries, R.: Agile Modeling: Effective Practice for Extreme Programming and the Unified Process. Addison-Wesley, Reading (2002)
6. El-Shinnawy, M., Markus, L.: Acceptance of Communication Media in Organizations: Richness or Features? IEEE Transactions on Professional Communication 41, 242–253 (1998)
7. Layman, L., William, L., Damian, D., Bures, H.: Essential Communication Practices for Extreme Programming in a Global Software Development Team. Information and Software Technology 48(9), 781–794 (2006)
8. Agile Project Management, Scrum, and Agile Development Tool, Version One, http://www.VersionOne.com
9. An Agile/Scrum Project Management Tool, ScrumPad, http://www.ScrumPad.com

10. XPlanner, http://www.XPlanner.org
11. Chau, T., Maurer, F.: Knolwledge Sharing in Agile Software Teams. In: Lenski, W. (ed.) Logic versus Approximation. LNCS, vol. 3075, pp. 173–183. Springer, Heidelberg (2004)
12. Auer, S., Dietzold, S., Riechert, T.: OntoWiki: A Tool for Social, Semantic Collaboration. In: Cruz, I., Decker, S., Allemang, D., Preist, C., Schwabe, D., Mika, P., Uschold, M., Aroyo, L.M. (eds.) ISWC 2006. LNCS, vol. 4273, pp. 736–749. Springer, Heidelberg (2006)
13. Korkala, M., Pikkarainen, M., Conboy, K.: Distributed Agile Development: A Case Study of Customer Communication Challenges. In: Agile Processes in Software Engineering and Extreme Programming, vol. 31, pp. 161–167. Springer, Heidelberg (2009)
14. Cubranic, D., Murphy, G.C., Singer, J., Booth, K.S.: Hipikat: A Project Memory For Software Development. IEEE Transactions on Software Engineering 31(6), 446–465 (2005)
15. Berlin, L.M., Jeffries, R., O'Day, V.L., Paepcke, A., Wharton, C.: Where Did You Put It? Issues in the Design and Use of a Group Memory. In: Proceeding of SIGCHI Conference. Human Factors in Computing Systems, pp. 23–30 (1993)
16. Richter, M.M.: Knowledge Containers. In: Watson, I. (ed.) Readings in Case-Based Reasoning, Morgan Kaufmann Publishers, San Francisco (2003)
17. Sutton, R.S., Andrew, G.B.: Reinforcement Learning: An Introduction. MIT Press, Cambridge (1998)
18. Schuetze, H., Pedersen, J.O.: Information Retrieval Based on Word Senses. In: Proceedings of the Symposium on Document Analysis and Information Retrieval, vol. 4, pp. 161–175 (1995)
19. Robertson, S., Walker, S., Jones, S., Hancock-Beaulieu, M., Gatford, M.: Okapi at TREC-3. In: Proceedings of the Third Text REtrieval Conference (TREC 1994), Gaithersburg, USA (1994)
20. Robertson, S., Walker, S., Hancock-Beaulieu, M.: Okapi at TREC-7. In: Proceedings of the Seventh Text REtrieval Conference, Gaithersburg, USA (1998)

Towards Understanding Communication Structure in Pair Programming

Kai Stapel, Eric Knauss, Kurt Schneider, and Matthias Becker

Software Engineering Group, Leibniz Universität Hannover,
Welfengarten 1, 30167 Hannover, Germany
{kai.stapel,eric.knauss,kurt.schneider}@inf.uni-hannover.de,
matthias.becker@stud.uni-hannover.de

Abstract. Pair Programming has often been reported to be beneficial in software projects. To better understand where these benefits come from we evaluate the aspect of *intra-pair communication*. Under the assumption that the benefits stem from the information being exchanged, it is important to analyze the types of information being communicated. Based on the Goal Question Metric method we derive a set of relevant metrics and apply them in an eXtreme Programming class room project. Data covering a total of 22.9 hours of intra-pair communication was collected. We found that only 7% of the conversations were off-topic (e.g. private), 11% about requirements, 14% about design, and 68% about implementation details (e.g. syntax). Accordingly, a great share of the information being exchanged in Pair Programming is on a low level of abstraction. These results represent a first data point on what kind of information is communicated to what extent during Pair Programming.

Keywords: Pair Programming, Communication, Empirical Study.

1 Introduction

When Kent Beck introduced eXtreme Programming (XP) it was considered to be the antithesis to document- and plan-driven software development [1]. Beck defined the XP practices in a provocant manner: Accordingly, all practices have to be *turned to ten*, i.e. best practices in software development should be practiced in an extreme manner. For example, Beck states that if reviews are good then all code should constantly be reviewed. Therefore, Pair Programming (PP) should be performed. Today, PP is one of the most prominent XP practices in use, even outside of XP. Many studies investigated the effectiveness of PP and its impact on code quality. PP is mostly considered to be superior to conventional single developer programming, because pairs produce better quality code, learning takes place, team building is speeded up, while development is about as effective as in the solo case [2,3,4,5,6]. These benefits are usually attributed to the intensive intra-pair communication that takes place when working in pairs. According to Lindvall et al. communication is one of the three most important success factors of PP [6]. Still, not many studies have invastigated the aspect

A. Sillitti et al. (Eds.): XP 2010, LNBIP 48, pp. 117–131, 2010.

communication in PP in detail. As a consequence, studying communication in Pair Programming and its effect on development success has been proposed by several research frameworks, e.g. by Gallis et al. [7] and Ally et al. [8].

In the work presented here we focus on analyzing intra-pair communication to better understand its connection to the benefits of PP. Two often mentioned benefits that are related to communication are learning and team building:

Learning: If one partner shares technical experience with his or her peer, learning takes place. The driver (the one who uses the keyboard) is even able to share tacit knowledge similar to the master-apprentice type of learning. Better educated developers are more likely to produce high quality code.

Team Building: If pairs closely collaborate and talk about off-topic issues, team building takes place. In addition, this kind of communication establishes a common context among partners which makes future communication simpler.

This paper is structured as follows. In Section 2 we discuss related work on measuring communication in software development and case studies investigating communication in PP. In Section 3 we define our research goals by applying the Goal Question Metric (GQM) method. This leads to the metrics we then apply in a case study with students in an XP class room project that is described in Section 4. Section 5 summarizes our results. In Section 6 we interpret our results and discuss their validity. Finally, we conclude in Section 7 and give an outlook on future work.

2   Related Work

Dutoit and Bruegge propose to use communication metrics to get project status information early on when no product related metrics are available yet [9]. They use digital communication media that is used for collaboration in class room software projects to derive communication metrics. For example, the number of messages per week in an electronic bulletin board are counted. These metrics are then applied in a series of software engineering project classes. The results are used to improve communication in the projects over time. Statistical analysis shows that bulletin board communication size and complexity has a significant positive correlation with project outcome. Here project outcome refers to source code as well as corresponding documents. In the work of Dutoit and Bruegge communication metrics are applied in non-agile projects and on non-verbal communication media. Still, counting and classifying communication events and using them as an early indicator for project outcome can also be applied in our agile setting on verbal intra-pair communication.

Sfetsos et al. investigated the impact of personality types on communication and collaboration-viability in Pair Programming [10]. They compared the effects of uniform versus mixed temperament type pairs on communication, collaboration-viability, and effectiveness using a controlled experiment with 42 pairs (84 subjects/students). Temperament types were classified according to

Keirsey Temperament Sorter (KTS). Communication was measured by counting communication events. Five different communication topics were considered: (1) Requirements gathering, (2) specification and design changes, (3) code, (4) unit tests, and (5) peer reviewing. The subjects (i.e. the navigator) had to self-report their communication activities as they were working on their tasks. Analysis showed that the number of communication transactions was significantly positive correlated with productivity (measured as points for correct solutions) and that mixed personality pairs communicated significantly more than uniform personality pairs. Although they have measured different types of communication similar to the classification we used (requirements, design, or code related, see table 3, M1.1-M1.3), they do not report their results concerning distribution of the topics and total amount of communication events. They also do not report about the durations of the communication events.

Bryant et al. analyzed 23 hours of pair programmers' dialogue and used the results as an indicator for collaboration of the pairs [11]. The dialogues stem from experienced professional pair programmers. They found that pairs had a high amount of verbal interactions. The pairs produced more than 250 verbal interactions per pair programming hour. Almost all tasks were contributed to by the driver and by the navigator in collaboration (more than 90% in 10 out of 12 task categories) with the driver contributing slightly more. They conclude that: "the benefits attributed to pair programming may well be due to the collaborative manner in which tasks are performed". As opposed to our study, off-topic dialogues were left out in the analysis. Therefore, they did not report the ratio of project relevant to off-topic conversations. Other differences to our study are that we observed students instead of professionals, that we had dedicated observers classifying the conversations on the fly as opposed to analyzing audio recordings afterwards, and that we had a different approach: we first chose how to classify communication and then measured it as opposed to first recording the communication and then classifying it.

3   Research Question

The main goal of the work presented here is to better understand the communication structure in Pair Programming. We chose the Goal Question Metrics paradigm [12] to refine this main goal to metrics that can be measured in a case study. In the first step we derived two GQM goals. For each GQM goal an abstraction sheet [12] was created. Based on these abstraction sheets the metrics for measuring communication in PP and finally a measurement plan were developed.

3.1   Goals

Our aim is to better understand the structure of Pair Programming communication. We decompose this into the following two GQM goals:

Goal 1. Understand the quality aspect *level of abstraction* of intra-pair communication in PP. In this context level of abstraction refers to the abstractness of the information according to the software development phase. For example, requirements are on a high level of abstraction whereas program code issues are on a low level. Program design and architecture are somewhere in-between. So this goal tries to address the question: Are the developers talking about requirements, design patterns, syntax, or off-topic issues?

Goal 2. Understand the quality aspect *interactivity* of intra-pair communication in PP. Interactivity is the distribution of the drivers' and the navigators' share of communication. So this goal addresses the question: Who is communicating more, the driver or the navigator?

Abstraction sheets help to find the relevant factors that directly make up or indirectly influence the quality aspect of a GQM goal. Abstraction sheets allow to derive reasonable metrics for these factors. In table 1 and 2 the abstraction sheets for the two GQM goals are shown. Table 3 shows the derived metrics.

In an abstraction sheet the factors that directly make up the quality aspect of a GQM goal are called quality focus (QF). For the first goal we identified 4 quality factors (see table 1): the number of conversations about requirements (QF 1), design (QF 2), code (QF 3), and off-topic things (QF 4). We expect the greatest proportion of the communication to be about code (QF 3), because the students in our case study were rather inexperienced programmers. If the developers are more experienced in the usage of the programming language, they do not talk about syntax topics as much. We also expect a lot of conversations about requirements (QF 1), since the Story Cards that were used in the XP project are rather brief and do not contain many details. Usually, in XP the details of the requirements are directly exchanged between the On-site Customer and the developers. If a pair is talking to the On-site customer about a requirement each developer might interpret the details differently. This may lead to the need for discussion in the pair later. Design issues (QF 2) and off-topic (QF 4) conversations will probably not make up a big part of the communication, because the XP course required the participants to apply the practice Simple Design and because the developers have never worked together in a project before and therefore were unfamiliar with each other. Still, we believed once the developers get to know each other better, they will talk more about private things. Another aspect that characterizes the communication is the duration of the conversations about one topic. For example, we expect the conversations about design issues to be longer than the conversations about syntax issues.

Besides the quality focus an abstraction sheet allows for gathering variation factors (VF). Variation factors are factors that indirectly have an effect on the quality aspect. For our first goal we identified 7 variation factors, which include the developers' experience in requirements analysis, program design, and programming in general (i.e. writing source code). The variation hypotheses in abstraction sheet 1 describe how each variation factor influences the quality aspects.

The second goal is to understand the interactivity of the communication between driver and navigator. Here, we investigate whether driver or navigator contribute more to communication. Also, the frequency of the questions being

Table 1. Abstraction sheet for GQM goal "level of abstraction"

Goal 1: Analyze *intra-pair communication in Pair Programming* for the purpose of *understanding* with respect to the **level of abstraction** from the perspective of the *developers* in the context of a *class room XP project.*

Quality Focus	Variation Factors
QF 1. Conversations about requirements	**VF 1.** Quality of requirements
QF 2. Conversations about design (e.g. module structure)	**VF 2.** Complexity of software design
QF 3. Conversations about code (e.g. syntax)	**VF 3.** Developers' experience in requirements analysis
QF 4. Off-topic conversations (non software development related, private)	**VF 4.** Developers' experience in program design
	VF 5. Developers' experience with programming
	VF 6. Knowledge differences between developers
	VF 7. Familiarity with other developers

Baseline Hypotheses	Variation Hypotheses

1. Because of the brief nature of Story Cards and the developers being not very experienced in requirements analysis we expect many conversations about requirements ($> 30\%$)
2. Because of the XP practice "Simple Design" we expect few ($< 10\%$) conversations about design topics. But if the developers talk about design the conversations will be rather long (> 3 min.)
3. Because of the inexperienced programmers we expect many ($> 50\%$) but short (< 1 min.) conversations about code topics
4. Because of the unfamiliarity with each other we expect a small proportion of off-topic or private communication ($< 10\%$)

1. More clear, thorough, and unambiguous, i.e. high quality, requirements lead to fewer communication about them (QF 1).
2. The clearer and simpler a software design is, the less communication is needed about design issues (QF 2).
3. Experienced requirements analysts talk less about requirements related issues (during programming), because their requirements are of good quality and have fewer room for interpretation (QF 1).
4. Experienced designers talk less about design related issues (QF 2), because best practices in program design like design patterns are common knowledge.
5. Experienced programmers talk less about syntax related issues (QF 3), because they do not make as many syntax mistakes as inexperienced programmers.
6. Higher differences in software development knowledge between the developers lead to a lot communication about requirements (QF 1), design (QF 2), and code (QF 3)
7. Good knowledge of the other person leads to a great proportion of private conversations (QF 4)

Table 2. Abstraction sheet for GQM goal "interactivity"

Goal 2:Analyze *intra-pair communication in Pair Programming* for the purpose of *understanding* with respect to the ***interactivity*** from the perspective of the *developers* in the context of a *class room XP project.*	
Quality Focus	**Variation Factors**
QF 1. Balance of communication proportions **QF 2.** Question frequency	**VF 1.** Number of navigators' clarification questions
Baseline Hypotheses	**Variation Hypotheses**
1. We expect the driver to talk slightly more than the navigator ($\approx 60 : 40$), because in a similar study the distribution between driver and navigator already was $60 : 40$ [11]. 2. According to Williams and Kessler [13] we expect a question at least every minute.	1. The number of the navigators' clarification questions is positively correlated with the question frequency (QF 2).

asked characterizes the interactivity. We expect the driver to talk slightly more than the navigator, because a similar study already found that the driver contributes slightly more to a given task [11]. Another assumption is that the pairs will discuss a question at least every minute [13]. A variation factor for the interactivity of the communication is the number of the navigators' clarification questions, which is positively correlated with the overall question frequency.

3.2   Metrics

The next step in the GQM approach is to create metrics based on the abstraction sheets. Metrics are needed to answer the questions associated with each goal. Ideally, at least one metric should be set up for each quality factor (QF) and each variation factor (VF). Table 3 summarizes the metrics we used in our case study. Each metric has an ID, a name, a scale type (e.g. ordinal, ratio), a range or value set, a "counting" rule that briefly explains how to measure it, and a reference to the corresponding abstraction sheet. The scale type is important for later analysis. For example, mean and standard deviation are not defined for ordinal scales. Hence, other characteristics like median and quartiles are needed for interpretation of results on an ordinal scale.

For the first abstraction sheet (see table 1) metrics for all but two factors were derived. We did not create a metric for the quality of requirements (VF 1), because we did not expect them to vary much. All pairs used Story Cards that the team created in collaboration with the customer at project start. Furthermore, measuring quality of requirements is a problem of its own [14]. We also did not explicitly measure the familiarity (VF 7) of the developers with each other. But, we know that none of them had worked in pairs with the others before. For the second abstraction sheet (see table 2) all metrics were created.

Table 3. Metrics

ID	Name	Scale type	Range	Counting rule	Abstract. sheet ref.
M1.1	Number of conversations about req.	ratio	$\mathbb{N}^+$	For each closed conversation about one requirement	Goal 1, QF 1
M1.2	Number of conversations about design	ratio	$\mathbb{N}^+$	For each closed conversation about one design topic, e.g. module structure	Goal 1, QF 2
M1.3	Number of conversations about code	ratio	$\mathbb{N}^+$	For each closed conversation about one program code topic, e.g. syntax	Goal 1, QF 3
M1.4	Number of off-topic conversations	ratio	$\mathbb{N}^+$	For each closed conversation about one not project relevant topic	Goal 1, QF 4
M1.t	Time of conversations	ordinal	short (< 1 min.), med. (1-3 min.), long (> 3 min.)	Map each closed conversation about one topic to a time interval	Goal 1, QF 1-4
M1.5	Complexity of design	ratio	$\mathbb{R}, \geq 1$	Average cyclomatic complexity over all classes per iteration	Goal 1, VF 2
M1.6	Req. analysis experience	ordinal	1 (very exp.), 2, 3, 4, 5, 6 (none)	Self-evaluation of developers	Goal 1, VF 3
M1.7	Design experience	ordinal	1 (very exp.), 2, 3, 4, 5, 6 (none)	Self-evaluation of developers	Goal 1, VF 4
M1.8	Programming experience	ordinal	1 (very exp.), 2, 3, 4, 5, 6 (none)	Self-evaluation of developers	Goal 1, VF 5
M1.9	Deviation in developers knowledge	ratio	$\mathbb{R}$	Standard deviation of average self-assessment grades	Goal 1, VF 6
M2.1	Proportion of drivers' share in conversation	ratio	$0\% - 100\%$	Mark on scale (see figure 1)	Goal 2, QF 1
M2.2	Number of questions per hour	ratio	$\mathbb{R}$	For each question asked	Goal 2, QF 2
M2.3	Nr. of navigators' clarification questions per hour	ratio	$\mathbb{R}$	For each question asked	Goal 2, VF 1

4   Study Design

We chose the eXtreme Programming (XP) course at Leibniz Universität Hannover, Germany to apply our metrics. This course is a mature XP laboratory [15] where students first learn the XP practices in theory - including Pair Programming - and then apply their new XP knowledge in a short XP project in practice. The following tool set was used in the project: Eclipse, SVN, Ant, and JUnit4. In 2009 we combined the XP course with an empirical study course. Before the actual XP project started the students had to prepare an empirical study. We had 2 XP teams with 7 developers each. In each team 6 developers formed 3 pairs. The 7th developer was the observer of the other team. The observers were switched every day. The development pairs had to switch regularly, at least every new day or after every finished Story Card. Intra-pair communication was measured just in one team. The project was a 5-day-project with 7 development hours a day. The first day was for a technical spike and requirements gathering. The students interviewed the customer and created the Story Cards. The remaining 4 days were 4 development iterations. An on-site customer with a real development task was available to the developers throughout the whole project.

4.1   Subjects

The observed team of this study consisted of 3 undergraduate (BSc level) and 4 graduate (MSc level) students. On average the students were in their 11.0^{th} (±2.8) semester in computer science. Their curriculum covered programming lectures, topics like requirements engineering or design patterns, and a non-agile software project. According to their self-assessment they were least confident in their design abilities and most confident in their programming skills (see table 4, M1.6-M1.8). All but one student were new to Pair Programming. They have never worked in pairs with each other before. Since the class was also an empirical study class (and because of the present observer) the pairs knew they were being measured, but they did not know what about.

4.2   Data Collection

Before project start the developers had to fill out a self-assessment questionnaire. Results from this questionnaire were used for the metrics M1.6 - M1.9. For all other metrics a data collection sheet was prepared (see figure 1). During the project an observer monitored a pair, classified their conversations, and filled out the data sheet. One data collection sheet was filled in for a single pair for a period of up to two hours. After two hours or when the pair switched the observation was stopped and a new data collection sheet with a new pair was started. During an observation the durations and topics of the intra-pair conversations were noted. Each conversation duration was assigned to a group depending on whether it was shorter than one minute, longer than three minutes or in between. A conversation has been considered *closed* once the pair had stopped talking or the topic changed. Then a stroke was made in the corresponding column and

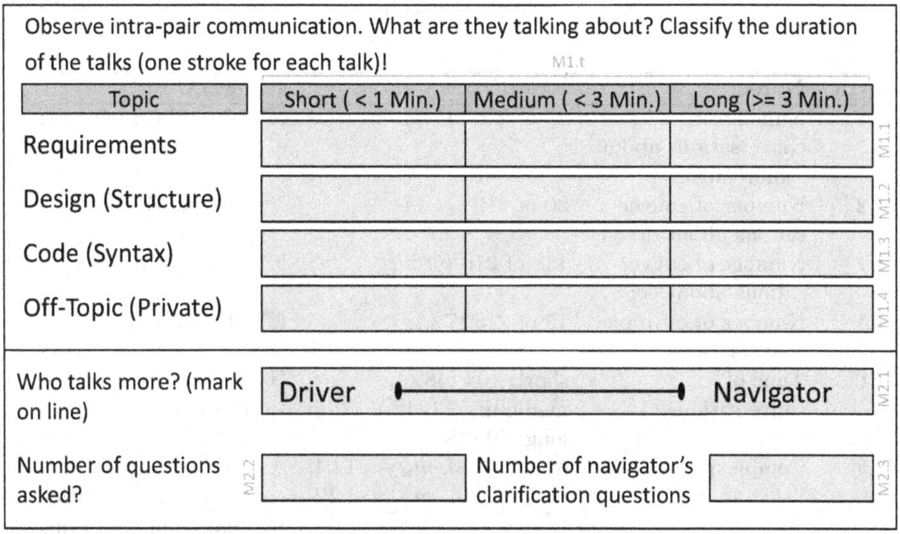

Topic	Short (< 1 Min.)	Medium (< 3 Min.)	Long (>= 3 Min.)
Requirements			
Design (Structure)			
Code (Syntax)			
Off-Topic (Private)			

Observe intra-pair communication. What are they talking about? Classify the duration of the talks (one stroke for each talk)!   M1.t

| Who talks more? (mark on line) | Driver ●————————————————● Navigator |
| Number of questions asked? | Number of navigator's clarification questions |

Fig. 1. Data collection sheet

in the row given by the topic. Corresponding to the metrics the available topics were requirements, design, code, and off-topic. Requirements covered conversations about functions or quality aspects of the software under development or preparations for a talk to the on-site customer. Design topics include dicussions about the program stucture, e.g. the module and package structure, or the usage of design patterns. Code topics include everything that is low-level source code related like syntax issues. Off-topic covers everything that is not software development related like private conversations. Parallel to this every question asked was noted in M2.2 and the number of clarification questions (the driver makes a decision and the navigator has to ask to understand it) was noted in M2.3. At the end of each observation the driver's share of the just monitored intra-pair communication was estimated by drawing a stroke on the line in M2.1, where the left end represents 100% and the right end 0%. According to the student's feedback the data collection sheet was easy to use. Putting an extra developer in the team for observation was a reasonable effort. There has been a short talk between the observers after they switched each morning to share experiences from data collection to ensure constant quality of the collected data.

5   Results

In total 22.9 hours of intra-pair communication were monitored. Out of the 21 possible pair combinations (7 developers forming pairs) data from 14 different pairs was collected and analyzed. Table 4 summarizes the results. In total, 216 conversations were observed. Almost half of the conversations were short (< 1 minute). The other half of the conversations was evenly split in medium ($1 - 3$

Table 4. Results

Metric	Name	Result	Range/Unit
M1.1	Number of conversations about requirements	23 of 216 (11%)	N^+ of total (in percent)
M1.2	Number of conversations about design	30 of 216 (14%)	N^+ of total (in percent)
M1.2	Number of conversations about code	148 of 216 (68%)	N^+ of total (in percent)
M1.4	Number of off-topic conversations	15 of 216 (7%)	N^+ of total in percent
M1.t	Time of conversations	short: 104 (48%), medium: 52 (24%), long: 60 (28%)	N^+ for each time interval (in percent of total)
M1.5	Complexity of design	$m_{it1} = 1.00$, $m_{it2} = 1.04$, $m_{it3} = 1.16$, $m_{it4} = 1.12$	Average cyclomatic complexity per iteration
M1.6	Requirements analysis experience		Boxplot (min, lower quartile, median, upper quartile, max)
M1.7	Design experience		Boxplot (min, lower quartile, median, upper quartile, max)
M1.8	Programming experience		Boxplot (min, lower quartile, median, upper quartile, max)
M1.9	Deviation in developers knowledge	$s = 0.9$	Standard deviation of average self assessment grades
M2.1	Proportion of drivers' share in conversations	$\approx 40\%$ ($\pm \approx 20\%$)	$0\% - 100\%$ ($\pm$ std. deviation)
M2.2	Number of questions per hour	9.9 (± 8.1)	$\frac{1}{h}$ ($\pm$ std. deviation $\frac{1}{h}$)
M2.3	Number of navigators' clarification questions per hour	2.1 (± 1.6)	$\frac{1}{h}$ ($\pm$ std. deviation $\frac{1}{h}$)

min.) and long (> 3 min.) conversations. Two out of three conversations were about code issues, 14% about design, 11% about requirements, and 7% about off-topic things. Figure 2 summarizes the results for the metrics M1.t and M1.1 to M1.4 by showing the overall distribution of the conversation durations on the left and the conversation topics on the right. Code analysis showed that the average code complexity of the software did not exceed 1.16 throughout the project. The self-evaluation metrics showed that the developers estimated their requirements analysis experience with a median of 3, on a scale from 1 to 6 with 1 being very experienced and 6 having no experience at all, to be slightly more

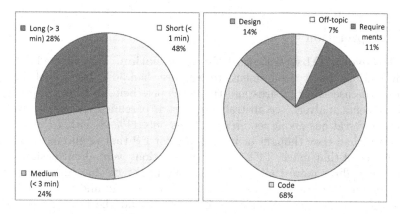

Fig. 2. Overall distribution of conversation durations (M1.t, left) and discussed topics (M1.1-M1.4, right)

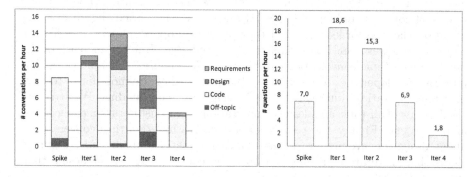

Fig. 3. Number of conversations per hour for each topic (left) and number of questions per hour (right) over the project time

experienced than the middle of the scale. With a median of 4 the developers were less confident in their design abilities. With a median of 3 and a lower quantile of down to 2 the developers were most confident in their programming skills. Still, they were far from classifying themselves to be very experienced programmers. The overall standard deviation of the combined measures of all software development related self-evaluation questions was 0.9. This means that about 68% of the developers ($\approx$ 5 of 7) self-evaluate their knowledge to be in a region that does not span more than 2 points, e.g. between 2 and 4. So, the majority of the students were on a similar level of knowledge.

On average the drivers' shares in conversations were approximately 40% with a standard deviation of approximately 20%. Over the observed 22.9 hours of inta-pair communication 227 questions were asked. Figure 3 (right) shows a decrease in the number of questions per hour over the course of the project. The navigators asked a total of 49 clarification questions.

6   Dicussion

6.1   Interpretation

Goal 1: Level of Abstraction of Communication. We expected the ratio of conversations about requirements to be more than 30%, because of the brief nature of the used Story Cards and the developers being not very experienced in requirements analysis (see abstraction sheet 1, baseline hypotheses). But the ratio of conversations about requirements was only 11%. So either the students were better than they thought or it is typical for PP that requirements are not being discussed that much. 14% of the conversations were about design issues, which was slighlty more than expected. This might be due to the fact that the students had not much experience in software design and therefore had to discuss these issues more. With a ratio of 68% by far the most conversations were about code. This is even more than the expected 50%. The students were not very experienced programmers, so this high value may be attributed to their need for learning low level programming. The decrease of conversations about code over the project time (figure 3, left) while the conversations about design remained constant and the decrease of questions being asked (figure 3, right) are also indicators for learning that took place. A proportion of 7% for off-topic conversations was even lower than the expected 10%. But the increase of the number of off-topic conversations in iteration 3 (see figure 3, left) indicates that once the developers get to know each other better they are more likely to have private conversations during PP. This is a sign for team building. We attribute the decrease of off-topic and design conversations in the last iteration to the stress at project end. Finally, the results support our assumption that conversations about design on average are longer than conversations about code. Figure 4 shows that there are more medium and long conversations about design than there are for conversations about code.

Goal 2: Interactivity of Communication. Along with the findings of Bryant et al. [11] we expected the driver to talk slighlty more than the navigator, about 60:40. But our results showed that it was the other way around. In our case it was approximately 40:60. So our assumption turned out to be wrong. The driver does not seem to constantly explain his or her actions. Maybe the navigator is guiding the programming by communicating the current and near future actions to take, while the driver is busy typing in the according source code.

Williams and Kessler state that driver and navigator communicate at least every 45 to 60 seconds [16], if only through utterances as in "Huh?". We could not confirm this finding. In our study either driver or navigator asked a question every 6.1 minutes on average. This large difference might be due to several reasons: First, an utterance is much smaller than a real question. So we might have missed the small utterances during observation. Second, the students were new to PP and unfamiliar with each other. So they might not have been as communicative as the professional programmers Williams and Kessler refer to. Despite of the bias of our more coarse measurement we believe that novice pair programmers are much less communicative than expert pair programmers.

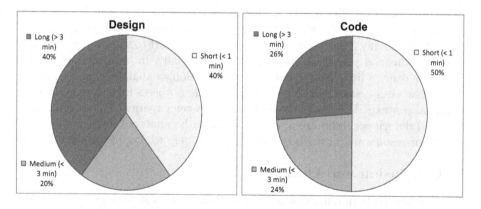

Fig. 4. Distribution of conversation durations for design topics and code topics

6.2 Threats to Validity

Conclusion Validity. The large standard deviations in some of our metrics indicate that we need a lot more data points, i.e. more pairs and longer observation periods, in order to increase conclusion validity. Another threat to conclusion validity is that the classification of the conversation topics was done subjectively by different observers. We tried to reduce that threat by setting some standards on how to classify the topics and had the observers discuss their experiences when switching. Despite the low number of data points and the subjectivity of our measures the results give a first indication of the structure and content of intra-pair communication.

Internal Validity. Internal validity is concerned with whether a treatment really causes the outcome of a study. The only treatment in our study was the fact that we observed pair programmers. The collected data and the observations of the supervisor show that the developers were actually working as pair programming suggests it [1]. Still, a threat to internal validity is that the distribution and frequency of communication also depends on other factors beyond PP. For example, personality types have already been shown to be significantly related to the frequency of communication in PP (see related work section) [10]. We did not measure personality types in our study. But, our data covers 14 out of 21 possible pair combinations, so the effects of personality types are partially evened out.

Construct Validity. The self assessment measures for the developer knowledge have a rather poor construct validity. They only reflect the developers' own opinion and not their actual knowledge. A second threat to construct validity is caused by the fact that the developers knew they were being observed. This might have had a distorting influence on the ratio of off-topic conversations, since observed developers tend to better follow the process (in this case PP) and do not talk as much about private things.

External Validity. There are two major external threats to validity: (1) We chose students that were new to PP and relatively inexperienced in programming at all. (2) The 5 day XP project might have been too short to show representative data for industrial pair programming settings. Usually, in industry developers know each other a little better and work together longer than 5 days. Despite of these threats our results can be used as baseline hypotheses for future studies in industrial contexts. Especially the difference between experienced pair programmers and deverlopers who are new to PP should be analyzed. Our assumption is that our results are most likely valid for developers who are learning PP.

7   Conclusion and Outlook

Our goal was to better understand the communication structure in Pair Programming. To reach this goal we applied the GQM method and derived relevant metrics to measure the intra-pair communication in PP. These metrics were then applied in a 5 day XP class room project with 7 students. 22.9 hours of communication were observed and analyzed. Two third of all conversations were about code related topics. This indicates that during PP neither design, requirements, or unrelated things are as important topics as communication about code. This holds at least for developers who are new to PP with programming experience at the level of a graduate student. Furthermore, the decrease of conversations about code over time, while conversations about design remained constant, and the decrease of the number of questions being asked indicates that learning took place. The developers increased their programming abilities and therefore did not have to talk as much about code issues anymore. Additionally, a small indicator for successful team building could be observed: Off-topic conversations slightly increased in the third iteration.

In future work we need to refine our measures further. Especially conversations about code need to be analyzed in more detail. Are syntax issues really dominating? If so, maybe Williams' and Kessler's "Myth 6: The navigator finds only syntax mistakes. How boring is that! Compilers can do that better than humans can anyway." [16] is almost not a myth after all. Maybe there is a chance to increase PP productivity even further by providing better low level code support and thereby allowing the pairs to concentrate their communication more on high level topics like design or even on requirements. Another interesting research question is whether some benefits of PP can be brought to solo programming by simulating a navigator, e.g. by using static code analysis data to provide more direct feedback about the code.

Finally, our findings could be useful for the design of tools that support *distributed* PP as described by Dajda and Dobrowolski [17]. For example, different support mechanisms for the different levels of abstraction can be created with an emphasis on low level code support.

Acknowledgements. We would like to thank all students who planned, executed, and participated in the study. This work was funded by the German Research Foundation (DFG project InfoFLOW, 2008-2011).

References

1. Beck, K.: Extreme Programming Explained. Addison-Wesley, Reading (2000)
2. Coman, I.D., Sillitti, A., Succi, G.: Investigating the Usefulness of Pair-Programming in a Mature Agile Team. In: XP, pp. 127–136 (2008)
3. Hulkko, H., Abrahamsson, P.: A Multiple Case Study on the Impact of Pair Programming on Product Quality. In: ICSE 2005, pp. 495–504. ACM, New York (2005)
4. Cockburn, A., Williams, L.: The Costs and Benefits of Pair Programming. In: Extreme Programming and Flexible Processes in Software Engineering XP 2000, pp. 223–247 (2000)
5. McDowell, C., Werner, L., Bullock, H., Fernald, J.: The Effects of Pair-Programming on Performance in an Introductory Programming Course. In: SIGCSE '02: Proceedings of the 33rd SIGCSE Technical Symposium on Computer Science Education, pp. 38–42. ACM Press, New York (2002)
6. Lindvall, M., Basili, V., Boehm, B., Costa, P., Dangle, K., Shull, F., Tesoriero, R., Williams, L., Zelkowitz, M.: Empirical findings in agile methods. In: Wells, D., Williams, L. (eds.) XP 2002. LNCS, vol. 2418, p. 197. Springer, Heidelberg (2002)
7. Gallis, H., Arisholm, E., Dybå, T.: An Initial Framework for Research on Pair Programming. In: Proceedings of the International Symposium on Empirical Software Engineering (ISESE 2003), pp. 132–142 (2003)
8. Ally, M., Darroch, F., Toleman, M.: A framework for understanding the factors influencing pair programming success. In: Baumeister, H., Marchesi, M., Holcombe, M. (eds.) XP 2005. LNCS, vol. 3556, pp. 82–91. Springer, Heidelberg (2005)
9. Dutoit, A.H., Bruegge, B.: Communication Metrics for Software Development. IEEE Transactions on Software Engineering 24(8), 615–628 (1998)
10. Sfetsos, P., Stamelos, I., Angelis, L., Deligiannis, I.: Investigating the Impact of Personality Types on Communication and Collaboration-Viability in Pair Programming – An Empirical Study. In: Abrahamsson, P., Marchesi, M., Succi, G. (eds.) XP 2006. LNCS, vol. 4044, pp. 43–52. Springer, Heidelberg (2006)
11. Bryant, S., Romero, P., du Boulay, B.: The Collaborative Nature of Pair Programming. In: Abrahamsson, P., Marchesi, M., Succi, G. (eds.) XP 2006. LNCS, vol. 4044, pp. 53–64. Springer, Heidelberg (2006)
12. Briand, L.C., Differding, C.M., Rombach, H.D.: Practical Guidelines for Measurement-Based Process Improvement. Software Process: Improvement and Practice 2(4), 253–280 (1996)
13. Williams, L., Kessler, R.R., Cunningham, W., Jeffries, R.: Strengthening the Case for Pair Programming. IEEE Software 17, 19–25 (2000)
14. Knauss, E., Boustani, C.E., Flohr, T.: Investigating the Impact of Software Requirements Specification Quality on Project Success. In: Proceedings of 10th International Conference on Product Focused Software Process Improvement (PROFES 2009), Oulu, Finland. LNBIB, pp. 28–42. Springer, Heidelberg (2009)
15. Stapel, K., Lübke, D., Knauss, E.: Best Practices in eXtreme Programming Course Design. In: Proceedings of the 30th International Conference on Software Engineering (ICSE 2008), Leipzig, Germany, May 2008, pp. 769–776. ACM, New York (2008)
16. Williams, L., Kessler, R.: Pair Programming Illuminated. Addison-Wesley, Reading (2003)
17. Dajda, J., Dobrowolski, G.: How to Build Support for Distributed Pair Programming. In: Concas, G., Damiani, E., Scotto, M., Succi, G. (eds.) XP 2007. LNCS, vol. 4536, pp. 70–73. Springer, Heidelberg (2007)

Continuous Selective Testing

Bastian Steinert, Michael Haupt, Robert Krahn, and Robert Hirschfeld

Software Architecture Group
Hasso Plattner Institute
University of Potsdam, Germany
`firstname.lastname@hpi.uni-potsdam.de`

Abstract. A manual and explicit activity, the frequent selection and execution of tests requires considerable discipline. Our approach automatically derives a subset of tests based on actual modifications to the code base at hand, then continuously executes them transparently in the background, and so supports developers in instantly assessing the effect of their coding activities with respect to the overall set of unit tests to be passed. We apply techniques of selective regression testing, mainly relying on dynamic analysis. By taking advantage of the internal program representation available in IDEs, we do not need to rely on expensive comparisons of different program versions to detect modified code entities.

1 Introduction

Test-driven development [5] (TDD) is a cornerstone of agile software development methodologies such as Extreme Programming [22] (XP). This technique suggests to write test cases before the code they are intended to cover. Written first, tests serve multiple purposes. First, they represent a specification for the system to be developed. Next, they document the system and help other developers in comprehending the system. Finally, they ensure that every single change violating one of the required features described in the executable form of a test is reported.

While testing is an important part of regular development activities, Integrated Development Environments (IDEs) have little support for selecting and (re)executing tests relevant with respect to modifications applied to the system under development [18].

There are a few approaches that support (re)running the test suite automatically every time a file is saved in the IDE [29,18]. However, *test selection* as such is traditionally not performed: it is always the complete test suite that is run, including irrelevant tests, leading to an execution overhead that is larger than it actually needs to be.

For that reason, developers often manually select a few tests that seem appropriate, run them explicitly, and wait for feedback. The manual, regular, and explicit selection and execution of tests requires considerable discipline. Moreover, success is guaranteed only if no relevant test cases are omitted in the selection. A solution that automatically selects test cases to be executed in the background based on the applied changes to source code is preferable.

A. Sillitti et al. (Eds.): XP 2010, LNBIP 48, pp. 132–146, 2010.

Approaches to test case selection are established: *Selective regression testing* [26] has long been a subject of research. Selective regression testing is concerned with reducing the set of tests that need to be executed to detect failures caused by recent modifications to the code base. However, researchers have not yet investigated the potential of integrating this technique into an IDE and having selected tests execute continuously in the background.

We suggest to select and execute tests *automatically* whenever the code status demands this. More precisely, it would be desirable to have support for TDD that, whenever source code is changed, *automatically executes exactly those tests that are affected by the actual modification*, giving developers *instant feedback* on whether the applied change breaks something or not.

In this paper, we propose our approach to *continuous selective testing* (CST) and present an implementation thereof in Squeak Smalltalk[1] [21]. Using an implementation of the suggested approach, developers will be supported as follows:

- Sets of relevant tests are selected based on dynamic analysis during the regular execution of tests.
- Relevant tests are executed continuously in the background after every modification to the code base.
- Developers are instantly informed about places in code that, resulting from an applied change, are no longer covered by tests.
- The introduction of new defects is made apparent immediately, which in turn lets developers focus on problems right away.

With that, our approach significantly improves on the way IDE tools provide immediate feedback in a development process adopting TDD. The main contributions of this paper are as follows:

- We present continuous selective testing as an approach relieving developers from the burden to select and run tests explicitly.
- We describe how test case selection in general can benefit from the internal program representation already available in IDEs and how differencing of two versions of a program can be avoided.
- We describe our approach to test case selection based on dynamic analysis, being not limited to statically-typed languages.

The remainder of this paper is organized as follows. The next section briefly summarizes TDD and presents the state of the art in tool support for it, providing further motivation for CST, which is presented and evaluated in Secs. 3 and 4. Related work is discussed in Sec. 5; Sec. 6 summarizes the paper and outlines future work.

2   Background and Motivation

In this section, we briefly introduce the terms and concepts of TDD. We then discuss current practices of developing tests and application code in accordance

---

[1] www.squeak.org

with TDD and point out the need for better tool support. Afterwards, we introduce the concepts of regression test selection and discuss current approaches.

2.1   The Three Phases of Test-Driven Development

Test-driven development distinguishes three phases of development [5]:

Red. Tests are written that specify new requirements on the system in an executable manner. When these new tests are run for the first time, failures or errors occur, as the system does not yet support the new requirements. An important guideline is to avoid writing application code if there is no test case that fails.

Green. The developer adds the required code to the system to make the failed test "green", i.e., run successfully. It is crucial that the developer write only code essential to the test in question. A successful test signals that the developer is done implementing the new requirement. It might happen that no code has to be added to make the test green, as the system already covers the newly defined requirement.

Refactor. The developer refactors towards the simplest design they can imagine. By definition of refactoring [13], new functionality must not be added during this phase. The tests can ensure that all required and specified features work after a refactoring. Running tests after each and every little change helps to avoid breaking features and provides instant feedback.

We can observe that tests and the regular execution of tests play an important role when developers employ the principles of TDD.

2.2   Tool Support for Test-Driven Development

Best practices in working with tests suggest to make only small changes and run tests immediately afterwards to get feedback. This suggestion is based, amongst others, on the following observations:

- Implementing new application functionality is a very complex activity. As every single step is inherently fault-prone, regular feedback is essential for detecting faults.
- Modifying source code without breaking existing functionality is also difficult. Adapting source code to new requirements or refactoring source code to a simpler design requires very detailed understanding, which to acquire is hard since source code abstracts from concrete execution paths. Having tests covering all parts of the respective code entities and running these tests regularly helps to detect faults early.
- The more steps are passed without getting feedback, the more difficult locating the source of a fault becomes. When a couple of source code entities are changed without running tests, and one ore more tests fail later on, isolating the modification that has caused the failure is not straightforward. Typically, developers are unaware of the complete set of modifications done before running the tests. Moreover, multiple failures might have different causes and

combinations of modifications might lead to completely unexpected behavior. To locate the defects, developers can revert modifications step by step or debug the current version. Both ways are tedious and time-consuming.

Running tests often and regularly helps developers to detect faults early, reduces the time required to localize defects, and gives confidence for the next adaptions and refactorings. However, running tests as often and regularly as suggested requires much discipline.

The necessary discipline is sometimes hard to bring up, for apprentices as well as experts. It is all too easy to ignore TDD theory, though well-understood and accepted, and continue modifying code without running tests. It is not necessarily only external factors, such as project schedules, that influence such decisions, but also internal ones like the strong will to finish a task. These aspects contradict with the required discipline.

Another issue with the theory of testing and test-first development is the implicitness of the relationship between test cases and application code they cover. When code is refactored or new features are implemented, existing code has to be modified. However, while developers are aware of recently implemented tests, they cannot know the set of all tests relying on a particular method. Hence, developers do not know the set of tests to be executed after a modification of a particular method. Consequently, all tests should be run after each modification, which is, however, increasingly time-consuming as projects grow. As a result of this, developers run only some tests regularly and the suite of tests is rarely executed, e. g., during integration builds.

Both aspects discussed above, the implicitness of the relationship between test cases and application code as well as the discipline required to run tests after each modification, question the usefulness of tests and test-first development. Our work provides tool support for TDD that alleviates these limitations and strengthens the benefits of testing.

3   Continuous Test Queuing, Selecting, and (Re-)Executing

In this section, we describe our approach to continuous selective testing called CST. It enables the continuous execution of selected tests directly after code modifications. Such automation relieves developers from the burden of executing tests manually. Selecting a subset of all tests and omitting those that cannot reveal faults reduces execution time and helps to provide feedback instantly. We have implemented the suggested approach in Squeak Smalltalk.

In the following, we will first introduce the concepts of regression test selection and then present the use of the IDE's program representation to detect and handle modifications to the code base. After that, we describe the queuing of tests and the selection and (re-)execution of tests according to the modification at hand. Finally, we present our extensions to the IDE providing instant feedback on test results.

3.1   Regression Test Selection

Regression testing refers to the practice of validating modified software; in particular, asserting that applied changes do not affect the software adversely [17]. The simplest approach to regression testing is to reuse the test suite used to exercise the previous version of the software. Fully running a large test suite can be unnecessarily costly, e. g., if only a few parts of the system were changed.

A technique to reduce the number of tests is *regression test selection*. It selects tests that have to be re-run to reveal a fault resulting from a particular change. Selecting an optimal set of tests is, however, generally inefficient [26]. Still, the set of tests traversing modifications can be computed efficiently. This set of *modification-traversing tests* can be considered a superset of the *fault-revealing tests* when the *Proper Regression Testing Assumption* [26] holds (P refers to a program and P' refers to the modified version of this program):

> When P' is tested with t, we hold all factors that might influence the output of P', except for the code in P', constant with respect to their states when we tested P with t.

A regression test selection technique is furthermore considered *safe* if it ensures to not omit tests revealing faults [17]. Several safe techniques have been proposed for purely procedural (e. g., [2,11,27]) as well as for object-oriented programming languages (e. g., [28,17]). Object-oriented programming is special as inheritance, polymorphism and thus late-binding have to be considered.

The most efficient and safe test selection technique is based on detecting modified code entities, such as functions or storage locations [26]. This technique was first implemented in TestTube [11] for software written in C. The technique is based on dynamic analysis [3]; test coverage information are recorded during each test run. For a new version of a software, the set of modified code entities can be detected. Based on coverage information, the technique selects and re-executes all tests that exercised the modified code entities in the previous version of the software. For object-oriented languages, the modified entity selection technique requires additional considerations due to language features such as inheritance and polymorphism enabling late binding.

Our approach, CST, is based on this technique of detecting modified code entities. CST records coverage information and selects tests on a method level. This procedure may select tests that do not traverse the modifications, because a test might only traverse unmodified parts of a method, for example. However, tracing on a more fine-grained level is much more expensive and does not pay off unless methods contain many control blocks [6].

3.2   Propagating Modifications to the Code Base

Most approaches to test selection are based on comparing the new with an earlier program version to detect change entities. Our approach takes advantage of an IDE's internal program representation. Fig. 1, on the left, depicts the setup of traditional approaches. IDE and test tools are not integrated and do not work

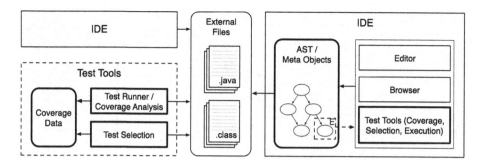

Fig. 1. The left-hand side shows a traditional setup where test selection tools and IDE work independently of each other. The right-hand side depicts CST integrating test selection into the IDE and taking advantage of the internal program representation.

together, each of them works rather separately on external program representations. In this setup, however, a test selection technique requires a comparison of program versions to detect modifications between two versions of a software. There exist differencing concepts and tool for both source code [1,17] and byte code [20].

We suggest to better integrate the tools for testing and test selection into the IDE as depicted on the right of Fig. 1. Every modification applied to the code base can produce an event notifying the IDE about the respective change. Using this notification mechanism, the test tools can process each modification to the code base. The tools are now able, for example, to automatically select and re-execute a set of test cases as necessary for the modification applied.

The set of events used to propagate code modifications to IDE tools has to be designed for the particular programming language and IDE, respecting the features of the language and the architecture of the IDE. In Squeak Smalltalk, for example, there are basically two operations to create or modify code objects. Sending a subclass-message to a class *c* creates a new or modifies an already existing subclass of class *c*. Sending the *compile:* message to a class object allows to compile a source code text of a method and puts it in the method dictionary of the corresponding class. Based on the effects of this two operations, the following change events can be defined for the Smalltalk [14] programming language, which is a rather simple language and does, for example, not provide any visibility modifiers; *class added, class removed, superclass changed, instance variable added, instance variable removed, method added, method modified,* and *method removed.* Note that class-specific ("static") state or behavior do not require special treatment as classes are also normal objects whose state and behavior are defined by meta-classes.

3.3   Queuing and Executing Tests for TDD

CST builds upon a well-defined set of different kinds of modification to the system. The event mechanism described above, with the possible modification

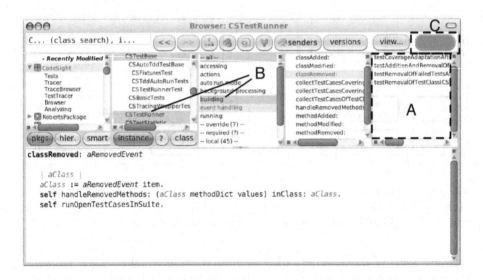

Fig. 2. An extended code browser in Squeak; having an additional panel on the right (A) that shows test cases covering the selected method named *classRemoved:*. Uncovered classes and methods are highlighted (B). A new widget (C) informs the developer on the current status of the test runner; whether it is currently running tests, and about the number of tests that have failed.

events it includes, allows for the continuous selection and execution of tests according to the current state of development.

Our approach distinguishes code entity modifications by their referal to test case code or non-test code. By convention, those methods of a class extending *TestCase* that are prefixed with *test* are treated as *test case methods*. Source code entities of test classes that are non-test methods, that is, attributes, *setUp*, *tearDown*, and other utility methods, are treated equally to application code.

When the creation of a test case method or modifications to one are reported, the developer is assumed to be in the red phase of the TDD cycle. The test runner will immediately execute the corresponding test case and provide instant feedback on the result. If the test fails, it will be queued. Failed test cases will be re-executed whenever a modification not related to a test method is reported. Now the developer is expected to be in the green or refactor phase, so the change has the potential to fix a test. All tests that still fail stay in the queue. A change of an entity can fix one or more tests cases, but the change can also introduce a fault that breaks other test cases. All test cases that might be affected by the reported change need to be re-executed. A technique to select the corresponding test cases is presented in the next subsection. The tests in the queue, failed before, are run first, providing earlier feedback on whether the current modification makes the failed test(s) pass.

To provide feedback on the test runs, we extended the tools for browsing and editing code. Whenever a modification is reported and the test runner executes

Table 1. Test selection procedures to be performed on entity modification events

Event	Application Class	*TestCase* Class
class c removed	for each method of c, perform procedure for removing non-test methods (see below)	for each test and non-test method of c, perform procedure for removing respective methods (see below)
superclass of class c changed	re-run tests covering non-test methods in c and subclasses of c	see left; additionally, re-run tests defined in c and subclasses of c

Event	Application Method	Test Method
method m added to class c	re-run tests covering overridden methods with dynamic type c and tests covering overriding methods	run corresponding test case
method m removed	re-run covering tests	remove coverage links; remove from list of failed tests
method m modified	re-run covering tests	re-run corresponding test case

tests, a newly introduced GUI widget will inform the developer about the test runner's activities and the current status of the test result (Fig. 2). The widget turns red as soon as one test has failed. Tests are executed in a background process allowing the developer to navigate to the next code entity of interest and start editing it.

3.4   Re-executing Selected Tests for OO Software

The set of tests to be re-executed for an applied change should be minimized. CST relies on collecting test coverage information, and using this information to select tests that might be affected by a modification.

Using this coverage information of previous test runs, the CST tools can determine the set of tests that is to be re-executed for any reported change. The algorithms for the different kinds of changes are provided in table 1. Selecting the test cases that might be affected by a reported change is a two-step procedure:

1. If a non-test method is modified, the test runner collects and re-executes all test cases that covered this method previously. Therefore, the test runner can simply navigate the coverage relationship between the corresponding method objects.
2. CST also deals with modifications such as adding a method or changing the superclass that might affect late-bound method invocations. When, for example, an application method m' is added to a class c', and m' overrides a method m in a superclass c, CST will execute tests that have covered m'. More precisely, it will select those tests that previously exercised m for instances of c.

As mentioned above, the set of meaningful events, which reports modified code entities, may vary between languages providing different sets of features. The algorithms to be applied to determine a safe set of tests may vary as well. If the language supports multiple inheritance, for example, the algorithms have to consider the possibility of multiple superclasses and the respective linearization order applied to method dispatch.

As pointed out in [17], a safe test selection technique for object-oriented software must also consider exception handling. CST allows to consider exceptions similarly to other code entities. A basic method constructing an exception object needs to be instrumented; for instance, default constructors in Java, or *basicNew* in Smalltalk. Using the receiver's dynamic type recorded for each method call, we can determine whether an exception was created and thrown during the execution of a test case. If the exception class hierarchy is changed, all test cases that might be affected can be identified easily.

3.5   Establishing a Coverage Relationship

Test coverage information used for test selection is collected during regular test execution. We decided to collect this information only for packages and classes of interest. This typically excludes basic development classes such as the collection or system libraries. The selection of relevant packages and exclusion of others avoids unnecessary overhead [15]. To record method coverage information, we use method wrappers [8]. Actual method code is wrapped in tracing code that records the call of the wrapped method in the context of the currently running test case, and forwards the sent message to the wrapped method afterwards.

Test coverage information is integrated into the IDE's program representation. In CST, we establish and maintain a coverage relationship between test case methods and methods covered during test execution, as depicted in Fig. 3. Here, we generally refer to objects representing methods in the IDE; Squeak Smalltalk provides so-called *CompiledMethod* objects to reflect upon and work with methods in the system.

Employing the test-first principle and using CST, tests run frequently and the coverage relationship has to be maintained for test runs. To avoid unnecessary

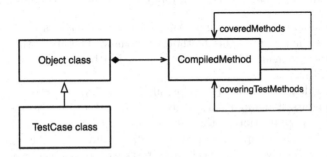

Fig. 3. The coverage relationship between test methods, included in *TestCase* classes, and application methods covered by them

start-up costs, tracing logic is installed incrementally after each compilation step. When the developer selects packages and classes of interest, wrapper logic is initially installed. If source code entities matching the selection criteria are added, they are wrapped directly after creation. This incremental approach avoids the need to instrument source code for each test run.

Using CST, developers can also be provided with instant feedback regarding test coverage. Classes and methods that are not covered any more are highlighted in the code browser (Fig. 2). The feedback supports developers in ensuring high method coverage. We further extended the code browser with an additional fifth panel (Fig. 2) that shows all test cases covering the currently selected method. This extension makes the coverage relationship visible and the applied test selection technique transparent for developers.

4   Evaluation

In the first part of this section, we describe our experience using CST, and its implementation in Squeak Smalltalk. After that, we report on our experiments for gaining insights into test set reduction.

4.1   Using CST in Developing CST

From early on, we used our CST tools to develop their next versions. This bootstrapping allowed us to get feedback on both the suitability of our approach and the quality of our implementation.

Unsurprisingly and as expected, we made mistakes during development and introduced defects into our code base in both unit tests and units under test, leaving us with both false positives and false negatives. Here, our tool served its purpose well by making us aware of unexpected results immediately after each method save. With that, and even if the problem itself was sometimes hard to understand, the cause of the problem becoming apparent was easily recognized as *the last change done to the system*.

Using our tools revealed another benefit in the form of obtaining instant feedback on test *coverage* after modifications. Getting this information right away helped to better understand the dynamics of our system and to remove code that was not needed any longer.

4.2   Test Set Reduction

We were interested in how effectively CST reduces the amount of tests to be run when a method is modified. We therefore conducted experiments on the following systems:

CST. The implementation of CST for Squeak Smalltalk (cf. Sec. 4.1).
XP-Forums. A groupware[2] supporting collaboration on artifacts specific to distributed agile software development.

---

[2] http://www.hpi.uni-potsdam.de/swa/projects/xpf

AweSOM. A virtual machine[3] for a Smalltalk dialect, implemented in Squeak.
Seaside 2.8. A Smalltalk-based Web framework.[4]

For these four very different software systems, we determined the number of tests
covering each method. These tests have to be executed when the corresponding
method is modified. The results and the overall number of tests for the systems
are presented in Table 2. The comparison shows that method coverage analysis
can significantly reduce the number of tests to be executed. It is also interesting
to see that some methods of the systems are only covered by one test whereas
other methods are covered by all tests.

Our test selection technique is the first to record dynamic type information
(DTI) to reduce the set of tests in case of subclass modifications. To evaluate our
assumption that collecting this information is useful, we performed the following
experiment on the systems:

1. Collect those application methods whose classes have at least one subclass,
   and which are not overridden.
2. Determine how many tests must be re-run in case a method is overridden in
   one of its class's subclasses.

The results, also presented in Table 2, show that using run-time information
about the actual receivers of a message can significantly reduce the test set size.
We conclude that our test selection technique is both safe, by considering late
binding in OOP, and still very effective.

Table 2. Results of evaluting the effectiveness of test set reduction on four projects

Project	Tests	Cov. Tests per Method			Savings Using DTI in %		
		min	max	median	min	max	median
CST	55	1	55	15	32	100	86
XP-Forums	98	1	95	24	0	100	38
AweSOM	124	1	124	23	3	100	97
Seaside	183	1	75	3	3	100	50

5   Related Work

In this section, we discuss related work on two major aspects considered in this
paper; tool support for TDD in general and regression test selection.

5.1   Tool Support for Test-Driven Development

The Ruby and Ruby on Rails community in particular is very committed to agile
methodologies. The community has reported the combination of several tools[5],

---

[3] http://www.hpi.uni-potsdam.de/swa/projects/som
[4] http://www.seaside.st
[5] http://www.zenspider.com/ZSS/Products/ZenTest/

such as Growl and autotest/autospec, to run tests when a file is saved and notify developers on test results. Coverage data are collected to reduce the set of tests to be executed. The applied test selection technique considers modifications on the granularity of files, thus it may select more than a modified-entity technique.

The authors of [24] present an approach to guide TDD which is complementary with our approach. TDD-Guide is an IDE-integrated tool that guides developers in applying TDD. Based on a set of rules, which can be adapted, the tool processes IDE information about the current development status and informs developers about compliance with rules; for example, whether they comply with adding new functionality only if a failing test exists.

The *continuous testing* approach [29] is especially interesting as it is close to our intentions. However, we observe notable differences. First of all, it does not select regression tests but only prioritizes them to allow for a more efficient test execution and more timely feedback. Change analysis focuses on files instead of single methods. Conversely, we do restrict the set of test cases to be executed to those actually covering changed methods.

5.2   Regression Test Selection

Regarding regression test selection, we restrict the discussion of related work to approaches that support object-oriented programming languages and constructs. Among these, we identify three dimensions of interest. First, approaches can be based on source code or binary formats. Second, static or dynamic analysis can be applied. Third, the granularity of application entities (files, classes, methods, single statements or expressions) is relevant. The selection strategy in CST is based on the *binary* format of compiled-method representations, applies *dynamic* analysis, and is *fine-grained* in that single methods are the units of analysis. To the best of our knowledge, CST is the first approach to combine these features.

A large family of approaches applies call graph analysis using source code [4,25,28,17,12,1] or a binary format [10,30,20] of the software. Dedicated mechanisms for object-oriented features, e. g., related to selecting test cases for subclasses, have also been devised [9,16,23,19,7].

The above maintain an internal representation of the program that enables a detailed and correct comparison. Call graphs allow for a very fine-grained analysis, down to single statements. Differencing algorithms in these approaches rely on static source code analysis, effectively restricting the approach to statically typed languages. Due to applying dynamic code coverage analysis, CST supports dynamically-typed languages.

Call graph-based approaches are also more precise than CST, which works at the granularity of single methods, but they are also more expensive [6] (cf. Sec. 3.1). Generally, good object-oriented programming style suggests to use small methods and few control structures—the liabilities our less fine-grained analysis brings about are likely to go unnoticed if these practices are applied.

One of the binary-format approaches mentioned above [20] is also fine-grained, regarding single methods as analysis units. The main difference to CST is that the latter applies dynamic analysis to extract actual method coverage data.

Regarding the *safety criterion* [26,17], we can report that CST is safe, since coverage analysis as applied therein selects all tests covering changes. In addition, object-oriented constructs and late binding are honored. Finally, we regard message receiver type information to limit the set of tests to execute upon subclass changes.

6   Summary and Outlook

We have presented CST, our approach to *continuous selective testing* and an implementation thereof in Squeak Smalltalk. Using a tool such as CST relieves developers from selecting and executing tests manually. Based on the actual modification, a selected set of tests is executed transparently in the background, reporting instantly on the effect of the applied change with respect to the overall set of tests to be passed. CST also takes advantage of an IDE's program representations and thus avoids differencing to detect modified code entities. The test selection technique that we apply is based on dynamic analysis and thus does not require a statically typed language. It is the first approach to test selection that makes use of run-time type information to reduce the test set in case of subclass modifications.

Future work on CST most importantly includes the investigation of techniques to prioritize selected tests and the integration of an appropriate candidate. We expect opportunities to reveal faults and inform developers about them even faster.

Acknowledgments. We gratefully acknowledge the financial support of the Hasso Plattner Design Thinking Research Program for the project "Agile Software Development in Virtual Collaboration Environments".

References

1. Apiwattanapong, T., Orso, A., Harrold, M.J.: JDiff: A differencing technique and tool for object-oriented programs. Automated Software Engineering 14(1), 3–36 (2007)
2. Ball, T.: On the limit of control flow analysis for regression test selection. ACM SIGSOFT Software Engineering Notes 23(2), 134–142 (1998)
3. Ball, T.: The Concept of Dynamic Analysis. In: ESEC/FSE-7: Proceedings of the 7th European Software Engineering Conference held jointly with the 7th ACM SIGSOFT International Symposium on Foundations of Software Engineering, London, UK, pp. 216–234. Springer, Heidelberg (1999)
4. Bates, S., Horwitz, S.: Incremental program testing using program dependence graphs. In: POPL 1993: Proceedings of the 20th ACM SIGPLAN-SIGACT symposium on Principles of programming languages, pp. 384–396. ACM, New York (1993)
5. Beck, K.: Test-driven Development: By Example. Addison-Wesley Professional, Reading (2003)
6. Bible, J., Rothermel, G., Rosenblum, D.S.: A comparative study of coarse-and fine-grained safe regression test-selection techniques. ACM Transactions on Software Engineering and Methodology 10(2), 149–183 (2001)

7. Binder, R.: Testing object-oriented systems: models, patterns, and tools. Addison-Wesley, Reading (1999)

8. Brant, J., Foote, B., Johnson, R.E., Roberts, D.: Wrappers to the Rescue. In: Jul, E. (ed.) ECOOP 1998. LNCS, vol. 1445, pp. 396–417. Springer, Heidelberg (1998)

9. Cheatham, T.J., Mellinger, L.: Testing object-oriented software systems. In: CSC 1990: Proceedings of the 1990 ACM annual conference on Cooperation, pp. 161–165. ACM, New York (1990)

10. Chen, Y., Probert, R.L., Sims, D.P.: Specification-based regression test selection with risk analysis. In: CASCON 2002: Proceedings of the 2002 conference of the Centre for Advanced Studies on Collaborative research, p. 1. IBM Press (2002)

11. Chen, Y.F., Rosenblum, D. S., Vo, K.P.: TestTube: A system for selective regression testing. In: Proceedings of 16th International Conference on Software Engineering, 1994, ICSE-16, pp. 211–220 (1994)

12. Clarke, P., Malloy, B., Gibson, P.: Using a taxonomy tool to identify changes in OO software. In: Proceedings of Seventh European Conference on Software Maintenance and Reengineering, 2003, pp. 213–222 (2003)

13. Fowler, M.: Refactoring: improving the design of existing code. Addison-Wesley Professional, Reading (1999)

14. Goldberg, A., Robson, D.: Smalltalk-80: The Language and its Implementation. Addison-Wesley, Reading (1983)

15. Gschwind, T., Oberleitner, J.: Improving Dynamic Data Analysis with Aspect-Oriented Programming. In: CSMR 2003: Proceedings of the Seventh European Conference on Software Maintenance and Reengineering, Washington, DC, USA, pp. 259–268. IEEE Computer Society, Los Alamitos (2003)

16. Harrold, M.J., McGregor, J.D., Fitzpatrick, K.J.: Incremental testing of object-oriented class structures. In: ICSE 1992: Proceedings of the 14th international conference on Software engineering, pp. 68–80. ACM, New York (1992)

17. Harrold, M.J., Jones, J.A., Li, T., Liang, D., Orso, A., Pennings, M., Sinha, S., Spoon, S.A., Gujarathi, A.: Regression Test Selection for Java software. In: Proceedings of the 16th ACM SIGPLAN conference on Object-oriented programming, systems, languages, and applications, pp. 312–326. ACM, New York (2001)

18. Harrold, M.J., Orso, A.: Retesting Software During Development and Maintenance. In: Frontiers of Software Maintenance, FoSM 2008, pp. 99–108 (2008)

19. Hsia, P., Li, X., Chenho Kung, D., Hsu, C.T., Li, L., Toyoshima, Y., Chen, C.: A technique for the selective revalidation of OO software. Journal of Software Maintenance: Research and Practice 9(4) (1997)

20. Huang, S., Chen, Y., Zhu, J., Li, Z.J., Tan, H.F.: An optimized change-driven regression testing selection strategy for binary Java applications. In: Proceedings of the 2009 ACM symposium on Applied Computing, pp. 558–565. ACM, New York (2009)

21. Ingalls, D., Kaehler, T., Maloney, J., Wallace, S., Kay, A.: Back to the Future: the Story of Squeak, a Practical Smalltalk Written in Itself. In: Proc. OOPSLA 1997, pp. 318–326. ACM Press, New York (1997)

22. Beck, K., Andres, C.: Extreme Programming Explained: Embrace Change, 2nd edn. Addison-Wesley Longman, Amsterdam (2004)

23. Kung, D.C., Gao, J., Hsia, P., Toyoshima, Y., Chen, C.: On regression testing of object-oriented programs. The Journal of Systems & Software 32(1), 21–40 (1996)

24. Mishali, O., Dubinsky, Y., Katz, S.: The TDD-guide training and guidance tool for test-driven development. In: The International Conference on Agile Processes and

eXtreme Programming in Software Engineering (XP), Limerick, Ireland, Springer, Heidelberg (2008)

25. Rothermel, G., Harrold, M.J.: A safe, efficient algorithm for regression test selection. In: ICSM '93: Proceedings of the Conference on Software Maintenance, Washington, DC, USA, pp. 358–367. IEEE Computer Society Press, Los Alamitos (1993)

26. Rothermel, G., Harrold, M.J.: Analyzing regression test selection techniques. IEEE Transactions on Software Engineering 22(8), 529–551 (1996)

27. Rothermel, G., Harrold, M.J.: A safe, efficient regression test selection technique. ACM Transactions on Software Engineering and Methodology (TOSEM) 6(2), 173–210 (1997)

28. Rothermel, G., Harrold, M.J., Dedhia, J.: Regression Test Selection for C++ Software. Software Testing, Verification & Reliability 10(2), 77–109 (2000)

29. Saff, D., Ernst, M.D.: Reducing wasted development time via continuous testing. In: ISSRE 2003: Proceedings of the 14th International Symposium on Software Reliability Engineering, Washington, DC, USA, p. 281. IEEE Computer Society Press, Los Alamitos (2003)

30. Zheng, J., Robinson, B., Williams, L., Smiley, K.: A process for identifying changes when source code is not available. In: MPEC 2005: Proceedings of the second international workshop on Models and processes for the evaluation of off-the-shelf components, pp. 1–4. ACM, New York (2005)

Applying SCRUM in an OSS Development Process: An Empirical Evaluation

Luigi Lavazza, Sandro Morasca, Davide Taibi, and Davide Tosi

Università degli Studi dell'Insubria
{luigi.lavazza,sandro.morasca,davide.taibi}@uninsubria.it,
davide.tosi@uninsubria.it

Abstract. Open Source Software development often resembles Agile models. In this paper, we report about our experience in using SCRUM for the development of an Open Source Software Java tool. With this work, we aim at answering the following research questions: 1) is it possible to switch successfully to the SCRUM methodology in an ongoing Open Source Software development process? 2) is it possible to apply SCRUM when the developers are geographically distributed? 3) does SCRUM help improve the quality of the product and the productivity of the process? We answer to these questions by identifying a set of measures and by comparing the data we collected before and after the introduction of SCRUM. The results seem to show that SCRUM can be introduced and used in an ongoing geographically distributed Open Source Software process and that it helps control the development process better.

Keywords: Open-source Software, OSS, agile methods, SCRUM, process improvement evaluation.

1 Introduction

The development of Open Source Software (OSS) products does not usually follow the traditional software engineering development paradigms described in textbooks. While classical development paradigms have been designed with Closed Source Software (CSS) in mind, OSS has inherent characteristics that make these paradigms hardly applicable. For example, OSS is often developed by a distributed community of developers and is freely distributed, as the source code is open and available to both developers and end-users under specific license policies.

As we now describe, an analysis of some inherent characteristics of OSS [13] on the one hand confirms that rigid development paradigms, such as the Waterfall model [14], are not applicable to OSS, while, on the other hand, it seems to suggest that agile paradigms [15] may help OSS developers improve the quality of their products. This is a result of the fact that the general principles behind the Agile Manifesto [2] are reflected in the way most OSS projects are developed and released to final users.

The short-term and non-commercial vision that characterizes many OSS projects implies that system analysis and product design are usually not pre-planned activities in OSS development. Also, many OSS projects were started to solve a user's particular

A. Sillitti et al. (Eds.): XP 2010, LNBIP 48, pp. 147–159, 2010.

problem, but they sometimes ended up deeply innovating the software field (this is the case of Linux, Perl, and the World Wide Web), even though they did not have a long-term vision, at least at their inception. The need for deep evolution of most OSS projects is usually perceived *after* they are successfully used by a large community of users. The success of an OSS product is usually unpredictable. It is directly related to the degree of attractiveness and usefulness that the project produces in the user community over time. It is thus quite hard to pre-plan the new releases of a system, except for the short term. These observations reflect the first two principles of the Agile manifesto [2]: "... satisfy the customer through early and continuous delivery of valuable software" and "Deliver working software frequently ...".

Moreover, OSS is characterized by an unstructured working environment, where the majority of OSS developers are volunteers who would not commit to hard deadlines and strict assignments. In CSS projects, team members are assigned tasks; in OSS projects, team members choose tasks. Due to this freedom, activities that are viewed as nuisances –such as project plan definition, system design evaluation, and requirements analysis– cannot be performed following traditional paradigms in the OSS community. Requirements that were not defined in advance by skilled analysts are continually discussed by the developers. Risks are monitored and managed during the project life-cycle in a natural way, as part of the "regular" development work. These OSS characteristics reflect the Agile principle "The best architectures, requirements, and designs emerge from self-organizing teams."

OSS is developed in a collaborative and distributed way [8]. OSS systems are developed in a large-scale cooperative context, where different teams, private users, a passionate core of developers, and virtual communities create the "unstructured company" (E. S. Raymond called it "Bazaar" [8]) that contributes to the project. Internet is the scaffolding and the desktop for these virtual software development organizations, and developers are coordinated by simple license policies without hierarchical supervision mechanisms as stringent as in CSS development. As a consequence, OSS developers hardly ever follow development methodologies as well defined as those followed by CSS developers. Furthermore, OSS is believed to be characterized by a faster growth [16] and more creativity than CSS [17], with the goal of satisfying and responding to user needs more quickly. This is primarily due to the unstructured and informal organization of the communities. Structure and rules may "inhibit innovative thinkers and drive them to the fringes," [17] while informality and freedom boost action and creativity. This implicitly requires the definition of architectures that are inherently modular and scalable, to guarantee the extensibility of a system and its interoperability across different hardware and software platforms. These observations reflect the seventh Agile principle "Build projects around motivated individuals. Give them the environment and support they need, and trust them to get the job done."

The massive use of the network and distributed resources fosters the dissemination of project knowledge via unstructured channels like mailing lists, forums, and chat logs, thus facilitating the communication between developers, final users, and managers. This partially meets the two Agile principles: "Business people and developers must work together daily throughout the project" and "The most efficient and effective method of conveying information to and within a development team is face-to-face conversation."

Thus, the work reported in this paper moved from two main considerations: 1) the development process of OSS products often resembles Agile or XP models in which each small-grained incremental development step is performed via a cycle involving test design, and execution; 2) while in the last few years several CSS developers have dismissed rigid development paradigms and embraced Agile or XP models, few works about the application of Agile paradigms in OSS development have been released (e.g., [10]).

We applied an Agile methodology to the development of an OSS tool in the QualiPSo project [18], and we performed measurements to evaluate whether it is possible to improve process productivity and OSS product quality via an environment that is more controlled than the one completely unstructured that characterizes OSS projects. Specifically, we applied the SCRUM [1] process to the development of MacXim (Model And Code Xml-based Integrated Meter), an OSS Java tool that extracts static measures from source code [3].

We describe a set of quality and productivity measures that were applied before and after the introduction of the SCRUM methodology in the development of MacXim. We then compare the data collected before and after the introduction of SCRUM, to understand if and how the SCRUM process actually affected the development, and we derive a set of observations on how to apply SCRUM to OSS products.

The experience shows that the introduction of SCRUM did not alter the productivity of our team significantly and the quality of our product. However, we were able to better control the development trend than in the non-SCRUM development period.

The paper is structured as follows. Section 2 states the hypotheses and the objectives of our experience. Section 3 describes the case study and the way we apply the SCRUM process to the development of MacXim. Section 4 reports about the results of our experience by introducing a set of productivity and quality measures, showing the data we collected, and discusses the results we obtained. Section 5 reviews related works in the field of agile methodologies. Finally, Section 6 contains our conclusions and an outline of future work.

2 Development and Research Objectives

MacXim is developed in the context of the activity of the QualiPSo project that is devoted to evaluating the quality of OSS, which, along with a set of other tools, it is used to evaluate the quality of the OSS products. Since we are interested in the quality of OSS products, it was therefore natural to include MacXim in the set of OSS products evaluated. As a consequence, the quality of every release of MacXim was thoroughly measured.

The development of the MacXim tool began in a rather unstructured way, that is, without following a well defined process. So, the measures of the quality of MacXim, along with the measures indicating the speed of the development progress, showed that the situation was not as good as we had hoped. Thus, our development objectives were to find the causes of such unsatisfactory performance and find and use mechanisms that could allow us to improve the development process and the quality of our OSS product.

The analysis of the development practice indicated that the main problem was in the too little amount of coordination among developers, who –also because of a lack of communications, favored by the physical distance among the developers– were not able to achieve a shared vision of the project and failed to act consistently.

It was therefore decided to improve the management of the project by enforcing coordination activities. However, we did not want to put too many constraints on the developers, but just to direct their efforts towards a common and shared target.

To this end, we decide to adopt SCRUM [1], a project management technique that allows developers to achieve a very good trade-off between effective coordination and process agility.

Measures concerning the 'pre-SCRUM' situation were available, so we could use those data as a baseline against which we could compare the results obtained after the introduction of SCRUM. Specifically, these measures could help us carry out a quantitative, objective evaluation of the impact of the introduction of SCRUM in an OSS development context. This evaluation led to three main research goals.

First, we wanted to verify if it is at all possible to switch successfully to SCRUM in an ongoing OSS development process. Our project started out following a different process, so it was unclear whether introducing SCRUM would actually be beneficial to the project.

Second, the applicability of SCRUM to a set of geographically distributed developers had also to be assessed: one of the basic practices of the SCRUM method is to attend daily meetings, which can be clearly problematic to organize if the participants reside far from each other.

Third, we wanted to verify the extent to which SCRUM helps improve the quality of the product and the productivity of the process. This objective could be effectively measured by means of the QualiPSo quality evaluation toolset. Section 4 describes the set of measures used to evaluate the productivity and the quality of MACXIM before and after the introduction of SCRUM.

3 The MacXim Case Study

The development of the MacXim prototype started in September 2007 without a clear development methodology in mind. After a few months, the project manager became aware that project requirements and deadlines were difficult to meet without a well planned work and without a dedicated development team. One year later, a dedicated team was formed and MacXim's development started to follow the traditional waterfall process, beginning from high-level requirements and going deep step-by-step. The MacXim team was composed of two junior developers and a project manager until May 2009, when a new junior developer was involved in the project. The team grew from three to four developers in the period June-October 2009, and it lost one developer in October. All the junior developers were involved full-time on MacXim's development, while the project manager is involved only partially (three days per week). Like many OSS development teams, our team was geographically distributed, with developers residing several kilometers away from each other. Problems in meeting deadlines surfaced when the size of team had grew to three people, mainly due to requirements volatility. As a consequence, the project manager recommended the introduction of an Agile methodology to alleviate these problems. As mentioned in

Section 2, we decided to adopt SCRUM because of coordination problems; in any case, we were ready to adapt SCRUM to our specific needs, mainly in order to take into account the distribution of the team. We started the introduction of SCRUM in the middle of July 2009 and we ended it with the V1.0 official release of MacXim at the end of October 2009. The SCRUM master (previously the project manager) suggested that the SCRUM process started with a trial period of two SCRUM sprints, each of two weeks. The trial period succeeded, so we decided to adopt the SCRUM methodology. Each sprint was supplied with a *Sprint Backlog* containing the tasks needed to implement a certain number of features in the Product Backlog. The SCRUM master, in collaboration of the team, assigned each sprint to the developer with the least workload and according to the set priority and the team member skills.

Because of the physical distribution of the MacXim developers, the daily meetings prescribed by SCRUM could not be attended in person. Therefore, we adopted an online-based approach, by using a forum and a videoconferencing system. We substituted morning meetings with an online forum. We structured our forum (see Fig. 1) by creating a thread per day where each developer wrote its comments by replying to three questions:

- What have you completed, with respect to the backlog, since last daily meeting?
- What specific tasks, with respect to the backlog, do you plan to accomplish until the next daily meeting?
- What obstacles got in your way of completing this work?

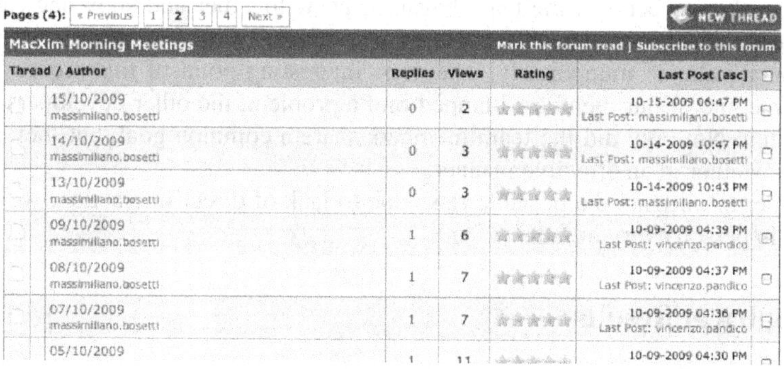

Fig. 1. Morning meeting list

Fig. 2 gives an example of a morning meeting post. The complete forum is available on http://qualipso.dscpi.uninsubria.it/forum (in Italian).

Every morning, each developer had to read all posts and, in case he had ideas on how to solve any posted problem, he was encouraged to suggest the solution.

At first, the team was uneasy about spending time in writing and reading the online morning meeting posts. Anyway, after a while, the team understood the usefulness of these virtual meetings, and both our SCRUM master and our "product owner" (i.e., the QualiPSo manager in charge of tool development) appreciated the possibility of keeping track of the work done on a day by day basis.

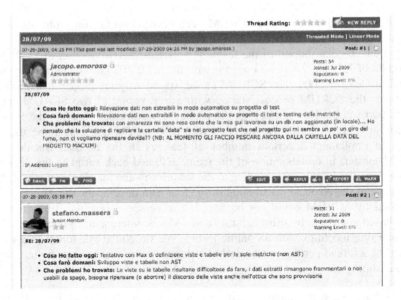

Fig. 2. Morning meeting example

We substituted also in-person sprint meetings with online reports via forum. Our team met online every two weeks: we had four hours meetings in video conference. The team leader was always in charge of writing the sprint retrospective on the forum.

During these meetings, the team began to grow together and show increasing involvement and project knowledge. The team completed a successful sprint, and began to cooperate almost immediately. The most interesting point of this process is that, every time one of our members bumped into a problem, the other developers quickly helped him. Not only did the team members share a common goal, but they actually worked together in an effective manner.

In order to mitigate the possible risks due to lack of direct interaction, we decided to meet in person every month.

4 Empirical Results

4.1 Data Collection

We started collecting data about quality and productivity measures in March 2009 and we ended the data collection at the end of October 2009 with the first official release of MacXim. For two weeks, at the end of June, we stopped the development of MacXim and started a quality and testing campaign to reduce the number of errors and warnings into the code. The campaign was organized both implementing a set of unit test cases and integration test cases, and also running third-party tools such as PMD [20] and Checkstyle [19] to improve code quality and adhere to coding standards. This activity ended at the beginning of July. In the middle of July 2009, we changed the development process and we kept on collecting data in the same way as we did in the previous period.

As fine-grained indicators to assess our initial research objectives (see Section 2), we considered measures for the following product and process attributes.

- Code organization. We expected that a better coordination among developers would lead to better structured code. We used the total number of packages, the average number of effective lines of codes (eLoc) per class and the total number of classes to measure the organization of the code.
- The pace of production. We used the number of classes to measure the "amount of product", as classes are more representative than LOC in an object-oriented development, though sufficiently fine-grained to show quantifiable progress on a weekly basis. In any case, we also take into account the productivity in terms of code produced and we used to eLoc measure to evaluate the productivity.
- Code quality. We used traditional measures for internal qualities, like Chidamber and Kemerer's measures of modularization [3] and McCabe's complexity measure [4], as well as elementary code assessment rules, which provide rather rough evaluations, but are expressive and easy to collect. Also, the amount of comments in the code, which is often a neglected concern, was considered as a quality factor.
- Sprint effectiveness. Finally, as a measure of the effectiveness of the project coordination through SCRUM we counted the percentage of user stories carried out in each sprint period, taking into account the evolution of the development team.

4.2 Case Study Result

At the end of the data collection process, we started the analysis of the data and we derive a set of charts as shown in figures 3, 4, 5, 6, and 7.

Fig. 3 shows the evolution of the measures we used to trace the evolution of project size and code organization. We collected the total number of packages, the average number of eLoc per class and the total number of classes. All these measures have been reported in the figure along with the evolution in the number of team members because of their correlation. Fig. 3 shows that the number of packages and the total number of classes increase after the introduction of SCRUM, while the average number of eLoc per class decreases. The behaviors of the number of packages and of the total number of classes show that MAXCIM's growth pace continued after the introduction of SCRUM, and the code seemed to be well modularized as far as size was concerned, since the average number of eLoc per class appears to be decreasing. Even though these trends seemed to exist even before its introduction, SCRUM was at least not detrimental to size aspects. Moreover, we can observe that the introduction of SCRUM leveled the max and min peaks we had in the previous period for the average eLocPerClass. This is probably due to the general SCRUM practice that suggests frequent intermediate deliveries with working functionality, like all other forms of agile software processes. So, the project can change its requirements according to changing needs, focus on small functionalities, and implement these functionalities into well modularized classes.

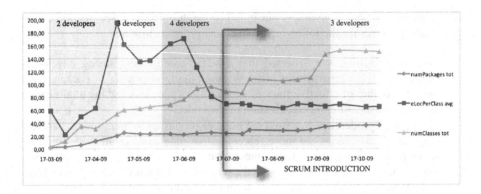

Fig. 3. Size measures over time

Fig. 4 shows the average number of lines of comment per eLoc. A preliminary observation of the chart suggests that this measure decreases after the introduction of SCRUM. This is not actually true because we can observe a growth only during the quality/testing period, which occurred around the end of June and the beginning of July 2009. The average number of lines of comment per eLoc was actually decreasing before that period, between mid-April and mid-June 2009. So, the same decreasing trend was confirmed even after the introduction of SCRUM, in the period from mid-July to mid-October 2009.

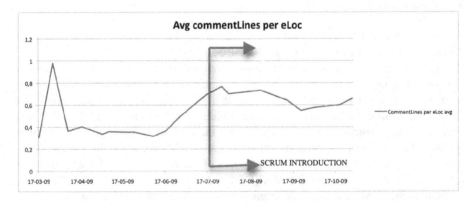

Fig. 4. Comment lines number per eLOC

Fig. 5 reports on code quality measures. We computed the average Lack of Cohesion of Methods metric (LCOM per class), the average Coupling Between Object classes (CBO per class), and the average Cyclomatic Complexity in the methods of each class. As stated in the literature, high values of these measures are undesirable, while low values suggest good internal quality of the object-oriented software product. In our experience, the Cyclomatic Complexity decreases slowly but constantly after the introduction of SCRUM, while the other two measures follow an increasing trend. As for CBO, excessive coupling between object classes is detrimental to modular design and prevents reuse. The more independent a class is, the easier it is to reuse it in another application. The larger the coupling, the higher the sensitivity to changes in other parts of the design, and therefore maintenance is more difficult. This is in contrast with the data we collected in Fig. 3, which seem to suggest an improvement of code modularization and as consequence code maintenance. The increment of CBO may be related to the high increment we had on the total number of classes after the introduction of SCRUM. In any case, the CBO value of MacXim is very low (e.g., a high CBO value is considered greater than 14 [21]). As for LCOM, the quality and testing activities performed just before the adoption of SCRUM strongly reduced LCOM from a value of 10 to a value of 4. This value suddenly increases after the introduction of SCRUM with a peak of value 7 at the end of September 2009. This negative value is occurs at the same time as the max value of the total number of classes, thus suggesting a relationship among the two measures. On average, the LCOM value computed during the Waterfall process is equal to the one computed during the SCRUM process.

In any case, the CBO and the LCOM values seem to suggest that the testing activity performed during the SCRUM process is not as efficient as the one performed during the previous quality/testing activity. This can be explained by the inexperience of our testers. Testers that are not skilled in processes that use iterative lifecycle may encounter greater difficulties when testing within each iteration, rather than at the end of a development lifecycle, deciding what to test when a product is still unfinished, and working with other team members to figure out what to test, rather than testing from requirements documents.

Fig. 6 shows the number of warnings per eLoc computed by means of PMD and Checkstyle. The number of warnings was very high during the Waterfall process (an average of 5 warnings per eLoc), sharply decreased during the quality check period (with the result of 1 warning per eLoc), and remained almost unchanged with a very slow and linear increasing trend (currently, 2 warnings per eLoc) after the introduction of SCRUM.

Fig. 7 shows the rate of successful sprints and the evolution of the developers number in our SCRUM team. With four consolidated developers the success rate

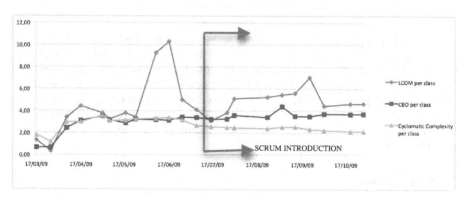

Fig. 5. LCOM, CBO and Cyclomatic Complexity

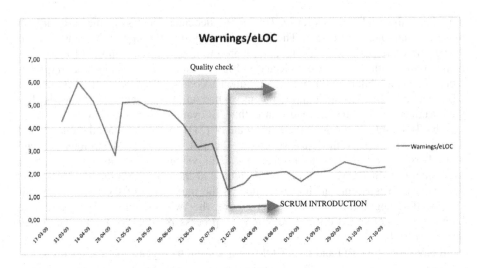

Fig. 6. Coding Standards Warnings / eLOC

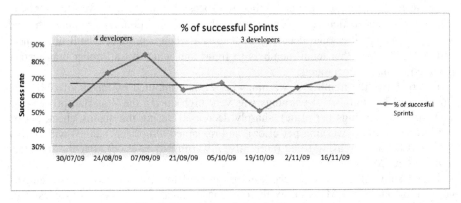

Fig. 7. Percentage of completed sprints

strongly increases from 55% of successful sprints to a rate of 85%. The success rate gets worse with the unexpected renovation of the team at the end of September. Probably, this renovation has invalidated the effort predictions and estimations the team set at the beginning of the SCRUM process. The linear trend of successful sprints (the light grey line in the chart) is almost constant to the rate 65%. Probably, a better definition of sprint backlogs and tasks could increase this rate. Unfortunately, the inherent characteristics of MacXim made difficult to break down its features into tasks of few hours of work.

5 Related Work

The vast majority of SCRUM's practices are not new to SW Engineering. The main idea of SCRUM is basically the same behind the Barry Boehm's Spiral Model [5]. SCRUM speeds up the requirement adaptability of the spiral model.

SCRUM aims at improving the quality of the software development process by means of short time boxes called sprints. In SCRUM, a sprint usually lasts from one to four weeks and a project lasts up to a few months. In this period, as in the spiral model, requirements are expected to change.

There are several studies reporting experiences on success stories in introducing SCRUM into a company but few studied the possibility of introducing SCRUM into a running Open Source process.

The experiment that is most similar to ours is reported in [5]. The adoption of SCRUM in a distributed open source project (PyPy) is reported. In particular, SCRUM was introduced in a project that had been "test driven" and had employed automated test suites and unit tests from the beginning. However, the development environment – with on-site customers, open workspaces and pair programming for each team– was quite different from ours. As in our case, the developers of PyPy were geographically distributed (i.e., several distributed sub-teams collaborate to the project), but they used only sprints to provide an accelerated and collaborative physical practice.

In [10] a two year long industrial case study shows that after the introduction of SCRUM into an existing software development organization, the amount of overtime decreased, allowing developers to work at a more sustainable pace, while, at the same time, customer satisfaction increased. This study differs from ours because of the nature of the team, which was located in a single site: they applied the classical SCRUM process, with in person pair programming and daily meetings.

An interesting work [11] shows the introduction of SCRUM in small teams, where the total number of developers was close to our team's. They found out that small teams can be flexible and adaptable in defining and applying appropriate variant of SCRUM.

Another interesting industrial report [8] shows the introduction of SCRUM in five companies with different sizes and different technologies, with positive results in all cases: SCRUM dramatically improved the communication and the delivery of code.

In general, this paper goes a bit further with respect to previous experience reports, since we do not just report a specific experience in introducing SCRUM. Instead, we suggest a new adaptation of SCRUM that can be used in distributed projects, where daily face-to-face communication is impossible.

6   Conclusions and Future Work

Here is what we may conclude as to the research objectives listed in Section 2. Our experience with MacXim's development suggested that:

1)   It is possible to switch successfully to SCRUM in an ongoing (OSS) development process. In effect, the analysis confirms that the introduction of SCRUM does not significantly negatively affect the values of the measures we computed and, in some cases, we had an improvement of these measures, for example for code modularization and Cyclomatic Complexity. Moreover, SCRUM seems to have made productivity more predictable, without min and max peaks, but with smoother curves than the ones we had during the Waterfall development.

2) It is possible to apply SCRUM to a set of geographically distributed developers. As one of the basic practices of the SCRUM method is to attend daily meetings, we replaced face-to-face meetings with online mechanisms of communication. In any case, SCRUM seemed to have significantly improved the communication among the developers.

3) With SCRUM, we obtained a code of high quality, without substantially altering the quality level we reached with the quality check activity, and we were able to meet the cutoff deadline for the first official release of MacXim.

As a final consideration, applying the pure SCRUM methodology to an OSS development community is not possible because of geographical, cultural, and communication problems. Often, developers with different cultures are located all over the world, generally in different time zones. Therefore, it is not possible neither to have morning meetings nor sprint reports together. In our team, we applied a slightly modified version of SCRUM and we substituted in person meetings with an online forum. Moreover, we think that SCRUM can be applied to OSS projects that are characterized by a limited number of contributors to allow a punctual communication among developers.

Currently, we are collecting new SCRUM data by monitoring the development of the next release of MacXim planned for the end of 2010. So, we will be able to compare these new data with the old ones and check whether we can confirm the conclusions we obtained with this first experience. Actually, we expect further process and product improvements as measured by all the measures we collect.

Acknowledgments

The research presented in this paper has been partially funded by the IST project Qualipso (http://www.qualipso.eu/), sponsored by the EU in the 6th FP (IST-034763); the FIRB project ARTDECO, sponsored by the Italian Ministry of Education and University; and the projects "Elementi metodologici per la descrizione e lo sviluppo di sistemi software basati su modelli" and "La qualità nello sviluppo software," funded by the Università degli Studi dell'Insubria.

The work reported was made possible by the enthusiast cooperation of the members of the development team: Marco Binda, Massimiliano Bosetti, Jacopo Emoroso, Stefano Massera, Vincenzo Pandico.

References

1. Schwaber, K., Beedle, M.: Agile Software Development with SCRUM. Prentice Hall, Englewood Cliffs (2001)
2. Beck, K., Beedle, M., van Bennekum, A., Cockburn, A., Cunningham, W., Fowler, M., Grenning, J., Highsmith, J., Hunt, A., Jeffries, R., Kern, J., Marick, B.C., Martin, R., Mellor, S., Schwaber, K., Sutherland, J., Thomas, D.: Manifesto for Agile Software Development, http://www.agilemanifesto.org/
3. Crisà, A.F., del Bianco, V., Lavazza, L.: A tool for the measurement, storage, and pre-elaboration of data supporting the release of public datasets. In: González-Barahona, J.M.,

Conklin, M., Robles, G. (eds.) Workshop on Public Data about Software Development (WoPDaSD 2006), Como (2006)

4. Chidamber, S.R., Kemerer, C.F.: A Metrics Suite for Object Oriented Design. IEEE Transactions on Software Engineering 20, 476–493 (1994)

5. McCabe, T.J.: A complexity measure. IEEE Transactions on Software Engineering 2, 300–320 (1976)

6. Boehm, B.W.: A Spiral Model of Software Development and Enhancement. IEEE Computer 21(5), 61–72 (1988)

7. Northover, M., Northover, A., Gruner, S., Kourie, D.G., Boake, A.: Agile software development: A contemporary philosophical perspective. In: ACM International Conference Proceeding Series, vol. 226, pp. 106–115 (2007)

8. Raymond, E.S.: The Cathedral & the Bazaar. O'Reilly, Sebastopol (2001)

9. Sutherland, J.: Agile can scale: Inventing and reinventing scrum in five companies. Cutter IT Journal. Cutter Information Corp. 14(12) (December 2001)

10. Düring, B.: Sprint Driven Development: Agile Methodologies in a Distributed Open Source Project (PyPy). In: Abrahamsson, P., Marchesi, M., Succi, G. (eds.) XP 2006. LNCS, vol. 4044, pp. 191–195. Springer, Heidelberg (2006)

11. Mann, C., Maurer, F.: A Case Study on the Impact of SCRUM on Overtime and Customer Satisfaction. In: Agile Development Conference, pp. 70–79 (2005)

12. Rising, L., Janoff, N.S.: The SCRUM Software Development Process for Small Teams. IEEE Software 17(4), 26–32 (2000)

13. Feller, J., Fitzgerald, B.: A framework analysis of the open source software development paradigm. In: Proceedings of the twenty first International Conference on Information systems (2000)

14. Ghezzi, C., Jazayeri, M., Mandrioli, D.: Fundamentals of Software Engineering, 2nd edn. Pearson, Prentice Hall (2002)

15. Northover, M., Northover, A., Gruner, S., Kourie, D.G., Boake, A.: Agile software development: A contemporary philosophical perspective. In: ACM International Conference Proceeding Series, vol. 226, pp. 106–115 (2007)

16. Mockus, R., Fielding, T., Herbsleb, J.: A case study of OSS development: the apache server. In: Proceedings of the International Conference on Software Engineering (ICSE), pp. 263–272 (2000)

17. O'Reilly, T.: Lessons from Open-Source Software development. Communications of the ACM 42(4) (1999)

18. QualiPSo portal, http://www.qualipso.eu (Accessed: December 2009)

19. Checkstyle tool download, http://checkstyle.sourceforge.net/ (Accessed: December 2009)

20. PMD tool download, http://pmd.sourceforge.net/ (Accessed: December 2009)

21. Sahraoui, H.A., Godin, R., Miceli, T.: Can Metrics Help Bridging the Gap Between the Improvement of OO Design Quality and Its Automation? In: Proceedings of the International Conference on Software Maintenance, ICSM (2000)

An Automated Approach for Acceptance Web Test Case Modeling and Executing

Felipe M. Besson, Delano M. Beder, and Marcos L. Chaim

School of Arts, Sciences and Humanities
University of São Paulo
03828-000 São Paulo, Brazil
{besson,dbeder,chaim}@usp.br

Abstract. This paper proposes an approach for modeling and executing acceptance web test cases and describes a suite of tools to support it. The main objective is to assist the use of *Acceptance Test-Driven Development* (ATDD) in web applications by providing mechanisms to support customer-developer communication and by helping test case creation. Initially, the set of web pages and relations (links) associated with a user story is modeled. Functional test possibilities involving these relations are automatically summarized in a graph, being each path of the graph a user story testing scenario. Once a testing scenario is accepted by the customer, a testing script is automatically created. A web testing framework then executes the script, triggering the ATDD process.

Keywords: testing automation, web testing, acceptance web test-driven development, agile methods.

1 Introduction

Web applications have become an essential part of many business strategies, and are therefore exposed to a highly competitive environment, surrounded by frequent changes in business rules. In addition, incremental deliverables, frequent customer's feedbacks, short deadlines and highly customized user requirements characterize the web engineering [1]. Taking into account these characteristics, agile software development processes are considered an effective approach for web application development [1].

One of the principles of agile methods is the *Test-Driven Development* (TDD), a software development strategy in which unit tests are developed for each unit of source-code before its implementation [2]. A drawback inherent to TDD practice is that tests are only written by the developer. According to Beck [3], one risk is implementing what the developer thinks the user wants, and not what s/he wants at all. In this context arises the *Acceptance Test-Driven Development* (ATDD), which is characterized by acceptance tests written by the customer to drive the software development process [4].

ATDD helps the developer team to deliver exactly what customers want when they want it while TDD helps to ensure the software's technical quality [5].

A. Sillitti et al. (Eds.): XP 2010, LNBIP 48, pp. 160–165, 2010.

The use of ATDD to validate user stories in eXtreme Programming (XP), for example, is needed to guide TDD practices [6]. This work proposes an approach that facilitates the use of ATDD in web applications and presents a suite of tools that implements it. The paper is organized as follows. Section 2 discusses the related work. Section 3 presents an overview of our approach and the tools supporting it. Finally, in Section 4, we draw our conclusions.

2 Related Work

Due to the importance of web applications several works on web functional test automation have been developed. A Web Testing Model is proposed by Qian *et al.* [7]. Initially a web application is defined in a PFD (Page Flow Diagram) which is converted into a PTT (Page Test Tree). Test case skeletons are then derived from tree paths, which should be completed with inputs and expected outputs. In the end of the process, the test cases are sent to a test translator in charge of modeling the request and the response for each page. A test engine finally executes the created script.

Concordion [11], Cucumber [12] and Fitnium [13] are tools specific for the ATDD pratice. Selenium RC [8] also allows ATDD practices, but the communication with the stakeholders is carried out by presenting the RC tests source code. On the other hand, Bromine [9] is able to run RC Selenium tests, presenting the results in a less technical way. Nevertheless, RC tests have to be developed and uploaded manually. In Concordion, acceptance tests cases are described using HTML and then linked to JUnit tests. Cucumber is a Ruby tool that provides a high-level interface that allows the customer to write acceptance tests in natural language; however, the connection between tests and source code should be written by the developer. Finally, Fitnium – an integration of FitNesse [14] and Selenium – provides an wiki interface for acceptance test specification. Subsequently, it automatically executes the tests modeled using Selenium RC.

The ATTD current approaches and tools require either the availability of the application [7] or the knowledge of programming and technical details for effective use [8,9,11,14]. The novelty of our approach resides in the graphical interface provided for customer-developer communication, the identification of testing scenarios, and the automatic generation of acceptance testing scripts.

3 The Approach

The goal of our approach is to provide mechanisms that (i) assist developers to automatically generate acceptance tests, (ii) supply a communication interface between the customer and the development team, (iii) automatically execute acceptance test cases, and (iv) organize software artifacts when ATDD is used in web applications. In this section we present the workflow and the tools that support the proposed approach.

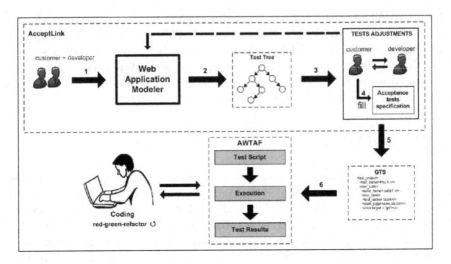

Fig. 1. The approach workflow

3.1 Workflow

The approach workflow is presented in Figure 1 and below we present in detail each of its steps.

To illustrate the steps of the approach workflow, let us consider an example of a virtual library that provides, among other features, a purchase of books functionality. As many e-commerce applications, initially, a book is selected and added into the shopping cart. Once the buyer has added how many books s/he wants, the order is closed. Then the buyer have to sign in or, if it is her/his first purchase, sign up. Finally, the type of payment (e.g., debit or credit card, checking account) is chosen. This flow will be used to illustrate how the approach works. Obviously, during the writing of acceptance tests in ATDD, the functionality modeled does not exist yet.

(Step 1). The approach describes a web application as a set of related pages where each page contains internal components such as a title, text inputs, forms, links, buttons, text content and so on, that are responsible for the information flow inside and outside the current page. The links connecting the pages are denominated relations. One of these pages is called "initial page", which is the first page showed when the web application is invoked. Taking into account the incremental development software process, the application will be modeled by functionalities, in other words, just a subset of pages belonging to the functionality under development needs to be modeled, not all pages at once. Figure 2 shows the modeling of pages that composes the "Book Purchase" user story.

(Step 2). Each user story (functionality) is then mapped into a graph, described by a triple $G(P, R, sp)$, where P corresponds to the set of pages (nodes), R represents the relations (edges) among pages, and sp is the root node; that is, the initial page of the user story. Following the creation of the graph, an

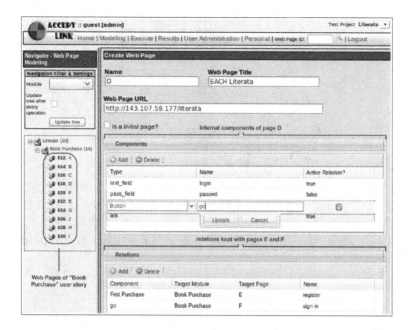

Fig. 2. Web page modeling

algorithm, based on Qian's work [7], removes the existing cycles and generates a direct acyclic graph (DAG) called *test tree*. Each path of a tree corresponds to a testing scenario (test path), while the tree as a whole represents a set of possible tests. A testing scenario corresponds to a logical sequence of interaction among those pages belonging to the user story modeled. In the example given, a purchase can be paid with debit/credit card or checking account, each one of these possibilities are considered a specific scenario. Figure 3 shows the graph and the testing scenarios derived automatically for the "Book Purchase" example.

(Steps 3 and 4). All the testing scenarios generated are displayed to developers which, in turn, select them for implementation. Following the ATDD practices, the customer and developers discusses and validates the logical behavior among pages and other characteristics of each testing scenario. If the customer considers a particular scenario correct, s/he will inform the inputs for that testing scenario, as well as the expected results. Otherwise, steps 1, 2 and 3 have to be performed again until the customer accepts the user story testing scenarios.

(Steps 5 and 6). Finally, the testing scenarios are converted into automated test scripts. As can be seen in Figure 4, the scenario "BookPurchase_611_13" which is represented by the path A→B→C→D→F→I→J is mapped into a GTS (Generic Test Specification). This specification is then interpreted by AWTAF tool to run the automated acceptance test case modeled.

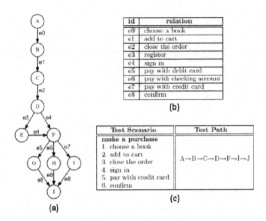

Fig. 3. Graph conversion: (a) Graph (b) Legend for relations (c) A testing scenario/path example

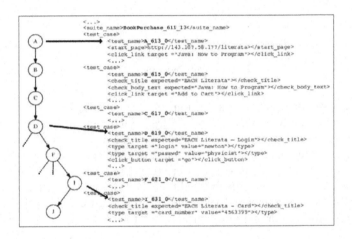

Fig. 4. Tree path mapped into a GTS

3.2 Tools Suite

According to the workflow proposed (see Figure 1), our suite is composed by two tools: AcceptLink and AWTAF, both open source.

AcceptLink: AcceptLink corresponds to a web application developed in PHP and Java. It is based on TestLink [10], a web application used to manage test artifacts. AcceptLink is in charge of steps 1 to 5 as can be visualized in Figure 1.

AWTAF (Automated Web Test Application Framework): AWTAF is a framework runnable in a desktop environment. Its main objective is to automate web functional tests execution using Selenium RC, HttpUnit or HtmlUnit, all open-source web test automation tools. According to the workflow (Figure 1), AWTAF is in charge of step 6.

4   Concluding Remarks and Future Work

This paper described an approach to assist the *Acceptance Test-Driven Development* (ATDD) use in web applications. Furthermore, two tools – AcceptLink and AWTAF – developed to support this approach were presented. The features presented in Section 3 have been implemented and are in operational use. In comparison to current ATTD tools, AcceptLink and AWTAF contribution resides in supporting customer-developement team communication and test scenario selection using a summary graph. We have conducted an exploratory assessment with the proposed approach. Although AcceptLink has shown usability problems, the tools had a positive impact on functionality understanding, test case modeling and creation, and customer-development communication. The usability problems raised are being addressed and new features allowing to test AJAX features are under study. Further experiments are planned.

Acknowledgements. This research is partially supported by QualiPSo Project (Quality Platform for Open Source Software), Grant Number IST-FP6-IP-034763, url: http://www.qualipso.org.

References

1. Mcdonald, A., Welland, R.: Agile Web Engineering (AWE) Process, Technical report, University of Glasgow (2001)
2. Crispin, L.: Driving Software Quality: How Test-Driven Development Impacts Software Quality. IEEE Software 23(6), 70–71 (2006)
3. Beck, K.: Test-Driven Development By Example. Addison Wesley, New York (2003)
4. Hendricksons, E.: Acceptance Test Driven Development (ATDD): an Overview. In: Seventh Software Testing Australia/New Zealand (STANZ), Wellington (2008)
5. Koskela, L.: Test Driven: Practical TDD and Acceptance TDD for Java Developers, Manning, Greenwich (2008)
6. Crispin, L.: The need for speed: Automating acceptance testing in an extreme programming environment. UpGrade - The European Journal for the Informatics Professional 3, 104–106 (2002)
7. Qian, Z., Miao, H., Zeng, H.: A Practical Web Testing Model for Web Application Testing. In: Third International IEEE Conference on Signal-Image Technologies and Internet-Based System, pp. 434–441. IEEE Computer Society, Washington (2007)
8. Selenium: Web Application Testing System, http://www.openqa.org/selenium
9. Bromine, A.: web-based QA tool for selenium, http://seleniumhq.org/projects/bromine/
10. TestLink: Test Management and Execution System, http://testlink.org/
11. Concordion: A Tool for writing Automated Acceptance tests in Java, http://www.concordion.org/
12. Cucumber: Behaviour Driven Development, http://cukes.info/
13. Fitnium: FitNesse and Selenium, http://www.magneticreason.com/tools/fitnium/fitnium.html
14. FitNesse: Acceptance Testing Framework, http://fitnesse.org/

Communication in Context: A Stimulus-Response Account of Agile Team Interactions

Nik Nailah Binti Abdullah[1], Helen Sharp[2], and Shinichi Honiden[1]

[1] GRACE Center, National Institute of Informatics, Tokyo, Japan
[2] Center for Research in Computing, The Open University, United Kingdom
{bintiabd,honiden}@nii.ac.jp, h.c.sharp@open.ac.uk

Abstract. Previous research has indicated that work artefacts commonly used by agile teams capture progress information, while functional aspects such as requirements are developed and sustained through the team's social interactions and communication channels. This paper reports an initial empirical study to investigate the relationship between agile work artefacts and communication during stand-up meetings and pair programming sessions, specifically focusing on gathering and clarifying requirements. Using Bateson's communication theory, we found that the work artefacts, and other individuals form an external event system which supports Agile teams during the gathering and clarifying of requirements. Using this communication theory together with Clancey's situated cognition, we predict that if the two do not exist together throughout the interactions, then teams members will form discoordinated actions together.

Keywords: Empirical study, stand-up meetings, communication, situated cognition, contexts.

1 Introduction

Agile practice emphasizes communication and downplays documentation. Most agile teams therefore rely on simple artefacts such as story cards and the Wall, together with frequent communication to help create and sustain a shared understanding of the product's requirements. Analyses of agile practice using distributed cognition [10, 14] and cognitive dimensions [8, 15] suggest that story cards and the Wall focus on capturing and displaying progress information rather than requirements issues such as problems, goals or functionality. Instead, requirements of the product reside in the social context and are sustained through communication and collaboration activities.

This paper progresses these earlier analyses by investigating what is achieved during an agile team's communication, and what role is played by the physical artefacts. We present the preliminary findings from a field study of one co-located agile team, focused on their communication relating to the activities of gathering and clarifying requirements.

The paper is organized as follows. In the next section we introduce some relevant related work in agile team communication and agile requirements. Then we describe the study setting, data gathering and analysis. Then we present our findings, followed by conclusion and future work.

A. Sillitti et al. (Eds.): XP 2010, LNBIP 48, pp. 166–171, 2010.

2   Related Work

Work focused on requirements engineering in an agile context often aims to integrate existing requirements engineering tools or processes into an agile environment. For example, Nawrocki [12] describe how to include requirements documentation into XP and how to enhance the planning game to take account of requirements engineering concerns. Grunbacher and Hofer [9] integrate requirements negotiation into agile processes. Gallardo-Valencia and Sim [7] investigate how agile teams handle requirements and conclude that requirements are constantly being validated which in turn strengthens team bonds.

Cao and Ramesh [5] provide evidence that the RE process for agile software development differs from that of traditional development – it is an iterative discovery approach – and they identify seven agile RE practices, the most important of which is the intensive communication between the customer(s) and developer(s). Yet few studies of communication in an agile team have been reported. For example Bryant et al [4] investigate collaboration in pairing by analyzing the verbalizations of pairs working together. In this work, the focus was on understanding whether pairs worked collaboratively and how collaborative they were. Moløkken-Østvold [11] focused on the role of the customer and found that where there was daily communication between developers and customers, there were fewer overruns. This latter study did not investigate the nature of those communications.

3   The Study and Research Methods

Our study was designed following an ethnographically-informed approach [13]. In particular, this approach aims to study practice without interference, treats all data as 'strange', and asks 'how' and 'why' and 'what are the characteristics of' questions. In this case, we intended to study the communication process of the agile team to understand the relationship between physical artefacts and communication during requirements activities. We therefore collected detailed data relating to the team's verbal and non-verbal interactions and analysed it.

3.1   The Study Context

The agile development team observed is based in a large telecommunications and media company in the UK; the observation lasted for four days in March 2009. The team had been together for over a year and several members of the team had worked together before. The team consisted of five developers and two customers. All the studies were conducted at the agile development team's office. The team's project was to deliver a prototype portal for cloud services. The portal needed to include some additional features, which were to be achieved by combining it with other systems that the team had been developing. It had to be demonstrated to the company's clients the following week. The request for additional features was made at the beginning of the observation period and it had to be delivered the day after observation ended. In this team stories were expressed as abbreviated labels such as 'USER ACCOUNTS'. The Wall was a filing cabinet, as shown in Figure 1.

Fig. 1. The team discussing story cards on the Wall during a stand-up meeting

3.2 Data Gathering and Analysis

The data gathered from our observations consisted of field notes, photographs, meeting audio recordings, short video recordings of group interactions in front of the wall, audio records of four pairing sessions, and post-observation informal interviews via email. In this paper we report our analysis of audio, video, interview and field note data from two stand-up meetings from the first and second day observations (22 minutes and 30 seconds in total), and four pair-programming sessions (3 hours 5 minutes in total) also from the first and second day of observation. The audio data was transcribed using symbols commonly employed in discourse analysis [1, 16]; in total we have transcribed about 7,410 lines of dialogue. We then aligned the transcriptions to field notes, photographs, and video interactions based on a timeline, and contacted the team members via email for clarification when necessary.

To analyse our transcripts, we used an approach that combines Bateson's communication theory [2] and Clancey's situated cognition [6]. Bateson's communication theory provides a framework for identifying stimulus and response patterns from everyday communication in which the patterns are associated to the notion of context. This theory focuses on the set of stimuli (called the *external event system*) that is responsible for a person's response(s) in a repeated manner during a specific context. Clancey's situated cognition was developed from the observation of work practice and explains how people form knowledge and experiences. Specifically, it looks into how people formulate coordinated actions by relating what people see and what they interact with in their environment to memory.

Our analysis approach [3] extracts stimulus and response patterns to uncover physical artefact-communication relationships. A *pattern* in our work refers to repeated responses exhibited by team members during similar contexts of communication [2]. The patterns are in the form:

<*external stimulus, internal stimulus, focus*> associated with a *context*.

where the tuple {external stimulus, internal stimulus and focus} is known as a feature, and each feature is then associated to a context. In our work, we were interested in contexts related to requirements *External stimulus* refers to some specific detail(s) from the environment (including artefacts) that caused the individual to react in the observed way at the present moment. There can be several external stimuli at any one time [2]. *Internal stimulus* refers to dialogue contents or thoughts associated with the external stimulus (i.e., associative thoughts), which can be inferred as remembering [2, 6]. *Focus* refers to the issue which a set of utterances is about [2]. Once we have extracted the physical artefact-communication relationships, we identify the basic stimuli that constitute the external event system of the agile team, and use situated cognition to explain what the basic stimuli represent for the team.

4 Findings

In this section we introduce the eight patterns that we found associated with the contexts of gathering and clarifying requirements. *Gathering requirement* is defined as when the utterance(s) indicates a response to customer's user story or developer's progress. *Clarifying requirement* is defined as when the utterance(s) indicates a question or an issue raised by the developer to another stakeholder. The eight patterns are listed below, in feature format, followed by an explanation:

Patterns from the stand-up meetings
Pattern 1 (8 instances): *<story card, associative thoughts, acceptance criteria>* associated with *clarifying requirements*.
> When an Agile member is about to start clarifying what he did yesterday, he refers to the relevant story card, and then he communicates.

Pattern 2 (22 instances): *<other individual's communication, associative thoughts, acceptance criteria>* associated with *clarifying requirements*.
> When an Agile member is clarifying what he did yesterday, his pair will contribute to his clarifications.

Pattern 3 (6 instances): *<story cards and group communication, associative thoughts, acceptance criteria>* associated with *clarifying requirements*.
> When members as a group confirm that there is no longer the need to clarify what they did yesterday, they look at the physical artefacts together, and then they communicate.

Pattern 4 (9 instances): *<the wall and other individual's communication, associative thoughts, new story>* associated with *gathering requirements*
> When a team member is about to start gathering details from a new user story, he refers to the physical artefacts, and then he communicates.

Pattern 5 (12 instances): *<other individual's communication, associative thoughts, system events>* associated with *gathering requirements*
> When a team member is contributing details to the new user story, another member will contribute to his communication.

Pattern 6 (2 instances): *<new story card and group communication, associative thoughts, the wall>* associated with *gathering requirements*
> When the team as a group decide that they have finished gathering requirements for the new story card on the wall, they look at the physical artefacts together, and then they communicate.

Patterns form the pairing sessions

Pattern 7 (29 instances): *<code and other individual's communication, associative thoughts, acceptance criteria/bug>* associated with *clarifying requirements*

When pairs get stuck during pairing, another member will contribute to the pairs' communication.

Pattern 8 (6 instances): *<code and other individual's communication, story card, acceptance criteria/bug>* associated with *clarifying requirements*

When pairs get stuck during pairing, one of them refers to the physical artefact, and then they resume their pairing.

In each of the eight patterns, the external stimulus was either the physical artefacts (i.e. story card or the wall), or another individual's communication. We can generalize that the physical artefacts and other individuals were the two fundamental stimuli that allowed the team members to start, *sustain* and end their requirements contexts throughout time. According to Bateson's definition, we say that the external event system for the team comprised the physical artefacts and other individuals.

5 Limitations

Our analysis is based on a very small set of data from one co-located team, studied for only 4 days. Our data came exclusively from a large commercial company in the UK, and the extent to which our results are valid for other companies or contexts is not clear without replication and further iterations. Additional data and further iterations are needed to verify, refine and expand this initial set of patterns.

6 Discussion and Conclusions

Using Bateson's communication theory [2] to account for how individuals react to the external world, we have identified that the external event system of the agile team comprises physical artefacts and other individuals. Bateson tells us that if we remove either one of the stimuli (physical artefacts or collaborating members), we can predict that an individual's response will be slightly different from what we expect.

According to Clancey's situated cognition [6], a person formulates coordinated action by relating what he/she sees in the environment to memory. During the construction of ongoing activity, knowledge, and experiences are formed, enabling team members to formulate coordinated actions together. In order to ensure that a group of people formulate coordinated actions together during work activity, they need to *communicate together* where *they are able to share what they physically see and do together in the environment situated to their ongoing activities*. We then may predict that if one of the team members is absent, or that the team members are distributed, then discoordinated actions may be formulated.

On the one hand, these implications are not surprising. However their significance lies in the fact that we have begun to relate the kind of communication that takes place in an agile team to theories of communication and learning. For agile practitioners, these preliminary findings indicate that we may be able to predict when discoordinated actions will occur, and suggest how to avoid or rectify them. For agile researchers, we have illustrated how communication theory may be applied to agile practice. Future work will analyse further communication data both from this team and from other teams.

Acknowledgements

We are grateful to the agile team members and customers for their participation, and the Agile Alliance who provided partial funding for this work. We are also grateful to Dr. William J. Clancey from NASA Ames Research Center, California and the Florida Institute for Human and Machine Cognition, and Dr. Robert GM Hausmann from Carnegie Learning Incorporation, Pittsburgh for their constructive comments on our study, helping us to move our study forward.

References

1. Atkinson, J.M., Heritage, J.: Structures of Social Action: Studies in Conversation Analysis. Cambridge University Press, Cambridge (1984)
2. Bateson, G.: Steps towards Ecology of Mind. Collected Essays in Anthropology, Psychiatry, Evolution, and Epistemology. University of Chicago Press, Chicago (1972)
3. Binti Abdullah, N.N., Sharp, H.C., Honiden, S.: A Method of Analysis to Uncover Physical Artifact-Communication Relationship. In: Proceedings of the 23rd FLAIRS conference. Special track: Cognition and AI: Capturing Cognitive Plausibility and Informing Psychological Processes. AAI Press (2010)
4. Bryant, S., Romero, P., du Boulay, B.: The collaborative nature of pair programming. In: Abrahamsson, P., Marchesi, M., Succi, G. (eds.) XP 2006. LNCS, vol. 4044, pp. 53–64. Springer, Heidelberg (2006)
5. Cao, L., Ramesh, B.: Agile Requirements Engineering Practices: An Empirical Study. IEEE Software, 60–67 (January/February 2008)
6. Clancey, W.J.: Situated Cognition on human knowledge and computer representation. Cambridge University Press, Cambridge (1997)
7. Gallardo-Valencia, R.E., Sim, S.E.: Agile Validation is continuous and collaborative: A field Study of Agile Requirements presented at Agile. Research-in-Progress Workshop (2009)
8. Green, T.R.G.: Cognitive dimensions of notations. In: Sutcliffe, A., Macaulay, L. (eds.) People and Computers V, pp. 443–460. Cambridge University Press, Cambridge (1989)
9. Grunbacher, P., Hofer, C.: Complementing XP with Requirements Negotiation. In: Wells, D., Williams, L. (eds.) XP 2002. LNCS, vol. 2418, pp. 105–108. Springer, Heidelberg (2002)
10. Hutchins, E.: Cognition in the Wild. MIT Press, Cambridge (1995)
11. Moløkken-Østvold, K., Furulund, K.M.: The Relationship between Customer Collaboration and Software Project Overruns. In: Proceedings of Agile 2007, pp. 72–83 (2007)
12. Nawrocki, J.: Extreme Programming Modified: Embrace requirements engineering practices. In: Proceedings of RE 02, pp. 303–310 (2002)
13. Robinson, H., Segal, J., Sharp, H.: Ethnographically-informed empirical studies of software practice. Information & Software Technology 49(6), 540–551 (2007)
14. Sharp, H., Robinson, H.: Collaboration and Co-ordination in mature eXtreme Programming teams. International Journal of Human-Computer Studies 66, 506–518 (2008)
15. Sharp, H., Robinson, H., Petre, M.: The role of physical artefacts in agile software development: two complementary perspectives. Interacting with Computers 21(1-2), 108–116 (2009)
16. Wood, L.A., Kroger, R.O.: Doing Discourse Analysis. Methods for Studying Action and Talk in Text. Sage Publications, Thousand Oaks (2000)

Understanding the Importance of Trust in Distributed Agile Projects: A Practical Perspective

Siva Dorairaj, James Noble, and Petra Malik

School of Engineering and Computer Science,
Victoria University of Wellington,
Wellington, New Zealand
{siva.dorairaj,kjx,petra.malik}@ecs.vuw.ac.nz
http://ecs.victoria.ac.nz

Abstract. Agile methods rely on face-to-face communication but are being used in distributed projects. We have conducted grounded theory research with Agile practitioners to collate the strategies they use to overcome the challenges in distributed projects. In this paper, we argue that trust is one of the key factors in determining the success or failure of distributed Agile projects, and describe how trust can be generated and sustained by increasing effective communication and understanding cultural differences.

Keywords: Trust, Agile Methods, Agile Project Management, Distributed Agile Project, Grounded Theory.

1 Introduction

The high success rate of Agile software development could have encouraged many organisations to incorporate Agile methods in their distributed projects [2]. One of the fundamental values of Agile is that Agile practitioners give great importance to individuals and interactions [9]. Agile methods, such as XP [3] and Scrum [13], typically require continuous face-to-face interaction between team members but this interaction is hard to maintain when projects are distributed [8, 14]. Although there is a wealth of literature in the area of distributed projects, the literature on the adoption and adaption of Agile methods in distributed projects is still scarce [4, 7, 12].

We have conducted a qualitative research with seven Agile practitioners to identify the key factors that determine the success or failure of distributed Agile projects, and collate the strategies adopted by them to manage distributed Agile projects. In this paper we report the result of our research: trust is one of the key factors in determining the success or failure of distributed Agile projects. We found that trust can be generated and sustained in the distributed Agile projects by increasing effective communication and understanding cultural differences.

2 Research Method and Participants

Grounded Theory (GT) [6] is a qualitative research method that emphasizes the generation of a theory from systematic analysis of data. GT was developed by Glaser and

A. Sillitti et al. (Eds.): XP 2010, LNBIP 48, pp. 172–177, 2010.

Strauss [6]. GT aims to discover the underlying concepts in the research phenomenon regardless of the time, place and people, rather than to describe the phenomenon itself [1, 6]. We chose to apply GT as our research methodology for three reasons. Firstly, GT allows us to study social interactions and behaviour of people, and Agile methods focus on people and their interactions in the team. Secondly, GT is suitable to be used in new research areas that have yet to be explored, and the literature on the distributed Agile projects is scarce. Thirdly, GT has been used successfully to study the social nature of Agile teams [5, 10, 15].

Although Glaser and Strauss [6] do not encourage preliminary literature review and a predetermined research "problem", yet a basic phenomenon of interest need to be recognized. Using the classical GT, we commence our research by choosing the phenomenon of interest (i.e. Distributed Agile Projects). We explore the nature of distributed Agile projects to identify the key factors that determine the success or failure of distributed Agile projects, and to collate the strategies adopted by the Agile practitioners to manage distribute projects.

We conducted semi-structured, face-to-face interviews using open-ended questions with seven Agile practitioners from the USA, UK, Argentina, Brazil and Germany. The interviews were all pre-scheduled and voice recorded where permission was granted. The participants are Agile Coaches (Scrum Masters and XP Coaches) and Developers from the computer software industry. Each of the participants has at least three years of hands-on experience in working with globally distributed teams using combinations of XP and Scrum. The interview questions focused on the participants' experiences, and around their roles and responsibilities in their distributed projects. We asked the participants questions in regard to the key factors that determine the success or failure of distributed Agile projects according to their real life experiences and the strategies they adopted to manage those projects. During the interviews, no question were asked directly relating to the strategies or key success factors in distributed agile projects as these would have drawn biased responses from them. Due to privacy and ethical consideration, we will only identify our participants using the codes P1 to P7.

After an interview is done, we transcribed it. The transcripts are analysed line by line to identify the codes, concepts and categories [6]. The concepts are constantly compared as we code more data so that the emerging categories can be seen coming from the concepts. Since the categories emerge directly from the data, the resulting theory is grounded within the context of the research data. Although the end product of a GT research is called a *grounded theory*, it is in fact an explication of the concepts that emerge from the data [1]. This emergent *grounded theory* is more conceptual than descriptive, and it defines the relationships between the emergent concepts and categories. From our data analysis, three categories have emerged; one category for the key factors that determines the success or failure of distributed Agile projects, and two categories for the strategies adopted by the Agile practitioners.

3   Results

3.1   The Importance of Trust

Trust is valued by all our research participants. At the same time, they realize that trust is not easily generated and sustained in distributed projects:

> *"Trust is very important! And, it is very difficult to establish [trust] across globally distributed teams." – P5, Agile Coach.*

Agile practitioners need to realize the effect of lacking trust in a distributed team:

> *"...a lot of things get down to trust, and if you are not able to establish trust or maintain trust, then you will not be able to get along [with your team]. It is very difficult to repair trust and therefore distributed teams have to watch out that trust related relationship is alive." – P4, Agile Coach.*

Trust provides a significant bond in a team's relationship:

> *"... all the team members should [trust that] we are all one whole team" – P7, Agile Coach*

Our participants identified two strategies to generate and sustain trust in distributed teams: increasing effective communication and understanding cultural differences.

3.2   Increasing Effective Communication

Agile methods rely on continuous face-to-face meetings and active interaction amongst team members. Our participants described how increasing effective communication increases trust:

> *"You cannot do [distributed projects] without honest communication. It's a matter of establishing [the team's] trust." – P2, Agile Coach.*

Even in distributed projects, the best way to communicate effectively is face-to-face communication. It is important to get all team members or at the least the key members to meet each other during the project kickoff, and from time to time.

> *"There is a number of ways that organizations do to go about [establishing trust]. One of the ways is to fly people around; bring people in [for group meetings]. Face-to-face communication is still the best!" – P5, Scrum Master.*

> *"I believe it is really important that you do have always possibility that people meet [from] time to time. I think it is really hard to maintain trust, especially harder to establish trust without having a face-to-face communication." – P4, Agile Coach.*

In a distributed team, face-to-face meetings are expensive and difficult to schedule. Therefore, video-conferencing is often used as an alternative rather than e-mailing, instant messaging (IM), IRC or Wiki. Video-conferences capture the visual aspect of communication, such as body language, allowing the team to communicate more effectively:

"When we started using video conferencing, we found the visual aspect in communication is so important that we encourage teams to, at least once or twice a month, have video conferencing." – P1, Senior Developer.

"...the first 15 minutes [of video conferencing] was open time and you could talk about anything you want. And, that's when we started seeing a very strong team building ...and that became probably the strongest thing we did as far as building team ...a really good model for allowing the trust, the opportunity for relationship, to build" – P1, Senior Developer.

We found that bringing all distributed team members into team discussions, especially using face-to-face conversation or through video conferencing, and facilitating casual socializing between team members before meetings commence, was important for building and sustaining trust in a distributed project.

3.3 Understanding Cultural Differences

Cultural differences are often a problem in distributed projects. Our participants also described how understanding cultural differences increases trust:

"Always, always, always [we face] cultural differences; cultural understanding of what the different words mean; what different things mean. You can increase the interpersonal relationship and overcome some of the cultural barriers being faced." – P5, Scrum Master.

One of the cultural differences faced by our research participants is the difference in national culture of the team members (i.e. India and the USA):

"When [the Indian team members] speak English, they would try to speak faster than what's comfortable for them because their understanding is that American talk fast and they too talk fast. We tell them to speak slowly and deliberately, their English is much better and communication got much better. That was another thing we just discovered after having enough trust." – P1, Senior Developer.

"One of the experiences is when asked a question [to the Indian team], the answer is always 'Yes' even though they didn't know it. We came to understand that 'Yes' means 'Yes, I heard you', not 'Yes, I am going to do it' or 'Yes, I agree to it'. Some of the Indians have the habit of shaking their head in circular motion which means 'Yes, I heard you', not 'Yes, I agree'." – P1, Senior Developer.

Another aspect of cultural differences is each individual's culture. Individual team members need to make positive changes towards accepting and practicing Agile methods in distributed Agile projects:

"Agile mentality is a cultural change. So, if you can make that change, the team's velocity and quality will immediately double! People have to change the behavior to execute [Agile practices]." – P3, Scrum Master.

"The biggest challenge has been cultural issue. I've tried to push and encourage people, to work in a collaborative way; think [in a] collaborative way" – P6, Senior Developer.

Many misunderstandings and confusions in distributed teams are the results of cultural differences. Deep understanding of intercultural team relationships will make a positive contribution to the success of distributed Agile projects.

4 Related Work

Several recent studies have argued that trust is an important factor in determining the success or failure of globally distributed projects. Moe and Smite [11] consider that it is essential to understand the importance of trust, and to increase the level of trust in order to understand what leads to lacking trust, and the effect of lacking trust in a distributed team. Moe and Smith find that face-to-face meetings, active communication, and socialization are commonly used for building trust in globally distributed teams. Young and Terashima [16] pointed out that building trust in globally distributed teams was not easy but making team members comfortable allowed trust to build naturally.

5 Conclusion and Future Work

Trust is one of the key factors that determines the success or failure of distributed Agile projects. Our participants discussed how trust can be generated and sustained in distributed teams. We have described two strategies that distributed Agile teams have adopted to build trust: increasing effective communication and understanding cultural differences. These strategies reflect actual practice by the research participants. Since our research participants are experienced Agile practitioners, we believe that these could be valuable to other Agile practitioners.

References

1. Allan, G.: The Use of the Grounded Theory Methodology in Investigating Practitioners' Integration of COTS Components in Information Systems. In: 28th International Conference on Information Systems, Montreal (2007)
2. Ambler, S.W.: IT Project Success Rates Survey Results: (August 2007), http://www.ambysoft.com/surveys/success2007.html (December 15, 2009)
3. Beck, K.: Extreme Programming Explained: Embrace Change. Addison-Wesley, Reading (2000)

4. Dyba, T., Dingsoyr, T.: Empirical Studies of Agile Software Development: A Systematic Review. Information and Software Technology 50(9-10), 833–859 (2008)
5. Ferreira, J., Noble, J., Biddle, R.: Up-Front Interaction Design in Agile Development. In: Concas, G., Damiani, E., Scotto, M., Succi, G. (eds.) XP 2007. LNCS, vol. 4536, pp. 9–16. Springer, Heidelberg (2007)
6. Glaser, B., Strauss, A.: The Discovery of Grounded Theory. Adline, Chicago (1967)
7. Hossain, E., Babar, M.A., Verner, J.: Towards a Framework for Using Agile Approaches in Global Software Development. In: Bomarius, F., et al. (eds.) PROFES 2009. LNBIP, vol. 32, pp. 126–140. Springer, Heidelberg (2009)
8. Korkala, M., Abrahamsson, P.: Communication in Distributed Agile Development: A Case Study. In: 33rd EuroMicro Conference on Software Engineering and Advanced Application, pp. 203–210. IEEE Computer Society, USA (2007)
9. Manifesto for Agile Software Development, http://www.Agilemanifesto.org
10. Martin, A., Biddle, R., Noble, J.: The XP Customer Team: A Grounded Theory. In: Proceedings of IEEE 2009 Agile Conference, Chicago, USA, August 24-28, pp. 57–64. IEEE Computer Society, USA (2009)
11. Moe, N.B., Smite, D.: Understanding Lacking Trust in Global Software Teams: A Multicase Study. In: Münch, J., Abrahamsson, P. (eds.) PROFES 2007. LNCS, vol. 4589, pp. 20–34. Springer, Heidelberg (2007)
12. Paasivaara, M., Lassenius, C.: Could Global Software Development Benefit from Agile Methods? In: Casper, L. (ed.) ICGSE, International Conference on Global Software Engineering, pp. 109–113 (2006)
13. Schwaber, K., Beedle, M.: Agile Software Development with Scrum. Prentice-Hall, Upper Saddle River (2001)
14. Vax, M., Michaud, S.: Distributed Agile: Growing a Practice Together. In: Agile 2008, pp. 310–314. IEEE Computer Society, USA (2008)
15. Whitworth, E., Biddle, R.: The Social Nature of Agile Teams. In: Agile'07, pp. 26–36. IEEE Computer Society, USA (2007)
16. Young, C., Terashima, H.: How Did We Adapt Agile Processes to Our Distributed Development? In: Agile 2008, pp. 304–309. IEEE Computer Society, USA (2008)

Values and Assumptions Shaping Agile Development and User Experience Design in Practice

Jennifer Ferreira, Helen Sharp, and Hugh Robinson

The Open University, Walton Hall, Milton Keynes, MK7 6AA, UK
{j.ferreira,h.c.sharp,h.m.robinson}@open.ac.uk

Abstract. Previous discussions concerned with combining User Experience (UX) design and Agile development have either focused on integrating them as two separate processes, or on incorporating techniques from UX design into an Agile context. There is still no rigorous academic view on the nature of practice in this area. Further, the many and varied settings in which Agile developers and UX designers work together, and how those settings shape their work, remain largely unexplored. We conducted two field studies to address this. The results suggest that the values and assumptions of decision-makers external to the teams shape UX/Agile practice. The current focus on processes and techniques falls short of providing the insight necessary to improve practice. Instead, our results indicate that improvement requires further explication of contextual values.

Keywords: Agile, Scrum, User Experience Design, Organisations, Values, Assumptions, Field Studies.

1 Introduction

The growing literature concerned with combining User Experience (UX) design with Agile development has highlighted the importance of this topic and exposed various challenges faced by practitioners. To date, these discussions have either focused on integrating two separate processes (e.g. [1,2]), or on incorporating techniques from UX design into the Agile context (e.g. personas [3], or scenarios [4]). Our research takes a different perspective, instead seeking to understand how mature Agile teams integrate with an established UX design community, on a day-to-day basis, embedded within organisational contexts. Tolfo et al. [5] and Wendorff [6] draw connections between Agile teams and their wider contexts, i.e. the organisations in which they are embedded, but this remains largely unexplored in the UX/Agile literature. Our analysis highlighted the importance of values and assumptions underlying decisions made by individuals who were external to the teams. These values and assumptions were found to shape UX/Agile practice in the ways that we explain in this paper. Explicating the values and assumptions gives insights into differing views on how "best" to create quality software and how "best" to create software combining the skills of UX designers and Agile developers.

A. Sillitti et al. (Eds.): XP 2010, LNBIP 48, pp. 178–183, 2010.

2 Methodology

We collected data via observations of daily work, supported by semi-structured interviews and studies of documents, records and other tools. The detail of practice was documented via contemporaneous field notes, records of interviews and photographs/sketches of the physical layout of the work area. The researcher observed the day-to-day activities of Scrum development, attended meetings and during natural breaks in the work asked questions to build an understanding of events as they unfolded. Interviews were conducted with key team members, identified at the time of the observations. We spent one Sprint (2 weeks) observing the first team, Team1. We observed the second team, Team2 for 3 days at the start and 3 days at the end of their Sprint.

Data was analysed thematically, emphasising validation through the seeking of confirming and disconfirming instances. The thematic analysis was complemented by feedback sessions with the participants in our study. Their comments have subsequently been incorporated into the analysis presented here.

3 Shaped by Decisions

Our case studies were both based in the UK, located within organisations that were mature in their use of Scrum and were committed to UX design as a significant discipline. Much of our understanding about the work practices of Team1 and Team2 has been informed by the visible activities that we as observers were given access to. We learned that these visible activities were the consequences of decisions by management roles external to Team1 and Team2, that is, Team1 and Team2 were *intended* to function in the ways we observed.

Team1: Valuing separation. Team1 were part of a large media organisation and comprised 14 Agile developers and two UX designers. The UX designers were responsible for creating wireframes[1] and visual designs[2]. The developers were responsible for transforming the UX designs into functional software. It was common practice for the UX designers to create the UX designs without the Agile developers' involvement, and then to email them to the developers. The UX designers also did not take part in the Sprint planning meetings, standups or retrospectives and worked on the floor above the developers in the same building.

For Team1, transforming the UX designs into functional software occured as distinct phases of activity. In the first phase the developers spent significant time becoming familiar with the UX designs and building up an understanding of what the designs meant in terms of working software — asking each other: Why does it look like that? How are we going to do that? The second phase of activity was referred to by the developers as "gap analysis": inspecting the designs handed over by the UX designers, comparing it to the software already

---

[1] By *wireframe* we mean the popular design tool as described by Garrett [7].

[2] By *visual design* we mean a non-functional representation of the website under construction, which conveys content, layout and graphical information.

implemented and identifying mismatches between them. In the final phase the implementation work had to be added to the existing Scrum backlog. Again, the developers systematically went through the design and broke its implementation tasks up into story cards, discussed the story's priority and inserted it into the Scrum backlog. In all three phases, when clarifications or changes in the UX design were required, the developers made a note of it and requested "feedback meetings" with the UX designers. The developers were not adapting the UX design themselves — they relied on approval or redesigns from the UX designers.

A member of Team1 informed us that the decision to separate UX designers and developers was put into effect by management in the UX division. This was based on their view that UX designers work best when they are separated from the issues of software construction, which hamper their creativity. In light of this decision and our observations of practice, we can explain management's view on how to achieve quality software, as well as the place of UX design relative to software construction, in terms of the following value:

Value 1. *Agile and UX disciplines should remain separate.*

In this view, UX design exists independently from construction. Optimal UX design is created in a "design phase" in which UX designers are free to apply their creative energies without considerations about whether the designs can be turned into functional software. Agile development applies to the "construction phase" during which UX designs are implemented as functional software. Agile development becomes the mechanism through which UX designs are turned into functional software. This view has nothing to say about UX design issues emerging from software construction and, consequently, it has nothing to say about the notion of emerging requirements. The expectation is that any emerging issues will require minimal input from the UX designers.

Advocates for this approach include Cooper [8], Constantine [9] and Beyer et al. [10]. The advantages they cite include a holistic approach to UX design: "...the overall organization, the navigation, and the look-and-feel — must be designed to fit the full panoply of tasks to be covered" [9]; concentrating expertise within each discipline: "The great strength of agile methods is that they focus the engineers on doing what engineers do best" [10]; and that a separate UX design phase saves costs by determining the correct solution before costly changes in the implementation phase are required: "Iterating in construction just throws your money away."[3]

Team2: Valuing togetherness. Team2 were part of a small organisation developing solely for the mobile phone and were building a chat application. Team2 was composed of 5 Agile developers and one UX designer. The UX designer created non-functional representations, or "screen mock-ups" which the Agile developers could refer to as they created functional software. The team was working in the same building, but spread across three floors: The Project manager/Scrum

---

[3] From Alan Cooper's keynote at the Agile 2008 conference, which can be accessed at `http://www.cooper.com/journal/agile2008/`

master, Product owner and UX designer were seated in a room on the second floor, while the developers were seated together in a room on the ground floor.

With Team2 there were no distinct and visible UX/Agile integration activities to observe. Instead, we observed how all roles on the project were taking part in frequent discussions, creating awareness and sharing decision-making responsibilities. Conversations spontaneously occured during Scrum activities, as well as resulting from testing activities. Team2's relaxed interactions contrasted with the systematically planned activities that prompted the conversations between the developers and UX designers of Team1. During the course of the day, UX design issues were generated and dealt with alongside technical implementation issues. Breaking up and prioritising the UX design work was no more remarkable to Team2 than carding and prioritising the non-UX related work. The UX designer was continually aware of the implementation issues of their designs and the developers were constantly aware of UX design decisions. Every role on the project was involved in UX design discussions, which led to decisions that took into consideration both design values and technical constraints.

In the case of Team2, the managing director of the company informed us that he hired individuals who could fulfil the responsibilities of their main role, but who were also able to contribute outside their roles, or who could learn to do that. In light of the managing director's decision and the practice of Team2, we gain insight into another view on how UX design and Agile development should be combined. This can be expressed in terms of the following value:

Value 2. *Agile and UX disciplines should work as closely as possible.*

Instead of pitting UX design against construction, there is an emphasis on the contributions of various roles and their continuous interaction throughout the project. Value 2 hinges on the assumption that each role has a valuable contribution to make to the overall product. If this were not the case, Team2 may have engaged in activities where boundaries between roles and between disciplines were maintained. This view acknowledges that UX design issues, along with technical issues, emerge throughout the project and are dealt with via the ongoing interactions between all the roles on the project.

Those who support this view promote favourable environments in which project stakeholders continuously interact in ways that are helpful in progressing with their work — through consideration of the team as a whole irrespective of the skills of the individuals, or through enhancing collaboration. Beck and Andres include the practice *Whole Team* in eXtreme Programming [11]: "Include on the team people with all the skills and perspectives necessary for the project to succeed." Highsmith connects collaboration between roles with project success [12]: "Collaboration, not eliminating specialty roles — like business or product specialists — is the key to success." Miller has provided a process model in which UX design work is interleaved with implementation work throughout the duration of the project, thereby ensuring input from the UX design role throughout [1].

Interpretation. On the surface, the teams in this study seem rather similar: both teams were embedded in organisations that recognised the combination of

UX design and Agile develpment (Scrum) as essential for software development, both teams had the UX designers sitting on separate floors to the developers and both teams included UX design roles. Yet, despite these similarities their experiences of practice were quite different. Practice was shaped by decision-makers external to both teams, around values and assumptions concerning how best to create quality software. Team1 was built around a value promoting separation between UX design and Agile development disciplines, manifesting as a systematic, separatist approach to integrating and coordinating the two disciplines. Team2 was built around bringing UX design and Agile development closer together, manifesting as a subtle ongoing effort promoting shared awareness of UX design values and technical constraints, as well as shared decision-making. In the case of Team1, the developers were expected to take direction from the UX designers whereas in the case of Team2 the various roles were negotiating what that direction should be.

Finding echoes of these views in the literature demonstrates that the values and assumptions shaping the practice of Team1 and Team2 are not only peculiar to these teams. Rather, the values and assumptions we have uncovered, are situated within a wider ongoing debate about how Agile development and UX design should work together. Kent Beck, creator of eXtreme Programming (XP) and Alan Cooper, creator of Goal-Directed Design [8] famously debated the place of UX design in XP [13]. Their debate drew much attention from academics and practitioners in the years that followed. While Cooper advocated UX design being done entirely before any implementation, Beck argued for a phaseless approach in which implementation work is as cheap as UX design prototypes, in terms of effort and time. This set the tone for subsequent discussions on the topic and publications continue making reference to this debate (e.g. [14]). Our analysis has shown how that debate persists in practice.

4   Conclusions and Future Work

This paper has demonstrated how the practice of two teams was shaped by the values and assumptions of decision-makers external to those teams. The conclusions we draw are two-fold. First, articulating these values and assumptions has allowed them to be discussed and compared, so (in)forming part of a wider, ongoing debate about how UX design and Agile development should be combined. Second, we conclude that the integration of UX and Agile in practice can not be characterised solely by adaptations of different processes and techniques. Rather, our empirically-based results demonstrate clearly that the nature of UX/Agile practice is characterised strongly in terms of the values of the organisations in which they are embedded. Therefore, instead of merely prescribing processes and adding techniques, improving practice requires also a shift in focus to the explication of contextual values.

Future work will include a deeper interrogation of the literature to identify the source of these differing values and assumptions. This will include literature that focuses on non-Agile software development as well as Agile approaches.

References

1. Miller, L.: Case study of customer input for a successful product. In: ADC 2005: Proceedings of the 2005 Agile Development Conference, Denver, CO, USA, July 24-29, pp. 225–234. IEEE Computer Society Press, Los Alamitos (2005)
2. Patton, J.: Improving on agility: Adding usage-centered design to a typical agile software development environment. In: ForUse 2003: Proceedings of the Second International Conference on Usage-Centered Design, Portsmouth, NH, USA, October 18–22 (2003)
3. Haikara, J.: Usability in agile software development: Extending the interaction design process with personas approach. In: Concas, G., Damiani, E., Scotto, M., Succi, G. (eds.) XP 2007. LNCS, vol. 4536, pp. 153–156. Springer, Heidelberg (2007)
4. Obendorf, H., Finck, M.: Scenario-based usability engineering techniques in agile development processes. In: CHI 2008 extended abstracts on Human factors in computing systems, pp. 2159–2166. ACM, New York (2008)
5. Tolfo, C., Wazlawick, R.S., Ferreira, M.G.G., Forcellini, F.A.: Agile methods and organizational culture: Reflections about cultural levels. In: Softw. Process Improve. Pract. Published online in Wiley InterScience, DOI: 10.1002/spip.436
6. Wendorff, P.: Organisational culture in agile software development. In: Oivo, M., Komi-Sirviö, S. (eds.) PROFES 2002. LNCS, vol. 2559, pp. 145–157. Springer, Heidelberg (2002)
7. Garrett, J.J.: The elements of user experience: User-centered design for the web. Peachpit Press, Berkeley (2002)
8. Cooper, A.: The Inmates Are Running the Asylum: Why High Tech Products Drive Us Crazy and How to Restore the Sanity. SAMS, USA (1999)
9. Constantine, L.L.: Process agility and software usability: Toward lightweight usage-centered design. Information Age 8(2) (2001)
10. Beyer, H., Holtzblatt, K., Baker, L.: An agile customer-centered method: Rapid contextual design. In: Zannier, C., Erdogmus, H., Lindstrom, L. (eds.) XP/Agile Universe 2004. LNCS, vol. 3134, pp. 50–59. Springer, Heidelberg (2004)
11. Beck, K., Andres, C.: Extreme Programming Explained: Embrace Change, 2nd edn. Addison-Wesley, Boston (2004)
12. Highsmith, J.: Agile Project Management: Creating Innovative Products. Addison Wesley Professional, Reading (2009)
13. Nelson, E.: Extreme programming vs. interaction design (2002), http://web.archive.org/web/20030621112434/http://www.fawcette.com/interviews/beck_cooper/default.asp (Last accessed December 11, 2009)
14. Kollmann, J., Sharp, H., Blandford, A.: The importance of identity and vision to user experience designers on agile projects. In: Proceedings of the 2009 AGILE Conference, Chicago, IL, USA, August 24-28, pp. 11–18. IEEE Computer Society, Los Alamitos (2009)

Introducing Agile Methods in a Large Software Development Team: The Developers Changing Perspective

Mary Giblin[1], Padraig Brennan[2], and Chris Exton[3]

[1] Athlone Institute of Technology, Dublin Road, Athlone, Co. Westmeath, Ireland
[2] Ericsson Software Campus, Cornamaddy, Athlone, Co. Westmeath, Ireland
[3] University of Limerick, Plassey, Limerick,
Co. Limerick, Ireland
mgiblin@ait.ie, padraig.brennan@ericsson.com, chris.exton@ul.ie

Abstract. NW Soft Solutions Ltd. (a pseudonym) is a large software development unit that develops large-scale network centric software solutions. NW Soft Solutions Ltd decided to adopt an agile development methodology. Martin Fowler in his article "The New Methodology" [1], states that in his opinion *"Since agile methods are so fundamentally people-oriented, it's essential that you start with a team that wants to try and work in an agile way"*. Using NW Soft Solutions as a case study, this paper sets out to show how the developers attitudes towards agile methods change during the adoption phase. We see a shift in focus from agile practices at a superficial level to the core values that underpin agile methods.

Keywords: agile, methods, adoption, large organization, developers, mindset, expectations, concerns.

1 Introduction

In this paper we look at the initial expectations and concerns of the developers and investigate how their views changed throughout the agile adoption process. Our goal was to build up a picture first of all of the initial concerns and expectations of the developers with respect to agile. Then as the developers gain experience and practice the methodology we can analyze if those initial concerns and expectations materialized or not.

Agile is not a tool-based technique that can be easily rolled out across a large organization. It is value based and needs buy-in. Craig Larman points out that *"Many confuse the heart of 'Agile' with practices rather than values"* [2]. He also states that *"Yet increasingly, we see "top down" mandated or forced adoption of these methods or practices ("You will adopt Scrum"). These are signs of people not understanding the core values and principles of the Agile Manifesto, and instead, focusing on the myriad surface practices that may support agility. This is a grave mistake."* [2] In a large organization there has to be an element of "You will adopt Scrum". The challenge then is to shift the focus from the surface practices to the core values. As we

A. Sillitti et al. (Eds.): XP 2010, LNBIP 48, pp. 184–189, 2010.
© Springer-Verlag Berlin Heidelberg 2010

look at the changing views of the developers, we keep in mind the question *"Are they focused on surface practices or core values?"*

The remainder of this paper is organized as follows. In Section 2, we review some related work. In Section 3, we present our research methodology and data collection techniques. Section 4 describes some background information on NW Soft Solutions Ltd and its agile adoption strategy. Section 5 contains our findings and finally the implications and conclusion are in Section 6.

2 Related Work

Whitworth and Biddle [3, 4] examine motivational and social aspects of agile teams. A survey by Cockburn and Highsmith [5], for example, found that agile methodologies were rated higher than other methodologies in terms of morale. High degrees of motivation and job satisfaction can be experienced in large Scrum teams, as evidenced by Tessem and Maurer [6].

A number of papers, case studies and experience reports produced on large scale agile adoption show that the adoption process takes time [7] and [8].

Research by Lindvall et al. [9] indicates that many companies – in particular large companies – are approaching agile methods with a high degree of scepticism due to the conflicting data regarding *"in what environments and under what conditions agile methods work"*. In [10] Cohn and Ford state that *"Most developers respond to the proposed introduction of an agile process with the appropriate combination of skepticism, enthusiasm, and cautious optimism."* In a previous study [11] we looked at the initial concerns and expectations of developers and our conclusion was that with respect to that case study *"the developers are approaching agile adoption with an appropriate combination of realism, cautious optimism and enthusiasm."*

3 Research Methodologies and Data Collection

The purpose of this research was to determine how developers were responding to the introduction of an agile methodology. Given the objectives, it was decided that a qualitative approach should be applied.

The first stage of the data collection took place at the very beginning of the agile adoption process. It consisted of one-to-one audio-recorded interviews with developers. There were eighteen participants and the level of software design experience of the participants ranged from less than 1 to greater than 10 years. Their level of knowledge of agile methods ranged from none to a 1-day course, a 5-day course, up to having worked for a few weeks in a team piloting agile. The interviews were semi-structured and each interview lasted between 15 and 25 minutes. A guideline questionnaire using open questions was used to steer the interviews.

Afterwards the interviews were transcribed and using a Grounded Theory based approach, Qualitative Data Analysis Software (Weft QDA) was used to capture and code the main themes that emerged from the interviews.

The second stage of the data collection took place ten months later. This time we had seven one-to-one audio-recorded interviews with developers. We also conducted group interviews with eight feature teams, where a systems engineer, developer and tester represented the team. The one-to-one interviews lasted for 20 to 30 minutes and the team interviews lasted for between 1 and 1.5 hours each. Again the interviews were semi-structured and steered by a guideline questionnaire. This time the questionnaire used questions to focus on the main themes from the 1st stage analysis while also including some open questions allowing for new phenomena significant to the teams and participants to emerge. Again the interviews were transcribed and Weft QDA was used to code the interviews.

4   Overview of Organization and Adoption Process

NW Soft Solutions Ltd. is responsible for the design, development and maintenance of Network Management solutions for the Wireless Access and Core Network. It employs in excess of 250 software developers, testers and systems engineers in this development unit and is part of a large multi-national organization.

NW Soft Solutions Ltd. embarked on an ambitious change program that included the adoption of a mixture of XP practices (User Stories, Pair Programming, Test Driven Development, Continuous Integration, Cross-Functional Teams) and Scrum (Sprints, Product Backlog, Estimating Effort, Product Owner, Scrum Masters, Daily Stand Up Meetings).

5   Results and Findings

The following sections outline key aspects of the comparison between the themes in the 1st stage of interviews and the stage 2 interviews.

5.1   Main Issues Raised Initially in the First Stage Interview

Documentation in general: Initially developers believed that the introduction of agile would result in less "non-code" documentation. Their existing process was document heavy and less documentation would be welcomed. They felt that with agile, more face-to-face communication and less "hard handovers" would result in the need for less documents. However in the agile way of working, there was only a slight reduction in the total amount of documentation but not by the amount they had initially anticipated.

Design Analysis Documentation: In the pre-Agile process, developers strongly indicated that they didn't see a value in some of the Design Analysis documents because the solution they would implement in code would invariably differ from what they specified in Design Analysis. However in the Agile process their view changed and they found the Design Analysis much more useful. They felt this was because it was done closer in time to the coding and focussed on smaller work items and also in a less formal way.

Unit Testing and Code Inspections: Developers felt that in the old process, time ran out for unit testing and code inspections and the practices of pair programming and test driven development should improve the situation.

However when using agile methods, there was a variation among feature teams with respect to the amount of test driven development employed and to the extent that pair programming was implemented and this expectation didn't materialize directly. There were issues with the availability of test harnesses for legacy code and difficulty automating GUI tests and while there was still work to be done in this area, the focus on quality heightened dramatically.

But teams that didn't have such good test coverage were becoming aware that they needed to reduce dependencies in they system and have less coupling in order to improve the testability.

Pair Programming

In the first stage interviews, developers expressed the view that there was a benefit in pair programming mainly from a knowledge transfer point of view, but there was much concern regarding personality conflicts.

Pair programming was on average used only about 30% of the time and generally between experienced and inexperienced pairs, but from analyzing the second stage interviews the main barrier to using it was pressure on resources. The teams felt that they could not afford the time to do it in all cases. The issue of personality conflicts was no longer seen as a problem.

Test Driven Development: When we conducted the initial interviews, a number of developers had completed a training course on test driven development and they felt that it would improve quality, but they were concerned about the lack of test harnesses for the legacy code and they were aware that TDD necessitated a change in mindset.

At the second interview stage the thinking in this area hadn't really changed. The lack of test harnesses for the legacy code was an issue and developers were having some difficultly with changing their way of working to write the test case first. However, there was a realization that too many inter-dependencies in the system architecture were making the stubbing of interfaces more difficult.

Frequent Deliveries: The initial reaction was that the frequent deliveries associated with agile methods would result in a more pressurised environment.

This concern did not actually materialise or at least not in the negative sense. In fact the conclusion was the agile environment was less pressurised, because it eliminated the big bang style delivery and integration that existed previously.

Open Plan and Co-location: In the initial interviews the subject of having an open plan team area provoked a very negative response, but after working with agile methods for a period of time, the requirement for co-location was strongly recognised by the developers. The work areas were not open plan as prescribed by agile, but also in some cases the Systems Engineer was not co-located with the Developers and Testers. Generally the Developers and the Testers were physically close together. The lack of co-location was highlighted as an issue showing a recognition of the value of spontaneous communication and an acknowledgement of what could be lost if conversations were not "*overheard*".

5.2 New Emerging Themes

The second round of interviews contained some open questions that allowed developers to give their views on

- o The best thing about working in an agile way
- o Any other negative issues related to agile
- o Preferences to continue to work in the agile way.

Best Aspect of Agile: When asked open questions on the benefits of agile, improved communication, more flexible way of working and quicker feedback were all seen as positive.

Negative aspects of agile: When asked if there were negative aspects to agile, the developers or teams didn't come up with specific aspects of agile itself that they felt were negative, but pointed out aspects of agile that they had to improve on to complete the transition to an agile way of working.

Continuing with agile: Out of all the developers and teams interviewed, apart from one team that was inconclusive, all of them most definitely wanted to continue working in an agile way. They felt that the adoption of agile methods was a correct choice for the organisation.

6 Conclusions and Summary

In summary we can conclude that in this study, developers initial concerns and expectations were mainly related to themselves as individuals and are primarily on a superficial level related to the practices. For example, the concerns that the open plan would be distracting, pair programming resulting in personality conflicts, less documentation to do, more pressure due to deadlines. What happened in reality was that these individualistic concerns didn't materialize. Take the documentation example; the document that developers initially felt was worthless became a valuable document in the agile world.

After working with agile for a period of time, the focus of the developer's shifted from individual concerns to principles and values that concern the whole team.

In [12], Kent Beck outlines the differences between values, principles and practices. We see that the thinking of the developers shifted from a surface level opinion about the practices, and after working in an agile way, the interviews show an emerging understanding of the core values and principles. *"XP embraces five values to guide development: communication, simplicity, feedback, courage and respect."* [12]. From Section 5, we see evidence of the appreciation of *communication* and *quick feedback*, which were mentioned as the biggest benefits of agile. Simplicity was not explicitly mentioned in the interviews, but the developers see the need for less class dependencies and focus on architecture with respect to making the unit testing more robust. They realized that the division of user stories makes them *"more manageable"*. *"Sometimes courage manifests as a bias to action. If you know what the problem is, do something about it."*[12] Developers are taking initiatives, and continuously trying to improve their processes. And *respect* is evident, as the contribution of the whole team working together was been acknowledged.

These results lead to a deeper understanding of how the adoption of agile methods can affect the developers in a large software development team.

References

1. Fowler, M.: The New Methodology,
   `http://martinfowler.com/articles/newMethodology.html,200`
   (Last accessed October 1, 2009)
2. Elssamadisy, A.: Patterns of Agile Practice Adoption the Technical Cluster, C4Media 2007 (2007)
3. Whitworth, E., Biddle, R.: Motivation and Cohesion in Agile Teams. In: Concas, G., Damiani, E., Scotto, M., Succi, G. (eds.) XP 2007. LNCS, vol. 4536, pp. 62–69. Springer, Heidelberg (2007)
4. Whitworth, E., Biddle, R.: The Social Nature of Agile Teams. In: Proceedings of Agile 2007, pp. 26–36 (2007)
5. Cockburn, A., Highsmith, J.: Agile software development: The people factor. IEEE Computer 34 (2001)
6. Tessem, B., Maurer, F.: Job Satisfaction and Motivation in a Large Agile Team
7. Goos, J., Mellisse, A.: An Ericsson example of enterprise class agility. In: Proceedings of Agile 2008 conference, pp. 154–159 (2008)
8. Sureshchandra, K., Shrinivasavadhani, J.: Moving from Waterfall to Agile. In: Proceedings of Agile 2008 conference, pp. 97–101 (2008)
9. Lindvall, M., Muthig, D., Dagnino, A., Wallin, C., Stupperich, M., Kiefer, D., May, J., Kahkonen, T.: Agile Software Development in Large Organisations. Computer 37(12), 26–34 (2004)
10. Cohn, M., Ford, D.: Introducing an Agile Process to an Organization [Software Developer], vol. 36(6), pp. 74–78. IEEE Computer Society, Los Alamitos (2003)
11. Giblin, M., Brennan, P., Exton, C.: A Theme Based Analysis of the Concerns and Expectations of the Developers Prior to the Introduction of An Agile Development Methodology in a Large Software Development Team. In: Proceedings of CAIA 2009. Wiley Publishing, Chichester (2009)
12. Beck, K.: Extreme Programming Explained-Embrace Change. Addison-Wesley, Reading (2004)

A Systematic and Lightweight Method to Identify Dependencies between User Stories

Arturo Gomez[1], Gema Rueda[1], and Pedro P. Alarcón[2]

[1] School of Computing
Blekinge Institute of Technology (BTH), Sweden
{argo09,geru09}@student.bth.se
[2] E.U. Informática
Technical University of Madrid (UPM), Madrid, Spain
pedrop.alarcon@eui.upm.es

Abstract. The order in which user stories are implemented can have a significant influence on the overall development cost. The total cost of developing a system is non commutative because of dependencies between user stories. This paper presents a systematic and lightweight method to identify dependencies between user stories, aiding in the reduction of their impact on the overall project cost. Initial architecture models of the software product are suggested to identify dependencies. Using the method proposed does not add extra load to the project and reinforces the value of the architecture, facilitates the planning and improves the response to changes.

Keywords: User Stories Dependencies, Agile Development, Dependencies Identification Method, Non Commutative Implementation Cost.

1 Introduction

The elements that comprise the system under construction interact with each other, establishing dependencies among them [1]. In Figure 1, element A requires element B, generating a dependency between them. Such dependencies are naturally inherited by the user stories (US_i cannot be implemented until US_j is implemented). Therefore, the natural dependencies between User Stories (US from now on) should be accepted as inevitable. In fact, only a fifth of the requirements can be considered with no dependencies [2]. The existence of dependencies between USs makes necessary to have some implemented before others [2] [3] [1] [4]. If the order of user stories implementation does not take into account these dependencies it may have a large number of preventable refactoring, increasing the total cost of the project needlessly. Identifying beforehand the dependencies increases the ability to effectively deal with changes. Therefore light systematic mechanisms, as shown in this paper, are needed to help identify dependencies between USs.

The rest of the paper is structured as follows. The second section describes the problem of dependencies. The third section defines the concept of dependency

A. Sillitti et al. (Eds.): XP 2010, LNBIP 48, pp. 190–195, 2010.
© Springer-Verlag Berlin Heidelberg 2010

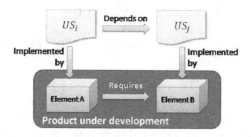

Fig. 1. Inherited dependencies by user stories

between user stories. The fourth section describes the method to identify dependencies. The fifth section presents an example applying the method proposed. The sixth section presents related work. Finally, the conclusions are listed.

2   Problem Description

The existence of dependencies between USs hampers planning [5] [4]. Not considering them increases the chances of not complying with the release plans [6]. Therefore, the sequencing of USs is seen as a challenge [7]. Depending on the established implementation order of USs the number of refactoring may increase. For example, suppose that at time t, once the user story US_i has been implemented, there is a database (DB) in production with the entity T_1 and primary key k_1. At time t+1, after implementing US_j, the data model shown in Figure 2 is obtained, in which the primary key of the entity T_2 is k_2. Given the cardinality, the primary key attributes from T_2 become part of the table generated for entity T_1. This will require a refactoring of the DB and all components that access T_1 and an update of all rows of table T_1. If US_j had been implemented before US_i there would be no need to refactor, so the refactoring cost would be zero. Hence, due to the existing dependencies, the total cost of developing a system depends on the order in which the USs are implemented. Therefore, the total cost of developing a system is non commutative. Generalizing, if US_j depends on US_i and being C the cost function of implementing a user story in a given time t, considering RC as the cost of carrying out a determined refactoring j, then: $C(US_j)_t + C(US_i)_{t+1} = C(US_i)_t + C(US_j)_{t+1} + RC_j$. Note that refactoring can become a complex process with a very high cost [8], which is directly proportional to the number of implemented user stories [9].

Fig. 2. DB in time = t+1

3   User Stories Dependency Concept

This section defines the concepts: Dependency on key (Definition 1) and dependency on service (Definition 2).

Definition 1. Considering an agile project P, and E as the data model of P. Given that US_i and US_j are user stories from P that respectively require data represented in the entities E_i and E_j belonging to E. If after E is transformed into the target model (usually relational model) the data structure generated for the entity E_i adds the primary key attributes of the entity E_j, then US_i has a dependency on key with US_j, and it is expressed as: $US_j \rightarrow US_i$. In Figure 3, the following dependencies on key are found: $K=\{US_2 \rightarrow US_1\}$.

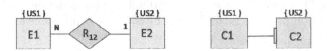

Fig. 3. Example of simplified conceptual data and component diagram

Definition 2. Considering an agile project P which has been represented by a component diagram C. Given that US_i and US_j are user stories from P, which are implemented respectively in the components C_i and C_j included in C. The user history US_i has a dependency on service with respect to US_j, if and only if C_j implements at least one service used by US_i in C_i, expressed as: $US_j \rightarrow US_i$. In Figure 3, the following dependencies on service are found: $S=\{US_2 \rightarrow US_1\}$.

Based on the above definitions, the complete set of depencencies is defined as: $D=\{K \cup S\}$. Note that D can vary because of changes in user stories.

4   User Stories Dependencies Identification Method

The dependencies cannot be clearly inferred from the definition of USs. Building an initial architecture (data and component models) helps to identify them. Both models are transversal to the USs, see architectural models boxes at Figure 4. The evaluation of the interaction of each user story with both models allows the identification of possible dependencies. The proposed method identifies USs dependencies. Its duration depends on the size of the project and the presence of the whole team is recommended during its application to gain a project overview. It is lightweight in the sense that it does not add load to the project, since the activities or products needed are carried out in initial stages. If the USs or models change, the identification method should be executed before starting the next iteration (see Figure 4).

To identify dependencies between USs: First, a quick study of user stories defined so far is suggested, generating a simplified data model (without attributes). The use of the entity-relationship model is recommended since it helps to generate an overall view of the system. It is usualy generated in software projects and

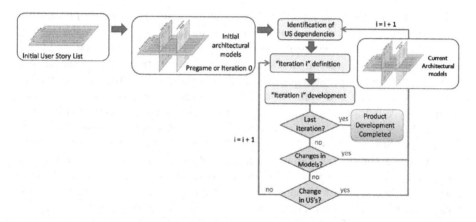

Fig. 4. Proposed method in iterative life cycle

therefore it does not add additional load. Notice that this diagram is not an objective in itself. Its purpose is to identify the elements from the data model that each user story requires to be implemented, writing its identifier next to the data element required. For example, brackets can be used as shown in Figure 3. Second, establish the set of dependencies on key from the diagram, according to Section 3. To do so, for example, the transformation rules from an entity-relationship model to relational model can be used. Thus, given two elements A and B of a model M, if element A migrates the primary key attributes to element B, then the user stories related to B will have dependency on key of the user stories related to A.

To identify dependencies on service it is proposed: First, use a simplified component model which will represent the list of user stories identified so far. This diagram will include the components identified as well as the service relationship between them. It has a high level of abstraction that allows to easily identify the dependencies on service. Its creation provides a global perspective of the system to the team, which is important for understanding the dependencies. As in the previous case, this diagram is not a goal in itself. It can be replaced by any other that allows identification of such dependencies. The USs involved in the implementation of each component should be written within brackets (see Figure 3). Second, identify the set of dependencies on service from the diagram, according to Section 3. Thus, given two elements A and B of a model M, if the element A implements a service required by B, then the user stories related to B will depend on the user stories related to A.

The mechanism to register dependencies is to record them using a directed graph like the one shown in Figure 5. Initially, all the USs are represented as disconnected vertices. As soon as $US_j \rightarrow US_i$ is identified, an edge pointing US_i is drawn between vertices US_j and US_i. This representation informs quickly about the dependencies among USs. Additionally, it helps to quickly identify dependency chains between USs. The graph generated can be used as basis to support planning or as an input for well known algorithms [1] [3] to generate an implementation sequence that reduces the impact of dependencies.

When interpreting the results, a vertex without incoming edges means that this user story has no dependencies. If a vertex (US_i) has incoming edges but these edges come from vertices representing USs already developed, it is also considered that US_i has no dependencies. From the technical perspective, a user story without dependencies can be implemented at any time or assigned at any release and business value would be the main factor when prioritizing and planning it. When planning, the development team must be aware that if a user story (US_i) is developed and it depends on other USs not developed yet, there could be additional costs associated with refactoring and other technical risks. The customer should be warned with this information before prioritizing the user story. When a user story changes or a new one is introduced, the directed graph must be checked to identify the USs that depend on the changed or new user story. The architectural elements associated to these dependent user stories are more likely to be impacted by this change. Therefore, the set of architectural elements that are likely to change is reduced, facilitating the response to change.

5   Example of Use

This section focuses on a subset of USs extracted from a real project in which the authors of this paper participated. This project included the development of a software tool called Agile Management Tool (AMT). The subset of user stories selected from AMT project is: US_1 (Create User Stories); US_2 (Create Iterations); US_3 (Create Projects). Due to the paper's size restrictions this section focuses only on the data model (see Figure 5). Following the identification method proposed, references to USs related to each model element have been included. Notice that when the simplified data model is transformed into relational tables, the primary key attributes from the entity *Project* (related to US_3) will migrate into the entity *User Story* (related to US_1), which implies that US_1 depends on US_3, therefore an edge from US_3 vertex pointing to US_1 vertex must be drawn. This way the team will continue identifying dependencies, generating at the end a graph like the one showed on Figure 5. Based on it, the dependency set is: D={$US_3 \rightarrow US_1$; $US_3 \rightarrow US_2$; $US_2 \rightarrow US_1$}. Then, from the technical point of view, since every user story depends on US_3, the recommendation to the customer would be implementing US_3 first. Otherwise, the cost of refactoring should be added to the cost of developing US_1, US_2 and US_3.

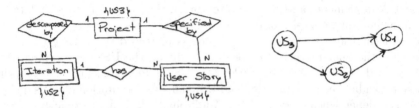

Fig. 5. Original scanned data model from selected US

6 Related Work

Some well known methods consider dependencies such as IFM [1] and Evolve [4][3]. Nevertheless none of them provide a systematic mechanism for identifying dependencies between user stories as the method proposed in this paper. In [2] is proposed a method to identify dependencies but it relies on pairwise assessment among the requirements. This is applicable for a small number of requirements but requires too much effort facing a large number of requirements. Mike Cohn states that if two user stories are dependent they must merge [5]. However, in practice it has been seen that large user stories that cannot be completed in one iteration, hinder the feeling of progress and therefore team motivation [7].

7 Conclusions

The implementation cost is non commutative due to the existence of dependencies between user stories. If this fact is obviated, it could generate overrun in the development of a product. This overrun comes from unnecessary refactoring that could have been avoided with a different implementation order. Two definitions of dependencies have been provided: dependency on key and dependency on service. This paper contributes with a very lightweight method that identifies dependencies between user stories, helping the planning and reducing the technical risks of the project, while reinforcing the architectural value as a lateral effect. Furthermore, if this method is applied at the beginning of the project, it helps to create a common perspective of the system. This method has been designed to fit in an agile environment, following the agile values and principles.

References

1. Denne, M., Cleland-Huang, J.: The incremental funding method: Data-driven software development. IEEE Software 21(3), 39–47 (2004)
2. Carlshamre, P., Sandah, K., et al.: An industrial survey of requirements interdependencies in software product release planning. In: RE 2001, pp. 84–91 (2001)
3. Greer, D., Ruhe, G.: Software release planning: an evolutionary and iterative approach. Information and Software Technology 46, 243–253 (2004)
4. Logue, K., McDaid, K.: Handling uncertainty in agile requirement prioritization and scheduling using statistical simulation. In: Agile 2008, pp. 73–82. IEEE CS, Los Alamitos (2008)
5. Cohn, M.: User Stories Applied: For Agile Software Development (The Addison-Wesley Signature Series), March. Addison-Wesley Professional, Reading (2004)
6. Babinet, E., Ramanathan, R.: Dependency management in a large agile environment. In: AGILE Conference, pp. 401–406 (2008)
7. Ton, H.: A strategy for balancing business value and story size. In: Proceedings of the AGILE 2007, Washington, DC, USA, pp. 279–284. IEEE Computer Society Press, Los Alamitos (2007)
8. Ambler, S.W., Sadalage, P.J.: Refactoring Databases: Evolutionary Database Design. Addison-Wesley Professional, Reading (March 2006)
9. Boehm, B., Turner, R.: Balancing Agility and Discipline: A Guide for the Perplexed. Addison-Wesley Professional, Reading (August 2003)

Agile Documents: Toward Successful Creation of Effective Documentation

Omar Mazni[1], Syed-Abdullah Sharifah-Lailee[2], and Yasin Azman[1]

[1] Applied Sciences Division, UUM College of Arts and Sciences,
Universiti Utara Malaysia, 06010 UUM Sintok, Kedah, Malaysia
{mazni,yazman}@uum.edu.my
[2] Department of Computer Sciences, Faculty of Computer Sciences and Mathematics,
Universiti Teknologi MARA, Arau Campus, 02600 Arau, Malaysia
shlailee@perlis.uitm.edu.my

Abstract. This paper presents the initial findings from an action research study in applying Extreme Programming (XP) activities and generating agile documents. The study was carried out in a university computer centre in Malaysia. Data were collected from four software engineering (SE) teams in this centre. Simple and practical agile documents were successfully created during the software project and received positive feedbacks amongst team members and the centre management. The results of this study suggest that a right combination of personality types in a team can influence team performance. These findings offer valuable insights into aspects related to agile approach and documentation that can be explored and understood to suit an organizational culture and team personality types.

Keywords: Agile documents, XP, SE teams, culture, personality types.

1 Introduction

Organizations need evidence that agile methodology can be well suited and applied in their working environment. Therefore, there is increasing interest among SE researchers in conducting empirical studies from industrial perspectives to provide more empirical evidences. Agile researchers in the industry were more focused on the agile perception [1-3] and comparison studies [4-6]. However, there are few studies on effectiveness of agile documentations in software industry.

Even though agile is people-oriented, and communication plays a vital role in software development, it does not mean that written documentation should be neglected. However, too much documentation is cumbersome and time consuming to produce and read. Often, nobody appreciates good documents until maintenance is needed. The culture of end-product orientation often pushed the documentation effort to a back burner. Therefore, this paper presents the authors' approach in educating and training four SE teams of one university computer centre in Malaysia to generate agile documents while simultaneously developing new projects.

A. Sillitti et al. (Eds.): XP 2010, LNBIP 48, pp. 196–201, 2010.

2   Related Works

The suitability of using agile practices in large organization was conducted by Lindvall et al. [7] at ABB, DaimlerChrysler, Motorola and Nokia. The study showed that XP allowed developers to gain positive experiences because this methodology was easy to understand and therefore increased team morale. However, these organizations needed to define an agile process tailored to their current software practices to avoid conflict of interests in developing software.

Sillitti, Ceschi, Russo, and Succi [4] conducted a survey of Italian companies. The study showed that agile companies were more customers centric and flexible, and therefore able to have satisfactory relationships with customer. Study by Greening [1] reported his challenging experiences in adopting XP practices in a document-centric company. Finally, after experiencing XP approach, the company decided to adjust their too many documents strategy and cater only high level documentation.

Often, software engineering teams failed to maintain software documentation as reported by Lethbridge, Singer, and Forward [8] because the surveyed SE teams were convinced that out-dated documentations remain useful. To accommodate this scenario, Selic [9] suggested that stable design requires more comprehensive documentation, but new project requires only adequate information to serve as communication purposes.

3   Methods

A university computer centre in Malaysia was selected for this study. In this study, four SE teams consisted of eight system analysts and sixteen programmers were selected to participate in 'Embracing XP Projects'. This project came about because one of the computer centre deputy heads who was in charged of applications was an 'XP convert'. The manager's prior involvement with XP started when he was one of the project advisor in earlier studies [10, 11]. He was impressed with XP effective documentation that were simple and practical because existing situation demands the computer centre to adopt this approach.

All SE teams were sent to agile workshops before the projects started since the approach was new to them. XP was chosen in this study because it is the most prevalent in agile software development methodology [12]. The workshops addressed the theory and the practical aspects of agile software development. During this workshop, agile documentation was introduced to facilitate team members in documenting the project development works. The documentation consisted of Unified Modeling Language (UML) use case diagram, entity-relationship diagram (ERD), object files, and interface designs.

3.1   Data Collection and Analysis

This study used action research approach. Data were collected through a series of interviews, short-term observations, and a personality questionnaire. The action research approach allows a flexible and responsive strategy that helps improve the learning experiences and practices of the participants. The observations were carried out for six-months to improve the understanding of the working culture in the computer centre under a natural setting. Interviews were carried out using semi-structured interviews with selected participants to ascertain that each team understood and applied XP practices as much as possible and document the projects meticulously. Every interview session lasted between five to 10 minutes. The interviews were audio recorded and transcribed after each session. Follow-up questions were asked via face-to-face meetings when clarifications were necessary. During the interview sessions, the problems that were encountered were discussed. Software quality delivered was measured using software quality metrics [13]. The quality was assessed by the top management of computer centre.

The Jung Myers-Briggs (MBTI) personality questionnaire test was used to assess the personality of each software developer. The personality test result was a combination of four dimensional pairs, which are Introversion (I) and Extroversion (E), Sensing (S) and Intuitive (N), Thinking (T) and Feeling (F), and Judging (J) and Perceiving (P). These four dimensions then make up 16 possible combinations of personality types as depicted in Table 1.

Table 1. The 16 MBTI personality types

ISTJ	ISFJ	INFJ	INTJ
ISTP	ISFP	INFP	INTP
ESTP	ESFP	ENFP	ENTP
ESTJ	ESFJ	ENFJ	ENTJ

A person can be classified into one of the 16 personality types based on the largest scale obtained. For example, a person scoring higher on Introversion (I) than Extroversion (E), Sensing (S) than Intuition (N), Thinking (T) than Feeling (F), and Judging (J) than Perceiving (P) would be classified as an ISTJ.

4 Results and Discussion

The results were discussed based on data gathered during this study. It explained factors contributing to the successful creation of agile documentations.

4.1 Creating Effective Agile Documents

During the planning game activities, all teams were able to discuss and write story cards. Even though some teams claimed the activity was easy, others found the story cards to be cumbersome. It was observed that the story card acts only as a foundation for starting a project, but as the project progressed, the story cards were not used because members realized, that story cards were difficult for tracking requirements and rescheduling projects. Instead, team members were more comfortable using interface design, because interface designs are diagrammatic in nature. Therefore, both developers and clients were able to discuss and visualize requirements better.

A decision was made to compile and document use cases, ERD, interface designs, and object files into formal project documentation called a Simple Design Document (SiDD). This documentation allowed work to be completed simultaneously, and therefore, team members were not burdened with additional documentation tasks. The documentations tasks can be upgraded easily by updating interface design and linking the source codes simultaneously during the design and coding phase. The simple and practical agile documents were appreciated and commented on by the members and management teams:

> *"It [simple design document] was easy, because it was simpler from what we have done before...last time we completed the documentation just for the sake of documentation but not to use or refer to..."* [Team member1]

> *"Let say, if after this other people take over, they will see the system flow, to find the scripts [source codes] is easy ....because it is link like this [the simple design document]* [Team member2]

> *"We have more current systems that do not have documentation, so we will use this approach [simple design documentation] as reference..."* [Application manager]

Document effectiveness was measured using Producing Quality Technical Information (PQTI) selected matrix [14]. The quality metrics were understandability, usability, and accessibility. The effective documentation was assessed by the organization manager. The management was very satisfied and confident that the approach can assist the centre in applying simple and practical system documentation.

4.2 Personality Factors toward Successful Creation of Agile Documents

Researchers showed that personality types play an important role in adapting new technology [15] and organizational change [16]. In this study, it was observed that a combination of personalities in a team encouraged XP to be easily accepted by the team members.

A majority of the members were combinations of Introverted-Intuitive-Thinking-Judging, INTJ; Introverted-Sensing-Feeling-Judging, ISFJ; Extroverted-Sensing-Feeling-Judging, ESFJ; and Introverted-Intuitive-Feeling-Judging, INFJ, personality types. Detailed combinations of personality types for each team are shown in Table 2. Earlier research has demonstrated that the predominant personality types of information technology (IT) professionals are introverted and thinking people [17-19]. In this study, Team C was the best team able to deliver effective documentation and quality software according to the deadline. A good combination of members' personalities for this team ensured that the team was stable and able to proceed with their project successfully. The team combinations in this study allowed the members to be more courageous and innovative when adjusting to the agile documentation and XP practices. This observation was supported by research on personality and job performance [20].

Table 2. Composition of SE team's personality types

TEAM	Member1	Member2	Member3	Member4	Member5	Member6
Team A	ISTJ	INTJ	ENTJ	INTJ	INTJ	ESFJ
Team B	ESFJ	ENTJ	INTJ	ISFJ	INFJ	INFJ
Team C	ISFJ	INFJ	INTJ	ESFJ	ISFJ	ENFJ
Team D	ESFJ	ESTJ	ESTJ	INTJ	ENFJ	ISTJ

5 Conclusion and Future Works

This study reported the initial findings of an action research study in applying XP practices and thereby generating simple but effective agile documents.

Agile documents were successfully created because they were generated simultaneously during the design and coding of the projects. Due to the simple and practical way of creating these documents, the person in-charge of documentation acknowledged that creating agile documents was not time consuming and troublesome.

A combination of good personality types amongst team members ensured that XP activities were easily accepted. Personality types, effective methodology, and organizational culture are important factors that must be considered in generating innovative teams, creating effective work culture, and delivering quality software. Further studies of these relationships would be valuable in creating a new generation of creative and innovative SE teams.

Future works will include analyzing psychological data, such as personality types, and work related well being in relations to software methodology. The study will look into how these data affected the acceptance of the evolving XP activities in Asian countries.

Acknowledgments. The authors would like to thank the computer centre management, staff and participants for their support and cooperation during this study.

References

1. Greening, J.: Launching extreme programming at a process-intensive company. IEEE Software 18, 27–33 (2001)
2. Aveling, B.: XP Lite Considered Harmful? In: Eckstein, J., Baumeister, H. (eds.) XP 2004. LNCS, vol. 3092, pp. 94–103. Springer, Heidelberg (2004)
3. Rasmusson, J.: Introducing XP into Greenfield Projects: Lessons Learned. IEEE Software 20, 21–28 (2003)
4. Sillitti, A., Ceschi, M., Russo, B., Succi, G.: Managing Uncertainty in Requirements: a Survey in Documentation-driven and Agile Companies. In: 11th IEEE International Software Metrics Symposium (METRICS 2005), pp. 10–17. IEEE Press, Como (2005)
5. Ilieva, S., Ivanov, P., Stefanova, E.: Analyses of an Agile Methodology Implementation. In: 30th EUROMICRO Conference (EUROMICRO 2004), pp. 326–333. IEEE Press, France (2004)

6. Layman, L.: Empirical Investigation of the Impact of Extreme Programming Practices on Software Projects. In: Conference on Object-Oriented Programming Systems Languages and Applications, pp. 328–329. ACM, New York (2004)
7. Lindvall, M., Muthig, D., Dagnino, A., Wallin, C., Stupperich, M., Kiefer, D., May, J., Kahkonen, T.: Agile Software Development in Large Organizations. Computer 37, 26–34 (2004)
8. Lethbridge, T.C., Singer, J., Forward, A.: How Software Engineers Use Documentation: The State of the Practice. IEEE Software 20, 35–39 (2003)
9. Selic, B.: Agile Documentation, Anyone? IEEE Software 26, 11–12 (2009)
10. Mazni, O., Sharifah-Lailee, S.-A., Holcombe, M.: Being Agile in Classroom: An Improvement to Learning Programming. In: National ICT in Education Seminar. Universiti Perguruan Sultan Idris (UPSI), Ipoh, Malaysia (2009)
11. Sharifah-Lailee, S.-A., Mazni, O., Mohd-Nasir, A.H., Che-Latifah, I., Kamaruzaman, J.: Positive Affects Inducer on Software Quality. Computer and Information Science 2, 64–70 (2009)
12. Cockburn, A.: Agile Software Development: A Cooperative Game, 2nd edn. Addison Wesley, USA (2007)
13. Pressman, R.S., Lowe, D.: Web Engineering: A Practitioner's Approach. McGraw-Hill International Edition, Singapore (2009)
14. Smart, K.L.: Assessing Quality Documents. ACM Journal of Computer Documentation 26, 130–140 (2002)
15. Vishwanath, A.: Impact of personality on technology adoption: An empirical model. Journal of the American Society for Information Science and Technology 56, 803–811 (2005)
16. Vakola, M., Tsaousis, I., Nikolaou, I.: The role of emotional intelligence and personality variables on attitudes towards organisational change. Journal of Managerial Psychology 19, 88–110 (2004)
17. Smith, D.C.: The Personality of the systems analyst: an investigation. ACM SIGCPR Computer Personnel 12, 12–14 (1989)
18. Capretz, L.: Implications of MBTI in Software Engineering Education. ACM SIGCSE Bulletin 34, 134–137 (2002)
19. Mourmant, G., Gallivan, M.: How personality type influences decision paths in the unfolding model of voluntary job turnover: an application to IS professionals. In: Conference on Computer Personnel Research: the Global information Technology Workforce. SIGMIS-CPR 2007, pp. 134–143. ACM, St. Louis, Missouri (2007)
20. Capretz, L.F., Ahmed, F.: Making Sense of Software Development and Personality Types. IT Professional 12, 6–13 (2010)

Structuring Complexity Issues for Efficient Realization of Agile Business Requirements in Distributed Environments

Richard Mordinyi, Eva Kühn, and Alexander Schatten

Space-based Computing Group
and
Christian Doppler Laboratory "Software Engineering Integration for Flexible
Automation Systems"
Vienna University of Technology
1040 Vienna, Austria
{richard.mordinyi,eva.kuehn,alexander.schatten}@tuwien.ac.at

Abstract. One of the ideas of agile software development is to respond to changes rather than following a plan. Constantly changing businesses result in changing requirements, to be handled in the development process. Therefore, it is essential that the underlying software architecture is capable of managing agile business processes. However, criticism on agile software development states that it lacks paying attention to architectural and design issues and therefore is bound to engender suboptimal design-decisions. We propose an architectural framework, that by explicitly distinguishing computational, coordinational, organizational, distributional, and communicational models offers a high degree of flexibility regarding architectural and design changes. The framework strength is facilitated by a) combining the characteristics and properties of architectural styles captured in a simple API, and b) offering a predefined architectural structure to the developer of distributed applications to cope with complexities of distributed environments. The benefit of our approach is a clear architectural design with minimal mutual effects of the models with respect to changes, accompanied by an efficient realization of new business requirements.

Keywords: Agile Business Requirements, Agile Software Development.

1 Introduction

Business constantly changes. Therefore, software architectures should be able to manage agile business processes and need to have the ability to meet future changes and business needs. The field of agile software development [1] addresses exactly the challenges of an unpredictable, turbulent business and technology environment. Thus, the main question [2] in software development regarding software architecture is how to handle these changes better, while still achieving high quality. On the one hand, how many various numbers of eventualities have

A. Sillitti et al. (Eds.): XP 2010, LNBIP 48, pp. 202–207, 2010.

to be taken into consideration, and therefore how much time and effort should be invested into design and implementation of components or layers with respect to a good architectural design to cover all these circumstances, which eventually at the end may be not used at all. And on the other hand, performing no or hardly any planning ahead, and at the same time bearing the risk of redesigning the existing architectural design from the scratch, once it is not capable of handling the latest requirement [3]. The former case means, that software developers a) do not really focus on realizing the current requirement, but b) develop components which might not be needed in future. This results in higher development time and costs. Problems regarding architectural and design issues in ASD have been discussed in several papers, like [4], [5], [6]stating that ASD lacks paying attention to architectural and design issues and therefore is bound to engender suboptimal design-decisions.

In this paper we propose the Architecture Framework for Agile business requirements (AFA)[1] in ASD, in which it is explicitly distinguished between computational logic, coordinational, organizational, distributional, and communicational models. The five categories are independent of each other and therefore AFA offers a high degree of flexibility regarding architectural and design changes introduced by agile business processes. In the proposed framework the categories are not implemented by means of the software layer pattern [7] but rather in a component-oriented style [8], while making usage of the interceptor pattern. This allows to keep changes local or extend categories individually. AFA can be seen as an abstraction layer between applications and architectural styles, and as such it provides loosely coupling between the applications and their way of coordinating each other, between applications and architectural styles, between the applications and the way they process, distribute, and exchange information.

2   Related Work

Distributed middleware are mostly based on either dataflow style, such as pipes-and-filters, on data-centered style, i.e. a repository, or on implicit invocations, like publish-subscribe or event-based [9]. A detailed description regarding the advantages and limitations of the combination of architectural styles can be found in [10].

Concepts for agile software development (ASD) have been created by experienced practitioners and can be seen as a reaction to e.g., plan-based methods, which attach value to "a rationalized, engineering-based approach" [11]. By contrast, ASD has been proposed as a solution to problems resulting from an unpredictable world, and several agile methods have evolved over time, like Dynamic Systems Development Method [12], or XP [13].However, there is also skepticism [14] regarding ASD with respect to architecture design and implementation issues. One of them is that agile development is an excuse for developers to implement as they like, coding away without proper planning or design [4], [2] and consequently causing suboptimal design-decisions [5], [6].

---

[1] An implementation of the framework can be downloaded at www.mozartspaces.org

Software architectures for distributed systems are a challenge in terms of software development and evolution. Yet it is known from experience that evolution is a key problem in software engineering and exacts huge costs, thus companies spend more resources on maintenance (i.e. evolving their software) than on initial development [3]. Experiences [15], [16] gained by several case studies revealed most influential risks and their affects on the design of the software architecture. The range of affects starts at a complete refactoring of the architecture e.g., in case of poor clustering and ends at adding architectural add-ons.

3 Architecture of the AFA Framework

The main components [17] of the AFA Architecture are Containers, Coordinators, and Aspects. A container is a collection of entries accessible via a basic simple synchronous and asynchronous API of read, take, write, and destroy operations. In case of read, take, and destroy, the operation may be blocked in case the queried entry is not available. Coordinators are programmable parts of the container and are responsible for managing their own view on the entries in the container. A container may host multiple coordinators which aim is to represent a coordination model and to structure and organize the entries in the container for efficient access. Finally, a container may be surrounded by a set of pre- and post-aspects, representing additional computational logic and deployed at specific interception points according to the interceptor pattern. They are executed on the peer where the container is located and are capable of changing or to extending the operation with further functionalities, e.g., to replicate container entries [18].

The three main concepts of the framework form a predefined structure for the developer of distributed applications to cope with complexity issues of distributed systems. These issues can be explicitly clustered and categorized resulting in models distinguished by their capabilities for managing computational, coordinational, organizational, distributional, and communicational requirements.

The computational category represents the application logic and thus the business requirement. It specifies the behavior of the application in case of receiving data and when to write new data into which containers. For the application a container may look like an endpoint known from ESBs [19]. However, an endpoint abstracts underlying protocols trying to map high-level process flows into individual service invocations. A container abstracts transportation protocols as well, but offers the capability to use other coordination models beside the FIFO coordination style representing simple messaging.

The coordination model is used to express the communication and synchronization requirements between applications. This decoupling allows to switch between coordination models [17] transparent to the application accessing the container by replacing the existing coordinator in the container. In traditional sense, the computational and coordination models are combined, since a lot of the systems rely on the pipes-and-filters or call-and-return architectural styles. This implies that the application itself also has to contain and implement the complexities coming along with the used coordination model. Furthermore, from the point of view of the application it is "'just"' reading and writing entries into a container. However, although the container has an entry - written by another application - it may still not be accessible since from the point of view of the coordination model the 'coordination strategy' may not be yet complete.

The organizational category hides from the application the various combinations of architectural styles [10], offers space for managing cross-cutting concerns, and abstracts resources. Architectural styles explicitly designed for coordination issues, like the blackboard style (see section 2), have already been taken into consideration in the coordinational category. A big contribution to this category is given by the aspects as they may contain any computational logic a) restricted to the aspect only, like filter functionalities, or b) logic that needs access to other resources, like in the case of aggregating events or logging operations.

The distributional category deals with transparency issues known from distributed systems, like location-, migration-, relocation-, and replication-transparency. From the application point of view it is not known whether the container is embedded, hosted locally, or on a single server or in a P2P network. Similar to an ESB, AFA enables to migrate a single container executed on a server to a replicated one. However, by means of aspects the container can be located and replicated in a P2P environment. In such case, aspects installed at every replica would define the replication technique and the consistency strategy between the replicas [18]. Since aspects may contain any code, for software developers it is not necessary to implement replication issues from the scratch. Aspects may contain already existing solutions to these issues, like realized in group communication protocols.

The communicational category allows to specify how the necessary information needed for coordination is exchanged between the participating containers. It describes how data from one container is transmitted to the other. The model may contain lower level protocols or higher level ones like P2P protocols. However, in case the developer decides to use group communication protocols, as mentioned before, AFA cannot modify the settings of that product, since it is not it the scope of AFA and thus the communicational category anymore.

4   Discussion

The proposed AFA framework explicitly distinguishes between five categories each responsible to manage specific complexity issues of distributed environments. This helps system engineers to identify only those components which are effected by a new business requirement, and thus minimize the effects of the implementation of the new requirement on other categories.

Todays middleware technologies represent a specific architectural style [10]. This implies that the middleware itself either does not have the ability or would require a lot of effort to satisfy business requirements the middleware has not been explicitly designed for. On the contrary, the AFA framework abstracts the combined power of several architectural styles and thus facilitates the implementation of new requirements by specific changes in the AFA structure (coordinators and set of aspects). The advantage of such a structure is that an average engineer [20] with limited knowledge about e.g., design patterns, object-oriented programming, or available frameworks operates with simple concepts in each category. This limits the numbers of design and implementation decisions an average engineer would have to make. This also means that in case of design mistakes and implementation errors the effects of the decision is limited to the category where it has been made. The limitation of the concept is that professional engineers may be restricted in their way of implementing. Since they have the right knowledge, they know how to tune frameworks or how to design architectures in combination with the right design patterns in order to a flexible and efficient software design. The AFA structure would limit they degree of freedom with respect to design decisions.

5   Conclusion and Future Work

In this paper, we described the concept of the Architecture Framework for Agile processes (AFA) as an abstraction framework in order to allow the efficient realization of new business requirements with minimal effects on other components in the architecture. The concept is capable of representing the characteristics of different architectural styles at the same time and by explicitly distinguishing between computational, coordinational, organizational, distributional, and communicational models, it offers a high degree of flexibility. The combination of a generic interface, containers, coordinators and aspects a) offers a predefined architectural structure to the developer of distributed applications to effectively cope with complexities of distributed environments, and b) allows to decouple the models resulting in minimal mutual effects in case of changes transparent to the application. Further work will include a benchmarking of the framework, i.e. to what extent does the additional abstraction layer decrease computational performance. A more comprehensive evaluation with respect to testing and development time is intended.

References

1. Highsmith, J., Cockburn, A.: Agile software development: the business of innovation. Computer 34, 120–127 (2001)
2. Hadar, E., Silberman, G.M.: Agile architecture methodology: long term strategy interleaved with short term tactics. In: OOPSLA Companion 2008: Companion to the 23rd ACM SIGPLAN conference on Object-oriented programming systems languages and applications, pp. 641–652. ACM, New York (2008)
3. Jazayeri, M.: On Architectural Stability and Evolution. In: Blieberger, J., Strohmeier, A. (eds.) Ada-Europe 2002. LNCS, vol. 2361, pp. 13–23. Springer, Heidelberg (2002)
4. Rakitin, S.R.: Manifesto Elicits Cynicism. IEEE Computer 34(4) (2001)
5. McBreen, P.: Questioning Extreme Programming. Addison-Wesley Longman Publishing Co., Inc. (2002)

6. Stephens, M., Rosenberg, D.: Extreme Programming Refactored: The Case Against XP. Apress, Berkeley (2003)
7. Kircher, M., Jain, P.: Pattern-Oriented Software Architecture: Patterns for Resource Management. John Wiley & Sons, Chichester (2004)
8. Heineman, G.T., Councill, W.T. (eds.): Component-based software engineering: putting the pieces together. Addison-Wesley Longman Publishing Co., Inc. (2001)
9. Taylor, R.N., Medvidovic, N., Dashofy, E.M.: Software Architecture: Foundations. In: Theory, and Practice. Wiley Publishing, Chichester (2009)
10. Mordinyi, R., Kühn, E., Schatten, A.: Space-based Architectures as Abstraction Layer for Distributed Business Applications. In: Track on Software Engineering for Distributed Systems at the 4th International Conference on Complex, Intelligent and Software Intensive Systems, CISIS 2010 (2010)
11. Nerur, S., Mahapatra, R., Mangalaraj, G.: Challenges of migrating to agile methodologies. Commun. ACM 48, 72–78 (2005)
12. Stapleton, J.: DSDM: Business Focused Development. Pearson Education, London (2003)
13. Beck, K., Andres, C.: Extreme Programming Explained: Embrace Change, 2nd edn. Addison-Wesley Professional, Reading (2004)
14. Dingsoyr, T., Dyba, T.: What Do We Know about Agile Software Development? Software, IEEE 26, 6–9 (2009)
15. Slyngstad, O.P., Li, J., Conradi, R., Babar, M.A.: Identifying and Understanding Architectural Risks in Software Evolution: An Empirical Study. In: Jedlitschka, A., Salo, O. (eds.) PROFES 2008. LNCS, vol. 5089, pp. 400–414. Springer, Heidelberg (2008)
16. Slyngstad, O., Conradi, R., Babar, M., Clerc, V., van Vliet, H.: Risks and Risk Management in Software Architecture Evolution: An Industrial Survey. In: Software Engineering Conference, APSEC 2008. 15th Asia-Pacific, pp. 101–108 (2008)
17. Kühn, E., Mordinyi, R., Keszthelyi, L., Schreiber, C.: Introducing the concept of customizable structured spaces for agent coordination in the production automation domain. In: Proceedings of The 8th International Conference on Autonomous Agents and Multiagent Systems, AAMAS 2009, pp. 625–632 (2009)
18. Kühn, E., Mordinyi, R., Keszthelyi, L., Schreiber, C., Bessler, S., Tomic, S.: Aspect-oriented Space Containers for Efficient Publish/Subscribe Scenarios in Intelligent Transportation Systems. In: The 11th International Symposium on Distributed Objects, Middleware, and Applications, DOA 2009 (2009)
19. Chappell, D.: Enterprise Service Bus. O'Reilly Media, Inc., Sebastopol (2004)
20. Hannay, J.E., MacLeod, C., Singer, J., Langtangen, H.P., Pfahl, D., Wilson, G.: How do scientists develop and use scientific software? In: SECSE 2009: Proceedings of the 2009 ICSE Workshop on Software Engineering for Computational Science and Engineering, pp. 1–8. IEEE Computer Society, Los Alamitos (2009)

A Literature Review on Story Test Driven Development

Shelly Park and Frank Maurer

Department of Computer Science
University of Calgary
2500 Univeresity Dr. NW, Calgary, AB, Canada
{sshpark,fmaurer}@ucalgary.ca

Abstract. This paper presents a literature review on story-test driven development. Our findings suggest that there are many lessons learned papers that provide anecdotal evidence about the benefits and issues related to the story test driven development. We categorized these findings into seven themes: cost, time, people, code design, testing tools, what to test and test automation. We analyzed research papers on story test driven development to find out how many of these anecdotal findings were critically examined by researchers and analyzed the gaps in between. The analysis can be used by researchers as a ground for further empirical investigation.

Keywords: Story Test Driven Development, Executable Acceptance Test Driven Development, Requirements, Systematic Review, Testing, Empirical software engineering, Agile software development.

1 Introduction

The Story Test Driven Development (STDD) is a way of communicating requirements using tests. The purpose of STDD is to facilitate better communication between the customers and the development team by reducing the ambiguities in the requirements. The testable requirements can either pass or fail, thus story tests reduce the ambiguities in requirements interpretations. This idea is currently called many names in the agile software engineering community: functional tests [1], customer tests [1], specification by example [2] and scenario tests [3], executable acceptance tests [4, 5] and behavior driven development [6] among many.

The idea of STDD has been in circulation in the agile software engineering community for a decade now starting with Beck's publication of his book [1] in 1999. For the last decade, we have seen the industry accept and practice many of the agile concepts in varying degrees despite their initial objections. For example, TDD has been widely accepted by developers in industry. However, comparably STDD is much less adopted and there is still a lot of confusion about what STDD is and where it should be used. The aim of the paper is to analyze the state of our knowledge on STDD. We want to categorize what people found to be the difficult points in practicing STDD and what research has discovered so far in our understanding of STDD. We performed a literature review on STDD papers published in conferences, magazines and

A. Sillitti et al. (Eds.): XP 2010, LNBIP 48, pp. 208–213, 2010.
© Springer-Verlag Berlin Heidelberg 2010

journals. We categorized them into lessons learned/experience papers, tool development papers and empirical research papers.

2 Result

This section describes in detail on STDD that are published in various publication venues in the past. We categorized the discussion points into 7 themes: cost, time, people, code design, testing tools, what to test, and test automation issues. We first describe the points from the lessons learned and tool development papers and describe the findings from the research papers. For references that start with [T], please refer to [7].

2.1 Cost

Budget is an important aspect of software development projects, especially when one needs to justify the cost of introducing a new process such as STDD into a development team. Authors in [T15, T16, T17] suggested that the benefit of STDD is to help keep the project within budget. Schwartz also states that the automated story tests can "run often and facilitate regression testing at low cost"[T16]. However, four papers [T15, T16, T18, T19,] stated that STDD may not pay off because the cost of writing and maintaining the tests is high. In addition, four papers stated that their teams did not have the budget necessary to automate the tests [T18, T19, T20, T21]. There were no research papers that explicitly analyzed the cost and budget aspect of STDD process or the STDD tools.

2.2 Time

Five points were discussed in the lessons learned papers as the benefits of STDD process: 1) The STDD can help check the overall progress [T15, T17, T18, T19, T22, T23, T24, T25, T26, T27, T28, T29, T68]; 2) adapt to requirements changes with the help of instant feedback, which can help keep the project on time [T18, T27, T30]; 3) continuous verification (test often, repeatedly)[T17, T25, T27]; 4) better estimation of the stories [T23, T31]; 5) immediate defect fixes [T28, T32]. However, some lessons learned papers identified three issues related to time: 1) writing and maintaining tests took considerable time [T17, T28, T29, T33, T34, T35], 2) it can take long time to execute the tests [T24, 34, 36, 37, 38], and 3) there can be a lack of time to build the necessary testing tools and infrastructures [T28].

There were two research papers that dealt with time on STDD. The research paper, [T72], discovered that the test subjects were able to write and test using story tests within an expected amount of time. The research paper, [T74], discovered that timing was a matter of discipline more than an actual timing problem.

2.3 People

Software is developed by people. Their commitment, skills and collaboration are important in the success of the development project. The lessons learned papers suggest there are five benefits: 1) better communication with the stakeholders [T17, T25, T31, T39, T40, T41, T42, T43, T63, T64], 2) confidence about the progress and deliverables [T17, T19, T28, T32, T38, T39, T41, T44, T45], 3) better awareness for testing in the team [T81, T35, T61, T17, T28, T68], 4) encouragement of collaboration between right people [T39] and 5) anyone can quickly understand what has been developed [T34, T35]. The lessons learned papers also identified two problems related to people. 1) The STDD affects everyone, which made the adoption difficult [T24]. 2) Some papers identified that there was no direct contact between developers and customers because the tests were too explicit [T34, T41]. In addition, there were some papers that discussed the people's skills. Some papers argued that it took too long to learn the STDD testing tool or the specification language [T27, T46, T55]. Some authors identified that lack of test automation experience in the team was the barrier [T25, T43, T46, T48, T69], but most of them overcame the problem quickly.

In terms of the responsibility of writing and maintaining the story tests, there were teams where the whole team was equally responsible for the tests [T19, T26, T35, T48], or a separate group of dedicated developers/testers were created for STDD [T18, 34]. One team used pair story testing method [T18]. In terms of who writes the tests, there were many variations. Some stated that the customers wrote the tests with the help of the developers and testers [T23, T24, T25, T27, T30, T36, T42, T49, T50]. In some cases, developers wrote the story tests with the customer collaboration [T20, T26, T27, T51]. In some teams, the QAs wrote the tests in collaboration with the customer [T19, T45].

We found seven research papers that looked into people related issues. [T67] performed an experiment on how quickly developers can learn to use a STDD tool and discovered that 90% of the test subjects delivered the Fit tests on time. However, the researchers in [T70] discovered that there was difficulty in learning some of the Fit fixtures, because the test subjects only used a very basic and limited number of fixtures types. The experiment performed in [T72] suggests that there was no difference in the quality of story tests produced by business graduate students or computer science graduate students. The research in [T73] suggests that experienced developers gain much more benefits from Fit tables in software evolution tasks, suggesting that previous experience does matter. The research in [T74] found that story tests alone could not communicate everything, because it didn't provide the context. The researchers in [T77] found that the story tests are the medium for communicating complex domain knowledge, especially in a very large software development team. The researchers in [T75] discovered that story tests written in Fit actually were more ambiguous to untrained test subjects, because they didn't know how to understand the Fit tables.

2.4 Code Design

The lessons learned papers identified that there are 1) a better design of the code for testability, such as separation of backend functionality from the user interface code [T15, T18, T33, T35, T38, T52, T53, T54, T55]. 2) Some discovered that the team produced quality code first time and discovered that STDD can drive quality [T21, T22, T41, T56, T71]. 3) The STDD can drive the overall code design [T17, T25,T56] and 4) developers had better understanding of their code [T45]. 5) Some papers argued that STDD also helped developers think about the user experience early [T22, T25]. There were no papers that identified the issues or concerns related to code for STDD.

There were four research papers related to the code design. The researchers in [T70] discovered that more quality code is produced the first time. The research in [T73] suggests story testing tools can help with software evolution, especially for more experienced developers who are coding alone. The researchers in [T76] confirmed that Fit tables can help developers perform code maintenance tasks correctly, because it ensures that requirements changes are implemented appropriately and the regression tests ensure that the existing functionality are not broken. However, the experiment performed by [T72] showed that there was no correlation between the quality of the story tests and the quality of the code.

2.5 Testing Tools

Many papers deal with tool support for STDD. The papers suggest that there is a lack of tools that can help facilitate STDD effectively. First, we present the discussions related to the types of tools that were used for STDD. Some used capture/replay tools [T18, T30, T51, T57, T58,]. However, most people voiced that the capture/replay tests are easily broken even with a minor/cosmetic changes in the user interface. Instead, some people use unit testing tools such as jUnit and nUnit [T15, T28, T36], because they give a lot of power to the developers for automation. Some people used word processors or spreadsheets for acquiring the story tests from the customers [T15, T18, T33, T45]. Some people used XML for the test specification [T18, T33, T43, T49, T59]. Some people preferred scripting languages or API based tools such as Selenium [T18, T28, T32, T38, T43, T55, T58]. But most people used tabular and fixture based tools such as Fit [T16, T17, T22, T25, T27, T30, T33, T34, T37, T39, T43, T44, T45, T46, T48, T49, T50, T59, T60, T61, T62].

In terms of ways people use these tools, some people argued that customers and developers ended up using different tools based on their familiarity of the tools [T21, T24, T29, T38, T45, T60]. Some people also integrated other testing, bug tracking, and/or domain-specific productivity tools [T42, T43, T60, T63].

In terms of features that people thought were important in story testing tools are automated test generation [T29, T36, T51, T58], automatic test data generation [T36, 58] and automatic documentation generation [T24, T31, T52]. In addition, some people thought important tool features include viewing the test result history [T29], refactoring of the tests [T18, T21, T25, T29, T65] and test organization features [T24, T25, T29].

In terms of research papers, [T78] analyzed whether annotated documents in story testing tools can help write better story tests. The researchers in [T79] also performed an annotation experiment on a medical domain. Their findings suggest that the participants who were given an annotation to follow created story tests with less missing elements than those groups that did not.

2.6 What to Test in STDD

We found that there are surprisingly many variations on what to test using story tests. They include the graphical user interface in order to simulate how user will interact with the system [T22, T41, T51, T57, T58], web services, web applications and network related issues [T32, T43, T49], backend functionality (functional requirements) [T31, T41], performance [T19], security [T19], stability [T19], non-functional requirements [T31, T36], end-to-end-customer's perspective of the feature [T17, T51], regression testing [T15, T21, T22, T24, T28, T32, T33, T38, T43, T48, T50, T51, T61], user interaction [T21, T25, T38, T57], concurrency [T41, T43], database [T43], only the critical features as judged by the developers [T27], and multi-layer architecture of software design [T54]. Finally, most people thought the purpose of STDD is not so much about testing, but to communicate the requirements with the customer in an unambiguous way [T17, T24, T25, T27, T29, T30, T31, T39, T55, T56, T62]. No empirical evaluation of this question exists in terms of story test driven development.

2.7 Test Automation Issues

Finally, we analyzed the issues involved with automating story tests. Some people identified that there is a real difficulty in maintaining the tests especially in large projects [T21, T24, T28, T29, T36, T51]. Similarly, there is difficulty in organizing and sorting the tests in order to see the big picture [T20, T21, T34, T38]. Some found that it is difficult to locate defective code [T18, T20, T21, T24], because a story was concerned with a bigger scope of a feature. There is a desire to automate at the user interface level [T18, T21, T25, T38, T40]. One author desires for better usability of the testing tools [T33]. Some people desired for more readable test specifications [T17, T21, T24, T25, T33, T34, T41, T42, T57, T66, T81]. Some people thought keeping track of the history of the tests is important [T34]. One author worried that the team ignored the tests because there were too many false alarms [T38], mainly because the tests relied on the GUI, which broke the tests easily even with only small changes to the user interface. Another concern is a lack of readily usable testing tools that can accommodate specific needs [T38, T45]. One author argued that the problem is with the incompatibility of different platforms and languages for the tests [T45]. Some people emphasized that tests should be written using more reusable objects and services [T34, T45, T61]. Some people argued for separation of test data and test code and the tool should help with the separation [T18, T32, T53]. No research paper analyzes these issues in relation to story test driven development.

3 Discussion

The review suggests that we need a lot more research done in the area of story test driven development. Just from the number of papers we found, we were able to discover 49 lessons learned papers and 8 tool development papers but only 8 research papers. There is no research done in the area of cost, test automation issues, or what to test. Much of the research done so far since the introduction of STDD focused on time, people and code design. The research is also done with a very small group of research participants and we still lack enough evidence to aggregate these findings into general knowledge.

We need better understanding of what can be tested by story tests and what should be outside the scope of STDD. The industry practitioners have a lot of concerns about the test automation and the lack of tools to facilitate STDD in a cost-effective and timely manner. Our findings suggest that the gap is very wide between what researchers were able to provide to the practitioners at the time and what are needed. Existing papers focused on time, people, code design and tools, but there are still many unanswered questions as well as conflicting results. Thus, a substantial amount of empirical research on STDD is needed to create a solid foundation for rational decisions in this area.

Acknowledgement. This research is supported by the National Research Council of Canada (NSERC) and iCore.

References

1. Beck, K.: Extreme Programming Explained: Embrace Change, 1/e. Addison-Wesley, Reading (1999)
2. Fowler, M.: Specification by Example,
   http://www.martinfowler.com/bliki/SpecificationByExample.html
3. Kaner, C.: Cem Kaner on Scenario Testing: The Power of 'What-If...' and Nine Ways to Fuel Your Imagination. Better Software 5(5), 16–22 (2003)
4. Melnik, G.: Empirical Analyses of Executable Acceptance Test Driven Development, University of Calgary, PhD Thesis (2007)
5. Park, S., Maurer, F.: Communicating Domain Knowledge in Executable Acceptance Test Driven Development. In: XP 2009, May 2009. LNBIP, vol. 31, pp. 23–32 (2009)
6. Behavior driven development, http://www.behaviour-driven.org
7. Park, S., Maurer, F.: An Extended Literature Review on Story Test Driven Development, Technical Report, University of Calgary, 2010-953-02

Improving Responsiveness, Bug Detection, and Delays in a Bureaucratic Setting: A Longitudinal Empirical IID Adoption Case Study

Caryna Pinheiro, Frank Maurer, and Jonathan Sillito

University of Calgary
Calgary, Alberta, Canada
{capinhei,frank.maurer,sillito}@ucalgary.ca

Abstract. This paper empirically studies a group of projects in a large bureau-cratic government agency that adopted iterative and incremental development (IID). We found that a project that followed IID since inception provided substantially better bug-fixing responsiveness and found bugs earlier in the development lifecycle than existing projects that migrated to IID. IID practices also supported managerial decisions that lead to on-time & on-budget delivery.

Keywords: Iterative and Incremental Development, Longitudinal Study, RUP.

1 Introduction

With the ascendance of Agile Methods it has become hard to find articles related to process improvements without hitting the words "Iterative and Incremental Development" (IID). Incremental means "add onto" and Iterative means "refine" [1].

This paper reports on a case study that was conducted to understand the adoption of an IID approach by a group of IT projects in a large bureaucratic government agency. The improvement efforts were motivated by concerns identified by the business clients of those projects, primarily: poor bug-fixing responsiveness and delivery delays. The focus of this work was to understand how effectively the process changes have been able to deal with these concerns. To this end, we explore the practices in the context of a new project in comparison with existing projects that migrated to IID, both quantitatively and qualitatively.

An industrial investigation of IID practices merits examination for various reasons. IID is often seen as the innovative response to traditional engineering practices [2]. Many believe that IID practices have hit the mainstream of application development [6]. Others believe that "we're not there yet" [7]. Perhaps these contradictory views are related to the fact that much of the evidence about Agile adoption has been decontextualized [4]. In addition, Dingsoyr *et al.*'s roadmap [3] calls for more industrial collaboration through Action Research and for more knowledge on how Agile principles, such as IID, work in different contexts. In our research, a governance model faced with strict conformance to rules and regulations resulted in formal decision-making processes. This culture and context led managers to adopt IID through a methodology with a higher degree of "ceremony and formality", the Rational Unified Process (RUP) [5].

A. Sillitti et al. (Eds.): XP 2010, LNBIP 48, pp. 214–219, 2010.

The IID adoption strategy we present in this paper followed a "go all in, but iterate first with some public display" [10]. IID adoption efforts were motivated by several "smells" [9] identified by the business clients of those projects (poor bug-fixing responsiveness and delivery delays). The adoption was top-down and mandated that all projects in the organization had to follow the new RUP practices, but the adoption path for existing projects was limited (discussed in a previous paper [14]).

2 Case Study

We collected data from a suite of three pre-existing complex projects in the largest IT program that migrated to IID practices (**Projects Transitioned**), and from a suite of four new applications developed using IID practices since inception (**Project New**). Table 1 presents some organizational context following Eckstein's five dimensions to categorize the largeness of a project [11].

Table 1. Jutta Eckstein five dimensions of largeness

People	900 employees in total. Ten IT programs with 191 IT professionals.
Scope	Real-time validation of complex government rules and regulations during on-line submission of data, with a user base of over 11,000 users.
Money	The projects under study had budgets of over $1.5 million dollars.
Time	One to three years for a first production release.
Risk	Innovative and unconventional systems. Specially, one of the web applications is considered a "state of the art" government application.

Due to external industrial factors, such as the Alberta oil and gas boom, development was fast paced and many releases were rushed or delayed. Fixed delivery dates forced unreliable acceptance testing schedules on the business clients. IT project teams quickly evolved from small groups of four to six developers to increased teams of over 15 developers. In less than three months the existing projects under study grew to 40+ team members. The result was poor software quality, low team morale, and loss of trust between IT management and business clients. Business clients communicated the need for better quality, better stability, better responsiveness, and more reliable testing schedules to management.

The introduction of process improvements in real life is a complex problem that involves many simultaneous factors. IT Management made a small number of process changes over a period of approximately 13 months to Projects Transitioned (discussed in a previous paper [14]). In this section we provide further contextual information about the process changes in the new project that followed IID since inception (Project New), to avoid decontextualization [4]. Specific practices adopted by this new IID project included: short iterations, iteration planning, scheduled iteration testing, iteration end demos, risk management, early prototyping, and external focus groups for user acceptance tests.

The reviewed RUP execution state used by Project New included: the iterative RUP lifecycle, Rational Tools, Role sets, and selected work products (approximately 13).

The team experimented with iteration length during the Inception and Elaboration phases. At the end of first Elaboration phase, the team decided to follow three-week iterations as more become known about the project. Transition iterations were an exception; they were seven weeks long. The team also started to hold daily stand-up meetings during the Elaboration phases and the developers implemented unit tests to prototype and evaluate the risk of project tasks. Later in the construction stages the team stopped developing and maintaining these unit tests. Manual testing occurred during the last week of an iteration. During the last week of Construction iterations code was delivered to a staging environment - the "Sandbox." A dedicated tester and the business analyst used this staging environment to test and validate the builds. The team prepared demos for the business clients at the end of each iteration. These demos presented the progress of the iteration to business clients for feedback by showing a working version of the system in so far.

2.1 Methodological Approach

The data presented is longitudinal. It extends over three years of data from Projects Transitioned and over two and a half years of data from Project New.

The Goal Question Metric approach (GQM) proposed by Basili *et al.* [8] was adopted in order to formalize the research goals and to find appropriate measurements to answer them. The question: "How long did it take to fix bugs?", resulted in two metrics: bug-fixing responsiveness in days (quantitative data) and subjective views of business clients (qualitative data). This question and metrics were applied twice: once for (Projects Transitioned) and once for (Project New).

Quantitative Data. Bugs were grouped based on priority. Mixing all the bugs together would lead to a less realistic representation of bug fixing responsiveness as higher priority items would most likely be worked on first. Bug priority was used instead of bug criticality because according to interviewees, a clear definition of a critical bug was not available until the later stages of the RUP adoption. We define bug-fixing responsiveness as:

$$\text{Bug-fixing responsiveness (in days)} = \text{The number of days between when the bug was submitted and when it was closed.} \tag{1}$$

Only bugs logged from the RUP Transition forward were measured for Projects Transitioned to allow a fair comparison of the affects of the IID adoption. Bug reports that did not include any action related to a developer analyzing and/or fixing the bug were excluded. As a result, we only included 958 bugs from Projects Transitioned and only 318 bugs from Project New in our analysis.

Qualitative Data. Data was gathered using field notes based on interview sessions with the project manager, technical lead, business analyst, and one developer from Project New. Three to four sessions were conducted with each of the participants for approximately 20 minutes each time. The questions were designed based on qualitative interviewing techniques [12] with probing questions [13].

3 Results

On-time & On-budget Delivery. The risk list document and iteration demos provided a more tangible way to manage and negotiate expectations. Business clients bought into the idea of having a subset of the project delivered first instead of prolonging the delivery timelines. Based on items of this risk list the business clients agreed to break Project New into two phases at the end of Elaboration Iteration 2. Although the project took longer than it first envisioned, both phases of Project New were delivered on-time and met the deliverables milestones.

This government agency has a set budget given to the IT Department at the beginning of each fiscal year. The budget for Project New was set during Inception. The interviewed business clients and the project manager stated that this project was on-budget. The interviewees indicated that no overtime was required or imposed to the project team.

This was confirmed by the overall perception of this project in the organization that this was *"the first IT project to be on-time and on-budget in six years."*

Better Bug Detection. A core goal for software is to deploy bug-free software. Bugs found before deployment are a sign that the overall process is working. As such, we analyzed where in the development process most bugs were being logged for both Projects Transitioned and for Project New. The bugs reports were grouped based on the staging environment where they were discovered. The ascending order of staging environment is: Dev (Development), Test (Testing) and or Sbx (Sandbox), UTE (External User Testing Environment), Act (User Acceptance), Prod (Production).

Figure 1 shows that during the waterfall days (Pre-RUP), 40% of all bugs were found after a production release for Projects Transitioned. A total of 47% of all bugs were found in the two latest staging environments (Act and Prod). During the RUP transition, the percentage of bugs found after a release dropped to 34%, and after the Partial RUP adoption, the overall numbers dropped to 25%. We do see an improvement in the amount of bugs found after a release (from 40% to 25%).

For Project New, Figure 1 shows that only 7% of all bugs were found after a production release. Close to 9% of all bugs were found in the latest staging environments. An interesting difference is that for Project New an external user testing environment (UTE) was set up for external focus group participants to test the application. 30% of the bugs reported were found during such testing.

Bug-fixing Responsiveness. Bugs were grouped based on priority. The arithmetic mean (average) in days, median, standard deviation, minimum (min), and maximum (max) number of days that it took to fix a bug were calculated for each group. Figure 2 illustrates the results. The values from Projects Transitioned and Project New are intercalated to facilitate comparisons. The averages and median values are substantially lower for the project that followed IID practices since inception.

The data was not normally distributed. The standard deviation was always higher than the averages. This variation in time to fix bugs within the same priority was not a surprise. The level of effort required to fix a bug is not always associated with its business impact and priority.

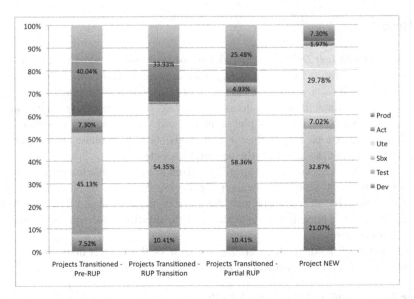

Fig. 1. Bugs breakdown per staging environment

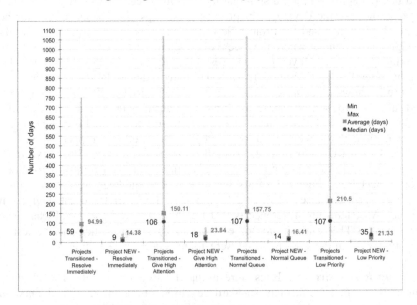

Fig. 2. Bug-fixing responsiveness - day to closure

A quick turnaround to address an issue showed respect and concern towards the business clients. The business partners felt they could trust the team to fix issues in a timely manner. To validate this sentiment, bug-fixing responsiveness was also measured relative to the iteration end dates. Project New's bugs labeled as "Resolve Immediately" were, on average, addressed within the iteration they were found. "Give High Attention" and "Average" bugs were addressed within the next iteration.

Unfortunately that was not true of Projects Transitioned where due to the high volume of bugs introduced before the concept of iterations was adopted, existing bugs competed against new ones in the queue to resolution. In average bugs were fixed well after the end date of releases in which they were found.

4 Conclusion

Through the analysis of bug-fixing data and qualitative data gathered during interviews, we discovered that IID practices allowed a new project to: provide support for managerial decisions that lead it to be the first project in six years to deliver on-time and on-budget; avoid quality and stability issues; provide substantially better bug-fixing responsiveness than projects that migrated to IID. IID practices in both new and existing projects allowed the teams to detect bugs earlier on in the development lifecycle.

References

1. Cockburn, A.: Incremental versus iterative development,
   http://alistair.cockburn.us/index.php/Incremental versus iterative development
2. Larman, C., Basili, V.R.: Iterative and incremental development: a brief history. Computer 36(6), 47–56 (2003)
3. Dingsoyr, T., Dyba, T., Abrahamsson, P.: A preliminary roadmap for empirical research on agile software development. In: AGILE 2008. Conference, August 2008, pp. 83–94 (2008)
4. Kruchten, P.: Voyage in the agile memeplex. Queue 5(5), 38–44 (2007)
5. Larman, C.: Agile & Iterative Development, A Manager's Guide. Addison Wesley, Reading (2004)
6. Ambler, S.: Agile adoption rate survey,
   http://www.ambysoft.com/surveys/agilemarch2007.html
7. Erdogmus, H.: Agile's coming of age.. or not, Software. IEEE 24(6), 2–5 (2007)
8. Rombach, H., Basili, V., Caldiera, G.: The goal question metric approach. Encyclopedia of Software Engineering 2, 528–532 (1994)
9. Elssamadisy, A.: Patterns of Agile Practice Adoption. Lulu.com - InfoQ (2007)
10. Cohn, M.: Patterns of agile adoption,
    http://www.agilejournal.com/content/view/734/111/
11. Eckstein, J.: Agile Software Development in the Large-Diving Into the Deep. Dorset House, New York (1983)
12. Rubin, H.J., Rubin, I.S.: Qualitative Interviewing: The Art of Hearing Data, 2nd edn. Sage, Thousand Oaks (2005)
13. The question man, What to avoid, What to do,
    http://www.ajr.org/articleprintable.asp?id=676
14. Pinheiro, C., Maurer, F., Sillito, J.: Improving quality, one process change at a time. In: 31st International Conference on Software Engineering (ICSE 2009). ICSE Companion 2009, vol. 31, pp. 81–90. IEEE, Los Alamitos (2009)

Dealing with Navigation and Interaction Requirements Changes in a TDD-Based Web Engineering Approach

Juan Burella[1,3], Gustavo Rossi[2,3], Esteban Robles Luna[2,3], and Julián Grigera[2]

[1] Departamento de Computación, Universidad de Buenos Aires
jburella@dc.uba.ar
[2] LIFIA, Facultad de Informática, UNLP, La Plata, Argentina
[3] CONICET
{gustavo,esteban.robles,julian.grigera}@lifia.info.unlp.edu.ar

Abstract. Web applications are well suited to be developed with agile methods. However, as they tend to change too fast, special care must be put in change management, both to satisfy customers and reduce developers load. In this paper we discuss how we deal with navigation and interaction requirements changes in a novel test-driven development approach for Web applications. We present it by indicating how it resembles and differs from "conventional" TDD, and showing how changes can be treated as "first class" objects, allowing us to automate the application changes and also to adaptively prune the test suite.

1 Introduction

TDD and its variants like STDD [4] mostly focus on behavioural aspects of domain classes, and since TDD is generally applied in a bottom up way, it tends to disregard important features of Web applications such as navigation, interface or interaction. As a consequence, usability, look and feel, and also navigation features may be checked too late, once the application has been already presented to the customers, thus delaying the correction process.

As a way to overcome the mismatch between "conventional" TDD and Web applications development, we present an approach for improving change management in the context of our TDD-like mehotology by focusing on changes that affect navigation and interaction aspects. Requirements are represented using WebSpec diagrams, which capture navigation, user interface (UI) and interaction application aspects. WebSpec diagrams are then automatically translated into sets of meaningful interaction tests the application must pass. While the developers work coding the solution, the support environment captures the changes in objects and associates them to the corresponding tests. Change objects can also help to semi automatically change structural parts of the Web application when a requirement is added or changed. In the same way, we can reduce the number of tests that must be run to those that exercise changed objects only, improving the overall development time. We illustrate the approach with a simple Twitter-like application and show an integrated environment built on top of Seaside (www.seaside.st) that supports this functionality.

A. Sillitti et al. (Eds.): XP 2010, LNBIP 48, pp. 220–225, 2010.

2 Background: A Test-Driven Approach for Web Applications

The key aspects of our requirements modelling stage are fast interface and interaction prototyping on one hand, and navigation modelling on the other. Prototyping is carried out with interaction mockups: simple HTML stub pages that significantly help to agree on the application's look and feel, and the way interaction must be performed.

We use WebSpec diagrams to specify navigation and interaction requirements more formally than with User Stories (US) [3]. These artefacts (based on UIDs [5] and Quickcheck [1]) capture navigation and interaction aspects in a similar way UIDs do, but adding the formal power of preconditions and invariants to assert properties in the interactions. A WebSpec diagram contains *interactions* and *navigations*. An *interaction* represents a point where the user consumes information (expressed as a set of interface widgets) and interacts with the application by using some of its widgets. Some actions (clicking a button, adding some text in a text field, etc) might produce *navigation* from one *interaction* to another, and as a consequence, the user moves through the application's navigation space. These actions are written in an intuitive domain specific language. Fig. 1 shows a WebSpec that will let the user tweet, see how many tweets he has, and allow him to logout from the application. From the Login *interaction*, the user can authenticate by typing its username and password and then clicking on the login button (navigation from Login to Home interaction). Then, the user can add messages by typing in the messageTF and clicking on the post button (navigation from Home to Home interaction).

Fig. 1. WebSpec of Tweet's interaction

From a WebSpec diagram we automatically generate a set of interaction tests that cover all the interaction paths specified in it, thus avoiding the translation problem of TDD between tests and requirements. Unlike unit tests, interaction tests simulate user input into HTML pages, and allow asserting conditions on the results of such interactions. Since each WebSpec *interaction* is related to a mockup, each test runs against it and the predicates are transformed into tests assertions. These (failing) series of tests set a good starting point for our TDD-like approach.

Once we have a set of tests for a specific requirement, it is time to develop the functionality to make them pass. Since interaction tests define the functionalities at user level, and we will drive the development from such tests, our approach will naturally follow a top-down style, rather than the usual bottom-up way of regular TDD. Nevertheless, we will use regular TDD as we dive into the application's underlying domain model.

Basing ourselves in the mockups, we recreate the same UI using widgets, but this time adding stubs for the dynamic behaviour in the places where the application will interact with the domain objects. Next, for every stub message left in the presentation and navigation classes, we code the model classes to fill the gaps.

At the time we engage in the development of the domain model classes, we follow a traditional TDD cycle by creating the unit tests first to establish the purpose of the new objects, which is in turn facilitated by the UI/navigation models which have already set specific requests for them. Once unit tests pass, we can run the interaction tests to check whether we have completed the necessary functionality for the current request. As usual, when tests do not pass, we keep working on the code until they do, and once this happens we can go on with the next requirement.

At times, some domain behaviour is needed, and it is not possible to state it as a UI requirement triggered by the user, or cannot be validated at the interaction level. In such cases, we capture the functionality using US and then create unit tests.

For the sake of conciseness, we will focus our explanation on navigation and presentation requirements, and therefore we will not talk about the effect of changes in "conventional" unit tests.

3   Our Approach to Change Management in a Nutshell

We borrow ideas from changeboxes [2] to make software changes explicit and manageable. We specifically focus on navigation and interaction changes in Web applications requirements to minimize the effort for satisfying their impact on the implementation. These changes are explicitly represented as first-class objects, and related to the artefacts in which they produce modifications, and as a consequence, we not only obtain better traceability features, but we are also able to automate some of these changes in the final application. Since navigation tests are also represented with objects, and we can determine the elements they access, and we can know exactly which tests are affected by a change. As a result, we can set apart the tests that will not check the new functionality at all, leaving only those that are really needed to check the new change and its consequences.

We have built a support tool that manages change objects and their relationships with the approach's artefacts. Being developed on top of the Seaside Squeak's environment (www.squeak.org), it allows to maintain these relationships during the whole life-cycle, helping to dynamically manipulate even application objects.

3.1   Representing Changes as First-Class Objects

As we show in Fig. 2, an application is developed by incrementally applying sets of changes (Step 4). Starting from the initial status, a first set of changes is applied in order to get an initial prototype. In further iterations, the application is extended with new sets of changes, fulfilling the requirements one by one. We stress that the main difference with "pure" TDD is that we automatically derive navigation and interaction tests from WebSpec diagrams, we actively use Mockups to derive the final application's interface, and we use interaction tests to guide the development of the application's behavior.

Fig. 2. A TDD-based Web Development Process

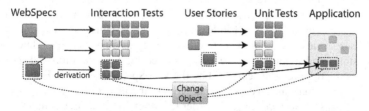

Fig. 3. Change Object's relationship with model and tests artefacts

Fig. 3 illustrates how the approach is improved using change management features. In the first stage, changes made in WebSpecs are captured into change objects. Then, changes made in the application's model are also captured into objects and associated with the corresponding test. We use these objects to reduce the set of interaction tests that drive the upcoming development steps to those affected by them.

WebSpecs can suffer different coarse grained changes, such as the addition or deletion of an *interaction* or *navigation*. These entities can be modified too, by the addition or deletion of widgets to an *interaction*, changes in invariants, etc. Regarding *navigations*, we can add or delete preconditions, change their source, target, or the action that triggers them. All these types of changes have been represented as classes.

3.2 Mapping Requirement Changes onto the Implementation

Some changes have direct effects on concrete application's artefacts; an important aspect of the corresponding change objects is that they can help to reduce the impact of these changes on the implementation. A *WebSpec* change object is associated to an effect on a Web artefact; this effect is also represented as a change object. These objects are able to produce the real modifications on their targets with the help of an *Effect Handler*. The *Effect Handler* is a component that knows how to perform changes on a concrete platform such as Seaside or GWT. For example, when a change modifies an interaction structurally, the page that represents this interaction must be modified: e.g. when a label is added to an interaction, it adds an equivalent label on the page represented by the modified interaction (Fig. 4).

Regarding *navigation* changes, we can change preconditions, sources, targets, or the actions that triggers them. The first type of change does not generate effects on the final application look and feel; in turn, if the *navigation* target changes, we can automate the effect of this change, for example linking the page associated to the new target *interaction*. Something similar happens when a *navigation* action is changed.

Fig. 4. A label addition change in action

4 A Proof of Concept

To illustrate our approach we describe how we put it into work in the Seaside framework, by implementing a specific *Effect Handler* for this platform. In the simplified Twitter-like application presented in Sect. 2, we started with a short sprint to capture the basic user stories: login and tweet. We will only discuss changes related with the tweet use story, and assume that we have finished the first iteration and the application satisfies the requirements captured by the WebSpec presented in Fig. 1.

Let us suppose that our customer wants to add the possibility to navigate from the home to a 'Terms of Service' page. In order to satisfy the new requirement, the development iteration starts with the requirements change (Step 1 in Fig. 2). We specify the *interaction* and *navigation* paths that we expect for the 'Term of service' requirement, which produces a set of change objects derived from the changes in the WebSpec diagram that express the link creation, the creation of the "terms of service" *interaction*, and the *navigation* between both *interactions* (Fig. 5).

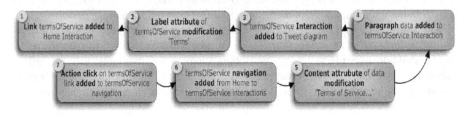

Fig. 5. Change objects associated with the "Terms of Service" requirement

We then derive a set of tests from the WebSpec diagram and find that it generates a new test that checks the terms of service navigation, while in the previous iteration we had two tests that checked the addition of valid and invalid messages. To avoid running all three tests, we ask the Change Manager to determine which are affected by this change. As the only affected is the new one (Step 2 in Fig. 2) we run it, and it fails (Step 3 in Fig. 2), thus we must implement the new changes to satisfy this test.

The process continues with the change effect management (Step 4 in Fig.2) iterating over each change to see how it impacts on the implementation. The first change generates a creation method for the link widget in the *WAHome* class; it represents the page for Home interaction, so it will be drawn each time a *WAHome* instance shows. The next one modifies the widget label attribute to display the correct link name 'Terms'. Fig. 6 shows these effects. Change number 3 creates the Seaside component *WATermsOfService* that represents the page for this interaction. The next change generates a creation method for the paragraph widget in the *WATermsOfServices* class,

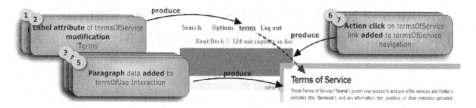

Fig. 6. Managing the effects of the "Term of Use" requirement

and the next one modifies its content attribute, in the creation method. The *navigation* addition change does not produce modifications, but the last change generates the necessary code for associating the *interaction* pages through the "terms" link. Finally, we run the affected test realizing that it passes because of the semi automatic changes we applied on the application, thus completing the iteration (Step 5 in Fig.2).

5 Concluding Remarks and Further Work

In this paper we have presented an approach to deal with navigation and presentation requirement changes in the context of a TDD process for Web applications. Our main strategy has been to reify these changes into "first class" objects, so they can not only capture the history of changes, but also trace the effects of changes in different development artefacts, such as tests and application components.

An integrated tool built on top of the Squeak environment allows us to manipulate these change objects, making them extremely useful in the development process. In particular, we have shown how to help the developer by automating some modifications at the presentation level, or advising him about the necessary changes. At the same time, change objects allow reducing the number of tests that must be run, as they maintain a trace with their corresponding tests. Notice that this kind of change-aware development environment is easier to implement in a reflective system like Squeak, though much harder in Java-based environments such as Eclipse. In this sense, we are working on a light version of our environment for the Eclipse platform.

References

1. Claessen, K., Hughes, J.: QuickCheck: a lightweight tool for random testing of Haskell programs. In: 5th ACM SIGPLAN international conference on Functional programming, pp. 268–279. ACM, New York (2000)
2. Denker, M., Gîrba, T., Lienhard, A., Nierstrasz, O., Renggli, L., Zumkehr, P.: Encapsulating and exploiting change with changeboxes. In: 2007 international conference on Dynamic languages: in conjunction with the 15th International Smalltalk Joint Conference 2007, vol. 286, pp. 25–49. ACM, New York (2007)
3. Jeffries, R.: Extreme programming installed. Addison-Wesley, Boston (2001)
4. Mugridge, R.: Managing Agile Project Requirements with Storytest-Driven Development. IEEE software 25, 68–75 (2008)
5. Rossi, G., Schwabe, D.: Modeling and Implementing Web Applications using OOHDM. In: Web Engineering, Modelling and Implementing Web Applications, pp. 109–155. Springer, Heidelberg (2008)

Adoption of Software Engineering Process Innovations: The Case of Agile Software Development Methodologies

Mali Senapathi

School of Computing and Mathematical Sciences,
Auckland University of Technology, Auckland, New Zealand
mali.senapathi@aut.ac.nz

Abstract. Though agile methodologies have gained widespread acceptance in the past decade, there are still a number of potential adopters who are yet to join the critical mass. Some of these adopters need assurance of whether agile software methodologies will continue to be the dominant software process technology of the 2010s and beyond. This study applies the Software Engineering Process Technologies Adoption Grid proposed by Fichman & Kemerer [3] to evaluate the adoption trajectory of agile software development (ASD) methodologies. The study concludes that ASD methodologies will continue to be the dominant software process technology of the 2010's, and adopted by more business organizations.

Keywords: software process innovation, agile, adoption.

1 Introduction

Agile methodologies have gained widespread acceptance in both the academic and industrial contexts with an increasing number of studies reporting their high adoption and success rates [2, 13]. However, most of these findings are mainly based on American and European data, and there are a number of potential adopters who are yet to join the critical mass.

The Diffusion of Innovations (DOI) theory suggests a total of five adopter categories: innovators, early adopters, early majority, late majority and laggards [10]. While innovators are willing to take risks in adopting an innovation, early adopters have the highest degree of opinion leadership of all adopter categories [16]. Of particular interest and relevance to agile methodologies is the third category, i.e., early majority, who pragmatically weigh the costs and benefits experienced by the early adopters to determine whether or not the innovation will be widely diffused. In their study of early adopters of agile methodologies, [13] found organizational resistance and managerial disinterest as key inhibitors to agile adoption. Therefore, in order to sustain the current high adoption rates, chief information officer (CIO)s and managers of business organizations who have currently adopted agile methodologies or who intend to do so in the future need reassurance of whether they will continue to be the dominant software process technology of the 2010's and beyond? In this paper, a robust process that should help organizations to answer this question is described. The current study

A. Sillitti et al. (Eds.): XP 2010, LNBIP 48, pp. 226–231, 2010.

uses Fichman & Kemerer's [3] adoption framework to evaluate agile adoption from two perspectives: diffusion of innovations and economics of technology standards. The brief description of the Software Engineering Process Technologies Adoption Grid in section 2 is adapted from [3]. It provides background and context to the current study. In section 3, the framework is applied to evaluate the adoption trajectory of ASD methodologies, and conclusions are drawn in section 4.

2 Framework for Assessing Software Engineering Process Technologies

The software engineering process technologies adoption grid proposed by [3] consists of two dimensions, each of which is based on a technology adoption perspective: the first dimension is based on the theory of diffusion of innovations (DOI) perspective, and the second dimension, the economics of technology standards perspective which is used to study the community effects of a process technology's inherent economic value [3].

DOI research is defined as the study of the dissemination of innovations through a population of potential adopters over time and within a particular social system. The rate of adoption of an innovation is impacted by five generic innovation attributes, i) *relative advantage* - degree to which an innovation is perceived as technically superior to its predecessor, 2) *compatibility* - degree to which an innovation is perceived as compatible with existing values, skills, and, work practices 3) *observability* - degree to which the results of an innovation's use can be easily observed , 4) *trialability* - may be experimented with on a limited basis without undue effort and expense, and 5) *complexity* - degree to which it is perceived as relatively difficult to understand and use [10]. All innovation attributes are positively correlated with the rate of adoption except complexity which is negatively correlated with rate of adoption.

The economics of technology standards perspective is based on the premise that the benefits of adoption also depend on the size of the current and future network of adopters. While the DOI perspective recognizes the effects of community adoption on how potential adopters perceive a new innovation, community adoption levels affect the inherent value of any class of innovation that has large increasing returns to adoption, where increasing returns to adoption is defined as the dependency between the benefits of adoption and the size of the community of other adopters. The important factors that help in the prediction of whether an innovation will achieve critical mass are: 1) *prior technology "drag"* - provides significant network benefits because of a large and mature installed base, 2) *investment irreversibility* -adoption requires irreversible investments in areas such as training and accumulated project experience, 3) *sponsorship* - sponsors exist in the form of person, organization, consortium etc., to define the class of innovations, set standards, and provide guidelines for practice for the community of early adopters and 4) *positive expectations* - innovation benefits from an extended period of widespread expectations that it will be pervasively adopted in the future.

3 Agile Software Development Methodology: Where Does It Fit?

ASD methodology is analyzed using the two dimensions of the software process technologies adoption framework. Figure 1 shows the unified framework based on the two perspectives on technology adoption: the vertical axis reflects the DOI view of organizational adoptability, and the horizontal axis reflects the economics of technology standards perspective of community adoptability. Each of the four quadrants defines a distinctive adoptive trajectory: **Niche -** adopters who have optimistic expectations about future levels of adoption, but adoption will fall short of dominance because of failure to achieve critical mass, **Dominant technology** - the innovation will face relatively low barriers to adoption, **Slow Mover** - it will diffuse steadily but slowly because of the difficulty of individual or organization adoption, and **Experimental -** will need to evolve before it is widely adopted as a dominant technology.

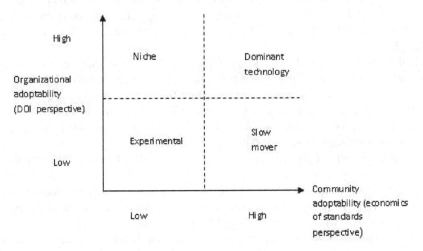

Fig. 1. Software Engineering Process Technologies Adoption Grid [3]

3.1 Organizational Adoptability

Relative Advantage: ASD methodologies claim to provide specific benefits such as lean documentation and moderate planning, in comparison to the heavy-documentation and highly restrictive planning requirements of traditional methodologies. ASD methods also claim to provide a number of benefits such as increased productivity, improved quality, reduced time and costs, maintainable and extensible code, improved morale, better collaboration, and higher customer satisfaction [13]. Therefore, the relative advantage of ASD methodologies can be rated as high.

Compatibility: ASD methodologies rate unfavorably on the compatibility dimension. The shift from the traditional approaches to agile methods entails major alterations to work practices, investment in tools that support and facilitate rapid iterative development, versioning/configuration management, JUnits, refactoring and other agile techniques [12]. The adopters will be required to learn and adapt to some challenging and controversial new practices such as test-first development. The emphasis on critical people factors for developers, such as amicability, talent, skill, and communication [4], and the need for consistent involvement of knowledgeable and committed customers add further challenges to compatibility. The ideas and practices of shared learning, and collaborative decision making may be overwhelming for developers who are accustomed to solitary activities or working with relatively homogeneous teams [12].

Complexity: Agile methods do not have any serious complexity issues. Many studies have reported that agile methods do not take long time to learn and are easy to use [1, 2]. Moreover, most agile methods require much less formal training than traditional methods, and practices such as pair programming are rather found to act as training aids where people tend to mentor and learn from each other [9]. In terms of learning the practices, entire books are now devoted by agile proponents and practitioners to presenting the practices, values, implementation details and guidelines for potential adopters, including a number of practitioner case studies. Agile methodologies, therefore rates favorably on the complexity dimension.

Trialability: Currently the most popular approach followed by organizations is by trialing a specific agile method or practice on either a single project or a small number of projects [1]. The number of studies that have been able to demonstrate value on a single project is consistently on the rise [2]. Hence, ASD methodology rates higher on the trialability dimension.

Observability: Agile methodologies rate high on observability, as a number of studies report on setting up projects to observe and learn about specific agile practices [14]. Many comparative studies have drawn comparisons between, for example, software developed using traditional and XP methodologies, practices such as test-first and test-last development, and individual versus pair programming [5, 7, 15].

In summary, the current perception on Agile methodologies can be summarized as having high relative advantage, low compatibility, low to moderate complexity, high trialability and high observability.

3.2 Community Adoptability: Economics of Technology Standards

Prior technology drag: None of the previous traditional approaches have taken a dominant mainstream position at any time [6]. Therefore, in the absence of any dominant and widely adopted prior methodologies, ASD methodologies do not have the risk of facing any major well-established base of prior methodologies. Therefore, the prior technology drag for ASD methodologies will be low.

Irreversible investments: The values and practices of most agile methodologies are derived from the 'lessons-learnt' by real practitioners in the industry, and are mainly based on prior known approaches such as rapid application development and iterative and incremental software development[12]. Therefore, adopting an agile methodology will entail making use of existing network of experienced personnel and a comprehensive spectrum of well known development tools and techniques, and will not require large irreversible investments in staff training, software, and other development tools and techniques. It is believed that "experience with actual building systems are much more important than experience with agile development methods" [9], and agile methods require less formal training than traditional structured methodologies.

Sponsorship and positive characteristics: On the sponsorship dimension, agile methodologies do not have one but many founding fathers such as Kent Beck, Ken Schwaber, and Alistair Cockburn. A number of books have been published which provide guidance in the use of many agile practices. For example, Schwaber has published books to provide guidance in the practices that characterize Scrum methodology, including the recently published 'Scrum Guide' that can be considered the formal definition of the method [11]. And the number of agile user groups is consistently increasing. For example, under the Agile alliance user groups itself, currently there are 70 groups under United States, 41 in Europe, and 16 in the Asia Pacific region. The main objective of these groups is to foster and encourage the use of agile methodologies in organizations. Companies such as IBM Rational® have also started providing a range of agile development solutions that organizations can choose from, to suit their individual specific business needs and requirements. Therefore agile methodologies rates favorably on this dimension.

Positive Expectations: The main strengths of agile methodologies such as emergent requirements and rapid change complements contemporary industry trends towards achieving business value by rapid delivery of systems [4]. They are also gaining popularity in the academic community [2], [15]. With consistent and growing support from both the commercial and the academic sectors, ASD methodologies possess many characteristics that will lead to an extended period of a number of positive expectations.

To summarize, ASD methodologies face a low prior methodology drag, low irreversible investments, and enjoy the benefits of a strong and wide sponsorship base, and positive expectations. Hence, the economics of technology standards view implies an easy community adoption of ASD methodologies.

Based on the combined ratings on ease of both organizational and community adoption the study places ASD methodology in the dominant quadrant of the framework.

4 Conclusions

Using the adoption framework proposed by [3], the study evaluated and analyzed the adoption trajectory of Agile Methodologies, and concluded that it is likely to continue to be the dominant software process technology of the 2010s and beyond. The current study should give reassurance to CIOs and managers of business organizations, who have currently adopted or intend to adopt agile methodologies in the future.

If it is accepted that agile methodologies will continue to dominate the next decade of systems development, then it should lead to a greater interest amongst researchers to i) conduct post-adoption studies to evaluate the effectiveness of their usage in organizations, and ii) gain deeper understanding of *"what the effects are of the changes that emerge in response to the adoption of agile development"*[2].

References

1. Bahli, B., Zeid, E.S.A.: The role of knowledge creation in adopting extreme programming model: an empirical study. In: ITI 3rd international Conference on Information and Communiations Technologies for the New Knowledge Society (2005)
2. Dyba, T., Dingsoyr, T.: Empirical studies of Agile Software Development: A systematic review. Information and Software Technology 50, 833–859 (2008)
3. Fichman, R.G., Kemerer, C.F.: Adoption of Software Engineering Process Innovations: The Case of Object Orientation. Sloan Management Review 34(2), 7–22 (1993)
4. Highsmith, J.: Agile Software Development Ecosystems. In: Cockburn, A., Highsmith, J. (eds.) The Agile Software Development Series, Addison-Wesley, Boston (2002)
5. Ilieva, S., Ivanov, P., Stefanova, E.: Analyses of an agile methodology implementation. In: Proceedings 30th Euromicro Conference, pp. 326–333. IEEE Computer Society Press, Los Alamitos (2004)
6. Johnson, R.: Object-Oriented Systems Development: A review of empirical research. Communications of the ACM 8, 65–81 (2002)
7. Layman, L., Williams, L., Cunningham, L.: Exploring extreme programming in context: An industrial case study Agile Development Conference. In: ADC (2004)
8. Lindstrom, L., Jeffries, R.: Extreme Programming and Agile Software Development Methodologies. Information Systems Management 21(3), 41–52 (2004)
9. Lindvall, M., Basili, V.R., Boehm, B.: Empirical Findings in Agile Methods. In: Proceedings of XP Agile Universe (2002)
10. Rogers, E.M.: Diffusion of Innovations. Free Press, New York (2003)
11. SA09. Scrum Guide, Scrum Alliance (2009), http://www.scrumalliance.org/resources
12. Sridhar, N., Radhakanta, M.: Challenges of Migrating to Agile Methodologies. Communications of the ACM 48(5), 73–78 (2005)
13. Vijayasarathy, L.R., Turk, D.: Agile Software Development: A survey of early adopters. Journal of Information Technology Management 19(2) (2008)
14. Tessem: Experiences in learning XP practices: a qualitative study. In: Marchesi, M., Succi, G. (eds.) XP 2003. LNCS, vol. 2675, pp. 131–137. Springer, Heidelberg (2003)
15. Wellington, C.A., Briggs, T., Girard, C.D.: Comparison of student experiences with plan-driven and agile methodologies. In: Proceedings of the 35th ASEE/IEEE Frontiers in Education Conference (2005)
16. Moore, G.A.: Crossing the Chasm: Marketing and Selling High-Tech products to Mainstream customers, New York, Harper-Collins (2001)

A Quantitative Comparison of Test-First and Test-Last Code in an Industrial Project

Burak Turhan[1], Ayse Bener[2], Pasi Kuvaja[1], and Markku Oivo[1]

[1] M-Group, Department of Information Processing Science,
University of Oulu, 90014, Oulu, Finland
{burak.turhan,pasi.kuvaja,markku.oivo}@oulu.fi
[2] Department of Computer Engineering, Bogazici University, 34342, Istanbul, Turkey
bener@boun.edu.tr

Abstract. This paper presents a comparison of test-first and test-last development approaches on a customer account management software of a telecommunication company. While the management had plans for initiating a process that enforces test-first development over test-last, they also had concerns about the tradeoffs. Therefore, an exploratory case study with quantitative analysis is carried out on a pilot project where the code metrics and estimated manual inspection efforts of both approaches are compared. Our results indicate no statistical difference between the two approaches in terms of design (CK) metrics. On the other hand, we observe that test-last development yields significantly simpler code in terms of cyclomatic complexity and less (though not significant) manual inspection effort. Hence, our initial results indicate no superiority of test-first over test-last development in the described industrial context.

Keywords: Test first, Test last, Code metrics, Case study.

1 Introduction

Test-first, or test driven development (TDD), is still a hot topic for both practitioners and researchers. From a practitioner's perspective, it is supposed to drive implementation and design via tests, resulting in shorter, simpler, more reliable, better maintainable and self-documenting code. On the other hand, there are conflicting research outcomes in terms of test-first's expected effects on design quality, programmer productivity and product quality (i.e. number of defects), which reflects the researcher point of view.

It is not the goal of this paper to investigate the conflicting outcomes of different research outcomes. However, it is worth mentioning considering the motivation of this research, that our industrial partner needs an answer to the following question: "Is it worth institutionalizing test-first development over traditional test-last?". The conflicting research outcomes suggest that the answer is not that obvious and an insight- possibly context dependent- can only be achieved through a comparative trial. This paper presents the results of our initial empirical study for answering the above question.

A. Sillitti et al. (Eds.): XP 2010, LNBIP 48, pp. 232–237, 2010.

This paper is organized as follows: We provide a brief discussion about research results related to our study, in the next section. Then the research setting is described in terms of context, data, methods and analysis. Before presenting our conclusions, we discuss the results and the limitations of our study.

2 Related Work

Empirical software engineering literature contains contradicting reports regarding the comparison of test-first and test-last methods. Siniaalto and Abrahamsson report five industrial case studies, where the traditional (CK and complexity) metrics collected from TDD and iterative test-last projects are compared [7]. They observe that depth of inheritance tree (DIT), response for a class (RFC) and McCabe's cyclomatic complexity (CC) are significantly lower in TDD projects, while other CK metrics are not significantly different. However, as they state, this is in contradiction with other results. Muller reports significant differences except for DIT and weighted methods for class (WMC) between test-first and test-last methods [5]. Vu et al. observe less WMC for test-first [8]. On the other hand they report, as well as Kaufmann and Janzen [3], no significant difference in CC. Further, Janzen and Saiedian reports significant increase in CC and no change in coupling between objects (CBO) when test-first is used [2].

Considering external quality, Madeyski reports increased number of defects as test-first is employed [4]. On the contrary, Williams et al. report 40% reduction in defect rates [9]. Then again Erdogmus et al. report no difference in external quality [1].

In summary, previous research report contradicting results in terms of complexity, design metrics and defect rates. Therefore, there is no convincing evidence regarding the effect of test-first on architecture, code complexity and test effort compared to test-last. In this sense, our case study provides further evidence to understand this issue.

3 Case Study

3.1 Context and Data

This research is carried out as a single exploratory case study on a small scale pilot project that has just been passed to the quality assurance (QA) team at the time of the analysis. The project is developed in Java and it consists of adding new features to the customer account management software of the telecommunication services provider. Two senior developers have worked on different parts of the project using the different development methods under examination, i.e. one developer followed traditional test-last while the other used test-first development. Before this project, the test-first developer had 3 months experience with test-first. They both performed iterative development and were co-located during the project with access to the same tools that they use in their natural

Table 1. Project summary

development	#classes	#methods	#devs	total loc
test-first	12	50	1	737
test-last	12	91	1	732
total	24	141	2	1469

Table 2. Descriptive statistics. (*lcom: lack of cohesion in methods,* rfc: response for a class, *wmc: weighted methods per class,* cbo: coupling between objects, *cc: cyclomatic complexity,* eff: estimated manual inspection effort, *p-value: p-value of normality test*).

metric	#data		mean		stdDev		median		min		max		p-value	
	tf	tl	tf	tl	tf	tl	tf	tl	tf	tl	tf	tl	tf	tl
lcom	12	12	2.25	2.58	3.44	3.08	1.00	1.00	1.00	0.00	13.00	10.00	**0.001**	**0.001**
rfc	12	12	7.08	8.50	6.84	8.02	4.00	4.50	2.00	0.00	26.00	24.00	0.078	**0.033**
wmc	12	12	4.16	7.58	5.21	8.02	2.00	4.00	1.00	0.00	17.00	24.00	**0.001**	**0.029**
cbo	12	12	1.00	0.83	0.95	1.11	1.00	0.00	0.00	0.00	2.00	3.00	**0.016**	**0.001**
cc	50	91	1.96	1.75	1.62	2.10	1.00	1.00	1.00	1.00	7.00	15.00	**0.001**	**0.001**
eff	12	12	31.75	8.66	53.04	20.28	0.00	0.00	0.00	0.00	157.00	55.00	**0.001**	**0.001**

setting. A summary of project attributes is provided in Table 1 along with their breakdown to test-first and test-last methods.

We have used a static analyzer tool (Predictive 3) for automated data collection from source code. The tool flags source code methods for manual inspection along with their risk assessment (high, medium, low), and also extracts code artifacts such as CK-metrics[1], McCabe's cyclomatic complexity and lines-of-code metrics. Since we do not have defect related data, we focused on inspection effort instead. We have used the length of flagged code methods as an estimation of manual inspection effort for the encapsulating class. The descriptive statistics of the collected data are provided in Table 2.

3.2   Analysis Methods

The independent variable in our analysis is the development method (i.e. test-first or test-last) and the dependent variables are the collected code metrics. We have postulated, and performed statistical tests on, six hypotheses corresponding to each dependent variable. Table 3 shows a list of these hypothesis. In each hypothesis, we have compared the distributions of the associated metric in test-first and test-last data groups, looking for significant differences and, if any, their directions.

Before applying a particular statistical test, we checked for normality in each distribution. We observed that none of the metrics are normally distributed in

---

[1] Inheritance was not used in neither test-first nor test-last part of the project. Therefore, DIT and NOC metrics have unique (i.e. zero) values and are discarded.

Table 3. Hypothesis. (tf: test-first, tl:test-last).

metric	H_0	H_A
lcom	$LCOM_{tf} = LCOM_{tl}$	$LCOM_{tf} \neq LCOM_{tl}$
rfc	$RFC_{tf} = RFC_{tl}$	$RFC_{tf} \neq RFC_{tl}$
wmc	$WMC_{tf} = WMC_{tl}$	$WMC_{tf} \neq WMC_{tl}$
cbo	$CBO_{tf} = CBO_{tl}$	$CBO_{tf} \neq CBO_{tl}$
cc	$CC_{tf} = CC_{tl}$	$CC_{tf} \neq CC_{tl}$
eff	$EFF_{tf} = EFF_{tl}$	$EFF_{tf} \neq EFF_{tl}$

both groups (Last column of Table 2 shows the p-values for the Kolmogorov-Smirnov normality tests, with Lilliefors correction). Therefore, we have used a non-parametric test, i.e. Mann-Whitney U Test, to check for statistical differences. In all tests we use the significance level $\alpha = 0.05$. All analysis are done in Matlab R2007a.

3.3   Results and Discussions

Table 4 summarizes the results of all hypothesis. We observe no significant difference between test-first and test-last groups in terms of design quality captured by CK metrics. Specifically, there is strong evidence for failing to reject the null hypotheses for LCOM and RFC and CBO. Though the average number of methods per class for test-last doubles that of test-first, there is not enough evidence to conclude for a significant difference in WMC.

The only significant difference is observed in the method level cyclomatic complexity. The direction is in favor of test-last, i.e. test-last generates simpler code than test-first. The reason becomes clear when we check Table 1 again. It is due to the equivalent size, yet different number of methods (i.e. a factor of 2) produced by the two approaches. Test-last's average method length is expected to be around half of the test-first's. We observe this difference possibly due to the fact that cyclomatic complexity is strongly correlated with method length [6]. We have conducted additional analysis that compares total and average cyclomatic complexity at the class level. However, there was not enough evidence for significant difference at this level.

Finally, we observe no difference in the estimated manual inspection effort, which is measured by the length of methods that are flagged by the static analysis tool. Though, there is no significant difference, the inspection effort for test-last is much less than the counterpart (i.e. 381 and 104 lines of code corresponding to 25% and 7% of the total size respectively).

3.4   Limitations

Our study has certain limitations that need to be considered:

- Our results are valid within the context of the case study that is described in earlier sections. Their external validity should be pursued with further empirical research methods in different contexts.

Table 4. Results

H_0	Reject	Direction	p-value
lcom	no	tf = tl	0.917
rfc	no	tf = tl	0.953
wmc	no	tf = tl	0.334
cbo	no	tf = tl	0.636
cc	**yes**	$tf > tl$	**0.047**
eff	no	tf = tl	0.239

- Though both developers are seniors, our results may be affected by their individual performances. It was not possible to control this factor given the nature of our study. Since both developers worked in their natural settings and have the same work title, we assume that the effect of this factor is at a minimum level.
- Conformance to the development practices could not be measured objectively. We do not know whether the test-first developer strictly adhered to test-first practices. This is a common issue for many reported results in literature, where the developers' self evaluations are taken for granted. Future studies may benefit from free tools, (i.e. http://csdl.ics.hawaii.edu/research/zorro), to overcome this issue.
- Number of data points in our analysis is few, especially at the class level, that threatens the validity of the statistical tests. Further case studies at larger scales are planned in order to overcome this limitation. We have used method level metrics in order to partially address this issue, whenever possible (i.e. CC).
- We have estimated the manual inspection effort based on the static analysis tool's predictions. However, to the best of our knowledge, several US based government agencies and private businesses employ this tool including NASA IV&V, NASA - Goddard Space Flight Center, U.S. Army, Intuit and Northrop Grumman, which can be considered as the industry's confidence to the tool's predictions.

4   Conclusions

We have presented an exploratory case study investigating the differences between test-first and test-last development methods. Our results indicate no statistical difference between the two approaches in terms of CK metrics. However, test-last code is found to be significantly simpler than test-first code in terms of cyclomatic complexity. Though not significant, we have observed less estimated manual inspection effort in favor of test-last development.

We believe that our contributions are relevant for both practice and research:

1. Based on the outcomes of this initial study, the company management decided to carry on further trials before making a decision about transition from test-last to test-first.

2. While the validity of case studies are limited within their context, a generalization of results is only possible by combining multiple results for the same question from various contexts. In this sense, we have reported a case study that describes a *real-life industrial* context.

Acknowledgements

This research is partially supported by: Tubitak under grant number EEEAG 108E014 and FLEXI project http://www.flexi-itea2.org

References

1. Erdogmus, H., Morisio, M., Torchiano, M.: On the Effectiveness of the Test-First Approach to Programming. IEEE Trans. Softw. Eng. 31(3), 226–237 (2005)
2. Janzen, D.S., Saiedian, H.: On the Influence of Test-Driven Development on Software Design. In: 19th Conference on Software Engineering Education and Training (CSEET 2006), pp. 141–148. IEEE Press, New York (2006)
3. Kaufmann, R., Janzen, D.: Implications of Test-Driven Development A Pilot Study. In: 18th Annual ACM Conference on Object-Oriented Programming, Systems, Languages and Applications (OOPSLA 2003), pp. 298–299. ACM, New York (2003)
4. Madeyski, L.: Preliminary Analysis of the Effects of Pair Programming and Test-Driven Development on the External Code Quality. In: Zieli?ski, K., Szmuc, T. (eds.) Frontiers in Artificial Intelligence and Applications, vol. 130, pp. 113–123. IOS Press, Amsterdam (2005)
5. Müller, M.M.: The Effect of Test-Driven Development on Program Code. In: Abrahamsson, P., Marchesi, M., Succi, G. (eds.) XP 2006. LNCS, vol. 4044, pp. 94–103. Springer, Heidelberg (2006)
6. Shepperd, M.J., Ince, D.C.: A Critique of Three Metrics. Journal of Systems and Software 26(3), 197–210 (1994)
7. Siniaalto, M., Abrahamsson, P.: Does Test-Driven Development Improve the Program Code? Alarming Results from a Comparative Case Study. In: Meyer, B., Nawrocki, J.R., Walter, B. (eds.) CEE-SET 2007. LNCS, vol. 5082, pp. 143–156. Springer, Heidelberg (2008)
8. Vu, J.H., Frojd, N., Shenkel-Therolf, C., Janzen, D.S.: Evaluating Test-Driven Development in an Industry-Sponsored Capstone Project. In: Proceedings of the Sixth international Conference on information Technology: New Generations (ITNG 2009), vol. 00, pp. 229–234. IEEE Computer Society, Washington (2009)
9. Williams, L., Maximilien, E.M., Vouk, M.: Test-Driven Development as a Defect-Reduction Practice. In: Proceedings of the 14th international Symposium on Software Reliability Engineering (ISSRE 2003), pp. 34–45. IEEE Computer Society, Washington (2003)

Product and Release Planning Practices for Extreme Programming

Gert van Valkenhoef[1,2], Tommi Tervonen[1],
Bert de Brock[1], and Douwe Postmus[2]

[1] Faculty of Economics and Business, University of Groningen, The Netherlands
{g.h.m.van.valkenhoef,t.p.tervonen,e.o.de.brock}@rug.nl
[2] Dep. of Epidemiology, University Medical Center Groningen, The Netherlands
d.postmus@epi.umcg.nl

Abstract. Extreme Programming (XP) is an agile software development methodology defined through a set of practices and values. Although the value of XP is well-established through various real-life case studies, it lacks practices for project management. In order to enable XP for larger projects, we provide the rolling forecast practice to support product planning, and an optimization model to assist in release planning. We briefly evaluate the new practices with a real-life case study.

Keywords: Planning, extreme programming, integer programming.

1   Introduction

Extreme Programming (XP) is one of the most "agile" software development methodologies. Unlike plan-driven methodologies (e.g. waterfall) that define software development as a process, XP defines it through values and practices proven to work well together in real-life software development [1,2]. A good project management process and strong customer involvement are critical to project success in XP [3]. Although XP provides a consistent set of practices, it almost completely lacks practices for planning [4]. Therefore, although XP has been reported to be tailorable for large-scale projects [5], it is generally considered more suitable for small projects. Moreover, the 'on-site customer' practice [1] is often hard to implement due to organizational or time constraints [6]. The XP customer is consistently under significantly more pressure than the developers or other participants in the project [7]. This causes the following problems (which become worse as projects get larger):

1. Lack of management context: XP does not address the larger context in which release planning takes place, or the long term project goals [4]. This means that the customer or the developers may loose track of the overall purpose of the system and consequently make sub-optimal planning decisions.
2. User story overload: the number of user stories to be considered in release planning can make the planning process too demanding for the customer.

A. Sillitti et al. (Eds.): XP 2010, LNBIP 48, pp. 238–243, 2010.
© Springer-Verlag Berlin Heidelberg 2010

3. Prioritization stress: the responsibility of prioritizing user stories may cause stress for the customer, even for a small number of stories. It is difficult to foresee the consequences and adequacy of the prioritization [7], and it is unclear whether the customer perceives business value in constantly managing the development priorities [8].

To address these problems, this paper proposes two new planning practices for XP. First, we assist in product planning with the new practice of rolling forecasts (Section 2). This practice helps to provide management context often lacking in XP (Problem 1 above). Second, we introduce an automated planning aid that can be used during release planning to reduce the customer workload by generating a suggested plan that satisfies simultaneously the constraints imposed by the customer and the limited development resources (Section 3). This addresses issues 2 and 3 identified above. After introducing the practices, we demonstrate their use in a real-life study (Section 4), before giving concluding remarks (Section 5).

2 Rolling Forecast for Product Planning

Expectation management is often the key difference between failed and succesful software projects [9]. XP originally proposes the 'system metaphor' practice for expectation management [1]. However, in practice, 'system metaphor' is difficult to apply and not useful, and is therefore often not implemented [6]. The 'system metaphor' has since been removed from XP [2], and there is no replacement practice addressing expectation management. The lack of an expectation management practice that is coherent with the rest of the methodology can cause additional project risks, especially if the customer is not constantly available on-site, as is often the case (see [6]).

Product planning should provide the context in which the release planning takes place [10]. In each release, before stories are elicited, the customers should have a rough idea of the current state of the system and the direction of development. This is promoted in XP by having the customer test and accept implemented stories and by frequently giving system demonstrations. However, it is unclear how a shared vision of the direction of future development can be established, especially when the customer does not clearly know what (s)he wants. As a consequence, an upfront rigid planning of the whole product in concrete terms is often almost impossible and can also become counter productive ('analysis paralysis').

To support product planning, we introduce the practice *rolling forecast*. At project inception, an overview of the *product goals* is drawn up by the customer together with the project manager. The goals should be stated in a functional format but in such a way that they cannot readily be broken into themes without further analysis and elicitation. The goals serve to provide a shared vision of the system and to form a basis for user story elicitation, but they are not requirements *per se*. It is advisable to re-evaluate the overall goals periodically, e.g. after every fourth release.

After defining the product goals, a *theme forecast* is created by the customer, project manager and a development team representative (e.g., an analyst or technical manager). A theme forecast consists of a set of themes, their likely implementation order, and a prediction of which themes will be realized in the coming two or three releases. The theme forecast can be adapted in preparation of every release planning (before story elicitation). Thus, a *rolling forecast* manages the expectations about the software by iteratively developing theme forecasts based on overall product goals. Then, in release planning, the theme forecast is taken into account when deciding on the themes and stories for the next release, while iteration planning takes into account (and adjusts) the release plan in choosing the stories and identifying the tasks for the next iteration, i.e., the normal agile planning practices are applicable at the release and iteration levels [10,11].

3   Supporting Release Planning Model

Our planning model is aimed to support release planning. The developers elicit stories from the customer and ask him/her to evaluate them with respect to their business value on an interval scale, e.g. 1–5. Then the developers evaluate the stories' implementation complexity in story points. The model provides a planning aid by maximizing the implemented business value, taking into account constraints on implementation complexity and precedence relations. A precedence relation is interpreted as a story not having value unless another (preceding) story is implemented. Moreover, in XP, related stories are often grouped into themes that represent larger pieces of related user functionality, and synergy effects occur when all stories within a theme are implemented [2]. We model such effects by awarding extra value to a theme of stories if they are implemented together in a single release. Note that not all stories need to belong to a theme, and that one story can belong to more than one theme. We don't allow themes to span multiple releases in order to prevent the supporting planning model being used for making longer term plans, that might lower the overall agility of the XP development process. Longer-term product goals should instead be handled with the other proposed practice, rolling forecast.

Our model assumes adherence to the standard best practices regarding story and theme sizes. Stories should be small enough that they can easily be implemented in a single iteration, and themes in a single release. Moreover, a theme should consist of the *minimal set of stories* required to achieve the aforementioned synergy effect. Not adhering to these guidelines may lead to inappropriate results from the model.

The story selection can be formulated as a knapsack problem (the complete integer programming formulation is given in Model 1). Let us denote by n the number of uncompleted stories. Each story i has a business value of b_i and implementation complexity of c_i story points. The total amount of story points that can be implemented during a release is denoted by p. The decision problem is to select the most valuable subset of stories to implement in a release (Model 1:

Model 1. The optimization model as a side-constrained knapsack problem

1. max $b_1 x_1 + \ldots + b_{n+m} x_{n+m}$
2. s.t. $c_1 x_1 + \ldots + c_{n+m} x_{n+m} \leq p$
3. $\quad x_j - x_i \qquad\qquad\quad \leq 0 \qquad$ for all i,j where $x_i \succ x_j$
4. $\quad \sum_{i=1}^{n} a_{ij} x_i - s_j x_{n+j} \geq 0 \qquad$ for $j = n+1, \ldots, n+m$
5. $\quad \sum_{i=1}^{n} a_{ij} x_i - x_{n+j} \quad \leq s_j - 1$ for $j = n+1, \ldots, n+m$
6. $\quad x_1, \ldots, x_{n+m} \in \{0,1\}.$

---

1), subject to a budget constraint on the maximum implementation complexity (Model 1: 2). For each story $i \in \{1, \ldots, n\}$, let $x_i = 1$ if story i is selected and $x_i = 0$ otherwise (Model 1: 6). Precedence of story i to story j is denoted by $x_i \succ x_j$ and can be incorporated into the optimization model by adding the following constraint: $x_j - x_i \leq 0$ (Model 1: 3).

To model themes, let m be the number of themes and let s_j $(j \in \{1, \ldots, m\})$ be the number of stories within theme j. Theme j can be included in the model by introducing a dummy story $(n + j)$, such that $x_{n+j} = 1$ if and only if all stories within theme j are implemented (Model 1: 4–5). The business value b_{n+j} associated with story $(n + j)$ represents the additional value that is awarded when all stories within theme j are implemented; its implementation complexity c_{n+j} is set equal to zero.

We implemented the supporting release planning model using R (http://www.r-project.org) and lp_solve (http://lpsolve.sourceforge.net). Our implementation is freely available online (http://github.com/gertvv/xpplan).

4 Real-Life Example

We are involved in a research project with external customers that expect us to develop software artifacts for the application domain of pharmacological decision support. Our development environment consists of 2 teams working part-time. In the following, we detail how we used the rolling forecast practice and our planning model in the development of ADDIS (see http://drugis.org).

Rolling Forecast. Although we didn't have clear requirements, we couldn't wait until the research results were present. In order to generate an overall view on the project and the first theme forecast, we interviewed the external customers of the research project. The initial forecast (Figure 1, top) was constructed considering 16 goals, such as "the system should provide drug efficacy and safety information". The theme forecast consists of a detailed set of themes for the next release(s) and a more global set of (likely) themes for the more distant releases. The forecast helped us to elicit stories in release planning meetings with the main external customer, who also chose the stories to implement. Figure 1 shows how our mutual understanding of the project evolved during the first half-year of development (only the most important themes are shown). We initially decided to focus on 'benefit risk' as a long-term goal. This defined our priorities

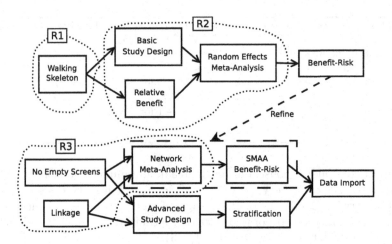

Fig. 1. The theme forecast for the beginning of the project (top) and the updated forecast (bottom) before release 3 (R3). A solid arrow from A to B indicates A has priority over B. The actually implemented themes from release 1 (R1) and 2 (R2) are shown, as well as the expected themes for release 3 (dotted lines). The dashed arrow indicates a high-level theme being refined as more information became available.

for the first two releases. We knew that to actually implement 'benefit-risk', research input would be needed. As these results became available only during the second release, the forecast was refined. Simultaneously, we were able to identify additional themes that also support our long-term goals, as well as two themes ('no empty screens' and 'linkage') that generate interest for our software through usability.

Planning Model. We did the first release (ADDIS 0.2) as a burn-in for velocity estimation and to create an initial end-to-end working system (also known as a 'walking skeleton', see http://alistair.cockburn.us/Walking+skeleton). Therefore we didn't estimate story business values while planning the first release. During the second release (ADDIS 0.4), we estimated story business values (scale: 1-5), story complexities (scale: 1,2,3,5,8), technical precedence relations (none were identified) and themes. In this release, we could identify 3 themes as being the most important. After the release was completed, we ran our supporting optimization model for release planning. We tested the sensitivity of the optimization model and differences between the model's solution and the stories we actually implemented by varying the theme value from 0 to 99. The results didn't differ much from our manually planned implementation order and the model showed to be robust with respect to changes in theme value: the only differences emerged when the theme value changed from 0 to 1 and from 10 to 11. When theme values varied between $1-10$ the same two out of three themes were included in the optimal solution whereas with theme value > 10 all three themes were included.

5   Conclusions

Lack of management context, user story overload, and prioritization stress cause high workload for the customer and hinder scalability of XP to larger projects. To overcome these limitations, we propose two new practices: rolling forecast for product planning and release planning support through an optimization model. We evaluated the applicability of our new practices in a software development project and found them useful. However, we do not have sufficient evidence to make claims about their suitability for projects with different customer profiles, numbers of developers, or levels of developer competency. Our ongoing development project cannot address these questions, and additional appropriate empirical studies should be initiated. Our future research will investigate how business value should be estimated for themes, and how uncertainty can be made explicit in the planning process.

Acknowledgements. This study was partly supported by the Escher project (T6-202), which is a project of the Dutch Top Institute Pharma.

References

1. Beck, K.: Extreme Programming Explained, 1st edn. Addison-Wesley, Reading (1999)
2. Beck, K.: Extreme Programming Explained, 2nd edn. Addison-Wesley, Reading (2005)
3. Chow, T., Cao, D.B.: A survey study of critical success factors in agile software projects. Journal of Systems and Software 81(6), 961–971 (2008)
4. Abrahamsson, P., Warsta, J., Siponen, M., Ronkainen, J.: New directions on agile methods: a comparative analysis. In: IEEE Proceedings of the International Conference on Software Engineering, Portland, Oregon, USA, pp. 244–254 (2003)
5. Cao, L., Mohan, K., Xu, P.: How extreme does extreme programming have to be? adapting XP practices to large-scale projects. In: Proceedings of the 37th Hawaii International Conference on System Sciences, Waikoloa, Hawaii (2004)
6. Rumpe, B., Schröder, A.: Quantitative survey on extreme programming projects. In: Proceedings of the Third International Conference on Extreme Programming and Flexible Processes in Software Engineering, Sardinia, Italy, pp. 26–30 (2002)
7. Martin, A., Biddle, R., Noble, J.: The XP customer role in practice: three studies. In: Agile Development Conference (ADC 2004), Salt Lake City, Utah, USA (2004)
8. Grisham, P.S., Perry, D.E.: Customer relationships and extreme programming. In: HSSE 2005: Proceedings of the 2005 workshop on Human and social factors of software engineering, pp. 1–6. ACM, New York (2005)
9. Boehm, B., Turner, R.: Balancing agility and discipline: a guide to the perplexed. Addison-Wesley, Reading (2003)
10. Cohn, M.: Agile Estimating and Planning. Robert C. Martin Series. Prentice Hall PTR, Englewood Cliffs (2005)
11. Beck, K., Fowler, M.: Planning Extreme Programming. Addison-Wesley, Reading (2001)

Launchpad's Quest for a Better and Agile User Interface

Martin Albisetti

Canonical Ltd, User Experience and Design
martin.albisetti@canonical.com
http://www.canonical.com/

Abstract. Introducing change into an established team with an aging code base is always a challenge. This paper is about my experience in shifting the Launchpad teams' focus to a more user-friendly mindset, evolving the existing processes to encourage constant improvements in the user interface and teaching developers to see their work from the users' perspective. We went from nobody owning the user interface to the developers feeling strong ownership over it, and I describe the ups and downs we went through as a team, what worked, what didn't, and what we could have done better.

1 Introduction

When I started working with the Launchpad team I was tasked with designing and rolling out a new interface using cutting-edge technology on a well established product and team. The existing processes and team structure made it very hard to roll out big changes while also ensuring consistency as time went by.

While the general designs and work flow changes were being fleshed out, I started to drive some change to the existing processes, enabling me to be successful at an objective that would take a year to accomplish, and unexpectedly, beyond that.

The project was 4 years old and had over 500 dynamic pages with different templates and layouts that had been left untouched at different points in time. The goal for the next year was to make the application easier to use, even enjoyable. I also had to make the UI consistent across the board, take the project from static HTML pages into the wonderful world of in-line editing, streamlined work-flows and predictable interactions. In parallel, fundamental features that had been developed were going completely unused and we needed to turn that around. A re-usable AJAX infrastructure had to be developed from the ground up, new features needed to be designed and delivered, and general navigation issues needed to be addressed.

However, this story isn't about the success of the roll out of a new interface, but rather the success in the process changes that evolved during that year and how the project went from nobody feeling ownership over the user interface, to the developers taking strong ownership.

A. Sillitti et al. (Eds.): XP 2010, LNBIP 48, pp. 244–250, 2010.

2   Project Background

Some changes in the process were particularly challenging because the Launchpad team is a fully distributed team of 34 people, across 9 different timezones, grouped into 6 sub-teams that focus on specific parts of the application. This involves a lot of people clustered virtually into small teams, so communicating project-wide changes is always hard.

It's an open source web-based project that serves as a tool for other open source projects to collaborate and manage their projects. It is also the key infrastructure behind Ubuntu, the popular Linux distribution, which means there are many stakeholders involved, at times with contradicting requirements.

The application is pretty large with more than 350.000 lines of Python and Javascript code, over 2 million visitors a month and does daily rolls out to an edge server which half of the most active users use. Roll-outs to production happen every 4 weeks, so changes are delivered to users on a frequent and regular basis.

3   The Road to UI Ownership

3.1   Nobody Owns the UI

The project had an amazing team of highly skilled and passionate software engineers. They focused on solving hard engineering problems while delivering features to users as quickly as possible. Everyone involved was a strong believer in agile processes, and proposals to evolve existing processes come up all the time with a general good predisposition to change.

While the team uses it's own application to develop, nobody uses all the features, and many times not even the ones they develop as they don't relate directly to the work they do.

One side effect of everyone being so narrowly focused and driven to release as early as possible, was that both the small details and the overall result frequently got overlooked. It's hard for a developer to justify on his own spending an extra day working on a feature so it's consistent with a different part of the application. That is, of course, if they know of the existing pattern at all.

The lack of consistency and polish created a general feeling with users that the application was hard to use, slow, and changed too often. Developers felt frustration as well since a lot of their hard work wasn't being appreciated.

The end result of this was that nobody felt enough ownership over everything that users interacted with, but rather specific features or pages, and focus was more on functionality rather than usability. Nobody felt like they owned the user interface.

The first step was to introduce user interface reviews at the point where the code was proposed for inclusion in the main code base. This mirrored the existing process of code reviews, where all code had to be reviewed by someone else before it was added to the code base, although this had a minor twist to it: they were optional. Each developer decided at that point if they needed a review or not. As you will see in a graph later on, this was not a very popular service to take advantage of. It turns out that developers don't normally like to go back and change code that is well tested and already proposed for inclusion.

While this was going on, myself with others outside of the team started to work on the general plan for the UI for the following year. It was mainly a set of interactions built as movies so we could present them individually to each sub-team and ensure that the end result would be consistent. It was also the time where I talked to existing users a lot in order to understand what their frustrations were, and try to prioritize the changes in a way that would address the biggest amount of users.

Some informal user testing was also performed, accompanied by reviews of existing work flows. I also started using more parts of the application in order to get a better sense of what our users were feeling.

3.2   I Own the UI

Having spent a few months planning and researching, I was quickly centralizing most of the information involving features, work-flows and usage patterns.

The whole team had a non-development 2-week sprint where I presented the general plan, short movies illustrating examples of what we wanted to do and the technology that was chosen to achieve it. We also started figuring out how we were going to achieve this on a technical level. The movies were very effective in conveying what we were aiming for. They were developed in Flash, showed a specific interaction on a portion of the page, and varied from 5 to 30 seconds in length. After that sprint, the team started working.

The fast pace at which development started happening made it very hard for me to ensure everyone was going in the right direction, so the optional UI reviews were turned into gate-keeping tool by making them mandatory. So for every piece of code that needed to be done, it had to have a code review signing off it was a good approach at fixing the problem, and a similar sign-off that the change that it introduced affected the user experience in a positive and consistent way.

A UI review would happen, for example, when a developer wanted to introduce a new feature that would let users subscribe to a certain event, and get notified via email when something changed. The review focused on where on the page this option was presented, with what text and icon, and the content of the email sent. The new option needed to be introduced in a way that made it clear what it would do. To address this. I would provide recommendations on how to do this, and work with the developer until we were both happy with the outcome. For example, here's a quote of something that would happen preparing for a UI review:

> "*Preparing for the UI review I discovered I neglected to put the batch navigator links into the page template. I've done that and updated one of the factories to allow a release to be re-used.*"

While it was a very effective at helping in the overall objective, it created some friction and frustration with developers who had tight deadlines and code they deamed ready to send, but were pushed back and in some cases needed days of work in order to be re-proposed. One example of this was a feature that had been delayed due to some unexpected complications in the code, and when it was proposed it had already doubled the time allocated to work on it, and yet the UI was not in an acceptable state. When I requested some changes to it the developer got very frustrated and raised the issue with his manager in order to get an exception.

Some of the frustration was addressed with negotiation, trading certain flexibility today, in exchange for some more complex work in the future. Another approach was to offer multiple solutions to the same problem, and work out together which would be the best balance between amount of work and best user experience. It can be a mix of both as well - "do this simple change today, but commit to developing the more complex one in a certain time-frame". Another reason for the frustration was that I sometimes became the bottleneck in the process, simply delaying work from sending it due to lack of time.

A key tool to remove friction also came inspired from what was done with code: pre-implementation meetings. Developers would bring up on a call or an email what work they were going to do, and we would work out together how it would look and behave. This made the UI review process flow much quicker as the biggest potential problems were usually addressed before the work was started.

Since all the conversations around UI were happening in a central place where I was always involved, it became easier for me to re-use existing patterns with new code, and gave me a place to plug into the process to slowly increase the general quality of the UI and raise the bar of what a minimum acceptable user experience was.

Five months into the process I had managed to sustain a reasonable speed in UI review turnarounds, as well as provide support in developing features, but this didn't completely address the bottleneck. The team was planning to focus entirely on the UI for 1 month. There was no reasonable way for one person to be able to deal with that amount of incoming change, and on top of everything, my vacations were coming up! We needed a new plan that would allow us to continue with the process that had already started to produce good results, but was scalable.

3.3   They Own the UI

While the process evolved, some developers had taken a special interest in UI patterns, rules of thumb for interactions and general design issues. The interest was so great that they were sometimes pointing out things I had missed in my own reviews with other developers or even the ones I did for them. It took me by surprise at first, but I quickly realized that I had found the solution to the heavy dependency on my day-to-day availability, and started looking into interesting places to go on vacation.

I picked 3 of the developers who had shown the most interest and good intuition, and talked them into experimenting with doing UI reviews for other developers, with help and support from myself. Interestingly enough, this mentoring process maps to the same process the team has for code reviews, where a new developer gets assigned a mentor that oversees all their reviews and makes sure they understand what they need to look for and how to ask the right questions in order to become an approved code reviewer.

The mentoring phase was very interesting. Developers had gained so much experience with UI reviews from the other side of the table that it took them only a few days until they were covering all the major issues by themselves.

What was really unexpected was what happened when we decided to start to bring in more developers into this new "meta-team". Against my better judgment, I brought in a few developers who had not been good at delivering UI but for some reason had an interest in participating in this experiment. After performing only 2 UI reviews, the same developer who had a hard time with changes to the interface, started to deliver code that showed thought and polish in the user experience. I was puzzled until one of them told me that doing a single UI review had completely changed the way he saw his work. Seeing the work of others from the perspective of somebody who doesn't care how brilliant the code is, but rather what was being used by people, seemed to have a profound impact on developers.

September was the month in which every single developer was going to work only on the user interface, to update current UI to the new design and layout that we had been building for months. Seeing how well developers had started to take over my daily tasks, I decided it was the perfect time to get lost in Europe on vacations for 2 weeks. Sometimes an image is worth a thousand words, so here's a graph of the number of UI reviews performed per month, separating my reviews from the ones from the developers:

That cycle of work was a success. All the changes that they had set out to make were done. By the end, the developers knew more about the pages and patterns that I had developed than I did. They had dealt with all the problems that had arisen from going from pictures and examples to actual code, had discussed them, made decisions, and even done a few iterations.

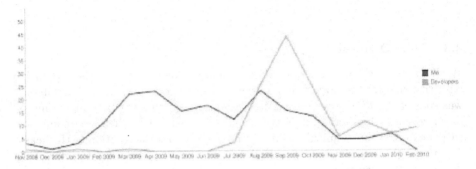

Fig. 1. This shows the number of UI reviews performed per month, distinguishing reviews done by developers from the reviews done by me

Developers started to feel very strongly about their UI, a quote extracted from a review portrays this well. Note the use of passionate words like "I am unhappy", and the person taking the advice agreeing that the extra work made it better:

Developer reviewing UI: "I create two branches in dev, then proposed a merge. I ran make sync_branches. The toggle works well, *but I am unhappy with the spacing between it and the download link. We use <ul class="horizontal"> in many places to normalize the space between user actions on a page (1.5em). I am not sure that this can be reused in the <div>. Can you experiment with the markup/CSS to make the spacing consistent with the rest of Launchpad?* "

Developer proposing the code: "I've done this, and attached an incremental diff. I agree this is a bit nicer. "

The trend of developers performing more UI reviews than user experience people continues to hold, the team feels it's a process that adds more value than it costs, and other teams across the company have started to adopt it.

In the future, I'd like to start working with all the teams to start performing cross-team UI reviews to build more shared knowledge across different applications and increase coverage of the reviewers available. I believe the process described here enables communication at the right times, and allows user experience practitioners to be able to hook into the development process in a way that fits in well with Agile software development.

4 Conclusion

This story covers a year and a half, quite an extensive period of time. If we had set out to implement this process from the beginning, I'm certain it would have taken only a few months, and some initial experience with other teams seems to indicate that adoption can be achieved in a shorter period.If you would want to implement this process, I would recommend:

- Don't recommend UI reviews, make them mandatory
- Be involved at the management level, it helps to be in line with the overall project strategy, and it's a good forum to bring up big changes (strong leadership can sometimes make up for lack of management involvement)
- Make sure that you can generally give immediate feedback. Having a very quick turnaround lowers the barrier for a developer to bring up issues before they get to the review stage
- The person who reviews the code, should not review the UI. They will understand the complexity behind the implementation and have a hard time proposing changes
- The initial adoption of the process will likely create friction, be prepared to deal with it and provide quick solutions to the problems created

- Be aware that you will need to negotiate: First bring up the problems with the proposed UI, then and propose more than one solution to the problem. The negotiation step also helps to gradually raise the bar of what an acceptable user experience is
- Pre-implementation calls and/or meetings removes friction created in reviews. Encourage these as much as you can, it will help everyone
- Build the specification of the UI with the developers. It will give them ownership over the feature and enables the experience to evolve beyond your initial concept

Something I regret not having done was documenting good patterns across the application as they came up in reviews. It would of made developers even more self-sufficient, and even would of reduced the time I had to spend in the end documenting the existing patterns.

Another success of this process was that it helped maintain the UI to an acceptable level through time and avoided the need for a big re-design, which at that point had been previously undertaken every year.

Acknowledgements

I would like to thank Charline Poirier for her unvaluable help in writing this paper, Francis J. Lacoste and Christian Reis for being so supportive and helping me drive this process, Angela Martin for all the encouragement and Elizabeth Whitworth for her guidance in writing this paper.

Distributed Meetings in Distributed Teams

Marc Bless

WEINMANN Medical Technology
marc.bless@computer.org

Abstract. Emails and phone calls are insufficient and most inefficient for distributed communication and meetings. It is impossible to let a team improve by these means.

This experience report presents how we dealt with the lack of communication in a distributed Scrum Team in three locations and two different time zones. We created a virtually colocated team by using video conferencing systems even for daily meetings and remote desktop systems for handling documents and tools. With such systems all necessary meetings and practices can be executed. It is even possible to support highly collaborative sessions like planning poker, pair programming, and retrospectives.

The necessary budget to set up such systems is outweighed by the obtained effectiveness and efficiency of team communication.

Keywords: distributed meetings, distributed teams, global development.

1 Motivation

One principle behind the Agile Manifesto is "The most efficient and effective method of conveying information to and within a development team is face-to-face conversation." [1]

This agile principle holds true maybe especially in distributed environments. Many agile practitioners and coaches have to work with distributed teams and yet do not know how to practice this principle.

This experience report shows ways to support tight collaboration of distributed team members.

2 Project Environment and Context

The project's goal was to create an update for an existing medical software system. Due to this medical field the project had to be implemented in a regulated environment.

The Scrum Team included up to 12 members who were dispersed over three different locations as shown in table 1.

Before this project was started the three locations have been in contact mainly by email, phone, and other shared documents and tools like bug tracking systems.

A. Sillitti et al. (Eds.): XP 2010, LNBIP 48, pp. 251–260, 2010.

Table 1. Locations and Team Members

Location	Time Zone	Team Members
Karlsruhe, Germany	GMT+1	1 Scrum Master, 3 developers, 2 testers
Hamburg, Germany	GMT+1	1 Product Owner
Tomsk, Russia	GMT+6	5 developers

The Scrum framework had been introduced to the organization for the first time with this project. Several agile workshops have been arranged for developers, testers, and product owners in the two German locations. The designated Scrum Master traveled to the site of the Russian developers to coach them in an intensive one-week workshop.

Sprint length has been decided by the team to be two weeks. Sprint turnover was on Wednesday, so overtime on weekends could be avoided (continuous pace is easier to achieve if team members do not have a possibility to get things done in a rush right before end of the Sprint).

3 Problems and Issues in Distributed Communication

Before the transition to Scrum face-to-face communication was completely missing in the organization between members of distributed locations. The few ways of communication were mostly indirect via email and via comments in a bug tracking system. Third choice of communication was via telephone if and only if both parties knew each other already. As many team members have not had a chance to get to know each other personally, people hesitated to initiate direct contact and preferred to communicate indirectly. This led to a single-point-of-communication way of information exchange: the project leaders were responsible for gathering, distributing, and deciding information of the projects. This habit was kept going on in the first time of the agile transition so that the Scrum Master was expected by the team members to take over this single-point-of-communication role.

After several attempts to facilitate Daily Scrum meetings via telephone, it became clear that this way could not lead to success. Neither one-on-one interviews nor group sessions could compensate missing face-to-face communication.

It was not possible for the team to reach a team-jelling state with these means of highly inefficient and ineffective communication. Other trust-building approaches had to be found to create a working and effective communication within the whole team.

4 Pragmatic Solutions to Difficult Problems

To keep things simple, pragmatic solutions to difficult problems have been implemented. The same involvement of all sites as well as direct, personal meetings provided a supporting structure for virtual meetings.

4.1   The Value of Tools

The first tenet of the Agile Manifesto says "humans and interactions over processes and tools" [2]. In a colocated environment humans are able to interact
face-to-face without any processes and tools. As only 42 percent of all agile development teams are colocated [3], the majority of project teams has to deal
with more or less distributed communication. The more dispersed a team is,
the more it is necessary to support humans and interactions with processes and
tools–people simply can't interact without.

This approach can be explained with a metaphor mentioned by Alistair Cockburn [4]: imagine the single terms of the Agile Manifesto have separate dials
which can increase or decrease these term's intensity. The Agile Manifesto gives
the freedom to adjust the intensity of "humans", "interactions", "processes",
and "tools" as needed for any specific project environment. In a distributed
environment it is not possible to communicate face-to-face continuously. So to
bring faces together on a regular basis a process (Daily Scrum meetings) and a
tool (video conference system or phone calls) is needed. This does not mean to
value processes and tools more than humans and interactions. Valuing humans
and interactions is still the primary goal. But to achieve this goal in a distributed
team a lot more of processes and tools are needed. (And mostly every communication in a distributed team needs a tool: even the plane to bring humans in
direct contact is a tool.)

The richer (hotter) a communication channel is, the more effective is its resulting communication as shown in figure 1. Working face-to-face at a whiteboard
is the most effective kind of communication, whereas written conversation like
email and paper has very poor communication effectiveness.

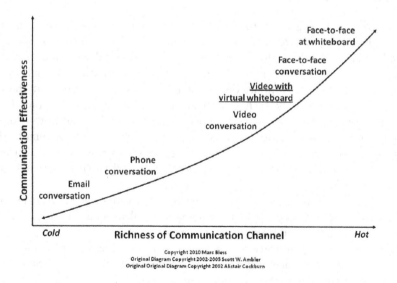

Fig. 1. Comparing Communication Channels

The only tool able to nearly catch up with face-to-face communication is a conversation via video. It is highly recommended by Ambler [5] and Cockburn [6] to use the richest communication channel available for the specific project situation. This approach maximizes the effectiveness of communication.

4.2 Video Meetings

Both locations in Germany were connected via a video conferencing system so the basic infrastructure already was available. The delivery and setup of a third camera and monitor in Russia lasted a few days only and took place right before the first meetings of the project.

A professional video conferencing solution was used to assure high visual and audible quality.

Costs. Cockburn calculates delays and lost-opportunity costs for projects that do not use face-to-face communication [6]. Let's assume the costs of one developer minute to be 1 Euro for an organization. Let's further assume everyone of the 12 team members needs only 15 minutes every day to get in contact with other team members for information exchange. (Example: Igor has a question and tries to call Michael who's absent at this time. Igor starts writing an email to explain his thoughts and question. Several minutes already are lost and both team members still had no contact at all. As a result the loss increases because an inefficient communication channel was created via email.) This results in $12 \times 15 \times 1$ Euro $= 180$ Euros per day. The used video conferencing system costs for a single location are about 5,000 Euros. So after 28 working days ($= 5,000/180$) the investment is break-even.

4.3 Shared Documents

Team members were in need to work with the same artifacts in their meetings such as the Scrum Board, the Product Backlog, and the Sprint Backlog. The natural, colocated way to work face-to-face at a physical whiteboard was not suitable in the distributed environment. The most pragmatic approach was not to search a new tool to support distributed artifacts but to use what the team was already used to work with: a typical office application suite consisting of word processor, spreadsheet, and a presentation application like PowerPoint.

As none of these applications was supporting distribution, a remote desktop system via Virtual Network Computing (VNC) [8] was used. With either TightVNC [9] or UltraVNC [10] it was possible for all three locations to work with the same application running on a host PC.

Most of the Scrum artifacts were transfered into spreadsheets. Backlog items with all their information could be managed in all aspects like prioritization, clustering, estimating, and refining.

The presentation application was used as a whiteboard replacement. Distributed retrospective meetings could be facilitated with this replacement, e.g. for visualizing timelines, writing and pinning virtual cards, and moving around objects on the board.

It was not appropriate to switch to fully distributed, multi-user office applications like Google Documents [11] due to following reasons: corporate IT security did not allow to store documents in an outside cloud, and compatibility and ease-of-use with the existing office application suite had to be provided.

5 How to Do Distributed Meetings

5.1 Rules and Practices

There have been no working agreements on special rules and practices for distributed meetings. It was intended that flaws of the meetings would be surfaced in the next retrospective meeting by the team itself.

5.2 Example: Retrospective Meeting

To follow the retrospective meeting structure by Derby and Larsen [7] offers a great variety of activities. In a colocated team many of these activities take place face-to-face at a whiteboard. Two examples show the usage of PowerPoint as a replacement for a physical whiteboard.

Figure 2 shows the result of the retrospective's "Gather Data" stage. It represents a timeline activity surfacing several virtual cards in the lower "improvable" area. Heavy interaction and participation of team members is required to create such a timeline. People constantly get inspired by input of others which leads to dispersed group discussions over the video system. Keyboards are switched between locations to enter actual ideas on the timeline.

An example result of the retrospective's "Generate Insights" and "Decide What To Do" stages is shown in figure 3. The virtual cards were taken from an earlier "Gather Data" stage and copied to the virtual board. As shown on some of the virtual cards, the "5 Whys" method [13] produced root causes which can be handled appropriately as action items in the next Sprint. A method like "5

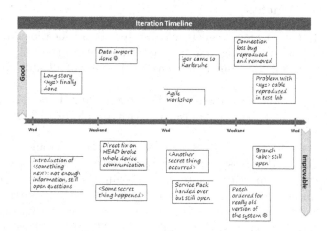

Fig. 2. Virtual board showing a retrospective's Timeline activity of a two weeks Sprint

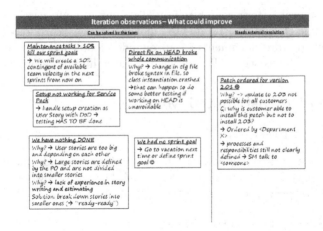

Fig. 3. Virtual board showing action items of a retrospective

Whys" depends on team interaction as it is an associative analysis. As already mentioned above such interaction between individuals was enabled by the video system and desktop sharing.

5.3   Example: Planning Poker

Story estimation was done by playing distributed planning poker. The user stories were edited via the shared desktop system while team members could discuss details with the Product Owner via video. Usual planning poker cards were way too small to be readable for everyone via video. The team created its own custom set of planning poker cards [14] which were printed two cards on a sheet of paper. This card deck was easy to handle by everyone and highly visible for the whole team.

5.4   Effective Benefits

The introduction of a video conferencing system in all locations and the usage of a VNC desktop sharing system made it possible to run fully distributed meetings with the whole Scrum Team. The involvement of all sites was given by these means.

Highly technical and educational sessions like coding dojos [12], and other development workshops could be realized with people of different sites and timezones.

The team was able to run all Scrum meetings via video and VNC. Scrum Review, Planning, and Retrospective meetings were facilitated successfully. Daily Scrum meetings took up to 45 minutes at the beginning, and after three months were finished in less than 15 minutes with 10 people actively participating in. This shows that virtual, distributed meetings (a) can be nearly as effective as their colocated counterparts with all resulting benefits, and (b) have no negative impact on learning and improving efficiency.

6   Pitfalls

6.1   The Worst Case

Imagine following situation. The team should meet for a short, time-boxed Daily Scrum at 9 AM in Germany (2 PM at the location in Russia). There's a team member in the first location to start the video system and boot the VNC machine five minutes before the meeting at 8:55. All team members of this location are in the meeting room at 9:00 so the time-box starts running. Unfortunately it is not possible to login with the wireless keyboard due to empty batteries. Someone runs out of the room to find new ones. Meanwhile the video system tries to connect to the other location but the system there seems to be switched off. Someone else calls a team member of the other location to get that fixed. At 9:04 the video system is running and connected, all team members can see each other. At 9:07 the keyboard is working again and login is possible just to realize that the IT department made a major system upgrade on this machine and the user login process gets frozen after several minutes. Some guy gets his notebook as replacement for the VNC machine. At 9:14 he can login and start the VNC service, so at 09:20 two locations are finally connected and ready for the meeting with 20 minutes delay.

This little story describes one of the worst cases of distributed meetings and their pitfalls. Following sections take a deeper look at pitfalls and reasons for failure.

6.2   Finding the Right Time

Sprint turnover meetings take quite some time and attention of the participants to be successful. According to the Scrum Guide [15] the length of meetings in a two-week Sprint should be as shown in table 2.

Figure 4 illustrates the 5 hours difference of timezones in Russia and Germany. A maximum of 4 hours is possible for meetings with all locations attending. Due to coffee breaks the effective duration of this time slot is reduced to 3.5 hours.

In a colocated setting it is easy to split these meetings over two days. For distributed team members this makes no sense as after planning and review meetings at the first day both sites would not have a Sprint backlog to work on for half a day. To avoid this situation, all Sprint meetings have to take place within that 3.5 hours meeting slot. This demands a very intense energy level and high discipline of the team.

Table 2. Meeting durations in two-week Sprints according to the Scrum Guide [15] and the real shortened durations in the project

Meeting	Favored Duration	Shortened Duration
Sprint Review	2 hours	0.5 hours
Sprint Retrospective	1.5 hours	1 hour
Sprint Planning Meeting	4 hours	2 hours

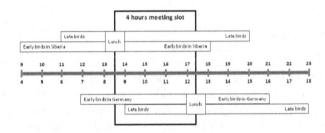

Fig. 4. Possible meeting slot of two different timezones

It is hard to keep up this level of energy for a long time. After a few Sprint turnovers the team learned by repetition to deeply focus on review and retrospective with useful output in the given time-boxes. Nevertheless full Sprint Planning could not be realized within the given time-box. Presenting and estimating the top priority Product Backlog, which normally are done in the first part of the Sprint Planning Meeting [15], were moved to an earlier date to the Sprint turnovers. The lasting two hours of the Sprint turnover day were primarily used to commit to top priority stories for the next Sprint and to create tasks in the second part of the Sprint Planning Meeting.

6.3   Preparation Time

It is hard to coordinate three locations to setup a daily video meeting. The more locations, the more preparation time is needed. To minimize preparation time the Product Owner did not participate in Daily Scrums but in separate meetings with the team once a week (phone conferences with desktop sharing between Product Owner and developers to clarify, detail, and estimate user stories).

The Scrum Master was responsible to prepare the meetings 10 minutes before start. All technical systems on the facilitator's site were activated and made ready for the meetings.

6.4   Human Flaws

Participants of distributed meetings need to have huge discipline in various fields. Timeliness is critical to hold the time-box which is shared with other distributed sites as well as responsibility for preparing and checking the infrastructure right before the meeting. Both emerged automatically after a while so that the Daily Scrum meetings could start and stop at the scheduled time.

A common issue is the language barrier. Some people feel uncomfortable to talk in a foreign language and try to hide in silence. Others have the courage to talk in languages they do not really know, so the audience has to guess the meaning. In most cases some team members function as translators for others.

Another common issue is the effect of side conversations or distraction in general. If such a conversation tends to bring important information for the rest of the team, one can decide to let it run at least for a while. Usually the Scrum Master raised his voice to get back attention and reorder the team's focus.

6.5   Technical Infrastructure and Tools

All machinery needed to run distributed meetings may somehow be out of order. This includes such simple things like empty batteries in wireless devices, and severe problems like broken network connections, or missing or removed equipment in meeting rooms. As other people use these rooms and equipment as well, the next step is to get dedicated technical infrastructure for all sites of the distributed teams. Then the team has control over it and is responsible for that equipment.

From the project's beginning some people had the ambition to find "The" perfect distributed Scrum tool for all needs of the team. Although lots of time was spent to investigate in tools, it did not lead to a better result than the mentioned solution with a common office suite. Neither the "face-to-face" principle nor the physical haptics of cards, pens, and pins could be provided with any more sophisticated software tool. Instead of searching for presumably better tools it is much more useful to let the team improve its interactions.

6.6   Avoiding Direct Meetings

Not arranging direct face-to-face meetings on a regular basis is a major pitfall. Direct, personal meetings are still necessary to keep up trust between all sites [16]. Therefore team members of the Russian site have been sent to Germany for several weeks every two or three months. German team members also made visits to the developers in Tomsk but on a more irregular basis. Nevertheless all team members had the chance to meet directly with other team members for collaboration and discussions.

The fact of knowing each other and the forming trust between team members made communication easier in distributed meetings. The high efforts to arrange direct meetings result in beneficial effects which hardly can be put into numbers. In the long term these efforts pay off due to their team norming nature.

7   Conclusion

Using video conferencing and remote desktop systems worked very well for this team and closed the gap to face-to-face communication. The investment in a video conferencing system was break-even after three iterations, so any project longer than a few weeks should receive benefits in distributed communication.

Next steps and improvements. The team should keep running a continuous virtual video window between all sites. Such windows could be placed at the coffee machine or a whiteboard in the team room. People should have the chance to meet there and just start a conversation.

Recommendation. If the common office time of all distributed sites is too short for all Sprint turnover meetings, move as many meeting activities to an earlier date as necessary. Estimating the top priority Product Backlog (normally done in the first part of the Sprint Planning Meeting) is a valid candidate for moving.

Despite all video communication tools, distributed team members have to meet regularly face-to-face to keep up trust and personal relationships. All team members should meet directly at the beginning of a project.

References

1. Principles behind the Agile Manifesto,
   http://agilemanifesto.org/principles.html
2. Agile Manifesto, http://agilemanifesto.org
3. Ambler, S.: Agile Practices Survey Results (July 2009),
   http://www.ambysoft.com/surveys/practices2009.html
4. Open Space session with Alistair Cockburn at XP-Days, in Karlsruhe, Germany. (2009), http://www.xpdays.de
5. Ambler, S.: Communication on Agile Software Projects,
   http://www.agilemodeling.com/essays/communication.htm
6. Cockburn, A.: Agile Software Development. Addison-Wesley, Reading (2001)
7. Derby, E., Larsen, D.: Agile Retrospectives. Pragmatic Programmers (2006)
8. Virtual Network Computing (VNC), Wikipedia definition:
   http://en.wikipedia.org/wiki/Virtual_Network_Computing
9. TightVNC website: http://www.tightvnc.com/
10. UltraVNC website: http://www.uvnc.com/
11. Google Documents: http://docs.google.com/
12. Coding Dojo: http://www.codingdojo.org/
13. Ohno, T.: Toyota Production System. Productivity Press (1988)
14. Bless, M.: Planning Joker,
    http://marcbless.blogspot.com/2009/08/planning-joker.html
15. Schwaber, K., Sutherland, J.: Scrum Guide, http://www.scrum.org/scrumguides
16. Eckstein, J.: Agile Software Development with Distributed Teams. Dorset House (2010)

Transitioning a Large Organisation: Adopting TDD

Padraig Brennan

Ericsson Software Campus, Cornamaddy, Athlone, Co. Westmeath, Ireland
padraig.brennan@ericsson.com

Abstract. Test-Driven Development (TDD) is promoted as a powerful technique for combining software design, testing, and coding to increase reliability and productivity. However the transition to TDD is not always easy. Is it worth the effort and what can really be gained from it? This report describes a useful transition strategy based on different TDD styles and identifies some key elements required for each style. It then identifies the main differences found on the code and designs that developed using these TDD styles. The differences are striking in their consistency and provide a strong indication that TDD is well worth the effort.

Keywords: Agile, Test-Driven Development, Code Complexity, Case Study, TDD style.

1 Introduction

This report details the experiences of the adoption of Test Driven Development (TDD) in the Ericsson Operation and Support System (OSS) development unit. The Ericsson Operation and Support System (OSS) is a Management System that supports Ericsson's radio network nodes. It consists of over 2000 employees in multiple international locations, supporting 500 different types of network nodes, and hundreds of features, some in legacy products some green field product development.

Test driven development was one practice that was introduced as part of a wider transition to Agile Development. This report focuses on the transition to TDD, the approach, the significant effects observed on code developed using TDD and key lessons learned.

The report is structured as follows:

- Overview of Organization and Adoption Process
- Transitioning with TDD styles
- Results from Teams that planned to use TDD
- Summary and Conclusions

2 Overview of Organization and Adoption Process

The OSS product has a strong track record of reliability and predictable delivery of a very feature rich product. Nevertheless in order to improve quality and efficiency a

A. Sillitti et al. (Eds.): XP 2010, LNBIP 48, pp. 261–268, 2010.

project was established to look at our current practices and process and determine possible improvements.

As part of this project one area of investigation was the status of the current code base and more particularly our approach and techniques for unit testing.

The following was the status quo

- **Test Last leading to unit test compromises -.** Unit tests were generally written after the code, usually at the end of the coding phase for a particular code module. As it was the last activity before delivery to a formal test phase it was the time that normally could get squeezed the most. This resulted in fewer tests which inevitably lead to less quality in the longer term. Simply stated this unit testing can be compromised or down prioritized over delivery schedules.
- **Test Activity-.** Unit Tests were a test activity and was not considered as an aid to improve designs or code.
- **Maintenance -.** Maintaining existing unit test suites was an issue and complaints of their brittleness were made in some cases.
- **Technical Debt -.** As some of the features had been developed over the previous 10 years, there was some technical debt building up which was a threat to improving productivity. The technical debt was in relation to existing unit tests and code complexity.

As part of the agile transition, TDD was one primary practice that could improve many of the observations made above. What we wanted was clean well designed code with a complete and maintainable set of unit tests. TDD seemed to be a step in the right direction as it promises the following:

- **Test First avoids unit test compromises-.** Building tests first ensures that unit tests are part of the coding and implementation activity rather than something done at the end. This should ensure that the activity is not compromised.
- **TDD promotes improved design-.** In particular the continuous refactoring and design in TDD promises to improve the code and designs, and with a good suite of tests refactoring is easier to do. This is because the tests provide more confidence and reliability for refactoring activities.
- **Maintenance-.** The TDD cycles promoted maintaining and refactoring tests regularly, therefore existing tests should not become obsolete or brittle.
- **Technical debt-.** Code should become easier to maintain and extend due to a more extensive suite of tests and due to the cleaner code that TDD promised.

In summary we wanted TDD to improve the quality of our code, improve maintainability and extensibility while reducing time spent bug fixing.

3   Transitioning with TDD Styles

In describing TDD at the start of our transition there was much discussion on how this tied into analysis and design, was there a design phase, how much design should be done before coding and so on.

The view that TDD drives all of the design caused a concern for a loss of governance and forethought over the design. How do we know that the team will TDD to reach an effective design? How do we track this and validate if the design can evolve, whilst at the same time how do we ensure that the team is not overly constricted by an initial design.

In order to help the transition we looked at TDD styles as some type of continuum from Test First Development to "Pure" TDD. This allowed us to be somewhat more precise on what we meant by TDD. The illustration in Figure 1 and subsequent explanation will be helpful to understand this continuum. It also provides a context for what is meant by TDD and TDD styles that are referenced throughout the report.

To the left of the continuum the development team expects the main design specification to be completed and code towards this design, perhaps not looking for shortcomings. In the middle the team expects to drive the design toward an initial semi formal design sketch, and makes adjustments along the way, whereas to the right the team is extreme in more continuous and ongoing design every day. We can define the styles as:

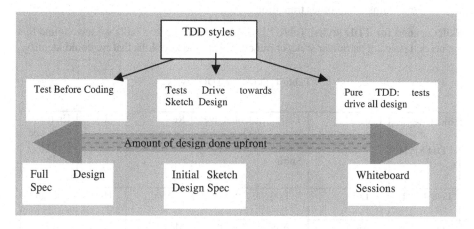

Fig. 1. TDD Styles

Tests First Style. To the left it shows that you develop a full design specification before coding starts. In this case the TDD style is actually Test written before writing code. If you will keep rigidly to the design specification the tests do not drive the design. When a design needs to deviate from the design specification some level of approval is normally required. The amount of refactoring that occurs will mainly be to improve the readability of the code, such as reducing method sizes, renaming and other low structural changes. It is stretching it to include this as a TDD style, but it is a potential starting point.

Tests Drive Towards a Design Sketch. In this scenario, around the middle of the spectrum is where there is some formal design specification created, this may be considered a sketch and not formally approved before coding starts. In this case the design specification is seen as one possible design and the team uses the tests to drive towards that design. However they believe and expect that some details will emerge.

Pure TDD. At the far right of the spectrum the team sketches a design, normally not much more than a whiteboard session. The initial sketches are concerned with the overall design of the solution, how the main components will interact. However the teams will use tests to almost fully drive the design. Aggressive refactoring to evolve the design is a key characteristic in this style. The team must also be very aware and tuned to how the code is evolving and should be comfortable with design changes as they gain greater insights into the solution.

There are a few main reasons why the above classification proves helpful, these are:

- To understand from an organisational and management level that there are some different flavours of TDD, awareness of this in itself avoids misunderstanding and misconceptions.
- The goals for adopting TDD can be used to help determine what flavour of TDD that can best achieve those goals.
- Choosing a particular flavour requires different skills and team skills in order to be successful. This is elaborated in the next chapter.
- It provides a framework for moving from Tests First to TDD, possibly allowing teams a smoother transition.

Skills needed for TDD styles. Table 1 is a summary of the key skills we have found that are needed for each particular style, or rather they are the key skills that we could identify.

Table 1. Skills for TDD Styles

Skills-> TDD Style | \\/	Pair Programming	Team Work/ Team Spirit	Collective Ownership	Re-factoring	CI	Unit Tests and Design Skills
Test First	Low	Low	Low	Med	High	High
Test drive to design sketch	Med	Med	Med	Med-High	High	High
Pure TDD	High	High	High	High	High	High

Table 1 shows that many of the skills seem to be quite similar, refactoring, design and unit test skills need to be good for all flavours of TDD, indeed for all development. They are only in the diagram to highlight the fact that you need all these skills almost regardless of TDD styles.

One of the most interesting things in the skill sets is that that Pure TDD requires a strong team spirit, enthusiasm and an eagerness to work together in pairs. It is about driving to the optimal design as the team learns more about the problem space; they react immediately and have to make key design decisions. Learning also seems to be amplified by this team environment.

The analogy to a sports team may be quite useful as this is indeed how any good sports team works. There is little certainty in a sports field as to how the game will progress, rather the team has a set system of plays and the team uses this rather than a full specification.

Although refactoring is an important skill regardless of what style is used, it tends to be used much more in pure TDD, whereas in the other styles there is less of a drive for refactoring to an optimal design. This can be explained due to the constant questioning of the design and the team focus on design improvement in pure TDD. It is worth clarifying that individuals using a Test First approach could do aggressive refactoring, the point is mainly that pure TDD makes it a very explicit team activity. It arguable provides a better organisational structure for good refactoring.

As Table 1 indicates that Pure TDD requires more teamwork than other styles, the expected benefit of this is that it produces code with some better design metrics than other projects that used the other styles. We'll go through those findings in the next chapter.

4   Results from Teams That Planned to Use TDD

In order to evaluate the effect of TDD we chose a number of key metrics to evaluate the designs. The metrics were primarily metrics that we used in our PMD toolset, namely cyclomatic complexity, excessive duplication, excessive class or method lengths. For the sake of brevity we mainly focus on complexity in this report, but the trend we observed for the other metrics are similar. We also recorded and used the unit test coverage. While we realised that the unit test coverage says little about the quality of the tests, we still felt it was an important thing to consider. The cases described below are representative samples of the findings. All teams received similar training in TDD and had either some TDD experience within the teams or used external consultants.

4.1   Case 1: New Development, Team Used Pure TDD

Development team were approximately 10 people. Duration of development was approximately 9 months. Functionality could be considered as relatively complex. Development was a new feature in an existing product; however the type of feature was quite similar to some existing functionality.

Team used PP, collective ownership, and had a high team spirit

In summary on this particular project, it produced a very high quality code, very low complexity, high level of unit test coverage with no external bugs reported.

Table 2. Metrics for new development using pure TDD

Measure	Agile project	Average/ or baseline
Complexity	1.32	2.9 Approx
Unit Test Coverage	90%	60% (or less)
Bugs report Internal	Minimal	High
Bugs report External	None	Medium

This case is especially interesting from a TDD perspective as TDD was used very extensively and the team felt that this was one of the main reasons for the product quality.

4.2 Case 2: Development with TDD of a Legacy Product

Development Team of approximately 10 people. Duration of development considered was approximately 7 months. The nature of the development of this product was that there were many small features or impacts to the existing product, rather than one large development. Features were of moderate complexity.

Team used Pure TDD (a little less so than case 1), some PP and had a good team spirit.

Table 3. TDD in Legacy Product, Metrics

Measure	Agile project	Average/ or baseline
Complexity	1.6 (new development)	3.143
Unit Test Coverage	90+%	60% (or less)
Bugs report Internal	Minimal	High
Bugs report External	Very low (1)	Medium

This table shows that all new code had very low complexity, almost full unit test coverage and there was negligible amount of rework required due to the new features developed. Due to the nature of the product, some of the new development would involve small changes to existing classes. Although TDD was applied where new classes or new methods were created, it was not always used when small changes were made to existing methods. For this reason we did not see as much change in the overall structure or design of the existing product as aggressive refactoring was not the goal.

It is worth noting that the product was an existing brittle product that required a high level of quality assurance activities. In the last year it has been a remarkably reliable and stable product. TDD is not responsible on its own for this stability and performance as much improved automated acceptance test as well as most other agile practices were introduced and now in full use within the team. Nevertheless the reduction in complexity of the code is striking as well as the extensive unit testing in place on all new code.

4.3 Case 3: Test Drive towards Sketch Design

Development Team of approximately 8 people plus 2 people were working on one part at a distributed location. Duration of development was approximately 7 months. The development at the distributed location did not use extensive TDD or indeed test first. Some of the development team at the home location used pure TDD, but it was not consistent within entire team, although the entire team did use extensive unit tests. Feature was of moderate complexity.

Onshore Team used Test first and TDD towards a sketch design, no PP and had a medium team spirit.

Offshore Team used no TDD, no PP and team spirit is unknown

Table 4. Metrics for new development, TDD drives towards sketch design

Measure	Agile project	Average/ or baseline
Complexity	2.1 (new development)	3.143
Unit Test Coverage	75%	60%
Bugs report Internal	Low-Medium	Medium
Bugs report External	n/a	n/a

Table 5. Metrics on new development, Unit Test after coding

Measure	Agile project	Average/ or baseline
Complexity	3.1	3.143
Unit Test Coverage	10% (->60% after QA)	60%
Bugs report Internal	Low-Medium	Medium
Bugs report External	n/a	n/a

This project showed that the project that used TDD had considerably lower complexity (50% less) than the project that did not use TDD. As part of QA activities a Unit test suite was developed after the offshore code was developed, this increased the test code coverage considerable to approximately 60%, but did not lower the complexity.

This again points to the trend where a TDD style reduces the complexity and promotes more extensive unit testing. The code complexity for the part that used a TDD style (either Test First or Tests to drive from Sketch) was slightly higher than the teams that were closer to a pure TDD. The internal bugs detected were also slightly higher.

4.4 Case 4: New Development, Test after Coding

Development Team were approximately 10 people. Development period considered was approximately 9 months. Little TDD used and unit testing mainly done after development.

Feature was relatively complex

Team did not use PP and had a medium-low team spirit.

This project had planned to use TDD, it had an external TDD mentor assigned and most of the team had received training in TDD, however it was not generally used. It had about the same experience levels and support in terms of training and mentoring for TDD as other teams. The development involved using new technologies which the team were not so experienced with.

Table 6. Metrics on new development, Unit Test after coding

Measure	Traditional project	Average/ or baseline
Complexity	2.6	3.143
Unit Test Coverage	50%	60%
Bugs report Internal	Medium	Medium
Bugs report External	Medium	Medium

Although there were some mitigating factors that worked against TDD in this project they were not insurmountable. The commitment to TDD seems largely related to the team spirit and cohesiveness. Such team spirit and cohesiveness will lead to adopting better to most difficulties. This is really the fundamentals of agile development and in particular Scrum, with its inspect and adopt mantra. Case 1 in this report had many of the same mitigating factors but still achieved high levels of TDD.

In summary the metrics on this project show that the complexity of code was higher, unit test coverage was lower, and the bugs reported higher than those that used a TDD style.

5 Summary and Conclusions: Transitioning to TDD Lessons Distilled

- Be as explicit as possible on what TDD is at an organisation level. Spend considerable time firstly understanding and then explaining what is expected, the expected benefits and then how to do TDD.

- Ensure that you identify someone or a group responsible for explaining TDD in detail and ensure that they are available to mentor teams for a short period before they use TDD.

- When it is a group of people that is responsible ensure that they have a solid and common understanding. A number of coding workshops is useful to build this consensus.

- External training on TDD is useful and necessary, but it must be supplemented by regular workshops with the people responsible for that discipline.

- Understand what type of TDD you would to achieve straight away. Test first as described in the report gives you some benefits and can be considered a reasonable starting strategy.

- Determine how exceptions to the TDD process are handled. Under certain circumstances a team may wish to reduce the initial design specification stage. Determine how to allow this in the organisation.

- Pure TDD requires a strong team spirit, enthusiasm and an eagerness to work together and in pairs. An eagerness to constantly look to refactor code smells. It is also important to have a champion in the team to ensure that shortcuts are not taken, however if the team is not working well together this champion role will not be successful.

- Be realistic, achieving pure TDD requires many aspects which many development teams will never achieve. Nevertheless, even a test first approach brings advantages and can be sufficient in many cases.

Finally, our experience is that we seem to recognise a trend where a TDD style lowers code complexity, tends to have a higher coverage of unit tests, and bugs tend to decrease. To get there requires strong skills, practice and a high team morale and spirit. We do not state that using a TDD style is the only means of achieving good designs or that it is a silver bullet, however the technique does seem to be a good organisation wide practice to adopt.

What Agile Teams Can Learn from Sports Coaching

Padraig Brennan

Ericsson Software Campus, Cornamaddy, Athlone, Co. Westmeath, Ireland
padraig.brennan@ericsson.com

Abstract. Experience from numerous agile teams in the transition to agile methods in the Ericsson Operation and Maintenance has shown that teamwork and collaboration are crucial to achieving success. This finding motivated a review of how sports coaches work to build effective teams. The review highlighted certain characteristics that sports coaches deem fundamental to success. This report details these finding and how we use these characteristics to helping teams improve.

Keywords: Agile, Teamwork, Coaching, Sports, Wooden, Pyramid of Success.

1 Introduction

This report details experiences on the applicability of sports coaching thinking to agile coaching and software development. Primarily the parallels are drawn as a result of the noticeable positive effects of high teamwork within agile software development teams. The proposition is that although agile development is definitely about high skills and knowledge on agile practices, the fundamentals of building these skills resolve around teamwork.

Much of the report focuses on the work of a number of renowned sports coaches. One of the most influential sports coaches is John Wooden, a former American basketball coach who won ten nationals championship and is widely viewed as one of basketballs most successful coaches. Wooden has written extensively on how to coach successfully and has developed a Pyramid of Success. This Pyramid of Success encapsulates the values required to achieve success, it is generally applied to sports but has also been used in business. The report details how we have found that this pyramid can be useful in agile teams. It also looks more generally at characteristics of sports coaches and how we are using these characteristics in defining characteristics of agile leaders and teams, some of which are perhaps not widely described in agile literature. Finally the report describes the impact seen from using this model of sports coaching. The report is structured as follows:

- Motivation for looking at how Sports Coaches work
- Wooden Pyramid of Success and Sports Coaches Characteristics
- The Importance of a Well Defined System
- Using Sports Coaching in Agile
- Agile Assessment Results
- Summary

A. Sillitti et al. (Eds.): XP 2010, LNBIP 48, pp. 269–276, 2010.

2 Motivation for Looking at How Sports Coaches Work

Although Individuals and Interactions is one of the principles of the agile manifesto the actual fostering of such good team work is quite a large and complex subject. Even the act of getting to a stage where productive discussions on correct behavior can initially require a certain trust and team work in place. During our transition we emphasized collaboration and teamwork as one of the practices, but found it quite difficult to highlight with everyday activities. After evaluating numerous teams, with similar technical skill, similar agile training and coaching, it was somewhat puzzling to understand why some teams were quite successful in using agile practices and others were not so successful. A pattern emerged where we found that teams with good communication and team work almost always worked better. These finding provoked some retrospection on how to re-emphasis the individuals and interactions mantra and what were the best characteristics of coaching and leading to achieve this principle. It seemed that the collaboration and collective ownership practices were too weakly defined to allow their importance to be emphasized and visualized. This motivated looking at how sports coaches work to build effective teams and teamwork.

3 Wooden Pyramid of Values and Sports Coaches Characteristics

3.1 Wooden Pyramid of Success

Coach Wooden describes the basic building blocks of his pyramid of success which is drawn in figure 1 and described in detail in [3]. The fundamental building blocks are:

- Industriousness: This is related to engaged and focussed work rather than any punching in of time. In order to achieve this, the next value is also necessary.
- Enthusiasm: Enthusiasm for the work you do is crucial for good performance it provides energy, enjoyment drive and dedication. Without this teams cannot be high performing.
- Friendship: This value is about camaraderie and respect. It is not about being buddies, but about having a spirit of goodwill, perhaps it is also about trust, or at least trust is a by product of this.
- Loyalty: Loyalty is often found in teams that care for each other and provide fairness, respect, dignity and consideration for others.
- Cooperation: The eagerness to cooperate. Cooperation is about listening sharing ideas and sometimes compromises.

While many different definitions can be taken for these foundation values the important aspects is that they are seen as building blocks to successful teams, even before technical skills. It is the visual nature of the pyramid that is quite powerful when using this to explain the role of teamwork.

This pyramid proves useful as a thinking tool and as a strong reminder of the need for teamwork. However even Wooden recognised that just talking and discussing were meaningless unless team members could see evidence of the pyramid in his own behaviour as a leader and coach. The need for the team leaders and coaches to demonstrate these values seemed key.

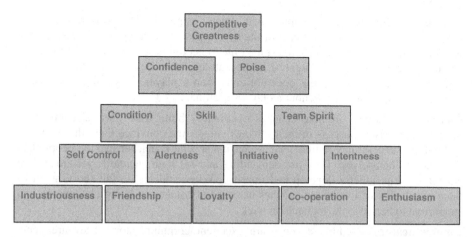

Fig. 1. Wooden Pyramid of Success

3.2 Characteristics of Successful Coaches

So while the pyramid is useful to describe values and their importance to successful teams, the characteristics of successful sports coaches themselves seemed key to building this teamwork. We experienced that these characteristics of successful sports coaches are the same as those required by agile coaches to be successful. These common characteristics are summarised below from Jansson and Dale in [1] the "Secrets of Successful coaches":

Character-based. Credible coaches seek to do the right thing. They are honorable people with high ethical standards and great integrity. They tell the truth to their athletes and never manipulate or play mind games with them. They conduct themselves in a professional manner and take pride in representing their teams and athletes with class. Credible coaches look to surround themselves with people of solid character because they know that character is just as important as talent in the long run.

Competent. Credible coaches have a thorough understanding of the strategies and fundamentals of the game. They know how to make the appropriate adjustments and are seldom out-coached. Despite their solid understanding of their sport they are highly inquisitive people who continually look for innovative and improved ways of doing things. They are lifelong students of the game. Further, they understand that admitting their limitations and mistakes is actually a sign of strength, not weakness. Even though they are highly capable and often revered people, credible coaches tend to remain humble and keep their success in perspective.

Committed. Credible coaches are highly committed people. They create successful visions for their teams and are more than willing to put in the time required to make them happen. They have a true passion for sport and coaching which fuels their intense drive and enthusiasm. They also have incredible reserves of energy and resiliency, which enables them to weather the inevitable storms of adversity. Credible coaches tend to be highly competitive people who really enjoy competing and winning at the highest levels.

Caring. Credible coaches care about their athletes as people. They sincerely want the best for their athletes in all aspects of their lives and are willing to help them in any way possible. Credible coaches invest the time to get to know each of their athletes on a personal level, showing an interest in their athletes' families, friends, faith, and future goals. Further, this caring does not end when a player's eligibility or career is over, but often extends throughout a player's lifetime.

Confidence-builder. Credible coaches continually build their players' confidence. They plant seeds of success in their athletes' minds and convince them that they can and will be successful. Credible coaches have a special knack for making people feel good about themselves. They are demanding and set high standards yet are patient enough to help athletes develop and improve. When athletes do fall short, as all of them eventually will, credible coaches use a good balance of being challenging and supportive to help people get back on track.

Communicators. Credible coaches are excellent communicators. They are open, honest, and direct when communicating with individuals and the team. They continually remind and refocus people on what they need to do to be successful. Credible coaches seek to involve their athletes as much as possible and value the input they receive from them. They have they remarkable ability to truly listen to their athletes. They take the time to understand where people are coming from and are able to make decisions accordingly. Because of their ability to listen, credible coaches are often aware of concerns and conflicts and proactively address them before they become major problems or distractions.

Consistent. Credible coaches develop a sound philosophy of coaching. This philosophy remains stable over time, but they are flexible enough to adapt to changing situations or personnel. Credible coaches bring a consistent mood to practices and games, regardless of whether their team is winning or losing. They control their emotions in the heat of battle and convey a sense consistency to their athletes by not letting the highs get too high or the lows get too low. Further, they maintain a consistent approach to the rules and standards of the team. They tend to have few rules, but are consistent in how they apply them whether a player is a starter or reserve. Finally, credible coaches tend to be highly organized people who take their practice and game preparation very seriously.

4   The Importance of a Well Defined System

Coaches tend to use the characteristics and pyramid of success to define, communicate and implement a system of play. The system used by all successful coaches is always extremely detailed, and the players work on that system everyday. It involves the entire team using the system. Phil Jackson[1] provides a detail explanation of a particular system that he deployed with one of his teams known as the "Triangle". He notes in [2] that *"This kind of movement requires complete coordination, with all the players thinking and moving in unison. Instead of following the dotted lines, they're*

---

[1] Phil Jackson was a sports coach with Chicago and Los Angeles basketball teams, winning 7 championships. Known for creating a secure open environment to develop character and chemistry of his players.

reacting to the defense, so each player must be totally aware of what is happening on the floor". Sports coaches work on this system of play relentlessly, constantly tuning and explaining it. Peter Jackson also noted [2] that having such a clearly defined system of play can have other advantages in that it

"relaxes the often tense relationship between a coach and his players. Having a clearly defined set of principles to work with reduces conflict because it depersonalizes criticism. The players understand that the coach is not attacking them personally when he corrects a mistake but simply trying to improve their understanding of the system"

Here there is a direct parallel between many of these aspects in sports and agile development. Primarily sports coaches understand the clear difference between a defined system of play and actually executing that system of play. A system of play in software development can be described as the software process that most organizations define, in this case Agile. However coaches know that formally describing such a process and actually understanding and doing it are completely different things. In order for a team to execute the process effectively requires practice, teamwork, on the spot coaching and complete coordination with all players.

5   Using Sports Coaching in Agile

Thus far we have primarily used the pyramid of success to communicate with agile leaders the importance of teamwork in any agile development. What we can communicate are more detailed values and characteristics. It has generally drawn a positive reaction. A number of leaders reflected that they had not fully considered the whole team aspects. Somehow such a visual tool seemed to raise the awareness and facilitated discussions on collaboration and teamwork. Providing a framework for discussions is quite powerful as it gives leaders something tangible to review. The pyramid itself does not provide any guidance on how to improve teamwork, but the characteristics of sports coaches described earlier helps in this regard.

The pyramid also prompted a review on how the other agile practices such as pair programming, user stories, and TDD were aids in building this teamwork, rather than just individual practices. The pyramid was subsequently modified to more adequately reflect the agile practices, it is shown below in figure 2 to provide some insight, although as with Wooden's Pyramid, this report cannot describe it in detail The framework is not to be considered as a complete framework, or even a completely correct one, it is more of a thinking tool and one to promote the importance of teamwork at this stage.

Although the framework is primarily discussed with agile leaders it will be used more with teams as it is now in the process of being included in our official agile process framework.

The framework has also prompted an additional focus on demonstrating and communicating in detail how practices such as TDD are defined. One result of this was that the agile assessment survey was improved to reflect the various levels or details of each practice. The assessment is now made of 16 different practices of agile development and contains an average of 10 levels, variants or steps on each practice. Some agile advocates may see this level of details as too prescriptive, but using the sports coaching mentality it is necessary details for teams. It helps them to understand their current state and next possible steps.

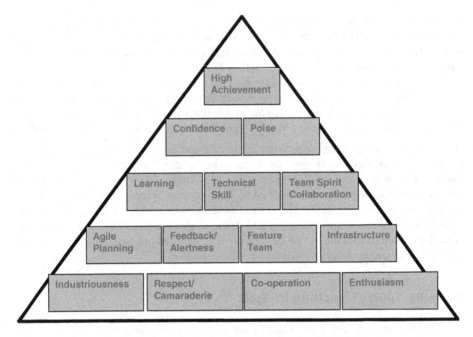

Fig. 2. Agile Pyramid of Success

Finally and possibly most importantly we use this framework with teams and managers that intend to use Agile. As a general rule we specify that if your team does not have the basic (bottom) blocks of the pyramid in place then Agile will not help, almost regardless of the other skills in the team.

5.1 Inspecting and Adopting Is Part of Sports Coaching

The analogy with sports coaching has also proved useful for some teams in understanding the importance of inspection and adoption and also to see how the inspection is aimed at improving the system (and interwork), rather than individual inspection.

Successful sports coaches are constantly inspecting the way the teams are playing. The inspection is continuous. What is under inspection is how the team is executing the system of play, as well as how the players are building their skills and interacting. Although the system of play is very detailed the coach will not have a written list of actions or remedies for every situation. There are too many variables, people are different and will develop differently, and situations will always have particular nuances. Much of the coaching is instinctive and relies on both a deep insight of the team and players as well as the system of play.

Managing and working with agile teams is much about defining, clarifying, and working with teams on how they collectively develop software. The team needs to collectively understand what other members are doing and how they are doing it. It is not a collection of individual practices with solo execution, but rather a set of interacting activities.

There is a natural link here to agile retrospectives, but agile retrospectives are normally seen as an event at the end of a sprint. It is perhaps better for the team and coach to think of it as a continuous activity, make changes as you go and use the retrospective meetings to review the overall position and larger changes.

6 Agile Assessment Results

As mentioned above we updated our agile assessment survey to help determine the teams that were developing or already using the characteristics described in this report and to determine what if any effect it had. The questions in the assessment were directed to determine:

1. If the teams had in place the values on the bottom of the pyramid. This was self assessment; it was partly aligned with other surveys on employee satisfaction in cases where the results were uncertain. It was completed mainly by a subset of the teams, including team leader (scrum master), project manager and some members of the team.
2. If the leaders and managers displayed the behaviour described above of sports coaches. This was partly self assessment, but the individual team members also replied on their team leaders and managers.

Table 1. is a summary of the results. These results are described briefly below.

Case 1 was a new development that has been doing agile for approximately 3 months to date. Previously they had some experience of agile while working in other teams. As this was a new team there was the opportunity to introduce the desired characteristics upfront. The survey found that they had a high level of characteristics on the bottom tier of the pyramid, noticeable above other teams. As the table also shows the other agile practices of this team were rated medium-high almost very early in the adoption of agile, even though they were relatively new to agile.

Case 2 represents multiple teams. It represents teams who have been working with agile for some time before the pyramid thinking was introduced. What is interesting is that they did not have as high a score as the team in case 1, suggesting that it may be more difficult to introduce this thinking to established teams.

Case 3 is an example of a team that were not introduced to the pyramid of values, it is noticeable that their agile practices were also considered low. It is intended to introduce the pyramid within these teams and evaluate if that has significant effects.

Table 1. Assessment Survey Overview

Type Of Project	Sports Characteristics	Other Practices	No. Developers
Agile Case 1	HIGH	MED-HIGH	18
Agile Case 2	MED	MED-HIGH	7+ (multiple teams)
Agile Case 3	LOW	LOW	12

A summary of this survey seems to be that the pyramid is most effective when introduced at the start of a team formation. When done in this way we have achieved good success in applying agile practices. Secondly, teams that do not have these core values are not likely to be successful.

Finally, it is worth noting that this was the first assessment since introducing the pyramid and it will take some time to fully evaluate its impact.

7 Summary

Our experiences in agile development identified team work and collaboration as a crucial aspect in successful teams. Ironically our experiences are also that this aspect is one of the least well defined parts of our agile practices. Wooden's Pyramid of Success is a useful tool in communicating and visualising the importance of teamwork. Combined with the characteristics of coaches it can be used to allow agile leaders and teams to reflect on their importance and how they can apply them.

Perhaps agile teams and coaches have or should have some similar ways of working, including:

- Always ensure the basics of teamwork are in place, these values are mostly represented by the bottom tier of Wooden's Pyramid. If they are not in place agile will not improve your capability.
- Demonstrate strong profession and successful coaching characteristics to your teams.
- Provide great details on the system of play/agile practices and demonstrate them.
- On the spot observations and adjustments must be made continuously, these adjustments are aimed at improving their system of play rather than any personal criticism.

In my personal view I believe it would have been very helpful if we had a model such as the pyramid during the earlier parts of our transition to Agile. We often tried to visualise how all of the agile practices were interdependent and drew complicated dependency diagrams that were impossible to follow. For me this model describes many aspects of agile in a succinct way, much better than any dependency diagrams.

While some or much of these values and characteristics are not on their own very new, it is still an area of Agile that perhaps needs to be re-emphasised and the sports coaching model is a very useful step in this direction.

Finally, it is worth reiterating our main motivation for looking at sports coaching: Although technical skills are crucial to agile development, it seems that without teamwork these skills are slower to mature or flourish.

References

1. Jansson, J., Dale, M.S.,, G.: The Seven Secrets Of Successful Coaches. Winning The Mental Game (2006)
2. Jackson, P., Rosen, C.: More Than A Game. Seven Stories Press (2001)
3. Wooden, J.: http://www.coachwooden.com/

Prototypes Are Forever
Evolving from a Prototype Project
to a Full-Featured System

Hugo Corbucci, Mariana V. Bravo,
Alexandre Freire da Silva, and Fernando Freire da Silva

Agilbits, Sao Paulo, Brazil
{hugo,marivb,freire,fernando}@agilbits.com.br

Abstract. Prototypes are a well known, widely accepted development practice but, if not carefully evolved, they can become a nightmare to maintain. This paper presents the experience of a four person agile team who successfully grew a prototyped system to a full-featured application without any clear transition in the project. The paper describes how the project started with a very simple prototyping goal, evolved through iterations and spikes to a partly working system and transformed, in the end, in a complete application widely tested and refactored.

Keywords: prototype, agile methods, refactoring.

1 Introduction

Prototyping is an activity that most developers have heard about. Fred Brooks mentioned it in The Mythical Man-Month [1] as one of the best ways to provide a quick view of a feature to the clients or users to help them make a choice. Many agile methods - Dynamic System Development Method (DSDM) [2] is heavily based on prototyping - adopt ideas related to this concept, like spikes [3] in Extreme Programming.

Successful software prototypes look very much like complete features given a certain execution path. Therefore it is common that the customers are so satisfied that they want to integrate the prototypes into the working system and move on. The problem is that prototypes are frequently created in a "quick and dirty" fashion and the result is not adequate to be incorporated in a full-featured system. Furthermore, it is quite hard to explain this fact to the stakeholders who usually do not want to invest any more money in this "already working" feature. The consequence is that they switch priorities, focus developer work efforts on other parts of the system and leave the rough prototype lost within the code base. In the long run, the prototype becomes a part of the system but it is filled with bugs, unhandled corner cases and, frequently, cruddy code. Nobody remembers what it was supposed to do or whether it is really important. Maintainability is deeply affected and developers get that natural and unpleasant I-told-you-so feeling.

A. Sillitti et al. (Eds.): XP 2010, LNBIP 48, pp. 277–286, 2010.

Developers who have been through the pain of maintaining dirty prototypes are no longer enthusiastic about prototypes. If they have to, they arrange their work so that there will be absolutely no way to integrate the prototype to the existing system. They often do this by either using a different platform, language or even creating prototypes in other media. This inflexibility can reduce the ability to respond to changes quickly and therefore harm the clients' interests.

This paper describes how a four-people collocated team managed to start a prototyping project and evolve it naturally into a full-featured application. We have organized this experience report in chronological order of the project's evolution. Section 2 will present the project as it was first introduced to the development team. Section 3 presents the work process established by the team to create the software based on prototypes. After some time, the team felt that the customer needed a full featured application. We describe this change in Section 4. The following section (Section 5) shows how the team adapted to evolve the prototype to a production ready application. Finally, Section 6 presents the current status of the project and Section 7 concludes with a summary of practices that we used to go through this experience without much pain.

2   Starting the Project

Back in March 2008, our company was hired to do some consulting for one of the largest movie production companies in Brazil. The client had a great idea for an application for movie-script writers but had absolutely no knowledge about software development. He wanted to investigate the idea and understand how much investment it would take to turn it into working software in order to establish his business plan. The company's job at the time was to scout the market, discover competitors and provide an estimation of the work required to develop the client's idea.

For this, a consultant was assigned the task of understanding the client's needs and desires and two developers were asked to analyze the existing script writing programs and evaluate possible development paths. After about 3 weeks of consulting and study, the team produced a deck of story cards with two estimates each, based on the use of two possible platforms. The first platform was an existing open source software with several features and a copy-left license[1]; the second one was an Eclipse Rich Client Application[2] developed from scratch using Eclipse's open source framework.

This initial estimate suggested that a four person team dedicating four daily work hours would be able to build a working prototype of each feature in approximately nine months using the existing open source software and in roughly one year using Eclipse's platform. The open source solution had the advantage of providing full functionality of several other features. For a complete system, the estimate was well over two years of work on the Eclipse version and about a year and a half for the open source one.

---

[1] http://celtx.com/ – Last accessed on 27/02/2010.
[2] http://www.eclipse.org/rcp – Last accessed on 27/02/2010.

After some discussion, the client opted for the Eclipse based solution due to a license restriction of the open source one which conflicted with his business plan. He also chose to develop only a prototype of the idea since two years seemed like too heavy of an investment for him.

After the exploration phase, the consulting contract ended and a new negotiable scope contract [3] with emphasis on development effort was signed. This new contract established a team of four developers working with an open scope that would be negotiated monthly, providing 160 hours of work each month. It specifically stated that the developers would work in pairs all the time and that the developed system should have automated tests for the production code.

The features initially presented to the team were organized by the client into three priority groups. The first group contained all features most critical to the client, the ones that would allow him to experiment with his "big idea". The second one consisted of some features already present in most script editors in the market, such as editing the script text itself. Most features in this second group were in fact epics [4]. The third group contained only the features needed to read and export to different file formats, such as those used by competing programs.

The project's goal was to create a visual high fidelity prototype with mostly faked or simplified features from the first group. The client would use this prototype to present his ideas to investors by October 2008. This meeting would either boost the project's development to a full featured system if the investors liked the idea or end its development in the case that they rejected it.

This was the team's vision of the project when development began, a short seven month project whose fate would be decided by its capacity to impress investors. Therefore, the main goal was to provide support for the client's demonstration to ensure the project's growth and success. The next section (Section 3) describes how the team organized itself to achieve this goal.

3   Prototyping Phase

Given the project's objective, the customer always prioritized new features considering only one specific usage scenario. This meant that, for most features, there were several cases which the team was asked **not** to handle. Regarding the source code, it meant that no verification or validation was written and the prototype would likely crash if the user did not behave as expected. We also incorporated several spikes as permanent solutions and did not handle a fair number of exceptions.

The team knew from the start that the client would change his mind over time. After all, it was partly to better understand his idea and its applicability that he wanted to build this prototype. This meant that features would be developed and later thrown away while code produced only for a quick spike was going to become part of the system. Therefore, the team invested only as much design, automated tests and refactoring as needed to keep the system flexible enough to receive the next changes. The team also made it clear to the client that some work would need to be done on features after he accepted them in order to polish the work.

From the start, the team installed a continuous integration server[3] to automatically build a new version of the system hourly. With this in place, the client could follow the system's evolution, test the features and provide feedback within a very short time span. This allowed for absolutely no surprises in review meetings and greatly improved the team's ability to tune each feature as it was released.

The first few iterations went quite smoothly, developing features from the first phase which involved importing a script in a text-only format marked with some meta-data and providing a simple way to manipulate and visualize this data. For these first features, it was easy to avoid inconsistencies since there were few business rules involved.

Meanwhile, the client's demonstration script was evolving as the prototype did and the team was able to use conditionals as needed to ignore cases he would not enter during his presentation to investors. By October 2008, the main features from the first group were ready for demonstration, although not finished and polished for real use. However, by testing and playing with these features, the client felt that the program lacked an important aspect of script editing programs: the text editor itself. It was an epic initially included only in the second group of features, but he wanted to see how the text editor would integrate to allow viewing and editing of the meta-data he was creating. Therefore, he prioritized the inclusion of an incipient text editor in the prototype and started to detail stories related to this editor.

As a result of this discovery, the client did not feel completely confident to present the software to the investors; even so, he started to make contact with a few people to schedule a meeting during December 2008. That date became our new deadline. All efforts were focused on making a prototyped text editor available for the demonstration.

At this point, the pressure for polishing the new features increased. Time was running out for the demonstration that would decide the project's fate. The customer wanted the team to ignore corner cases, speed up delivery and ensure the demonstration would run smoothly. The excitement from this important presentation to other people (only our client and us had seen the software so far) was strong motivation for the development team to deliver all features the client had asked for. Yet, despite unit testing and pair programming being mandatory rules, the general will to quickly deliver the features decreased the code quality considerably. However, external interference was about to change the situation. Section 4 will explain how the project got affected and what new direction those changes pointed to.

4   Changing the Rules

December 2008 came and went without any meeting. The company that the client was in contact with had just been acquired by another one so any project presentation was useless until things settled down. This relieved the pressure of

---

[3] http://www.jetbrains.com/teamcity/ - Last accessed on 27/02/2010.

the upcoming deadline and we finally acknowledged the burden of unhandled technical debt. All members of the development team agreed that the code was getting complex and the quality was decreasing. This had a negative effect on productivity and speed which complemented the client's request for a more complete text editor, with fewer mock-ups and simplifications. The first iteration of 2009 was dedicated entirely to refactoring the prototyped editor we had so far, and the iterations that followed further developed this editor to include more business rules.

Although the meeting with investors was mentioned in this period, again it did not take place. The general feeling the development team had was that the project was no longer aimed at a simple presentation to investors. It was slowly becoming a more elaborate end-user oriented application. This seemed to be confirmed by two important and concomitant changes that happened between June and July 2009.

In that period, the client was asking for a much more complex and full-featured text editor. At the same time, he was exploring and wanted to develop new features to evolve his previous idea. At this point, the client started to understand the dilemma that the developers had felt so far. How could we keep a good rhythm of new feature delivery and still cover most of the use cases for current features?

The team estimated that it would take at least three full iterations to have an editor with the more complex functionality expected by the client. He did not welcome this news, since it would mean that no new features would be added for a while and he wanted to explore them with the investors' meeting still in mind. We then decided to investigate other possible solutions for the text editor rather than just developing from scratch. After some research we discovered an open source Eclipse Rich Client WYSIWYG (What You See Is What You Get) HTML editor[4]. The editor relies on a reimplementation of Eclipse's `StyledText` component which is responsible for rendering text within Eclipse editors. This project was close enough to the one we needed to implement, having some of the functionality our client wanted on our application, and it was maintained mostly by one Russian company. We suggested the possibility of outsourcing the development of the underlying text editor infra-structure to this company, thus enabling us to continue working on the new features the client wanted. He accepted this idea and this was the first change that confirmed the shift towards a more full-featured system.

At the same time, the team learned that the client had formed a dramaturgy experts group to help him better understand how to structure the application, the existing features and the new ones. The software was now going to have a set of beta testers and it needed to perform decently to allow the users to suggest improvements. However, the current development approach would not be able to support this new use of the system. The change had to be clear to the client so that development efforts would be directed to address this new way of working.

---

[4] http://onpositive.com/richtext/ – Last accessed on 20/02/2010.

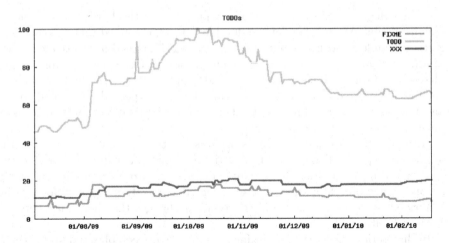

Fig. 1. Evolution of FIXME, TODO and XXX marks in the source code

Evidence of the software's deficiency came quickly from the dramaturgy study group. They started having trouble with several known and unknown corner cases, unexpected behaviors and just plain old bugs. The client recognized this problem and, despite the fact that it would mean new features delivered more slowly, decided it was time to invest more in usability and user experience. This was the second change that confirmed the shift in the project's purpose.

Meanwhile, the development team was concerned with the increasing complexity so they started to track some data from the source code. The first metrics were the amount of FIXME, TODO and XXX marks in the code. Since the beginning, the development team had added those marks everywhere they felt a corner case or a behavior existed but was not handled. Each mark had a small comment associated and the kind of the mark determined the criticality of the problem. Figure 1 shows the evolution of those marks during the project.

It is noticeable that the first data collection of those marks is dated for mid July 2009. It took the team some time to consider this metric was important enough to be automatically tracked. To consciously acknowledge that the team needed to track complexity was step one to adapt to the new direction. The next section will present other practices that allowed us to handle this shift.

5   Adapting to the New Rules

The amount of TODO marks was fairly high but the team still had to develop new prototyped features and therefore they decided to just track it and try to keep it under control. While this gave the team some idea of code complexity, it did not help to show if this complexity was being tamed by tests.

By the beginning of August 2009, the client decided that it was important for him to be able to see the evolution of the work done by the Russian team and he asked to have two editors available on the application. The first one was

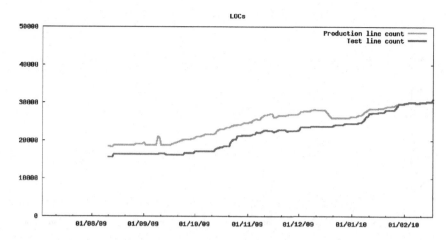

Fig. 2. Evolution of production lines of code and test lines of code

our original simplified one and the second one was based on the new outsourced component. At this point, we introduced a lot of code duplication because features available in the original editor were supposed to be also available on the new editor.

The result was a huge increase in the marks tracked as well as an increase in lines of code. The team suspected tests were not following this trend. A very simple script was written to count the lines of production code and test code. Figure 2 shows how both metrics evolved over time. It starts at the same date as Figure 1 to facilitate comparisons.

As with the TODO metric, the lines of code showed the team a small issue regarding testing but it was not addressed immediately. It was well known that the code did not have much coverage. There were no User Interface (UI) tests and quite a few features were related to the way data was shown. However, the team had a feeling that the effort to test the controller and model should have produced more test than code.

By this time, the customer brought up the idea of a presentation to the investors again, the project had been going for quite some time and he was feeling he had spent enough money and needed some external investment. Therefore the old investor meeting pressure appeared within the team and the deadline was, again, the end of the year. The goal was to quickly integrate the outsourced component and tune a few features for the much expected meeting.

Because of the rush to deliver new features, the code had reached a critical situation. TODO marks were amazingly high and distance between tests and code was at its highest level. During this period, the work was being roughly divided in three tasks: fixing bugs, implementing new features and integrating the outsourced component. Around September 2009, the team also suffered the loss of a member who was required for full time consulting work. The team went from two pairs to one pair and an extra person, and the velocity decreased.

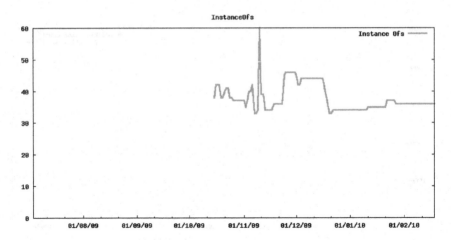

Fig. 3. Evolution of instanceof in the code

Figure 3 shows yet another complexity metric used by the team. Counting the number of occurrences of the `instanceof` Java reserved word led the team to understand the level of special cases unfactored in the code. The team felt reducing this number would lead to better factored code.

Curiously, as with the two previous metrics, the effect of tracking the number of `instanceof` was not immediate. More interestingly than that, in a short time span, having the metric did not stop it from getting worse. In the rush to produce the features, the team was becoming reckless with code quality. Something had to be done or the project was going to become very hard to maintain and the client's demonstration would surely suffer from it.

With three persons working at the end of the year to match two pairs velocity and reducing complexity, the team had to calm down, step back and rethink about agile values. Section 6 presents the resolutions the team adopted and their impact on the current version of the system.

6   Current Status

December arrived and it was time to perform a full integration of the outsourced component and throw away the team's first solution. Along with this came a considerable decrease in `TODO` marks, `instanceofs` and lines of production code. A large source of duplication was erased. By that time, the team was mostly working with just two persons pairing full time since the third developer was involved in other projects and rarely managed to pair up with the others.

The team decided to profit from this fact and instituted a merciless refactoring policy. No matter how small or how big the refactoring was, it had to be done and it was to be included as a regular part of each task and not as a separated task. Corner cases were not to be left unhandled and the execution of any user behavior which the client had not prioritized was to be logged to the application error log.

The impact of those policies was fairly clear by the end of the month. All metrics had improved and more bugs were being identified by the development team.

The month passed and no meeting was scheduled. The famous deadline was, once again, a myth. With code quality increasing, `TODO` marks decreasing, test code improving and bugs being caught by the development team (instead of the users), the team felt an extra developer would help increase velocity and so started to train one to join the team in January. The general feeling was that the client was getting ready to wrap up the project since he was quite happy with the software and was considering he had invested too much already on this idea.

However, in the next meeting, the client presented an officially hired beta tester that was going to support the team in order to improve the usability of the system. He also presented the team with many new features and usability improvements that he wanted to have done. The client also mentioned that he was seriously thinking about dropping the quest for investors and releasing the product by himself. In order to do so, bugs needed to be eliminated. All bugs found were immediately given the highest priority and should be solved in some way as soon as possible.

Since that time, the beta tester has helped the client to identify some inconsistencies in the business rules. Thanks to the experience that the client had accumulated so far in the project, he allowed himself to experiment with a few solutions and alternatives to these problems until he felt more comfortable with the way features worked, allowing him to seek consistency, conceptual integrity and the certainty that other choices were not as good as the one he had made.

7   Conclusion

Successful software prototypes need not always be completely thrown away. This fact comes from the very nature of software and the ability to easily and quickly merge pieces of code together to produce a working program using agile methodologies. Agility relies on this fact to allow for incremental evolution of the system and, therefore, supports that fact that prototypes can grow to complete features.

By embracing the idea that, if your prototypes are successful, they will be incorporated into the software, you can be prepared to maintain that code. It does not mean that prototypes should be developed exactly as well known complete features. Prototyping should allow you to explore different solutions and as they survive the selection process they should be refactored and evolved in a similar fashion to the set-based lean approach [5].

Refactoring, testing and decoupling are essential to allow code evolution and should be practices that are strongly enforced as the prototype starts to transform into a working feature. Unhandled exceptions, cases or behaviors should be documented with tests or some other mean that allows for quick listing and search.

Although prototypes are not first class production code and much of their value comes from this lower class status, they are likely to turn into essential features of the system. It is very important to track this evolution and provide the necessary support to maintain quality. Even so, there should be no fear about throwing away code either. The value provided by prototypes resides deeply in the knowledge they bring to the customers, which means the code is much less valuable then we give it credit for. In our experience, using prototypes to experiment with different ideas for the same feature proved invaluable, and many accepted prototypes were able to evolve to production code in the application.

References

1. Brooks Jr., F.P.: The Mythical Man Month: Essays on Software Engineering. Addison-Wesley, Reading (1975)
2. DSDM Consortium: DSDM: Business Focused Development. Addison-Wesley, Reading (2002)
3. Beck, K., Andres, C.: Extreme Programming Explained: Embrace Change, 2nd edn. Addison-Wesley, Reading (2004)
4. Cohn, M.: User Stories Applied: For Agile Software Development. Addison-Wesley, Reading (2004)
5. Poppendieck, M., Poppendieck, T.: Implementing Lean Software Development: From Concept to Cash. Addison-Wesley, Reading (2009)

Put It to the Test: Using Lightweight Experiments to Improve Team Processes

Michael Keeling

Institute for Software Research
Carnegie Mellon University
Pittsburgh, PA 15213, USA
mkeeling@neverletdown.net

Abstract. Experimentation is one way to gain insight into how processes perform for a team, but industry teams rarely do experiments, fearing that such educational excursions will incur extra costs and cause schedule overruns. When facing a stalemate concerning the use of pair programming one industry-like, academic team constructing a commercial-grade web application, performed a lightweight experiment comparing pair programming and programming alone using Fagan inspection. Through the experiment, the team learned that pair programming was not only faster than programming alone, but also required less effort and produced code of more predictable quality. Conducting the experiment required only eight hours of effort over six weeks (a mere 0.5% of the total effort during that time frame) and afforded crucial information for choosing the best practices for the team. As demonstrated by this experience, lightweight experimentation is cost effective and does not threaten project schedules.

Keywords: experimentation, Extreme Programming, pair programming, process improvement, process tailoring, scientific method.

1 Introduction

When faced with the choice of continuing to use pair programming, the Square Root team was divided. Half the team was dead against continuing on grounds that there wasn't time to waste in the schedule by pairing up. They suggested we drop pair programming and adopt Fagan inspection [1], a highly structured peer review technique, instead. The other half of the team enjoyed pairing and wanted to continue the practice, pointing to research that showed it can be faster than programming alone [2] and can produce code of similar quality to Fagan inspection [3]. Of course the research cited, like many software engineering studies, was based on work performed by undergraduate students working on toy projects and the results may not be applicable to industrial teams. Polarized, the team chose to put pair programming to the test by conducting a lightweight experiment. This paper will tell Square Root's story and demonstrate how simple it is to set up lightweight experiments for validating intuition coming out of retrospective meetings.

A. Sillitti et al. (Eds.): XP 2010, LNBIP 48, pp. 287–296, 2010.
© Springer-Verlag Berlin Heidelberg 2010

2   Project Background and Context

The SQUARE project was completed as part of Carnegie Mellon University's Master of Software Engineering (MSE) program [4]. The MSE program uses a capstone element, the Studio Project, which allows students to practice concepts that were learned through coursework in a realistic project setting. The team consisted of five members, all students in the MSE program.

While the project was conducted in an academic setting, the client was considered a paying customer and the students were all experienced engineers. Team members began the program with two to five years experience and varied technical backgrounds including quality assurance, data analysis, project management, and development on desktop applications, web applications, and real-time distributed systems. The project lasted four semesters (16 months) with varying time commitments from 9 hours to 48 hours per week depending on the semester. The project had a strict timeline, a budget of 4,800 engineering hours, and was monitored by two senior faculty members of the MSE program.

During the construction phase of the project, the team used Extreme Programming (XP) [5]. No team members had prior experience with XP; however most had used at least some of XP's practices in their previous jobs. At least one team member had experience with each of the following: Test Driven Development, refactoring, pair programming, creation and use of a coding standard, continuous integration, and incremental development. Team members also had experience with a variety of other software processes, most notably the Personal Software Process, the Team Software Process, Scrum, and the Rational Unified Process.

SQUARE (Security Quality Requirements Engineering) is a nine–step process for eliciting security requirements [6]. The result of the project was a commercial-grade, web-based tool currently used by the Software Engineering Institute (SEI) for research and education, and by business customers using SQUARE on real projects [7]. The client was a senior member of the technical staff at the SEI and is the principal investigator for SQUARE.

3   Framing Lightweight Experiments with the Scientific Method

During one of the team's iteration retrospective meetings, team members were divided about whether pair programming should continue due to schedule concerns. Since the team still desired some form of peer review, Fagan inspection was suggested as an alternative to pairing. As we were unable to decide whether pair programming or programming alone would be a better choice for the team, we decided to settle the dispute by collecting objective data.

Following the decision to conduct the pair programming experiment, two team members volunteered to plan and monitor the experiment. These team members became known as the "experiment champions." In planning the experiment, the

Step in the Scientific Method	Square Root's Application
Ask a question	Is pair programming efficient enough to finish the project on time with the desired level of quality?
Do background research	Projections based on research indicate that the schedule will be tight. Other research indicates Fagan inspection and pair programming are about the same in terms of quality.
Construct a hypothesis	The Square Root team should be able to approximately achieve results from previous, academic experiments.
Test the hypothesis in an experiment	Use GQM to identify data, metrics. Identify and mitigate risks introduced by the experiment. Divide work into test groups so the groups are roughly equal for comparison.
Analyze data, draw conclusions	Analyze collected data and calculate metrics identified with GQM.
Report results	Present results at team retrospective meeting. Discuss how the team will improve processes based on the results.

Fig. 1. Summary of Square Root's experiment

champions fell back on a key lesson from grade school: the scientific method, a means of inquiry in which objective data is collected through observation to prove or disprove a hypothesis (see figure 1).

Since the greatest sources of apprehension surrounding pair programming concerned schedule and quality, we chose to focus on those areas in our experiment. To make these ideas measurable, we turned them into a series of hypotheses to be proved or disproved through data. We hypothesized that the team would be able to approximately reproduce the results of previous academic studies which examined pair programming [2] [3]. Specifically that

- Pair programming produces code of similar or better quality than individual programming with Fagan inspection,
- Pair programming requires 15 – 80% more effort to complete a feature than individual programming on features of similar size, and
- Pair programming requires 60 – 80% less calendar time to complete a feature than individual programming on features of similar size.

Why these hypotheses? Since we had the information from prior research, we felt it would be better to have a more precise benchmark for comparison. Less precise hypotheses, (e.g. pair programming will require more effort but be faster) would likely have worked just was well. The point of having a hypothesis at all was to create a catalyst through which we could understand what data needed to be collected.

3.1 Data Collection

The experiment champions used the Goal Question Metric (GQM) approach [8] to identify metrics necessary for measuring the outcome of the experiment. In the spirit of XP, metrics were kept as simple as possible. To assess quality we decided to count the number and type of issues discovered through inspection and pair programming as well as the number of defects discovered during acceptance testing. Issue and defect data was normalized by size, in this case method lines of code. To assess time and effort, we examined the number of hours spent developing features.

Balancing data collection and agility was a primary concern, so we strove to use as much of our existing data collection methods as possible. We needed enough information to objectively evaluate our hypotheses but did not want to negate the agility of XP. As the team was already using Microsoft SharePoint to track tasking effort, we simply added a checkbox to the task form to indicate whether task time was executed alone or as a pair.

While time and effort information was relatively easy to collect, defect data turned out to be more challenging. Since XP does not give specific guidance for classifying defects, the team borrowed defect classifications from the Team Software Process [9]. The greatest challenge was determining how to fairly compare the effectiveness of Fagan inspection to pair programming. Comparing the number of defects discovered during acceptance testing is straightforward, but only addresses functional defects. One of the greatest benefits of peer reviewing code is that it helps uncover issues that might otherwise go unnoticed, such as coding style or design issues. The Fagan inspection process naturally captures this sort of information, but pair programming is designed to eliminate interruptions and decrease the amount of time necessary to execute a code-inspect-fix cycle. Issues

Programmer 1: _Marco_   Estimate (hours): ___
Programmer 2: _Michael_   Estimate (hours): ___
date: _7-16-2009_   Start Time: _5:36_   End Time: _7:39_
Milestone/Feature: _Create Project_   Task Points: ___ (Low/Medium/High)
Task Description: _Dialog Boxes_

Data / Documentation	Syntax	Build / Package	Assignment	Checking	Interface	Function	System	Environment
Comments, coding standard/style	Things that don't compile	CM, file maintenance, package stuff	Declarations, duplicate names, scope	Business rule violations, verify inputs	I/O, Method calls and references	Logic, algorithms	Performance, Timing, Java, design	Compile, test, hot keys, support
ЖҢ			7Ж	ҬҢ	\\	|||		|

Instructions: Record defects in real-time according to the type of defect detected by marking the appropriate column. The current co-pilot should record the defects. This paper should be traded for the keyboard and mouse between the pair.

Fig. 2. A tally sheet used to record issues discovered during a pair programming session. Each tick mark is an issue discovered by the co-pilot.

introduced during a pair programming session should not be present in the final artifact. Thus, we needed to collect data concerning caught issues through pair programming in real time. To accomplish this, the champions created a simple issue tally sheet (figure 2). The co-pilot recorded caught issues on the tally sheet as the pair worked. The tally sheet was traded for the keyboard and mouse throughout a pairing session. Using the tally sheet turned out to be a fun and effective way to collect data, and helped keep the co-pilot engaged throughout a pairing session.

4   The Experiment Work Plan

Normally scientists create independent test groups (e.g. control and experiment) to isolate variables in an experiment. While it would be ideal from a scientific perspective to have two teams building the same software project, one using pair programming and the other programming alone, for obvious business reasons this ideal scientific environment doesn't make sense. Rather than paying two teams to build the same software, we divided the remaining project work into two test groups: programming alone and pair programming.

The team agreed unanimously that our quest for information should not prevent us from shipping working software to our client. To ensure that the experiment did not negatively impact our ability to ship, we explicitly managed risks associated with the experiment using methods pioneered by the SEI [10].

The greatest risk we identified concerned the effectiveness of pair programming. There were doubts among the team as to whether pair programming would allow us to ship on time. To mitigate this risk, rather than apply pair programming exclusively during an iteration, we implemented features using both pair programming and individual programming with Fagan inspection during the same iteration. This way, if pair programming negatively impacted the project, we retained our ability to ship at least part of the desired features for that iteration. If two iterations in a row failed to ship promised features, the experiment was to be immediately terminated.

In order to maintain the desired test groups for the experiment and mitigate the pair programming risk, we modified our planning process as shown in figure 3. At the beginning of each iteration, our client chose the features to be completed during an iteration using XP's planning game. We articulated features as use cases and estimated the relative size of each use case with use case points [11]. Before starting the iteration, each of the picked features was assigned to one of the test groups based on point values so that each test group had approximately the same number of points. Because we used points as an estimate for size, it was easy to divide the work for each iteration into test groups. To complete the analysis, we used the actual size of developed features since the estimates may not accurately reflect how much code was actually created.

The experiment work plan was stored in the team's wiki alongside our other team processes so it would be highly visible and easily accessible. The experiment wiki page included the hypotheses, the GQM analysis, complete instructions for

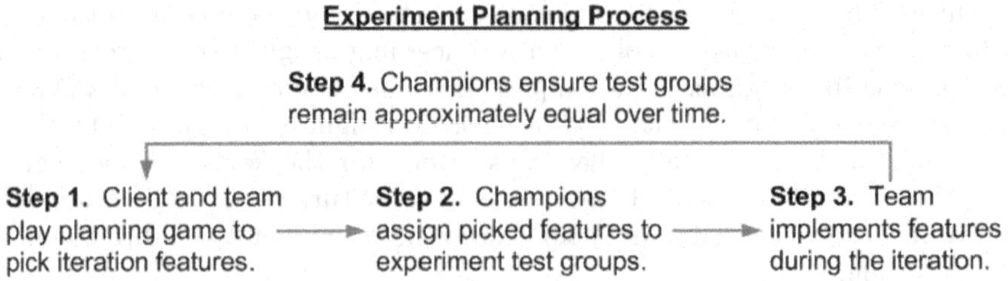

Experiment Planning Process

Step 4. Champions ensure test groups
remain approximately equal over time.

Step 1. Client and team
play planning game to ────▶ pick iteration features.

Step 2. Champions
assign picked features to ────▶ experiment test groups.

Step 3. Team
implements features
during the iteration.

Fig. 3. The modified team planning process for accommodating experiment test groups

data recording, the experiment work plan, and definitions for what it meant to "pair" or "work alone." Real time pair programming tally sheets were collected daily and the raw results published on the team's shared documents repository. The updated experiment feature list was also made publicly available [12].

5   Experiment Results and Discussion

The experiment required a total of three iterations to complete. Preliminary results were discussed during the team's iteration retrospectives, providing immediate feedback. Complete results[1] were presented to the team at the conclusion of the experiment.

5.1   Observations about Software Quality

We found that code produced using pair programming allowed slightly more defects to escape to acceptance testing than programming alone (figure 4). Reflecting on the results during our retrospective meeting, one team member noted, "I feel like I am more focused on finding issues during inspections than I am while pair programming." Other team members agreed that the focus when pairing is on writing working code, not finding issues. This intense focus on functionality could explain why more defects escaped when pairing.

We also observed that pair programming had a higher issue yield according to our real time statistics than Fagan inspection. While this may seem contradictory (since more defects escaped with pair programming), this observation is likely a byproduct of the real time issue tracking. Specifically, since tally sheets were only used to measure pair programming in real time, we don't know how many issues were uncovered and fixed during solo programming before an inspection. Certainly some issues are uncovered and fixed when programming alone. In addition, certain issues, such as those related to the environment, simply can't be uncovered during a Fagan inspection.

---

[1] Though the experiment proved to be extremely valuable for the Square Root team, the specific experiment results and our conclusions on pair programming and inspection may not apply generally because the sample size consists of only a single team.

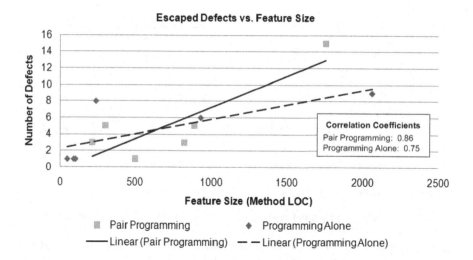

Fig. 4. The correlation coefficient was 0.86 pair programming and 0.75 for programming alone

The team was pleased to discover that code produced using pair programming had more predictable quality as a function of size (figure 4). In other words, though slightly more defects escaped to acceptance testing, we could better predict how many defects would exist. This is likely because programming in pairs overcomes individual biases in experience, mood, concentration, and other variable facts of day-to-day life that might cause quality to differ when programming alone. The team agreed that having a partner helped maintain focus on the work.

5.2   Observations about Effort and Schedule

We hypothesized, generally, that pair programming would cost slightly more but allow us to develop code faster. Much to our surprise, these hypotheses turned out to be wrong, in a good way. As hypothesized, pair programming allowed us to develop code in less time. Surprisingly pair programming also required less effort in most cases. Specifically we found that pair programming required 11% – 40% less effort than individual programming with Fagan inspection. Dropping inspection altogether, pair programming would have required between 26% less and 12% more effort than programming alone, less than hypothesized. In terms of calendar time, we found that pair programming required 54% – 62% less calendar time to complete a feature than programming alone, slightly less than hypothesized. This data is summarized in figure 5.

With this information in hand, there were no doubts that pair programming would have an extremely positive impact on our schedule, and that without pair programming we may not have been able to complete the project on time!

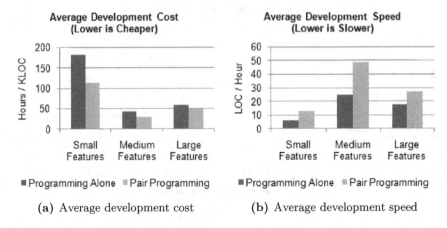

(a) Average development cost   **(b)** Average development speed

Fig. 5. Summary of effort and speed results. Pair programming consistently out–performed programming alone in both cost and speed.

5.3   Additional Observations

In addition to the hypotheses we set out to test, the team noticed other interesting things about pair programming throughout the course of the experiment. Pair programming is popularly touted as an alternative to inspection in which all code is peer reviewed; however we did not find this to be true. The standing order in our experiment was for features from the paired test group to use "100% pair programming." Recognizing that this was not realistic, we set an experiment threshold stating a percentage of effort that must be spent pairing for a feature to be considered "paired." In spite of this standing order, pairing never consumed more than 95% of the effort and averaged only about 85% of the effort for a paired feature. Prior to the experiment, pair programming was encouraged, but the team paired for only 60% of the effort for a given feature when we did pair. No matter what peer review technique is used, peer reviewing all code is difficult to achieve.

Knowledge sharing is another commonly known benefit of both Fagan inspection and pair programming, and the team made several observations about this as well. Generally the team felt that Fagan inspection was better at sharing high-level information, such as design strategies and systemic architecture concerns, while pair programming was better at sharing low-level, detailed information related to the environment, programming language, and programming in general. Team members also observed that it was more difficult to fix issues discovered during Fagan inspection due to a lack of context. One team member noted at our iteration retrospection meeting, "I hate going back and fixing the issues we discover during inspections. The issues come up days after I've banged out the code and it takes me forever to remember the context." Indeed, inspection meetings always lagged behind the completion of a feature to allow time for the inspection team to prepare.

6   Conclusion

Once the experiment concluded and the data was analyzed, the team chose to stick with pair programming. Though pair programming allowed slightly more defects to escape on average, predictability and consistency were more valuable. In terms of cost and schedule, pair programming was the clear winner. Setting up and executing the experiment turned out to be an easy and fun way to resolve an otherwise difficult conflict by turning a battle of wills into a comparison of data.

It took two people one hour to plan the experiment, a negligible amount of effort to adjust the experiment plan between iterations after the planning game and to collect data as we worked, and two people three hours to analyze data once the experiment concluded. All told, this accounts for only 0.5% a percent of work conducted over three iterations. This time investment was a small price to pay to validate gut feelings, boost team confidence through knowledge, and settle process disputes with data.

In executing this experiment there were a few key ideas that helped us keep the experiment light. The experiment itself was relatively small. The variables under test were kept to a minimum. Rather than comparing whole processes we compared only two practices. We chose to focus on a small handful of related hypotheses. We leveraged our existing data collection practices heavily. We planned the experiment so that it would require only a few iterations to complete, though in hindsight it would have been better if the experiment had ended after two iterations (four weeks).

Scientific thinking, scaled down, is an excellent way to gain insight for team retrospectives, but hard data is no substitution for team discussion and group reflection. Science is a method of discovery. Teams should consider running experiments to learn more about the processes they use and how those processes really work for the team. This sort of intrinsic curiosity is healthy for teams and might even strengthen work in other engineering areas. Further, lightweight experimentation is an excellent means for guiding continuous process improvement.

Given the inherent gap between research and industry, publishing experiment results in the form of whitepapers and blog posts would benefit the software industry as a whole. Think about how great it would be to see results from other industry teams experimenting with design practices, unit testing versus inspection, user stories versus use cases, or estimation techniques. As this experience demonstrates, statistical significance, strict control groups, and lofty academic goals are not necessary to make great gains in knowledge. All that's needed is a touch of science.

Acknowledgments. I would like to thank my fellow Square Root teammates (Sneader Sequeira, Marco Len, Yi-Ru Liao, and Abin Shahab) for their work on the SQUARE project. I would also like to thank our studio mentors, Dave Root and John Robert for their guidance throughout the project.

References

1. Fagan, M.: Design and Code Inspections to Reduce Errors in Program Development. IBM Systems Journal 15, 182–211 (1976)
2. Williams, L., Kessler, R.R., Cunningham, W., Jefferies, R.: Strengthening the Case for Pair Programming. IEEE Software 26, 19–25 (2000)
3. Phongpaibul, M., Boehm, B.: A Replicate Empirical Comparison between Pair Development and Software Development with Inspection. In: First International Symposium on Empirical Software Engineering and Measurement, pp. 265–274. IEEE Computer Society, Washington (2007)
4. Garlan, D., Gluch, D.P., Tomayko, J.E.: Agents of Change: Educating Software Engineering Leaders. IEEE Computer 30, 59–65 (1997)
5. Beck, K.: Extreme Programming Explained: Embrace Change. Addison-Wesley, Boston (2000)
6. Mead, N.R., Hough, E.D., Stehney, T.R.: Security Quality Requirements Engineering (SQUARE) Methodology. Technical report, Software Engineering Institute (2005)
7. SQUARE Tool, http://www.cert.org/sse/square-tool.html
8. Basili, V., Caldiera, G., Rombach, H.: The Goal Question Metric Approach. Encyclopedia of Software Engineering 1, 528–532 (1994)
9. Humphrey, W.S.: Introduction to the Team Software Process. Addison-Wesley, Boston (1999)
10. Nelson, C.R., Taran, G., Hinjosa, L.d.L.: Explicit Risk Management in Agile Processes. In: Agile Processes in Software Engineering and Extreme Programming, pp. 190–201. Springer, New York (2008)
11. Cohn, M.: Estimating with Use Case Points. Methods and Tools 13(3), 3–13 (2005)
12. Square Root Project Archive and Experiment Data Set (available indefinitely), http://dogbert.mse.cs.cmu.edu/MSE2009/Projects/SquareRoot/

Kanban at an Insurance Company (Are You Sure?)

Olav Maassen[1] and Jasper Sonnevelt[2]

[1] QNH AD&S, Zeist, The Netherlands
olav.maassen@xs4all.nl
[2] ASR Insurance, Utrecht, The Netherlands
jasper.sonnevelt@asr.nl

Abstract. ASR Insurance, one of the top 3 insurance companies in the Netherlands is transitioning their IT maintenance and operations from a more traditional approach to Kanban. They started small with 1 team and slowly increased to 7 teams to gain experience. Due to the positive results they are now in the middle of transitioning 200 people to their new environment. This experience report highlights the experiences gained by the first implementing during the initial phase of the Kanban implementation. This report reflects both the practicing perspective and the coaching perspective.

Keywords: Kanban, ASR Insurance.

1 Introduction

"You were not in control. You had no visibility: maybe there was a car in front of you, maybe not." – Alain Prost

How did a business that is in its very nature risk averse (insurance) in a conservative industry (finance) in a reserved country (the Netherlands) end up choosing to use a fairly new methodology, Kanban?

In December 2009 ASR Insurance has chosen Kanban as the methodology for their IT operations and maintenance departments. This means that at the writing of this paper ASR is in the middle of that transition. This transition of 200 people is not part of this paper.

This paper answers the question of how a risk averse company ended up choosing a fairly new methodology for a crucial part of their IT. It focuses on the organization, the team coordinator in his new role and the coach.

This paper exists of four sections. The first section (chapter 2) explains the context that led to this choice and what influences played a part. The second section (chapters 3 and 4) is about the road that took ASR from where it was to a position where large scale deployment of Kanban was the logical choice. Included in this section is also a description of how Kanban was implemented in the first team. The third section (chapter 5 and 6) provides information on the challenges we faced during the introduction phase and how we tried to resolve these. The final section (chapter 7) highlights our personal experiences from our role (team coordinator and coach) and our recommendations.

A. Sillitti et al. (Eds.): XP 2010, LNBIP 48, pp. 297–306, 2010.

2 Context

ASR Insurance is one of the top 3 insurance companies in the Netherlands. ASR has several business lines each responsible for their own label and their own budgets and goals.

Most of the software is developed in house by the IT department that works exclusively for ASR. Because of the size of the IT organization the department was made up of several teams each responsible for their own specific technology. When new applications needed to be developed members were drafted from the teams based on the technologies required for that project. When the project was done the responsibility for the maintenance of the resulting application lies with the individual teams. So if an application is developed in J2EE, Microsoft dotNet and Oracle each of these teams would have the maintenance and operations responsibility for that part of the application.

The IT infrastructure and physical operations was the responsibility of another department (I&O). This department carried out all the deployments to Acceptance and Production environments. This infrastructure department was located at another location which complicated cooperation.

Because of the complexity of the application landscape releases were normally done only a couple of times a year during a weekend. During this weekend all the changes were performed on the live systems at the same time. This way the client has as much up time as is possible with little disruption. If a project misses the deadline most likely the change would have to wait till the next release.

In 2006 and 2007 there was an increase in the number of change requests. When this number of requests increased it became harder for the organization to keep up with the rate of releasing changes in production. While a project normally would have only one client, teams doing maintenance have several. This leads to conflicts over priorities as each client needs his change the most.

With this increased rate of change requests it happened every now and then that a change didn't make the deadline for a release moment. Missing a deadline can result in lowering the trust between the two parties. Lead times were in no relationship to the actual amount of work that was asked. Something needed to be done.

In 2007 initiatives had started to increase the quality and productivity of development teams. The J2EE team started using Scrum with two teams (red and blue). The results with these teams and their new methodology were positive. At the end of 2007 IT management started an Agile Adoption Program to help other teams and projects to start using Scrum. The number of teams using Scrum within the ASR organization slowly increased. These teams provided more visibility and predictability than other traditional project approaches. By the spring of 2009 Scrum had become the standard for most starting projects as methodology of choice.

While most projects that were using Scrum reported being successful, other Scrum teams were having some difficulties. The commonality between these projects was most of the time that they were involved in operations work or small maintenance. The work was hard to distribute properly over sprints and often needed to be changed more frequently than the 2 week sprints allowed. What the client wanted was more flexibility and more control over the immediate results.

Other influences that played a part in the decision making process of management are a desire to improve continuously, a need for visual management to increase visibility and a driving desire that things could and should be better. Also another program was running at the same time to increase Lean practices within the whole company.

ASR wanted to keep the agile mindset and at the same time do something more appropriate for maintenance and operations so that they too can cooperate with the rest of the IT departments and projects.

In June the first conversations about Kanban started.

3 Implementing Kanban in Pilot Project

Scrum had cultivated the continuous improvement mindset in a number of people in IT management positions. They recognized the potential Kanban had for their organization. To validate their assumptions and not wanting to believe just presentations and articles a pilot project was selected. This team would need to be tasked with maintenance and operations for several applications using multiple technologies.

The J2EE department had just merged with System Integration (SI) and seemed the best choice. The team was new in working together using multiple technologies. In order to be able to start quickly and keep the scope manageable business and infrastructure were not represented in the team as team members. The team consisted of SI developers, J2EE developers and agile testers.

Kanban uses only 3 principles: [1]

- make work visible
- limit work in progress
- help work to flow

3.1 Make Work Visible

To be able to see what a team is doing it is essential to make everything the team does visible. The J2EE team started mapping their process and from that mapping they created their progress board. Each major step in the process had its own column. To make the team feel the ownership of the board it was very low tech. They used a whiteboard, post-its and magnets. The whiteboard allows for very quick changes to whatever is on the board increasing the odds of the team actually making changes.

When the board was created they put all their current work on the board so that everybody could see the actual status of all work in progress and start almost immediately.

Other ways of making work visible included having different colors of post-its on the board to signal different kinds of information. Currently they have 5 different colors in use to help the understanding. For instance orange means work that has been released by the team as done and was send back because it wasn't good enough. Knowing just this is enough to realize that a team is having problems if you see a lot of orange.

The other colors for the post-its are yellow for regular work items, green for problems (finding solutions for root causes), purple/pink for impediments the team can't solve on their own and white for high priority production incidents requiring immediate attention.

The team also came up with another way of visualizing when they found out that certain pieces didn't progress and hadn't noticed that for a while. They came up with a simple solution, they now put a dot next to each post-it each day. If a work item stays in the same place for a long time it accumulates many dots. Doesn't mean it's bad, it just means it needs attention.

3.2 Limit Work in Progress

By limiting the amount of work that the team is working on at the same time the team will focus more on the items they can work on. This increased focus leads to better results in lead time, quality and cooperation.

The team implemented the limits in 2 ways. They set limits for each step in the process as it was drawn on their Kanban board. There wasn't any experience yet as to what a good limit would be, so they decided to use the formula: (2 * amount of people doing the work) − 1. Although this was just used as a general rule of thumb it turned out to be quite accurate. When anybody from the team wanted to pick up some work they could only do that if they wouldn't exceed the limit for that particular column.

The other way to limit work was by representing each member of the team by magnets (also visualizing) and only have two of these magnets. Members can only start new work if they have finished whatever it was they were doing before.

Another benefit of limiting the amount of work is that problems become visible more quickly. Bottlenecks become apparent as they hold up everybody's work. It is not possible to hide any more. An example of this was when there was a testing capacity of four in one team and of those four three were blocked by impediments. This effectively meant that the possible testing throughput was severely restricted to only 25% of the normal capacity. These impediments blocked the progress of work items for the whole team and thereby the progress of the whole team. This experience really led to a much better understanding and cooperation between our developers and testers. They sat down together and worked out ways in which they can work and cooperate better. By more actively involving testers during development and developers during testing they improved the flow of the whole team. Without limiting the amount of work this wouldn't have happened. Limiting the amount of work in progress is forcing cooperation.

3.3 Help Work to Flow

Helping work to flow means that a team should pay attention that they make actual progress all the time. Work should stream continuously from start to end. While we would like to release work into production, the release schedule and policies didn't allow for this. To prevent the team from getting needlessly stuck the team inserted some "wait" columns where work could accumulate until either other teams are ready to move forward or there was a release weekend.

To monitor the Kanban board frequently the team was using a daily stand up for sharing the current status with each other. During a standup the team asks about status for each step in the process instead of asking each member. What we see is that these stand-ups are almost always completed within 10 minutes and everyone is up to date. Problems visible on the board (impediments, work items staying in one place, bottlenecks) are discussed immediately to find out what the cause is and how it could be used or fixed.

Another way the team helped work to flow was by practicing continuous improvement. They had their bi-weekly retrospective to take a step back and discuss anything that might need improving. And even outside the retrospective improvements are made when necessary.

3.4 Observations

When the team started they had some problems they expected. Cooperation with infrastructure was thought of that that might be labor intensive to set up. The team added an extra step in their process to be able to cope with this extra effort. The team showed the infrastructure group what they were doing and could demonstrate that they would provide a constant stream of deployments to the acceptance environment if only infrastructure would be able to deploy. They agreed that a phone call would be sufficient and the deployment was done within 30 minutes.

We observed a much better understanding and cooperation between developers from different technologies for each other as well as with the testers. This increased the performance of and spirits in the team tremendously. Members who started out reluctantly became enthusiastic about this way of cooperating.

4 Growing Kanban

The successes of the first team using Kanban were communicated to other teams, by management, coaches, team members wherever we could. These stories made other teams eager to start using the same thing and try and achieve similar results. This started a pull for Kanban coaching.

The approach we chose for ASR was to grow slowly and coach teams intensively when they start for 3 weeks to get them to a good start. When the team was rolling the coach would stop by once or twice a week and share his observations with the team and the team coordinator.

Each team creates their own process and Kanban board and really feel they own the process. Each team has its own pace and this should be respected. It's much better to go to slow than it is to go to fast. Most teams are up and running within 3 weeks, Some take a bit longer. .Going too fast results in a team that does what is asked of them and they don't feel ownership. Reestablishing that ownership takes a long time.

At the start we only help the team to visualize their work without changing other things. This reduces the resistance to change even of the most reluctant members as we are just creating insight without change. By visualizing impediments in their work we add value for them and a reason to have a conversation about improving their process. Gradual change trumps resistance.

By the end of 2009 ASR had 7 teams working with Kanban at the same time. The teams that started later started including members that were from the infrastructure or the business departments further increasing the cooperation and understanding.

5 Challenges in Adopting Kanban

Change is never easy. We were able to extend the pilot from 1 team to 7 teams and around 50 people within 4 months. During this period we came across many different challenges. While not specific to Kanban, Kanban helps make these problems visible much quicker than before. The following is a list of challenges we experienced when coaching teams. These challenges were mostly local to that team.

5.1 Team Challenges

The teams have had closest contact with the benefits of using Kanban in a maintenance and operations environment. Still they have their own reservations and their own change process to go through.

Working within limits not needed *"I don't need these limits, I can do multiple tasks simultaneously without a problem."*

Multiple research results have shown that we lose focus with every task we pick up other than the first. Our general response is to ask the person who has this objection to try this and focus on only one task without the distraction of other tasks.

We have seen situations where we actually needed to raise the amount of work per member. This happens when that member has to wait on many other projects and resources, but it should be the exception.

Limits reducing personal productivity *"What if I can't continue because we hit the limit?"*

What we have encountered when investigating these objections is that these team members wish to be engaged in work activities and otherwise feel they aren't contributing. It is a drive to remain efficient for the company. *"I'm here 8 hours so I must be busy 8 hours a day."*

It is important for team members to know that they contribute by being part of a team and only team results matter. It's only when they see this, they will cooperate. If your colleague doing the testing and you cannot start a new task you are familiar with, ask the tester how you may assist him. Team members are forced to communicate and increase each other's understanding without feeling forced.

Less than 80% allocation *"I can only be at the stand up on Tuesday during the odd weeks."*

Team members that are not working for the team at least 80% of their workweek are disrupting. This disruption is often bigger than the benefits they bring to the team.

In one of our teams some team members were specialists that were only available for 1.5 days a week. They were needed because they held specific knowledge of the systems while at the same time they violate one of the key principles *"help work to flow"* by not being available for the team when needed.

The 80% rule is a general rule, we have had exceptions to this. When we know we only need infrastructure 30% of the time and that is predictable, we want somebody from infra for 50% of the time.

No input from sources *"Yes, we know you have started, but Joe is on holiday for 3 weeks and he is the only one that can help you."*

This problem was mainly with clients to teams. The cause for this lies in old behavior. The ASR organization had become accustomed to an IT organization where it takes a long time (months) before anybody works on it due to the amount of other work that also needed to be done.

A solution we applied was really easy and that was communication. The team coordinator would call the requester of the change and verify that it is still valid. The next question is who has the knowledge the team needs and is he/she available for questions. If not, this work will be postponed until he/she is. This communication shields the team from unnecessary waiting and the client gets a better feeling as he is more involved and informed.

Members approached directly *"I didn't complete anything because I had to help on project A, B and C to help avoid disaster."*

Project managers will do anything they need to do to complete their project successfully. This includes calling any developer or tester they know when they have a problem. This problem we see with developers mostly. Developers like challenges and puzzles and they want to help, it's their profession.

Around the time we started using Kanban there was one project within ASR that was critical for cost reduction. One of the developers from that project transferred to a Kanban team. He stopped working for the other project, but was still called daily by people on the project with questions. The team member spent more time juggling the project and other assignments than doing actual work.

This is where the team coordinator needs to help his team. First of all the team needs to acknowledge that this is a problem for the team and their progress. With several teams we struck a deal that if the work would take less than 15 minutes they could do it. Otherwise the project managers need to go to the coordinator. Aim is to have all the work flow into the team through the coordinator.

The best results are achieved when all members act the same way and refer to the coordinator. And even more importantly the coordinator needs to show positive result for using the proper channel. It is a bit of a nuisance at the start and when people are aware of this the process flows much smoother.

Tired of change *"Last year it was scrum, now it is Kanban..."*

Sometimes people are just tired of yet another approach to how they should do the work they have been doing for many years.

Here the approach we took is similar to others: inform and show and let the experience and share the results.

5.2 Organizational Challenges

Administrative processes *"We understand, you still have to fill in these forms."*

Kanban is practiced only in parts of the company. The rest still uses the previous practices and methods. Kanban teams still have to comply with the rules for overall planning for releases and administration of the hours worked. These processes are time consuming. We have found no proper way to solve this yet.

One of these processes is the process of creating hour estimates for every assignment even it is relatively small. The estimating can be time consuming and disproportional to the actual work. This estimating is valuable to the client and can help him assess whether the change is worth it or not compared to the benefit. It is the process that is a challenge.

Multiple locations *"I can be at your location tomorrow."*

ASR has IT teams distributed over 3 locations. This results in a communication barrier, even when people are willing to travel between locations. Telephone and email are not rich enough media to be able to communicate well.

Nothing beats a team that is sitting in the same room next to each other. Even desks between team members disrupt communication in various ways. One team was scattered around a room with 40 desks and they were sitting roughly in the same area but not within talking distance. When we sat them at desks that were all next to each other, their joy and productivity increased although they say they communicate just as much as before.

All the teams found a place of their own sitting all team members together.

Separation in departments *"Not my problem. I did my part well, let them fix it."*

By defining what someone's responsibilities are, you are defining even more what it is not. And if you hold someone accountable he will do that job excellent and just that job.

Within Kanban the whole team is responsible for the end result. Kanban visualizes the whole stream of activities that need to be completed for the feature to be done and fully productive. It is not possible to "hide"; everybody needs to take ownership of what he or she does and take ownership as a team. When you hand off work that is not properly done, it is clear to everybody that others will suffer as a result. Trust and group pressure enforce responsible behavior.

Understaffed departments *"Yes, I'd love to help you. You are number 92 on my highest priority list."*

Certain departments were required by every other department and team and had to deal with many requests. More requests than they could handle. They were structurally understaffed. This resulted in high work pressure for their employees and to be able to cope with this pressure they rigorously applied policies as a way to deal with the work load and still help others.

The value Kanban provides in this situation is visibility. When there was a bottleneck for the flow of features it became apparent immediately and work would halt. Instead of piling on more work, new request and work was only added when there was room to service these requests.

We weren't able to solve this. What we did do is visualize the problems that are being caused by this situation.

Prioritization between multiple clients *"My feature is more important than yours."*

When there are multiple business lines within a company each with their own budget, goals and responsibilities prioritization can be a major issue. Most teams have no problems with prioritization either because they have only one client or it's divided evenly between the respective clients. Problems arise when a team has a multitude of clients and while there is a planning one of these clients has an urgent rush job.

This one surprised us. And was solved quite easily. The teams establishes a default priority for instance order by sequence of date submitted to the team. This policy is communicated to all clients and the progress is visible to everybody.

If somebody wanted to deviate from the default order all they had to do is pick up the phone and agree with the other clients that they would be allowed to take priority. For the team it was only a matter of distributing the clients phone numbers and they miraculously self organized. Most of the times it was resolved only in a matter of minutes where previously used to be weeks to reach a compromise.

The solution to most of these challenges is communication. Both on a team level, help people communicate with each other and on a corporate level. We have had many conversations with people, held presentations, visited successful teams to show others that this can work. Share the successes with others; the team, partners, managers, their boss and their bosses boss.

The thing that was the hardest was changing actual work process. It is like steering an oil freighter. People are willing to adapt to new ways of working, but habits executed for many years are hard to break.

6 Results of the Adoption

Kanban was successfully applied to 7 IT teams. This success gave IT management the confidence in Kanban that this could solve the challenges they had experienced so far. It builds trust by constantly being transparent about almost everything. People enjoyed their work more as the negative pressure was replaced with a sense of being part of a group. Each of the teams made their work visible and by hanging the information on the walls this information was available to everybody who was interested. They were all very transparent in what they were doing and their status.

Continuous improvement was executed by almost all the teams both by holding retrospectives to look back and by making adjustments on the fly where needed.

The way of planning for a Kanban allows for flexibility needed for maintenance and operations while still providing predictability.

When one of the teams faced the possibility of being split again based on their role the team revolted and resisted heavily. Despite the problems they had encountered along the way they wanted to maintain Kanban as their way of working including sitting next to each other.

Clients and team members valued Kanban as a valuable way of building features in maintenance and operations. Given the choice they would either choose Kanban again or be neutral about it.

7 Conclusion and Recommendations

The chosen approach for introducing Kanban at ASR by moving slowly and share results worked very well. A short and intensive introduction prepared team coordinators for what was coming and helped start the teams in the right direction. Team coordinators appreciated the freedom and responsibility they had been given while still enjoying the coaching and mentoring of a Kanban coach.

Each team creates their own process and Kanban board and they really feel they own the process. Each team has its own pace and this should be respected. It's much better to go to slow than it is to go to fast. Kanban enables teams to build trust by constantly providing transparency and results and thereby improve relationships with and between stakeholders. Clients and team members valued Kanban as a valuable way of building features in maintenance and operations.

The thing that was the hardest was changing actual work process. It is like steering an oil freighter. People are willing to adapt to new ways of working, but habits executed for many years are hard to break. When problems arise it is all too easy to slip back.

Kanban creates atmosphere of trust, openness, transparency, continuous improvement. The results of these pilots were so successful that ASR has chosen to transition their maintenance and operations department to working with Kanban. The transition of 200 people is now in process.

Our recommendations for transitioning an organization to Kanban:

- Start small with one dedicated team, build on existing experience, make it as easy as possible, continue to monitor principles.
- Go slow. Only introduce new practices when the team and organization is ready for it. This is really a matter of personal observation and judgment.
- Let the team own the process and Work in Progress board from day one.
- Perform the stand ups from right to left and ask whether there is an update for that column. Asking individual members their status will disrupt the flow of both the board and the meeting.
- Standardize the meaning of colors of work in process items (often post-its) across multiple teams. Failing to do this confuses people who interact with multiple teams.
- White board and post-its are sufficient tools for the first three months of a team switching to Kanban. There are many drawbacks to the use of electronic tools.
- Communicate! (Interviews, coffee corner conversations, presentations).
- Create and use support provided by management.
- Share the success with your team and your manager(s).

Acknowledgements

David Anderson for starting and continuing to explore the Kanban movement.

Reference

[1] http://www.kanban101.com (accessed February 28th, 2010)

Automated Acceptance Testing of High Capacity Network Gateway

Ran Nyman, Ismo Aro, and Roland Wagner

Nokia Siemens Network, PO Box 1
FI-02022 Nokia Siemens Networks
ran@rannicon.com, ismo.aro@nsn.com, ro.wagner@gmx.net

Abstract. In this paper we will explore how agile acceptance testing is applied in testing a high capacity network gateway. We will demonstrate how the organisation managed to grow agile acceptance testing testing from two co-located teams to 20+ multi-site team setup and how acceptance test driven development is applied to complex network protocol testing. We will also cover how the initial ideas that we had of agile acceptance testing evolved during product development. At the end of paper we give recommendations to future projects using agile acceptance testing based on feedback that we have collected from our first customer trials.

Keywords: automated acceptance testing, scrum, organizational change.

1 Introduction

At the end of 2007 we started having a discussion how to build a high capacity network gateway from scratch. We faced two fundamental risks. First, the technology was completely new and has never been used before in Nokia Siemens Networks. Second, the use cases for first commercial deployments were not completely defined at program start - It became clear that we need to adapt feature content heavily throughout the program. Applying Scrum appeared to be the appropriate response to these major risks.

The initial idea was to build broad band network gateway and after few months of development we realized that there would more market demand for a gateway for 2G/3G and long term evolution (LTE) enabled mobile networks. Luckily we had chosen agile methods to develop the product and these methods provide us the flexibility to change the direction smoothly. The hardware (HW) and software (SW) platforms we selected were totally new and in the beginning of the development they were not available. So we used HW that had the target CPU but was totally different from the ATCA blade architecture that we would use in commercial product. We used same approach with the platform SW because the high availability SW platform was not ready.

2 Organisation and Growth

Selecting Scrum as agile development framework was easy; implementing it in practice was hard work. The first challenge was to convince all parties that feature teams

A. Sillitti et al. (Eds.): XP 2010, LNBIP 48, pp. 307–314, 2010.

are better than component teams. The feature teams that we decided to use, after long debate, are long-lived, cross functional teams which complete many end-to-end customer features [1].

When we started the product we started with people coming from two totally different backgrounds. The first team had used Scrum over one year and successfully created a product. The other team came from a traditional waterfall organisation that had failed to apply Scrum and had resistance in trying it again. The failed Scrum implementation was not real Scrum implementation it had just consisted of renaming waterfall development to Scrum. So the approach that we used was to mix the teams so both teams would have members from waterfall development background and agile development background. We put all development people in a room and asked them to organise themselves into two feature teams.

At first, the teams did not want to use feature teams because they claimed that the feature teams lead to bad software quality. An Agile coach present in the meeting asked gently what is the quality of the code that the component teams had created in their previous project? The answer was that a mess. So after some discussion we agreed to see how the code would end up when using feature teams. After the teams agreed to try feature teams the forming of teams went very smoothly and it took under one hour. The newly formed teams were allowed to select their Scrum masters from two available Scrum masters.

We had our first teams and development could start. In the literature the recommended approach is to start with one team and then grow when you have enough infrastructure built [2]. We decided to start with two teams. This led to huge arguments between teams and very slow start in development because there were so many different opinions how the architecture and infrastructure should be done. In the beginning there were difficulties in planning, because in a sequential life cycle model there is a long planning and specification period. Jumping into agile style where only minimum amount of work is planned was hard for people who did not have agile development background.

2.1   Growing First Wave

The first growth point was to add two more teams. It was a challenge since they were transferred from traditional organisation. One of these teams refused to learn new testing tools and new way of working. They did not produce anything that could be considered done for several sprints in row. The team argued that the testing tools in their previous environment were much better and resisted the learning of new tools and did not want to write unit test. In retrospect one crucial point that caused the resistance was that we did not provide the sufficient training and the reasoning why things are done differently when using iterative development. Also the new teams should be able to influence the ways of working that have been agreed so they can feel the rules as their own.

The only good thing in adding new team without breaking existing teams was that the velocities of the existing teams did not suffer any significant impact because of the new teams. We added still few more team to our main development site and adding them did not cause so much troubles as adding the first two teams.

2.2 Growing Second Wave

Adding teams to the same site was easy compared to next step where we decided to add teams at a second site to speed up development because the market demand for the product that we were creating was suddenly emerging. Here we found out that using iterative development and automated acceptance testing really paid of. We trained the subcontractor in our ways of working by having them spend several weeks with our local team doing work as team members until we were confident that they could work by themselves.

The same coding and testing rules were applied to subcontractor that were for our own teams. They had to write unit test, create automated acceptance test for all code and use the central continuous integration system. The biggest challenge in working with second site was the distance. It was hard to communicate the requirements and in the first half a year we had one person working as product owner proxy for other site to reduce the misunderstandings in requirements.

2.3 Current Team Structure

After adding several teams we have now over 20 teams and the majority of the teams are developing and documenting features. We have couple of teams in supporting roles like performance testing, system testing, coaching and continuous integration (CI) team. CI team is taking care of building and automation system. The system testing team is focusing on executing test that can not be done by Scrum teams because the need of the real network elements which we have only a limited amount and coordinating the usage of them between several teams is not feasible. The coaching teams main responsibility is to support in modern engineering practices, help teams to solve difficult technical challenges and in general help the organisation to learn faster.

2.4 Expert Coaching

In the beginning we realised that we need expert coaches that can help us in using modern SW development practices. First we had two consultants who helped us to set up the CI environment that was not so straight forward because the building and installing the build to target HW was complicated. To get the first teams in speed with unit testing and test driven development (TDD) we used one world class consultant helping in setting up the unit testing framework and teaching teams how to test drive their code. TDD was not widely accepted in teams but unit testing was found useful by the teams. We used also help in teaching people acceptance test driven development that helped the teams to understand the concept.

3 Test Automation Strategy

It was clear in the beginning that we did not want to write legacy code that has no test as legacy code is defined in [3]. So we decided to have unit test coverage target and our aim was to automate all acceptance tests. We are now in situation where all user stories are unit tested, acceptance tested automatically and exploratory testing is done based on agreement with the area product owner. This has led to situation where almost all testing is done automatically and any manual testing done by teams is an exception.

3.1 Regression Tests

Regression tests consists of unit tests, smoke test and all automated test. For every commit unit and smoke tests are executed and if those test cases fails, commits to code base are not allowed until problem has solved. During night time we execute whole regression set that contains all acceptance tests. The regression set consists of all automated test cases that we have developed. As defined in [4] there is no cost in adding all automated test in regression set and test from regression set should be removed only if the functionality they test becomes obsolete. There is agreement with product owner and teams that all acceptance test cases should be passing at the end of the sprint.

3.2 Acceptance Test Driven Development (ATDD)

The idea of ATDD [5] was already known to some of the people and they had also experience in applying it in product development. The idea of ATDD came from Robot Framework [6] developers Pekka Klärck, Juha Rantanen and Janne Härkönen. The basic idea is to acceptance test every requirement which comes into the sprint and at that the moment acceptance tests are discussed for the first time and planned at a high level. The initial idea in ATDD was to have ATDD-meeting after each sprint planning where test cases are clarified and agreed how they will be implemented. Currently ATDD practices vary team by team but only acceptance tested requirements are considered as done.

3.3 Structure of Test Cases

In the previous project where we piloted Scrum, we started writing test cases at a very technical level and it was extremely hard to understand what test cases were doing without deep domain and tool knowledge. Then we found out that this approach was not working and started writing tests in business language. This was our experience and we wanted to try the same approach in this project, but there was huge resistance to create higher level language to test cases. Reasoning was that it does not give any value and also the way of how we use protocol tester does not support this kind of step by step presentation. One more reason for dropping this more readable way of writing test cases is that our test cases usually don't test any end to end functionality that has business value (see conclusions) and they are not read by product owner and area product owners.

4 Test Automation and Continuous Integration (CI)

There were two options what to use as testing framework when we started the development. HIT which is an in house test scripting tool and Robot Framework. There was not any formal decision by anyone and two initial teams started using Robot Framework because its usage was much simpler than HIT and it was easily integrated to CI environment. After it was already in use it was decided that it would be the testing framework for this product. Robot Framework is a generic keyword driven [7] testing framework so we also needed protocol tester.

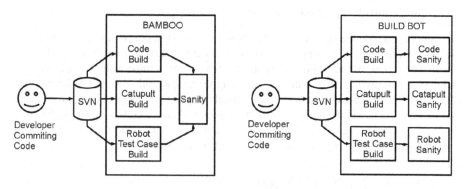

Fig. 1. Initial CI System   **Fig. 2.** Current CI System

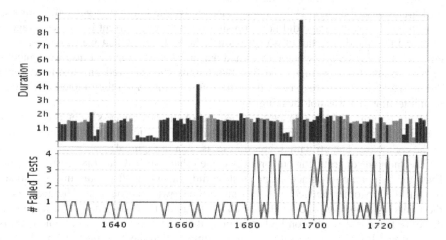

Fig. 3. Build status (gray is successful build) and failed test cases per build

Catapult [8] was chosen because there was no previous experience of acceptance testing this kind of product and Catapult was used successfully in previous, non Agile developed products as a protocol tester. The Robot framework is executing long catapult scripts. There has been now discussion of changing way of using catapult or even replace it, because how we are using it at the moment does not support ATDD.

In Figure 1 is our initial testing environment and in Figure 2 is the current environment. Currently we have switched most of the builds from Bamboo CI system [9] to Build Bot [10] system. Builbot executes build, which includes compiling and unit testing. Builbot executes also our sanity tests. Sanity tests represent smoke testing [11]. Buildbot is executing Robot Framework where those sanity test are. At the moment we have three different sanity builds, one for our Robot Framework test material, one for product code and one for catapult. When there is change in one these diffrened parts only that sanity is executed. Sanitys are executed in series, so only one commit is tested in one sanity run. There is dedicated environment for sanity testing.

4.1 Continuous Integration Practices

Teams are using their own development environments to test pre commit changes to avoid breaking builds on CI. This practice is crucial since we have so many teams and having each team to commit to trunk without first verifying the change would lead to situation where the build would all the time broken and the cause of failure would be hard to find. When we had fewer teams we committed directly to trunk and let the CI system to inform possible problems but we had to modify the practice when we grew bigger than 10 teams. In Figure 3 we can see the daily build success rates that we have currently and the number of failing test cases in case the build fails (black bar in picture).

5   Analysis of Achieved Results

Having unit test coverage as target backfired and we found out that people were writing unit test just to get the coverage but not testing anything. Having targets seems to backfire as described in [12]. We decided to remove the unit test target and to our surprise the unit test coverage did not drop significantly. Our current branch coverage is 75% and the mandatory target was previously 80%. It seems that we should have focused on training people when they joined our product development instead of having targets on unit test coverage. The first two teams who received unit testing training did not have time or necessary skills to train new teams when they joined and it lead to unit testing that was not meaningful.

Having automated acceptance test was one of the key success cafeterias why we managed to grow the development to multi site and still to maintain the high quality of the code base. The growing regression set is seen in Figure 4.

The moment of truth for our product came when we had our first customer trial. Even the huge amount of acceptance testing did not save us from missing functionality that the customer noticed in their trial in their own environment. The analysis of the faults and missing functionality revealed to us that we must have end to end acceptance test cases written on higher level so that they test the customer functionality and that we should have the same network elements that the customers have. Many of the findings in customer trial were incompatibilities with the customer elements because we had different interpretation about the specification than the other network element vendor. When we fixed the findings in customer trial we created new test case that we can be sure that the functionality that we create will also work with future modifications.

We tried to patch our lack of end to end test by having separate system verification team but even they were not able to find the missing parts of the functionality due to two reasons. They were not collaborating with the teams developing the functionality close enough so they would have clear picture what to test and they also lacked HW that the customer had.

We also found out that the feature teams that we created in the beginning were turned to functionality area teams and were not able to create end to end functionality inside one team. The functionality areas that we have are interfaces towards other system facing our gateway product. It seems that the product that we create is so big that one team can not handle the incoming and out going interface so they would conform to feature team definition that was our goal. Now when we have most of the interfaces in working shape we will try again to move more towards feature teams.

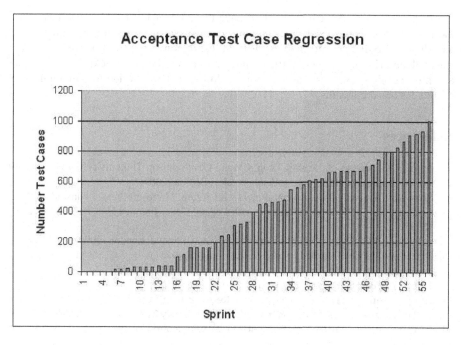

Fig. 4. Regression set growth

6 Conclusions

The selection of Scrum and agile development methods significantly accelerated the time to market and gave us flexibility that our traditional development methods never offered. The previous gateway product where we used sequential life cycle model took twice as long to develop and the sequential life cycle would not have allowed us to change direction of the product development as fast as agile methods. Automated acceptance testing helped us significantly when we added new teams to development to keep the code base in high quality.

One easy thing that were we should have put more effort was the speed and reliability of the CI system as the feedback speed from each code change should be as fast as possible as mentioned in [13]. Also the CI system should have been planned more carefully as it did not sustain the adding of new teams as easily as we thought.

On testing side we should have had more focus on exploratory testing. We were too excited about 100% automated testing and only automated testing. It came obvious after the first customer trials that we need to amplify the usage of exploratory testing [14] in teams to ensure product quality.

We also found out that splitting user stories to very small parts so they could fit in the one sprint leads to situation that testing is done at very low level. That makes problematic to have really end to end test cases which give real business value. We should bring acceptance testing more closer to customer, and use acceptance tests as a communication tool between all stakeholders [4], from customer to the developers and testers. This would also give us better visibility what functionality is ready ship and what not.

There is also one other big reason to have these upper level acceptance test cases: these test cases should verify that nothing has lost because of splitting requirements and also ensure that no information has been lost in communication between different stakeholders. Having system verification team to patch the lack of exploratory testing and missing high level test cases is not a solution that works due to communication challenges between teams.

References

1. Larman, C., Vodde, B.: Scaling Lean & Agile Development: Thinking and Organizational Tools for Large-Scale Scrum. Addison-Wesley, Boston (2009)
2. Schwaber, K.: Agile Project Management with Scrum. Microsoft Press, Redmond (2004)
3. Feathers, M.C.: Working Effectively with Legacy Code. Prentice Hall PTR, New Jersey (2005)
4. Adzic, G.: Bridging the Communication Gap. Neuri Limited, London (2009)
5. http://testobsessed.com/wordpress/wp-content/uploads/2008/12/atddexample.pdf
6. http://robotframework.org
7. http://en.wikipedia.org/wiki/Keyword-driven_testing
8. http://www.ixiacom.com/products/display?skey=ixcatapult
9. http://www.atlassian.com/software/bamboo/
10. http://buildbot.net/trac
11. http://en.wikipedia.org/wiki/Smoke_testing#Smoke_testing_in_software_development
12. Austin, R.D.: Measuring and Managing Performance in Organizations. Dorset House Publishing, New York (1996)
13. http://www.martinfowler.com/articles/continuousIntegration.html#KeepTheBuildFast
14. http://en.wikipedia.org/wiki/Exploratory_testing

So You Think You're Agile?

Colm O'hEocha[1], Kieran Conboy[1], and Xiaofeng Wang[2]

[1] National University of Ireland Galway
{c.oheocha2,kieran.conboy}@nuigalway.ie
[2] University of Limerick
{xiaofeng.wang}@lero.ie

Abstract. Some agile projects succeed, some fail miserably. Research shows that time does not necessarily cure such ills and there can be many complex underlying reasons. Evaluating the ways agility is supported across three supposedly agile projects reveals a myriad of organizational, human and political issues. Using a novel approach to assess agile projects from first principles, this paper outlines several key findings and recommendations beyond mere compliance to textbook methods.

Keywords: agile methods, adoption, assimilation, experiences, assessment.

1 Introduction

When adopting an agile information systems development (ISD) method, organizations will normally select one or more the defined 'textbook' examples such as Scrum or XP. These provide varying levels of prescriptive practices and tools which can be implemented directly and promise team agility as a result. When a team adopts such methods, they normally 'cherry pick' practices and adjust them to suit their project context. There is often little thought of dependencies between practices, and how the use or non-use of one could affect others. For example, how useful is continuous build without an automated test suite? Similarly, the way in which the practices are implemented can vary widely, such as daily stand-up meetings that last an hour and take the form of upward reporting versus a team 'touch base' that takes 10 minutes. Regardless of the practices selected, or how faithfully or effectively they are implemented, the projects tend to be generally regarded in the organization as 'agile' and management will expect to see the perceived benefits such as more flexibility, better quality and faster delivery. However, with many initial adoptions these benefits can be elusive with the result that the value of agile methods and their general perception in the organization can be called into question.

Such early faltering can lead to various 'agile assessment' attempts to try to identify the source of the problems. However, these tend to measure compliance to the 'defined' method, assuming that if everything is implemented as per the documentation it will resolve the problems. This approach fails to take into account the particular organizational context of the implementation, and often will encourage adoption of practices which are defined in the method but may not be appropriate in the particular case. Furthermore, it does not address the manner in which the practices are

A. Sillitti et al. (Eds.): XP 2010, LNBIP 48, pp. 315–324, 2010.

implemented, which can vary widely from project to project. In this paper we present the experience of a global financial services firm with a novel agile assessment approach, where the true contribution of each practice to the agility itself, rather than compliance to a defined agile method, is evaluated.

The firm in question has approximately 45,000 employees worldwide. Up to 10,000 of these are IT personnel developing systems to support the business, distributed across multiple sites in the US, Europe and India. With a history of using highly formalized, waterfall methods over many years, and with a strong emphasis on process predictability, the organization has developed programs for CMMi compliance, ITIL adoption and so on. More recently, agile and lean methods have gained traction in pockets of the organization. This led to early, ad-hoc trials of Scrum and XP in some teams. A newly developed proprietary method incorporating many principles and practices from agile methods such as Scrum is currently being piloted in several sites. This adoption is being sponsored as part of a larger 'IT Transformation' initiative and is being driven by the global IT organization. In a collaborative research initiative with practitioners in the company, the authors have assessed three such trial projects located in an Irish office between July and September 2009. All were part of distributed teams, but with the majority of analysis, development and test based in Ireland. One was a 'green field' project with some US members and a small, inexperienced team of five. The other two were larger (10-20) with US and India based members and were part of larger enterprise wide programs.

2 Assessing Agile Projects

Across the three selected projects, the agile method was being implemented differently in each. To establish how agile each project was we chose not to look at compliance to the documented method, but rather look at how each practice supported or inhibited agility. For this we used a 'conceptual framework' for agility which defines the underlying aspects of an agile team such as creativity ad simplicity. Therefore, the agile methods in use could be assessed effectively regardless of the particular practices each project did or did not implement, or indeed how the project implemented each practice. This approach allowed effective comparison of the three projects using three different agile implementations – in effect allowing us compare 'apples and oranges'. Therefore the assessment involved answering the following questions for each project:

1. What are we meant to be doing? This we call the *defined* method
2. What are we actually doing? This is the *method-in-action* [1]
3. Is what we are doing helping us be 'agile'?

We found that the *defined* method is a 'hybrid' combining both formal, deterministic elements from the Rational Unified Process (RUP) and agile elements from Scrum and, to a lesser extent, eXtreme Programming (XP). It can be regarded as an "iterative rigorous process" [2]. It has well defined disciplines and practices, and an overall iterative process within which they are executed. The method is expressed as concrete procedures, guidelines and templates designed to execute the implementation steps of a well defined project. The method is prescriptive in that it defines inclusive rules rather than generative [3]. For example, it defines how requirements should be documented and how peer reviews should be executed. It could not therefore be regarded as providing only 'barely sufficient process' [4].

We then established the *method-in-action* for each project through interviews with project managers and senior team members. Research has shown that work methods are never implemented exactly as defined, varying by project, team and organizational context [5]. Agile methods generally acknowledge this explicitly, citing the 'tailoring' of methods to ensure effectiveness in specific situations. The *method-in-action* for each project was found to be quite different. Different sets of practices were used, and each of these was used differently depending on development context, team context and rational and political roles the applied method plays. Table 1 below gives a snippet of the different method-in-action in the three projects regarding the iteration planning practice.

Table 1. The different method-in-action in the three projects (iteration planning practice)

Practice	Text book definition	Method-in-action		
		Team A	Team B	Team C
Iteration Planning	- Define scope, tasks & tests for the team. - Design Iteration Stories. - Team owns estimates. Estimates in finer detail.	- 3 week iterations are used. - Scope, tasks, estimates and detailed design are completed by each track before iteration planning meeting. - Planning Meeting is more of a brief review of stories. - Iteration is planned to deliver a fixed number of story points – it is not 'overloaded' with additional stories	- Iterations of 4 weeks are used. - Planning day is used to create user stories and link them to use cases. - Each user story is assigned an owner, who breaks it into tasks & leads detailed design - Early iterations in a release are 'overloaded' with story points to ensure there is always work planned	- 4 week iterations, long enough for largest use cases. - Received ABPs and existing iteration schedule dictate the use cases to be included in the iteration planning. - Joint design of lower level use cases/user stories and breakdown to tasks. - Iterations are planned to complete 100% of capacity – ie no overfilling, even though some level of overfilling has been introduced later on.

Once the method-in-action was established, the third phase involved a half-day focus group session with each team to establish how each practice supported or inhibited agility. From a foundation of organizational agility, and with reference to agile software development, the core contributory concepts of agility have been distilled [6]. Creativity, proaction, reaction, learning, cost, quality and simplicity are the foundations of agility. Table 2 below shows how the three projects perceived the contribution of their version of iteration planning to agility. Depending on how the method is implemented in each project, different project teams perceive differently the contribution of the method-in-action to the overall agility of the team. In the following discussion we take iteration planning as an example to further illustrate this.

In the case of Team A, the iterative planning is regarded negatively in terms of creativity – the iterations of 3 weeks are regarded as *"tight"* to deliver the end to end functionality required for a user centric story. Also, several comments indicate there are considerable story and scope changes within the iteration, which is likely to consume what should be implementation time, and further restricting latitude for creativity. However, proaction and reaction are supported through iterations, though the need for detailed design and changes within iterations indicates shorter cycles may be beneficial from this viewpoint. One concern is that stories are often not completely finished or 'done done' within an iteration which could reduce the ability to address new circumstances effectively through the iteration practice, evidenced by this comment: "*Tough to start an iteration with a clean sheet. Often some queries or issue from a previous area you worked in crops up which knocks you off*". As with estimation practice, learning can be inhibited due to the same developers being assigned tasks similar to ones they previously completed. Story implementation design is carried out before the planning meeting, with only a review and estimates shared with the larger team. Additionally, learning is constrained by the lack of on-going customer feedback: "*The result of an iteration is sometimes meaningless since customer is not engaged and not testing the deliverable of an iteration*". Initially, iteration planning meetings lasted most of a day and included joint design of stories by the whole team. However, they were found to be long-winded and '*boring*'. Now track leads are asked to perform task breakdown and estimation before the planning meeting, which now lasts less than two hours. This is perceived by the team as a cost saving since all members do not have to sit through the minute of each story. However, deployment of each iteration to QA environment is seen as a significant cost, and one that must be born for each iteration. Together with re-estimation of stories mid-iteration and problems accommodating these changes in the management tools, additional cost is added to the iteration practice. This effect is likely to reinforce the pressure to extend iteration durations, which in turn may exacerbate the overhead of managing them – in effect creating a 'vicious cycle' effect. There was no perceived effect on the quality or simplicity due to the iteration planning practice.

Table 2. How iteration planning is seen to affect agility across the three projects

Practice: Iteration planning	Agility						
	Creativity	Proaction	Reaction	Learning	Cost	Quality	Simplicity
Team A	Poor	Good	Good	Poor	Poor	No Perceived Effect	No Perceived Effect
Team B	Poor	Good	Good	No Perceived Effect	Good	Poor	No Perceived Effect
Team C	Conflicting Opinions	No Perceived Effects	Poor	Good	Poor	Conflicting Opinions	No Perceived Effects

In Team B, contrary to the defined method, iteration planning appears to be exclusively dedicated to firming up estimates and delivery expectations from the iteration. The detailed design is either performed by the tracks individually before the meeting, if the user story is understood, or a "*placeholder*" is used if not. A firm commitment of deliverables is given to program management at this stage, "*expectation is set at the start as to what features will be delivered*", with failure to deliver as planned viewed negatively, "*customer wanted the story points to match up with functionality delivered, it was a big issue if it didn't match*". In attempts to avoid such shortfalls, project management front load the release to deliver more than the teams sustainable capacity of story points in early iterations, thereby creating a '*buffer*' to absorb unforeseen delays later in the release cycle. Two contrary views on the effect of this on creativity are expressed. The first calls for longer (e.g. 2 days) iteration planning which "*would help in triggering the learning and creative thoughts in team*" and "*all team members participate and focus is on finding creating/innovative solutions for stories*". But another comment claims "*creativity is helped here by limiting time to define & deliver solution*". The method as defined calls for detailed design to be done at the iteration planning stage which aids with accurate estimation and occurs in a team setting before the iteration deliverables are committed and the 'clock is ticking'. This context may provide more scope for alternate approaches to be solicited and evaluated than the time-boxed iteration tasks allow. Where "placeholders" or "scope-less stories" are concerned, detailed requirements are not understood until the individual tasks are being executed within the iteration – at this stage estimates and deliverables have been committed which may again limit opportunity for creativity. Another concern with iteration planning is suggested by the comment "*too many stories to be closed out at the end of the iteration can have a negative impact on quality*". According to one comment, the ability to be proactive and reactive is enhanced for "scope-less stories" since these are not designed until mid-iteration, just before they are implemented; that is 'just-in-time' design. Interestingly, there were no perceived effects on learning. Progressing through the planning, design, development, test and deployment tasks might be expected to offer a strong learning opportunity. However, it is possible that these effects were attributed to the estimation practice. Initially, planning meetings were a full day for the entire team and this was regarded as a high cost – the length, and perceived cost of these has been reduced. However, the work of design, task breakdown and estimation still must take place – but only the people directly involved in implementation do this before the planning. Therefore, this cost could be considered to still exist but has been displaced from this practice. Another factor is that all team members do not contribute to these tasks for all user stories – this may also reduce the real cost of this exercise, but to the detriment of creativity and learning.

In the case of Team C, the team have different opinions on the impact of this practice in terms of creativity. Since the whole team get together for the planning day, with "*war room allocated*" and "*shared network*", the team members get good opportunities to discuss issues and tasks, "*think of new ways and better ways to do things*", and thus be more creative. There was a perceived negative impact on reaction. One developer commented that the ability of responding to change may be compromised if the plan was "*treated as in stone*", especially by the project management. The fact that the iteration plan already exists before the planning meeting may be the factor that influences the attitude of the project management towards the plan, and eventually impedes the team's ability to respond to changes. Iterative planning turned out to be a good learning experience for the team on how to "*gauge work*". As one developer comments, the team's ability to plan has been improved and they get more accurate estimates from iteration to iteration, which may lead to higher quality of resulting plans. However, since the team use 4-week iterations, typically iteration planning is done for 4 weeks, which is not easy and makes the planning day very busy and intensive. Quality of resulting plans may be hampered when people are hurrying to get the big planning done in one day. The team members feel that it is a huge cost to spend a full day on planning, basically due to the overhead involved with the project tracking tool associated with the method. Increasing effort such as loading estimates and stories and maintaining the tracking tool takes more time than necessary, and the team felt it impacted negatively on simplicity.

3   Findings and Recommendations

Although considerable data was collected for each of the twenty two defined practices in the method (as per the iteration planning described above), due to space limitations we can only provide a summary here (due to confidentiality concerns of the company please contact the authors directly for further access to detail data from the study). Analysing input from across the three project teams, a number of common 'themes' emerged. Three of these major areas are discussed here, along with actions being taken to improve them. The recommendations have led to improvements in the three projects, but more importantly, in the enterprise wide agile adoption program.

3.1   Iterative Development Is Not Agile Development

Performing planned but iterative development does not equate to agile development. The method studied here is a variant of the Rational Unified Method (RUP) and combines up-front planning with iterative development. This is sometimes described as 'Serial in the large, iterative in the small' and is often justified as an enterprise scalable approach to agile development. It includes up front commitment to a release plan with major features agreed with the customer, and detail to be added later. However, the method cannot be considered highly agile, even though it does allow for the iterative delivery of applications. This is reflected in developers comments such as *"Feels like we're doing mini-waterfall instead of agile"* and *"Agile development, waterfall everything else"*.

A fundamental concept in agile methods is an effective feedback loop – where plans are frequently evaluated against current reality and adjusted accordingly. In the projects studied, iterations did deliver software, but not necessarily working software whereby customers could interact fully with it. User stories often required coordination of several tasks across various 'component teams' and the hand-offs and synchronization involved meant end-to-end functionality could not be completed in a single iteration. Therefore, reflection on the iteration was normally confined to the development team rather than involving all stakeholders, and adaptation was therefore limited.

As implemented, the proprietary method lacks an effective feedback loop. Customers are not involved in the process on a continuous basis, developers are pressured to comply with original plans and schedules rather than adjust them based on current experience, and even feedback between dependant projects in the same program are not synchronised. This lack of ongoing communication intensity leads to a reversion to 'management by plan', which, in turn, severely limits agility of the method.

To tackle some of these problems, several recommendations were made. The intensive face to face 'visioning' and planning session used at the start of the project, although getting initial development off to a great start, is no substitute for ongoing customer involvement. This 'group solve' process [7] involved all stakeholders in extended, co-located and facilitated workshop sessions over a period of six weeks which served to form relationships across the team and define and prioritize requirements. Such intensive, face-to-face communication should be made a mandatory step in the initiation of any major project. However, this must be followed by on-going, rich (ideally face to face, but at minimum video based) communication between stakeholders, especially customers. Such an ongoing arrangement could mean a shorter and less costly initial planning phase. The cost of keeping stakeholders aligned would be spread throughout the project, rather than focused in a single intense effort. The time and resources to facilitate this critical stakeholder feedback must be built into the project plan. Senior management must understand the necessity and value of this practice and ensure it doesn't lapse later in the project. In addition, the root causes why user stories cannot be shortened should be investigated and debated. Are component teams the best organizational structure if agility is the end goal? End of iteration customer checkpoints should be made mandatory, and only 'done done' stories should be demonstrated.

Where the project is a minor development, the use of a Project Charter type document jointly developed and owned by the various stakeholders is a cost efficient, though not as effective, alternative to establishing a baseline for the project. This document should include business objectives, how business value from the project will be measured and communicated, and a high-level release plan and associated themes. However, ongoing, effective communication with customers is still essential.

To underline the importance of embracing change in agile projects, the 'change control boards' for the projects should be renamed to 'change facilitation boards' or another title that doesn't cast change in a negative light. This would support the agile manifesto principle whereby we should "harness change for customer competitive advantage".

3.2 Focus on Value Delivered, Not Effort Expended

Planning on the projects was focused on estimating Level Of Effort (LOE) and creating a plan accordingly. The role of project manager was little different from the waterfall approach with establishing and driving the plan still very much in evidence. Story points are based on the time taken to complete work. Tracking of the project progress is based on the number of story points completed. In one project, management insisted that the iteration deliver exactly (or more) the story point capacity of the team.

This approach leads the team to focus on the cost of delivery, rather than the customer value being delivered. This adversely affects several important agile principles. Delivering early & continuous value flow through short iterations of working software is important for maximising value, but has little affect on LOE. The tenet of 'Quality is not Negotiable' is undermined in preference to maximising the scope delivered, and hence story points. In Lean thinking, the creation of WIP is discouraged as it consumes effort, even though it creates no value. In one project, so- called 'administration stories' are created by the team to cover tasks such as code reviews. These were initially included as a task in the user story, but it was found to be more efficient to review several stories in one meeting. So to allow story points for the work done on these before they were code reviewed, the task was moved into an administrative story. Although it may be easier to manage, this encourages WIP and ignores customer value flow concerns.

Another finding was a perception by some that the method was being used to 'micro-manage' development. Senior developers and project managers are requested to provide initial estimates at project and release planning stage. These are based on limited information of requirements or context. Project plans are drawn up based on these estimates and agreed with senior management and customers. During development, when reality does not reflect these plans, it is the responsibility of the developers to justify the divergence. Some comments on this topic included "any deviation from estimates has high visibility with restrictive results for the team" and would be seen "in a negative light" Team members felt this leads to pressure on development, and unnecessary overhead and stress when variances have to be explained.

It is difficult to see why the initial plans, based as they are on limited information, and with little buy-in from those performing the work, should be treated as the benchmark for the project. Interestingly, several senior developers emphasized with pride how their estimates had become increasingly accurate throughout the project. The attention given to the estimates indicated their high importance to the team and likely underscores how they are perceived as a measure of performance.

Since all projects faltered in getting a viable customer feedback loop in place, it is easy to see that measuring effort expended is easier than value delivered. This in turn drives 'efficiencies' such as grouping code reviews for several stories into a single meeting and making user stories large enough to allow developers get a 'good run' at a certain area of code. It also undermines the imperative to automate testing as this becomes an 'occasional' rather than 'continuous' activity.

Recommendations to tackle these issues included refocusing on user stories that are customer centric and deliver the smallest feature of value to the customer, delivering 'done done' stories from each iteration, driving training and resources into automated testing and establishing transparent and common test coverage metrics across projects.

'Epics', 'themes' and 'stories' should only define the bare minimum of detail required at the time, acknowledging that changes will occur as the project progresses and premature detail will be a wasted effort. These agile constructs should also express requirements in terms of customer value rather than application functionality and are fundamental to achieving continuous, early value flow and implicit traceability of requirements to implementation. Move from up-front, contractually-oriented scope definition to a more collaborative, scope-variable approach where shared ownership and responsibility are the norm. Innovation starts with requirements, and elaboration should include diverse perspectives and skills including end customer, developers and testers.

The ability to continuously integrate and automatically test all sub-systems of an enterprise solution should be invested in as a critical IT competency. CI is a cornerstone of agile development and must be recognised as such by senior management, with necessary resources provided to arrive at effective, re-usable technologies and to provide for their implementation in any substantial project.

Establish a mechanism to measure test coverage that is common across projects. For unit tests, develop guidelines on how coverage should be measured (lines of code, method calls, functions, boundary conditions, etc) and coverage targets. The measure should aim to ensure priority is to test critical code and to avoid writing test code merely to meet coverage targets. Where targets are less than 100%, justification for this should be required (if the code isn't used – remove it). Similarly, for acceptance tests, coverage of user stories should be measurable in a consistent manner.

3.3 Agility Needs More than Agile Development Practices

The introduction of agile software development in the case organization focused on the new method and associated practices. Other organizational and people aspects received scant attention. Traditional roles such as project manager, team lead, developer, tester, analyst and the demarcation of responsibilities they represent still persist. Attention to individual capabilities and diversity of teams is not evident. There is little evidence of self-organising teams, or evolving from manager to facilitator roles. Tactics such as rotating team members between tracks, roles and projects to support diversity and cross team learning have not been adopted. Objective setting, performance reviews, training and other HR related activities do not seem to reflect the move to a new way of working.

In addition, the agile way of organizing work seems confined to the software delivery teams – portfolio and program management continue to work to predefined plans. One of the projects studied involved a component team building services to be called by front-end user applications which were being developed by other IT groups. Although these groups were nominally using the same ISD method, coordination between the projects was by plan rather than an agile reflect-adapt feedback loop. As reality impinged upon the project, the synchronization plan became irrelevant. The feedback loop between the component team and the front end feature team could not be maintained. As both teams belonged to different IT organizations, a very 'cautious' relationship developed as neither wanted to appear to fail to execute to plan. Some 'arms-length' solutions such as one project running an iteration behind the other were attempted but these do not seem to have resolved the difficulties, and have led to 'mini-waterfalls' in some cases. This failure indicates a need to apply more agile and effective co-ordination at the level of the portfolio, product or program.

A re-examination of the roles in the project was recommended, including a move from management to facilitation and the development of self-organizing teams. From simple measures such as rotating the role of facilitator in team meetings, to a re-examination of the role of the project managers and a move away from component based to product, project or feature centric organizational structures were recommended. To increase information redundancy and thereby increase team cohesion and resilience, job rotation within long life teams were advocated. Task estimation should be a team activity, using planning poker or a similar technique, rather than being the preserve of the 'expert' in the technical area involved. To encourage continual learning, tasks should be allocated as people become free, rather than on the basis of expertise, which reinforces the development of silos and indispensable 'heroes'.

4 Conclusions

This study used the method-in-action framework to characterize how an agile method had been implemented differently across three projects. Although all three were regarded within the organization as using the same agile method, there were significant differences in how it had been implemented. By evaluating each project against a set of underlying agile concepts on a practice by practice basis, we were able to assess how each supported or inhibited agility. This approach revealed that, although adopting the agile method had led to improvements in certain areas, it could not be regarded as highly agile. An incomplete feedback-adaptation loop, a focus on effort expended rather than value delivered and a lack of attention to people and organizational structure aspects severely limited the agility of the method. The 'cherry-picking' of practices without due consideration of how they inter-relate, along with wide variances in how each practice was implemented, led to an agile method adoption delivering little agility. Agile adopters need to focus on achieving underlying agility by carefully choosing and implementing practices, but also looking at people, roles and organizational structure, as well as dependencies between practices and how they work together.

References

1. Fitzgerald, B., Russo, N., Stolterman, E.: Information Systems Development: Methods in Action. McGraw-Hill, London (2002)
2. Ambler, S.: Choose the Right Software Method for the Job,
   http://www.agiledata.org/essays/differentStrategies.html
3. Highsmith, J., Cockburn, A.: Agile Software Development: The Business of Innovation. IEEE Computer (2001)
4. Highsmith, J.: Agile Software Development Ecosystems. Pearson, Boston (2002)
5. Madsen, S., Kautz, K., Vidgen, R.: A framework for understanding how a unique and local IS development method emerges in practice. European Journal of Information Systems 15, 225–238 (2006)
6. Conboy, K.: Agility From First Principles: Reconstructing The Concept Of Agility In Information Systems Development. Information Systems Research 20(3) (2009)
7. Takats, A., Brewer, N.: Improving Communication between Customers and Developers. In: Agile Development Conference (ADC 2005). IEEE Computer Society, Los Alamitos (2005)

From a Timebox Tangle to a More Flexible Flow

Jørn Ola Birkeland

Bekk Consulting AS, N-0102 Oslo, Norway
jorn.ola.birkeland@bekk.no

Abstract. Flow-based software development (FSD, a.k.a. lean, pull-based, or kanban) is attractive in certain types of software development projects, e.g. maintenance projects. This experience report shows one project team's attempt at moving from a timebox-based development process (scrum) to a flow-based process.

Keywords: Lean, kanban, flow-based development, WIP limit.

1 Background

The software development team had run a Scrum-based development process for several years. The main product was a custom-made web-based content management system (CMS) for a Fortune 500 industrial company. The team consisted of developers, design and user experience specialists, and project management. The product had been developed and enhanced since 1999, including a partial transition to a new platform in 2005. The codebase was estimated to be equivalent to around 400 KSLOC C#.

The practices were modern, and included continuous integration, automated, nightly build and deployment to QA servers, and suites of automated unit and integration tests. Developers and a group of domain experts ran functional and regression test manually.

1.1 The Iteration

Even with relatively short iterations (2 weeks), there were frequent mid-iteration changes. The main reasons were high-priority support requests, production system problems, or business reprioritization due to new information.

The work items were rarely correlated, and in combination with frequent changes, we found limited value in iteration planning. Estimation was problematic because a relatively high number of the work items were bug fixes. In addition, the system had a high degree of "legacy code", which often caused unexpected additions to the development work. As a consequence, the productivity of the team appeared to fluctuate a lot. In addition, core team members often specialised in certain parts of the system, and they would pick work items related to their specialty, regardless of the priority in the iteration. The underlying assumption was that all planned work items would be finished, which normally did not happen. Finally, the team had a number of part-time resources, and their

A. Sillitti et al. (Eds.): XP 2010, LNBIP 48, pp. 325–334, 2010.

availability varied substantially between iterations. This variability was somewhat invisible and often manifested itself as minor, but frequent interruptions.

We used burn-down charts to track progress within an iteration. Because of the frequent changes, the scrum master spent a significant amount of time on gathering current status and on updating the chart. The changes were reflected in an erratic burn-down curve, and neither the team, nor the product owner found much value in the charts.

The product owner was pleased with the responsiveness of the team and did not demand commitment to what would be implemented during an iteration. He did, however, find it problematic to prepare for iteration planning, as it was unclear how much the team would deliver. As a safeguard, both the product owner and the team prepared a larger number of work items than could realistically be completed. The team also accepted ill-defined work items, which also contributed to mid-iteration re-planning. Often we could not finish all the work item within an iteration and had to carry them over to the next.

The customer was not co-located, and stakeholders reviewed work items in the QA environment when required. The team did not find much value in an internal demo, so it was rarely held. The retrospectives ran at the end of each iteration were considered useful, but the suggestions for improvement were often local to the team, with typical examples being "do more pair-programming", "pay more attention to the build screen", and "do more test-driven development".

1.2   Release Cycle

A release cycle most often consisted of three 2-week iterations followed by one test week and one stage week before deployment to the production environment. In the test week, the development team and the domain experts did manual regression testing and work item testing in the QA environment. The domain experts did final validation and verification in the stage week, this time in a scaled-down but otherwise identical replica of the production environment. It was costly to deploy to the stage environment because a 3rd party had full control over it, and all changes required detailed instructions. The release dates were set half a year or more in advance and required co-ordination between resources in five different countries and careful alignment with company events.

Because of the problems with scope change within the iteration, some work items were often not completely finished when the test week started. Closing up on the release, there was often a strong push from the stakeholders to include new work items before the window of opportunity closed. The team faced two problems: the test week was used to complete work items, leaving little time for testing, and the rush to complete items often introduced errors, which had to be fixed before the end of the same week. In short, the test week was very stressful for everybody involved, and more often than not this carried over into the stage week: bugs were detected, and a second, and even a third very costly deployment to the stage environment had to be carried out. Quite often users also found problems in the production system. These late bugfixes were generally done as quickfixes, short-circuiting established process and coding practices. The general idea was that the quickfixes would be properly re-implemented or cleaned up afterwards to prevent technical debt from accumulating. We created entries in the change request system, but often they were never prioritized, because they had no business value as such, had little urgency (the code worked), and because the original context was lost after a while.

The next release cycle started in the stage week of the previous one. In theory, only final verification would happen in the stage week, and this would be handled by the team of domain experts. Thus the developers should have been able to begin the next iteration. However, the noise in the test and stage weeks often disturbed the start of the next release, forcing the team to handle unplanned issues already from the beginning.

2   The Move to Flow-Based Development

Early 2009 we decided to look for a process that better fitted our environment and that could provide a foundation for improving our way of working. A growing number of books, articles, and experience reports were showing how flow-based development (e.g. lean and kanban) could be approached in real-life projects. Table 1 shows core elements of some approaches to flow-based software development.

Table 1. Core principle, properties, and axioms from a selection of representatives/members of the kanban/lean community

Core properties for Kanban[1]	Primary Practices of Kanban[2]	Seven Principles of Lean Software Development[3]
1. Limit WIP 2. Visualize process workflow 3. Measure and manage flow 4. Make process policies explicit 5. Use models to recognize improvement opportunities	1. Map the value stream 2. Visualize the Value Stream 3. Limit Work in Progress 4. Establish a Cadence 5. Reduce the Kanban Tokens	1. Eliminate waste 2. Build quality in 3. Create knowledge 4. Defer commitment 5. Deliver fast 6. Respect people 7. Optimize the whole
Two axioms of lean software development[4]	The Principles of Product Development Flow[5]	Lean production - five principles[6]
1. Work can be divided into small value-adding increments that can be independently scheduled 2. Value-adding increments can be developed in a continuous flow from requirement to deployment	1. Use an economic view 2. Manage queues 3. Exploit variability 4. Reduce Batch Size 5. Apply WIP Constraints 6. Control flow under uncertainty 7. Use fast feedback 8. Decentralize control	1. Value: Identify what really matters to customers 2. Value stream: Ensure every activity adds customer value 3. Flow: Eliminate discontinuities in the value stream 4. Pull: Initiate production by demand 5. Perfection: Retain integrity via *Jidoka* and *Poka-Yoke*

It was immediately clear to us that many of the core ideas behind flow-based development could prove valuable to us, but still many of the practicalities needed to be fleshed out. After several iterations, we arrived at the following core concepts for our flow-based development implementation:

1. Schedule individual, value-adding work items
2. Define a workflow
3. Limit work in process
4. Same-size work items
5. Establish holistic key performance indicators
6. Visualize all the work and the entire workflow
7. Improve relentlessly

2.1 Schedule Individual, Value-Adding Work Items

Motivation. The frequent mid-iteration changes suggested even shorter iterations, but we were already struggling to fit some work items into the two week timebox. Frequent changes and unexpected work forced us to co-ordinate frequently and find development tasks on-the-fly. The work we had planned often never got started. For all practical purposes we were already scheduling individual work items, so it was a small step to formalize it.

Execution. We suggested replacing the iteration preparation and planning with a work item priority queue. Instead of three 2-week iterations before the test and stage weeks, the six weeks would be an uninterrupted development period. The product owner's role would be changed from biweekly finding work item candidates for the next iteration to keeping the queue non-empty. The team and the product owner were positive to the idea, and once decided it was implemented in a couple of days.

At any point in time the product owner now could add work items to the queue, or remove or reprioritize existing ones. The developers would pull work items from the top of the queue as soon as they became idle. If required, they would then contact the product owner, domain experts, or other stakeholders for clarifications. The first setup of flow-based development kept the idea of defining development tasks from work items. It turned out to never be used, so it was eventually dropped.

Result. The change was more of a formalization of the actual way of working. Both the team and the product owner reported that the new process worked better for them. Skipping the timebox also solved problem of having to use iterations of irregular length in order to fit the predetermined release schedule.

2.2 Define a Workflow

Motivation. Our original driver was to identify steps, natural to our way of working, with a limit to work in progress (WIP) for each step. When the WIP-limitation strategy changed (see below), we kept the idea, but changed the reasoning: in a flow-based setup the drive is to move work items through the workflow quickly, and a defined workflow ensures the work items are "slowed down" enough to have quality built in.

Execution. The development work was split into a four-step workflow, where each step was given clearly defined exit criteria:

1. *Analysis.* In the past, it had been a problem that work items were allowed into the development process without being properly defined, and that work items were inadequately tested due to missing or incomplete acceptance criteria. As a remedy, we introduced the explicit analysis step. A criterion for exiting the step was that the work item's acceptance criteria were defined in the form of acceptance tests. If acceptance tests could not be identified, or the work item was too big, the work item would be pushed back to the work item queue. We captured the acceptance tests as test cases in a dedicated system.

2. *Implementation.* This step was not changed. Code was developed in TDD fashion and continuously integrated.

3. *Code review.* This step ensured that all code changes were seen by at least two persons. The primary purpose was not to spot bugs, but to ensure that technical debt was addressed early. The developers were made responsible not only for their own changes, but also for cleaning up sub-standard and/or untested code that came in their way. Only the most experienced developers on the team did the review. The reviewers created a checklist and made it public to all developers in the team wiki. If a work item failed the review, it was pushed back to the implementation step.

4. *Test.* During the test step, a team member ran the acceptance tests (manually), and did some exploratory testing. If the test cases were missing or inadequate, the tester sent the work item back to the analysis step. If a test failed, the tester moved the work item back to implementation.

Result. The team received code review surprisingly well, and together with better defined acceptance criteria and more systematic testing, the new workflow reduced the number of bugs significantly over a six-month period. On the other hand, productivity declined in the same period (see fig. 1). This was anticipated, but the expectation is that productivity will at least be recovered over time due to less interruptions by bugs, and better code maintainability.

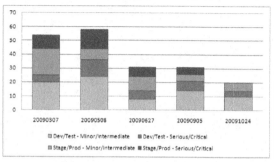
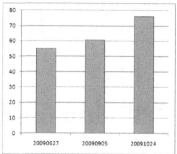

Fig. 1. Bugs per release (left) and work hours per change request (right)

2.3 Limit Work in Process

Motivation. WIP limits were introduced to put a cap on the amount of unfinished work. We expected that limiting WIP would be a more visible and effective control variable than team capacity and amount of work[5].

Execution. From the start we established a CONWIP[7] system, i.e. a single WIP limit for the defined workflow. We considered introducing WIP limits for each work step (kanban), but after running lots of computer simulations based on our process and resources, we concluded that CONWIP would be as effective as kanban and simpler to administrate. The simulation also indicated that setting the WIP limit around the same level as the number of resources (or pairs) would give good performance, i.e. short cycle time for a given throughput level.

Result. When WIP limits were enforced rigidly there was a visible reduction of unfinished work and significant reduction in cycle time. Over time the WIP limit has been enforced with less rigor, and the result can be seen as an accumulation of work in process, more interleaving of work and increased cycle time.

2.4 Same-Size Work Items

Motivation. We wanted to introduce metrics to improve and manage the workflow more quantitatively, but found that judgment-based size estimation like ideal hours opened up for "gaming" the numbers. If the work items could be considered equal, size judgement could be replaced by merely counting work items. Setting WIP limits would also be significantly simplified.

Execution. A random sample of 100 work items was investigated, and it was determined that 80 of them were virtually indistinguishable in terms of effort/schedule required to complete them, considering the resource and task uncertainty. To handle the remaining types of work items, the developers were encouraged to reject work items deemed "too large", so that they could be broken down.

Result. As fig 2 shows, work item effort and cycle time exhibited large variability. We analyzed the work items and concluded that the variation could not be explained by size information that was available up-front.

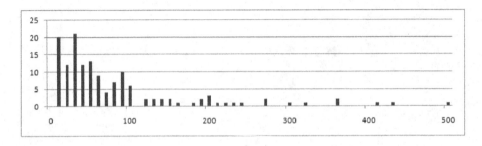

Fig. 2. Distribution of cycle time for 130 work items. Cycle time in work hours.

2.5   Establish Holistic Key Performance Indicators

Motivation. From the start we knew that flow metrics like lead time, through-put, and productivity were useful metrics, but not enough to capture the entire state of the product and the process. We wanted a set of key performance indicators (KPIs) that were reasonably high-level, practically obtainable, and useful for reporting and performing improvement work.

Table 2. KPI model

	Process Quality	Product Quality
External View	– Cycle time – Throughput – Productivity	– Bugs
Internal View	– Back-flows – Waiting – Hand-overs – WIP	– Test coverage – Maintainability index – Code duplication

Execution. After several iterations we arrived at KPI model in table 2. The idea was the quality had two sides to it - product and process, and that there were two viewpoints - external and internal. Customers, users and other external stakeholders represented the external viewpoint. The internal view was generally not available to them. This gave us a 2x2 matrix and we identified KPIs for each of the quadrants:

- *External process quality.* This quadrant included the well-known flow metrics: cycle time and throughput. They answer the stakeholders' question about when they can expect to get things, and how much they will get. The productivity metric is the ratio between effort and throughput in a period.
- *External product quality.* Bugs were costly and a major headache, so we made this the primary product quality indicator.
- *Internal product quality.* Technical debt was a concern. We were already collecting some internal product quality metrics, but now it became more systematic. Test coverage was included under the assumption that tested code would be more maintainable than untested code. The development environment provided different static code metrics, from which we chose one, the maintainability index[8]. Finally, we used tools to the check the amount of code duplication present in the codebase.
- *Internal process quality.* Cycle time and throughput provide no information about the underlying cause. Back-flows measure the number and length of

backward moves in the workflow. Hand-over count the number of work step transitions. One type of waiting is the amount of time a work item spend in completion queues. Since we also track effort per work item, we can also calculate waiting as the difference between effort and cycle time.

Result. We've found that the current KPI model provides a good oversight over the process and product. The fundamental observation is that the four quadrants are heavily interconnected, and the improvement work must consider all of them simultaneously. Gathering and analyzing data and presenting results require a non-negligible amount of work.

2.6   Visualize All the Work and the Entire Workflow

Motivation. At the outset we knew that the new workflow was sub-optimal in terms of flow. The initial focus was the work that previously was done in the iteration, but we wanted to get the full "concept to cash" perspective to avoid improving towards local optimums in our workflow. Only 30%-40% of the effort could be tracked back to work items. The rest of the effort was spent on handling support requests, operations issues, and a range of customer requests. We wanted to make more of these activities visible.

Execution. The first iteration of our process kept the whiteboard virtually unchanged. We used a plain whiteboard with post-its. The post-its were moved between columns representing the workflow steps.

The second round moved the visualization from the manual whiteboard to an electronic version that was continuously synchronized with the change request system. This helped working remotely, which was common, and collecting flow metrics. More importantly, we added all the worksteps up until and including production deployment to the whiteboard.

As the currently final iteration, we included bug reports on the whiteboard. Previously these had been handled outside the normal process. Now the team could pull bugs through the same workflow as other work items. The next iteration will also include support requests.

Result. Visualizing work items from when they are scheduled until they are deployed has made large batches and long waiting times inescapably visible. Previously hidden work is now handled using the same workflow, and by making it visible it can now be addressed by the entire team, and prioritized against other work.

2.7   Improve Relentlessly

Motivation. One of the major shortcomings with the previous way of working was that there was no clear direction in the improvement work. We held retrospectives, but it was never clear if they resulted in actual, customer-valued improvements. Occasionally the customer asked for an assessment of the quality of our work and our productivity, and we could only give a qualitative response. With a set of KPIs established we had a way to give more quantitative answers, and a foundation on which we could build improvements.

Execution. As a supplement to regular retrospectives, we started to look more closely for improvement opportunities in the day-to-day work. The KPIs could be used as a starting point, as described in the following.

1. *Bugs.* We started to systematically analyze all major bugs to find the root cause. Moving to flow-based development in itself significantly reduced the number of bugs introduced by the developers, but analysis showed that a large number of the remaining bug reports were caused by environment and 3rd party issues outside the development team's immediate control. We started to work to try to fail-proof the entire process. An example was to enhance the deployment tools to do environment checks before deployment to ensure that prerequisites were met.

2. *Cycle time.* We observed that the tail of the cycle time probability distribution was long, and started to analyze slow work items. Often a process flaw was the cause. One class of process issues we discovered was late UI changes. We are considering to add an explicit user experience check-off in the analysis phase. By "working the tail" we hope that the mass of the probability distribution is shifted to left, and that the variability is reduced.

3. *Waiting.* We identified different types of waiting. For example, we found our local build and test times to be so long that the waiting disrupted a good development flow, so we started to look at ways to reorganize code to reduce dependencies, tools to run local building and testing in the background, etc. We also have big batches of work items waiting in front of QA, stage, and deployment because of a predefined schedule. We're looking into ways of fully automating deployment of at least some components of our solutions to be able to deploy more frequently.

4. *Flow-backs.* We observed that over half of the work items were returned from review. We were expecting that the review return rate should have gone down as developers became more familiar with what was expected. This has not happened, and we've tried to encourage more pair-programming to prevent issues from being introduced in the first place. Pair-programming requires a change in work habits, and has not been a success so far.

5. *Work in process.* WIP limits prevent development work from accumulating in the workflow, but WIP can accumulate in other places as well. An example is that we spent a significant amount of time on analyzing bugs, technical debt and support issues, only to add them as low priority entries in the issue tracking system. If these items were ever prioritized, the analysis mostly had to be redone. We introduced a "fix or forget" policy stating that issues should either be fixed immediately, or if they were unimportant, they should be closed with a "won't fix" status.

6. *Repeated work.* The process required a work item to be tested three times. In addition, flow-backs often caused work-items to be re-tested. This is expensive when testing is manual. An obvious improvement would be to remove

the seemingly redundant testing and/or automate the tests. We tried two things: first, we worked up-front to prevent bugs from being found in late tests, so that the redundant testing justifiably can be removed, and second, to reduce the cost of testing. Automated regression tested is a goal, but as a first step we're trying out tools that assist the testers. Examples are browser screenshot comparison tools, link checkers, and record-playback tools.

Result. A mindset change is required to relentlessly pursue continuous improvement. Although we have made some initial attempts, we have long way to go. One important element of flow-based development is not only that improvement is encouraged, but that it can be done focused and methodically.

3   Summary

We have found that it is fully possible to run agile software development without timeboxes by using a continuously updated work item priority queue instead. WIP limit is a good control variable compared to controlling capacity and scope of work under high variability, and a single WIP limit (CONWIP) works well. We believe that flow metrics alone is not enough to manage product and process, and should be supplemented with other metrics. Although the transition to some of the flow-based concepts can be done rather mechanically and yield good results, full benefits requires a cultural change over a period of time.

References

1. Anderson, D.: Yahoo Group Kanban Development (February 8, 2010),
   http://finance.groups.yahoo.com/group/kanbandev/message/6954
2. Scotland, K.: AvailAgility blog (June 30, 2009), http://availagility.co.uk/
   2009/06/30/the-fifth-primary-practice-of-kanban/
3. Poppendieck, M., Poppendieck, T.: Implementing Lean Software Development. Addison-Wesley, Boston (2007)
4. Ladas, C.: Scrumban. Modus Cooperandi Press, Seattle (2008)
5. Reinertsen, D.: Principles of Product Development Flow. Celeritas Publishing, Redondo Beach (2009)
6. Middletion, P., Sutton, J.: Lean Software Strategies. Productivity Press, New York (2005)
7. Hopp, S.: Factory Physics. Irwin/McGraw-Hill, Boston (1996)
8. Vitaly's WebLog, http://www.vitalygorn.com/blog/post/2007/11/
   Code-Metrics-in-Visual-Studio-2008.aspx

Stakeholder Engagement in the Evolutionary Design of an API

Ken Power

Cisco Systems, Inc., Galway, Ireland
ken.power@gmail.com

Abstract. Iterative development of non-GUI software in general, and APIs in particular, in an agile context presents a number of challenges, not the least of which is effective engagement with people outside the development teams as the API evolves. We use two strategies to overcome these challenges. The first strategy is effective stakeholder engagement. This paper describes how we identify stakeholders in our product's API, who those stakeholders are, how we engage with them, and how we incorporate feedback on a continuous basis. The second strategy is the development of an API Test Client Application that allows many different stakeholders to use the product directly as it evolves. The Test Client Application evolves in parallel, iteration by iteration, with the main product. The experiences described here can be of benefit to anyone developing an API product with multiple consumers, for example an in-process library, an out-of-process service, a Web Service, or a service in Service-Oriented Architectures.

Keywords: API, architecture, stakeholder, test, agile, evolutionary design.

1 Introduction

Regular feedback on running, tested software is one of the hallmarks of effective agile development. Involving stakeholders in the evolution of the software, and incorporating their feedback, is a key benefit of the short iteration cycles that we adopt. This can be challenging enough when your application has an intuitive user interface, such as a Web page that your users interact with via a Browser as it evolves, or a desktop application. However, not all software has a graphical user interface (GUI) so we need to find suitable techniques to make these agile practices and principles work even when our products do not have a GUI. This paper describes some of our experiences at Cisco Systems, Inc. (NASDQ: CSCO) developing a middleware application that serves multiple consumers by aggregating access to multiple back-end services. The consumers of the API are typically developers of user-facing applications. The middleware product resides on a client computer, such as a PC. The product has entered its third year of development, and is approaching its third major external product release. The high-level system design is shown in Figure 1. The middleware product exposes an API that is consumed by client applications.

A. Sillitti et al. (Eds.): XP 2010, LNBIP 48, pp. 335–343, 2010.

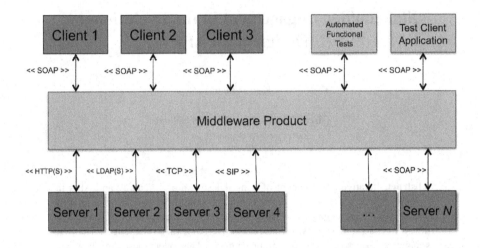

Fig. 1. High-level system design

The middleware product presents a unified API to consumers, and abstracts the details of communicating with multiple backend servers. These backend servers can include call processing servers, directory servers, messaging servers, and other infrastructure.

Developer testing (including unit testing, integration testing, Test Driven Development, and Mock Objects) is an ingrained part of our development habits, and these techniques are applied in the development of the product. However, the middleware core product is a real-time telephony and messaging product that is highly event-driven. It requires multiple client endpoints and several backend servers to test even the most basic scenarios. When it comes to end-to-end testing of the system, we found we needed a solution to compliment these developer test strategies and help us test the API end-to-end in a real environment as it evolves. We also needed a reliable way to demonstrate the API product to stakeholders outside the development team, and to allow those stakeholders to use the core product interactively and independently. Their goals may include interest, evaluation, exploratory testing of the core product, validation, or regression testing. These goals are outside the scope of developer tests. We wanted to allow stakeholders outside the development team to use the core product, independently of a consumer client application.

2   Stakeholder Engagement in API Design

Identifying stakeholders in the product API is critical. We broadly classify stakeholders in the API as those people or groups that affect or influence our product's API, or that are affected by, or are influenced by, the product's API. The diagram in Figure 2 shows some of the basic stakeholders in our API product. We consider two tiers of stakeholders. Primary stakeholders have a more immediate or a higher stake in the development of the API. Secondary stakeholders tend to have less input into the API as it evolves. For example, there are Client Application development teams that consume our API early and integrate with our core product at the end of each iteration, or even during the current iteration. We consider these groups to be primary stakeholders. There are groups that consume the API at various milestones such as a major or minor product release. We consider these to be secondary stakeholders. Both are important. Primary stakeholders tend to provide the earliest feedback, and hence have a bigger impact on shaping the API as it evolves.

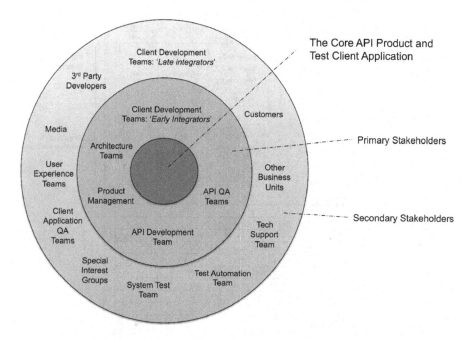

Fig. 2. API Stakeholders

The type of quantification helps us to understand the needs of multiple stakeholders. Later sections in this paper describe how we address their needs continuously, balance stakeholder needs when not everyone can get exactly what they want all the time, and evaluate and quantify stakeholder claims on the API structure, definition, and direction.

3 Test Client Application

We made the decision very early in the development of the middleware product to also develop a Test Client Application. We had been discussing the trade-offs for the first two development iterations. One of the deciding factors was that another team was building a client application in parallel, and they would consume the output of each iteration. Therefore we needed a way to validate our product before delivering it at the end of the iteration. Because of the complexity of the deployment environment, involving multiple backend servers, it was proving difficult to automate end-to-end tests at the functional level. Many of the tests involve evaluating voice and video quality, for example. Developers of the middleware product needed a way to exercise the product as they were developing it. Therefore in iteration 3 we started developing the Test Client Application. The Test Client Application quickly caught up with the API of the product, and has remained in synch with the product API ever since. The diagram in Figure 3 shows a sketch of the Test Client Application GUI.

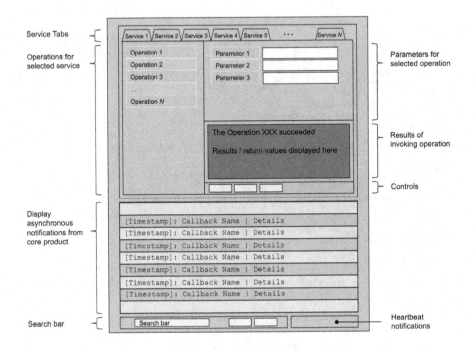

Fig. 3. Sketch of Test Client GUI

The overall UI of the Test Client Application reflects the API of the core product. There is a tab for each Service in the core product. The list of operations provided by that service is dynamically updated when a user selects a tab. The list of parameters for an operation is dynamically updated when the user selects that operation. A user can invoke any operation on any service and the results will be reflected in the results area. In keeping with red/green/refactor tradition, the results box turns green if the operation succeeds and red if it fails. Asynchronous notifications from the core product are displayed in the lower half of the UI. This displays a time stamp, message sequence number, callback listener interface name, callback operation, and any details associated with the callback. The core product itself is highly event-driven. The callback API is used to notify clients of application data and state changes, events from backend servers, and general service information such as server health notifications (e.g., if we lose connectivity with a backend service). The core product also provides a facility for sending heartbeat notifications to Client applications. These are updated in a dedicated notification area to avoid cluttering the main notification display. The event data is searchable from the UI to make it easy to filter on the data.

3.1 Design of the API Test Client Application

The diagram in Figure 4 shows the design of the Test Client Application, and its interaction with the core middleware product API.

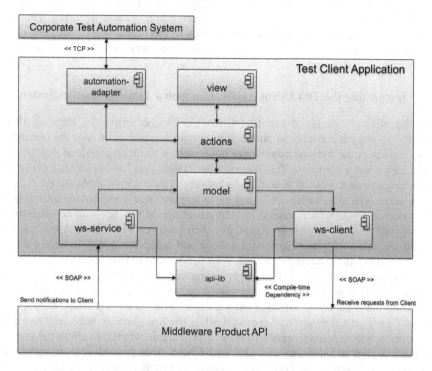

Fig. 4. Design of Test Client Application

The **view** component implements the graphical user interface of the Test Client Application. The **actions** component provides an abstraction for every request, or action, that can be executed against the middleware product API. The **model** component implements some basic client logic and some basic session and context management. The **ws-service** component implements a callback interface that listens for notifications from the middleware product. The **ws-client** component implements a Web Service client that sends requests to the middleware product.

3.2 Shared API Component

Whenever there is a change to the product API we want that change to be reflected in the Test Client Application. The development team uses Maven for automated builds (http://maven.apache.org/), Hudson for continuous integration (http://hudson-ci.org/.), and the Artifactory repository manager for managing build artifacts (http://www.jfrog.org/). The diagram in Figure 4 shows a component called **api-lib**. This represents the component that contains the API definitions for the product. This component is built and deployed as a JAR file, and, as with all the product's components, is deployed to a central

Artifactory repository. The Test Client Application references this component, and so, when a new version is deployed, the build scripts for the Test Client Application are updated to reference the new version of the shared component. This generally causes a compile-time error in the Test Client Application source code. Typical API changes that cause this include a new method added to a service interface, a new callback method added to a callback interface, or a change to a method signature. This forces the developer to make the appropriate changes in their local workspace, and commit to version control when ready. The continuous integration server will validate that the changes were successful.

3.3 Integrating the Test Client Application with a Test Automation System

We intentionally designed the Test Client API to be scriptable, knowing that we wanted to integrate it with an automation system at some point. All the concrete action classes in the **actions** component implement a common interface that facilitates this. Cisco has a corporate Test Automation System that has hooks into a number of reporting systems, as well as test hooks for other Cisco server applications. A System Test team typically writes TCL scripts to execute test scenarios against this Test Automation System. We wanted to take advantage of this automation infrastructure rather than invent our own approach. For their part, the Test Client Application provided the automation test team with a clean and ready-made way to access our core product API without having deal with Web Services, SOAP and XML.

To integrate with this system, a given product must provide a hook for the TCL-based execution environment. At Iteration 8 we engaged with the automation team to integrate our Test Client Application with their TCL-based test automation environment. The Test Client already provided all of the functionality necessary to exercise the core product. All we needed to do was provide an adapter to allow the test automation system to integrate with the Test Client. This proved very straightforward because the design of the Test Client application had already separated the user interface from the rest of the application. A member of the system test automation team was able to write an adapter that acts as the interface for the test automation system. This is the **automation-adapter** component in Figure 4. They worked in the same version control environment and the same iteration cycles as the core product development team, and reaped all the benefits of continuous integration.

3.4 The Test Client Evolves with the API

The product development team develops and maintains the Test Client Application. It began life as a side-project for one developer on the core product team. In part, the motivation for developing the Test Client was to give the API development team a reliable way to perform end-to-end tests. The product team was working closely with another team that would take the API product at the end of each iteration and consume it into their Client UI application. In the first two iterations we got a lot of defect reports from the Client UI team. There were scenarios that the API product team had not considered, or that proved too difficult to test through standard unit testing, and defects were escaping from our iterations. The Test Client was developed to allow the API developers to execute complex scenarios against the API, and to allow them to get rapid feedback as they developed new services and operations.

For the first release, it was primarily one person that developed the Test Client Application for a percentage of their time, as well as developing the Service API for the core product itself, and contributing to the implementation of a number of the vertical services. This had the advantage that not everyone on the team needed to become proficient with SOAP, WSDL and XSD, and we could easily maintain some level of consistency in the API. For the second and subsequent releases of the product, the number of services and operations grew, as did the size of the team. We decided to split the responsibilities so that whoever is responsible for developing the vertical services is also responsible for implementing the corresponding functionality in the Test Client Application. This had the advantage that we could split end-to-end design of the product, including the Test Client, vertically and have co-located teams at different sites working on vertical slices.

3.5 Users of the Test Client

The developers of the core product use the Test Client on a daily basis to test their service implementations end-to-end. Testers that are part of the delivery team use the Test Client to perform manual testing against the product. Testers from other QA functions use the Test Client's automation hooks to write and execute automated system tests. The Test Client has proven invaluable in debugging to isolate the root cause of a problem. It is used in resolving defects, and to determine whether a defect exists in a given client application or the middleware product. As other stakeholders took interest in the core middleware product and its API, we were able to give them the Test Client Application as well. This served two purposes. First, it gave them something they could use to directly interact with the API product. Second, it gave them a reference implementation in the Test Client source code so that they could get a feel for what it is like to write applications against the API.

4 Stakeholder Engagement during an Iteration

4.1 Iteration Planning

Iteration planning for the core product evolved to include a focus on the API of the product. We have user stories that relate directly to new services provided by the API. The tasks for these user stories generally include a task for updating the Test Client Application to support the new API changes, as well as tasks to update call flow documentation that describe the core services of the middleware product.

4.2 API Design Meetings

Our iterations include one or more API design meetings. We go into these meetings with an understanding of the requirements that the middleware product must deliver, and translate these into API definitions. Attendees include representatives of the API's primary stakeholders as depicted in Figure 2. These include members of the core middleware product team, as well as developers and managers from one or more client applications that will consume the API. The goals of these meetings are to define the service operations, callbacks and type definitions that the API must provide.

After the meeting the middleware developers take responsibility for specific user stories that include API implementation, write the API and develop the core API implementation. Another specific goal of this meeting is to ensure consistency of the API as it evolves. At a basic level this includes naming of operations, callbacks, types, and services. It also includes making sure we have the right services defined, that operations belong to the correct service, and that we don't have duplicate or redundant service operations. A critical aspect of these design discussions is making sure we do not put logic in the middleware API that more correctly belongs in a client application, or that the middleware API is not unjustly biased in favor of the needs of one client at the expense of others. We find it is best to have these meetings before the iteration planning meeting, so that they can contribute to the backlog grooming and preparation.

4.3 Early Integration with Client Applications

We often provide a skeleton implementation of the API that we are working on in the current iteration so that clients can begin to consume it right away to test their own application and to provide feedback on the API. The early feedback we get from both the API design meetings and the early integration with the client applications is very useful in helping us to shape the API as it evolves, and making sure it remains relevant to their needs.

4.4 Product Demonstrations

The Test Client Application has been a central part of our mid-iteration reviews, show & tell sessions, end-of-iteration reviews, and other product demonstrations with stakeholders since it first became functional. The first demonstration of the core middleware product used two Test Clients acting as communication endpoints. The middleware API implementation typically is completed faster than any of the consuming client applications, so the development teams for the middleware application use the Test Client application to demonstrate progress, and show running, tested features.

5 Conclusions

Evolving an API incrementally is not only possible with agile development, but is a very powerful way to make sure your API remains relevant to its stakeholders.

- Understand who are the stakeholders in the API. Involve them in the definition of the API. Engage with them early and continuously. Balance the needs of your API's stakeholders over time. Invite stakeholders to API design meetings. This is a good forum to understand the perspectives of different stakeholders. Listen to their needs; incorporate their feedback, while ensuring the API stays true to its design goals as you evolve its design through successive iterations.
- Build a test client application in parallel with the API product. This gives you a feel for using the API as it evolves, and also gives you a concrete way to test the services you are developing, as you develop them. This is particularly useful if you

are working in an environment where setup of test fixtures is expensive, and you need real-time feedback as you develop the service.

- Use the feedback and synchronization points offered by agile development processes to demonstrate the API in action. Use the test client in iteration reviews and other product demonstrations. It gives people outside the delivery team a sense of progress. This is particularly useful if you do not yet have a consumer that has integrated the latest API features in their UI.

- Evolve the Test Client with the core product API. Never let them get out of synch. Configure your build environment so that the Test Client automatically picks up changes to the API.

- Make the Test Client easy to develop and evolve. The core service definitions, operations, parameters, and asynchronous callback events can all be determined from the API definition. This is particularly straightforward if you are using a service description language such as WSDL or IDL.

- Take the design of the test client as seriously as the core product. Make it extensible and automatable. You never know when another group might be able to make use of it.

These guidelines will help you incrementally evolve the design of an API product, or any non-GUI product, using an agile process.

From Chaos to Kanban, via Scrum

Kevin Rutherford[1], Paul Shannon[2], Craig Judson[2], and Neil Kidd[2]

[1] Rutherford Software Ltd, 26 Hamble Way, Macclesfield, Cheshire SK10 3RN, UK
kevin@rutherford-software.com
[2] Codeweavers Ltd, 11 Imex Technology Park, Trentham Lakes South,
Stoke-on-Trent, Staffordshire, ST4 8LJ
paul.shannon@codeweavers.net

Abstract. Since late 2007 the software development teams at Codeweavers UK have been incrementally improving their ability to deliver motor finance and insurance web services. This two-year journey has taken the company from chaos to kanban-style single-piece flow, including Scrum briefly along the way. This paper charts that journey, showing the benefits gained from a simple "inspect and adapt" cycle in which the teams tackled their biggest problem at each stage.

Keywords: agile, kanban, scrum, continuous improvement, inspect-adapt.

1 Introduction

Codeweavers is a UK business of approximately 20 people, delivering motor finance and insurance web services. The software development team comprises 8-10 co-located developers. At the start of this process Codeweavers was losing money on a monthly basis. In addition to the development team Codeweavers also has a web designer, customer support team, server/database administrator and a sales team - all working with the Managing Director.

The development team predominantly use a Microsoft .NET environment with C#, developing using Visual Studio on Windows.

1.1 Defining the Chaos

In the beginning Codeweavers consisted of two teams of around 4 developers. Each team worked on a separate set of products using completely separate codebases. There was little cross-over between teams and each developer had his own to-do list and worked on tasks independently.

Tasks were given to each developer as the Managing Director and Development Director required, with their respective backlog of tasks being known only to them. Development tasks were split between 50% fixing problems or small changes and 50% spent on new features, speculative work and manual testing.

This attitude to planning and development resulted in no predictability, which frustrated management and clients because deadlines were vague and frequently missed. Stress levels increased following each deployment because limited, manual testing and write first, test later development let bugs slip out to customers unnoticed.

A. Sillitti et al. (Eds.): XP 2010, LNBIP 48, pp. 344–352, 2010.

Developers often needed to ask the Managing Director for tasks to work on when their todo lists were empty - this often resulted in work on speculative ideas which rarely added value to the business. There was a build-up of legacy code as a result and developers had no way to plan or design for the future.

2   Timeline

The state of chaos at Codeweavers worried both the development team and management alike, so ideas were discussed and new avenues explored.

In the final quarter of 2007 the development and planning processes at Codeweavers could be described as Complete Chaos (see §1.1). Development was slow as the low software quality meant "fire-fighting" was consuming development hours and work wasn't being done on the business' core value streams.

> *Response:* After investigating other planning techniques we decided that Scrum would best address our problems so a developer from each team attended a Scrum CSM course with the Development Director. The next day the newly Certified Scrum Masters introduced Scrum to the rest of the team and together we followed the handbook meeting schedule after merging all of our to-do lists into a backlog. We took tasks from emails, Outlook task lists, hand written lists and from memory, and put them into Scrumworks software, sorted by urgency. We used planning poker cards for estimation and had separate planning/estimation/stand-up meetings per team, with a joint retrospective. We also adopted Test Driven Development and Pair Programming using books and online resources to help us help each other.

In subsequent months we varied the sprint length from 1 week to 3 weeks to 2 weeks; we were spending a lot more time in meetings because we were closely following the Scrum methodology; tasks were hidden away inside Scrumworks and the backlog was inspected only rarely. Test driven development was progressing but the initial learning curve was steep.

> *Response:* To address our desire for better coding technique and to get some direction with regard to planning we hired an Agile Coach. We dropped Scrumworks, instead opting for a task board and paper cards. The teams had separate boards, and work was broken down into User Stories written in the "*As a ... In order to ... I would like ...*" form. Each board was organised with columns for "Not Started", "In Development" and "Done"; cards were moved into "Done" when the card's development work was complete and unit tested. We installed CruiseControl on a continuous integration server. Planning poker was dropped in favour of "pair hours" as a unit in planning which shortened meetings. Instead of holding a planning meeting every Tuesday, say, the team opted for a "just in time" planning meeting whenever the "Not Started" column on the board looked nearly empty.

2.1 Development Focus

All these changes enabled the team to regain some momentum and fresh energy. By 2008 Q3 the feeling in the teams was good and our planning and development techniques were working as developers were happy and user stories were being completed on time.

There was notable tension due to team rivalry as the teams developed different personalities. Support was becoming more difficult because there was too much specialism and knowledge silos in each team. Fundamental knowledge was duplicated between the teams and code was not shared effectively.

> *Response:* We began swapping one developer between teams for a week at a time.

2008 Q4 brought problems with our planning. The User Stories we used on the work in progress board were large, technical, development tasks and were difficult to demonstrate, thereby increasing the length of our feedback loop. Slow progression of stories through the development process was demotivating.

> *Response:* Simplification seemed to be the answer so we moved from user stories in favour of smaller engineering tasks. These promoted better team working and more frequent demonstrations, helping us fail faster and address quality issues earlier. Tasks moved independently across the board, much as the User Stories had done.

2.2 Time to Merge the Two Teams

Swapping one person each week between the two teams was not popular, and did little to break up the knowledge silos. Duplication of design and planning meetings, code overlap and the use of two boards all indicated that two separate teams may not be ideal. Our retrospective meetings, although involving both teams, were too specific so one half of the team would sit silently while issues were discussed between the others.

> *Response:* A major customer had an urgent request that involved just one team's codebase. We decided that the two teams would need to merge to get our customer's urgent requirement delivered in time, and organised the work as a special-case workshop event. With the extra energy brought about by the over-dramatisation a feeling of "all hands on deck" swept through the team and a single focussed development was started. We merged the two teams into one large team with a single board, creating a single plan to swarm on. To ensure further integration each pair consisted of one member from each team, which also helped with knowledge sharing. When the emergency was over the effectiveness of the single team approach was much applauded and the decision was made to continue as a single unit.

Although we'd made regular changes to our planning procedure it was noted that we were still spending too much time in meetings, particularly in planning.

> *Response:* We addressed this problem directly and stopped estimating task duration. Instead we ensured that tasks were designed so that each card covered a similar amount of work.

2.3 A Focus on Quality

By 2009 Q2 the single team was now the standard practise but we still noticed skill silos. A lack of focus emerged as developers had a tendency to refactor legacy code rather than delivering value. A disconnection arose between development and the business and the team didn't notice the amount of wasted time/yak shaving.

The work in progress board worked effectively for development but visibility up and down-stream was reduced. The board only had 3 columns and once a task was done it was effectively "thrown over the wall". This resulted in partially developed features being deployed, or conversely, a finished feature to be held up for deployment by code under development.

A kaizen activity on our value stream highlighted that most of our stream was never looked at as it wasn't on the task board.

> *Response:* We mapped our value-stream beginning with a customer order and ending with the income following a successful deployment. This helped us to expand the columns on the task board to add in space for internal acceptance, customer acceptance and live. We also included buffer columns between each acceptance state so that we knew when tasks were ready to move.

Tasks were still not getting attention outside the development column as it became clear the current board layout was more environment based that state based. Adding to this we found deployments were not approved for weeks as downstream activity caused a build up with the Product Owner, and the whole process was bottlenecked by approval.

> *Response:* We adapted morning meetings to use a pull system that pulled cards from the right - to help us focus in these meetings we moved the meeting to the right hand side of the board, helping us see the tasks from the customer's point of view. We were then able to take on customer approval tasks providing additional value where normally the product owner would have to take over. We added WIP limits[4] to the board with low WIP limits in the acceptance columns and a limit of 1 in each buffer. When a pair became free they would move to the board's downstream end and search upstream for work. No new tasks were moved to development until all reasonable effort had been applied to customer and internal acceptance.

2.4 Moving to Minimum Marketable Features

The downstream bottleneck into live deployment disappeared. We started measuring mean task flight time at this point and over the next month it dropped from 29 days to 6 days, then stabilized at 10-12 days.

In 2009 Q3 a key member of the management team left the company. This meant our Product Owner had less time to focus on his role within the development team. He was responsible for internally approving completed tasks and the development team handled customer acceptance.

Deployments were still not going smoothly, because quality wasn't seen as a priority. Our 10-stage board meant the feedback loop was very long: occasionally a task would be rejected in one of the downstream acceptance stages and moved back to development; this would lead to partial features in the codebase, and thence to either deploying incomplete features or holding up deployment while waiting for delayed tasks.

Response: To solve the above problems with co-dependent tasks we began batching them into Minimal Marketable Feature-Sets (MMFs). Quality was moved upstream and the team was responsible for approving the quality of an MMF before moving it to customer acceptance. This alleviated the bottleneck with our Product Owner as we employed "corridor testing", demonstrating smaller chunks of work to him when he was available rather than at the end of the feature. The board changed to reflect this and consisted of "Development", "Done", "Demo", "Live" and we removed the WIP limits as the discipline was no longer needed. Individual tasks moved from "Development" to "Done" (which continued to have its old meaning); when all of the tasks in a batch were Done, the whole MMF moved into "Demo", and then either into "Live" or back into "Development". At this time we might have 2 or 3 MMFs in flight at any one time, often working on different products.

A bottleneck became apparent when gaps in the flow appeared as the development team felt unable to prioritise tasks or create new ones due to a lack of information, while the Product Owner was still too busy.

Response: The Product Owner attached a value to each task card by adding 1 to 5 dollar signs. The team knew which cards to do next as those with more dollar signs were worth more to the company and helped us work towards the overall goal of making money for the business.

We became reluctant to deploy features due to lack of confidence in quality. MMFs were moving through customer acceptance quickly but our own confidence halted them. Support issues and bugs were not being reduced as we had hoped and time was being wasted combating these issues directly following deployments.

Response: We began to introduce automated regression tests. We thought this magic bullet would ensure that anything we hadn't unit tested would be covered and bugs would be caught before deployment to the customer. It didn't work though, and the amount of time spent on automating these tests was not justified by the benefits. We had "false positives" on one hand and additional work when regression tests randomly failed on the other. Following a retrospective on the subject, we decided that manual regression testing was a better solution as our codebase and understanding was not ready for automation. We created test plans and an overall agreement to do more manual testing was reached.

In 2009 Q4 incomplete MMFs could still get deployed. We were measuring flight time of tasks but not that of MMFs which created pressure to get tasks out resulting in a severe lack of code quality. Task cards could still be co-dependant and there was no improvement in legacy code.

Response: Acceptance criteria and swarming on quality had partially addressed the continued deployment of bugs but this wasn't enough. Our first change was the introduction of Single Piece Flow. At any time the team would have exactly one MMF in flight. Increased slack time meant we had more time for refactoring legacy code and manual regression testing. By measuring waste (recording time spent when our "Blue Lights"[1] were off) we identified problems in waiting for deployments so the board was refined to reduce columns; ending with: "In Development", "Done" and "Customer Acceptance". Tasks were moved to "Done" when the feature was complete and the code had been refactored to improve quality but would only move to "Customer Acceptance" when all tasks on the MMF were Done and the whole team was happy with the quality of both the feature and the code; if one person was unhappy we swarmed on the quality and didn't deploy.

Responsibility driven design[2] through CRC[3] sessions was our next addition which helped test coverage, code quality and design. During each CRC session we recorded interactions between objects and started TDD by testing the responsibilities and interactions on each CRC card in the code. We used mocking to ensure only the methods on the card were under test.

Although pairs swapped daily there were still specialisms within MMFs and new recruitment meant knowledge sharing became a priority

Response: We introduced a "least knowledgeable developer" rule. During daily stand-up meetings the developer who had worked on an area the least would volunteer for that task and they would select a pairing partner based on who had the most knowledge. The least knowledgeable developer would then start the task as the driver in the pair, ensuring no work was done without both developers having a full understanding of the code they were producing.

The "To-Do" column just ahead of development suddenly emptied one day, partly because a potential sale failed. We discovered that the product owner had no process for deciding which of the many other customer requests to prioritise. We introduced a new board upstream of development, representing a cost/benefit matrix to help sort cards for business requests before they were moved onto the development team. Although prioritisation was now adequate on the cost/benefit board for a month, there was no visibility of priorities upstream so the development team didn't know which MMF to bring in next. This became most apparent when the Product Owner was not available due to a spate of sales meetings.

Response: We introduced a new value based hopper board to feed the development board with MMFs. Cards were prioritised by placing high value cards at the top and cards that are ready to be developed to the right. We now knew where effort should be placed to get MMFs ready for development; this information was previously known only to the Product Owner.

A period of frequent changes meant that the development team had stabilised so our process improvements were extended to the server admin and database admin as wasted effort was evident in that team.

Response: A conscious effort was made to move that team into the MMF WIP board. All the database or server admin tasks were added to cards and tied to MMFs. This worked initially and knowledge was shared as developers worked cross-team, however, it was proving hard to maintain as the two conflicting work styles did not coordinate well and we deemed that perhaps the admin team needed an update to their own process first and we should revisit the integration later.

2.5 Increasing Flow

With an ineffective attempt at alleviating bottlenecks around the development team we decided that we'd focus again on the speed of MMFs moving through the development board.

We noticed we were not getting features out as fast as we wanted, waste wasn't being reduced and frustration was building when waiting for builds and deployments, causing a loss of focus in the value stream.

> *Response:* Using one of our whiteboards, we started recording reasons why we were wasting time, and then the amount of time wasted. This enabled us to start swarming on build and deploy times which halved the amount of waste. We also noticed that legacy code was a bottleneck in one particular product - our broker finance application - which was measurably slower to work on as this code had largely been produced in the early days of the company.

Towards the end of development on an MMF we noticed that swarming wasn't as efficient as it should be. It clearly needed an optimisation in organisation and communication.

> *Response:* A second stand-up meeting was brought in at 2pm every day to ensure tasks were worked on as things developed. New tasks were spawned regularly if we thought that a concurrent unit of work could be done on a particular part of the feature. Developers were encouraged to stand up and "pull the andon cord", if problems were found, so that we could all effectively swarm on adding value. A practical problem with the second stand-up emerged in that differing lunch times weren't always compatible with the new meeting time so we arranged for a lunch time alarm to sound synchronising developers.

As sales increased and new customers were added to our roster we noted that support loads increased and profitability diminished because clients needed help to integrate our solution into their websites.

> *Response:* A proactive approach was taken here as we started to go out to clients and help on-site. We also invited any new customers to come to the office to learn more about our processes while also getting a tutorial on the integration of our services. We attempted to improve their processes using our experience in addition to improving our support documentation, and improve the service to ease client implementation.

3 Discussion

Looking back over the journey so far, we notice some patterns in the kinds of changes made at different times. Throughout 2008, most changes were improvements to our programming techniques and general team organisation. During 2009 we focussed mainly on improving the flow of value through the organisation, which also involved giving a lot of attention to our approach to quality. In the most recent two quarters the development team's focus has again returned to programming technique, perhaps indicating that the team and business have found a "sweet spot" in their ability to collaborate responsively and effectively.

Our look back over the last two years also reveals patterns in Codeweavers' overall approach to problem-solving:

The team coach often used theatrical means to increase the apparent urgency of the team's problems, effectively "stopping the line" in order to get everyone's attention and perform whole-team root-cause analysis. Gradually the team learned to "swarm" when a crisis occurred, self-organising and stopping development in order to focus for a brief period on a single problem. During these stoppages, some pairs would work on fixing immediate symptoms, while others would analyse and address deeper causes. The team developed a consensus approach to quality that also transferred to development of MMFs: deployment of a feature or fix is now only permitted when everyone is happy with every aspect of its quality. Consequently, defect rates are at a record low, and continue to fall. You can see our current defect count on our support site[5].

Sometimes the team would agree on a process change, but would subsequently find that the change failed to "stick". It turns out that the most successful changes were always those that involved a physical or tactile component. For example, the team found it difficult to remember to focus on pulling value through the whole value stream; then someone suggested that everyone stand near the downstream end of the kanban board during stand-ups, so that all work in process was viewed from the customer's point of view!

Often, discovery of a problem led to a period of data collection, so that the team could decide how and what to tackle based on actual evidence. Sometimes the data collection itself served to create a culture in which the observed problem naturally disappeared.

Finally, as the focus on flow and throughput became more deeply ingrained, the developers' view of the value stream gradually increased. First we looked only at the "in development" column; later we lifted our gaze to look downstream to ensure our code was accepted and deployed to customers. Later still we looked further downstream, helping customers to adopt the new services, and upstream, helping the business decide what was needed and how to prioritise it. Recently the focus is expanding even further, into the company's sales and marketing functions.

3.1 Future Directions

The Codeweavers development team has a number of improvement goals for the coming year, including: solving the problem of automated end-to-end integration tests; expanding the philosophy to cover sales, marketing, administration, customer care and suppliers; reducing the amount of legacy code we have; and reducing defect levels to zero. The team also believes it can probably still halve overall feature cycle times by eliminating more queuing, waiting and waste.

Codeweavers plans to double the size of the development team during 2010, and is confident that the current kanban-based process will scale without problems.

4 Conclusions

Codeweavers has adopted a very simple inspect-adapt cycle of continuous gradual improvement, which has taken us from chaos to kanban, and from loss-making to consistent month-on-month profitability. We are getting better faster by stopping production and swarming on problems, and it is important to note that every change has been made in response to a genuine business need. We are having unprecedented levels of success with a development process based on lean principles, no estimating, promiscuous pairing and the least knowledgeable developer rule. We are also confident that our lean principles will scale well and support us as we expand their scope to encompass the whole company (and beyond).

References

1. Fox, K.: TOC Stories #2: Blue Light creating capacity for nothing,
   `http://theoryofconstraints.blogspot.com/2007/06/`
   `toc-stories-2-blue-light-creating.html`
2. Wirfs-Brock, R.: Responsibility-Driven Design,
   `http://www.wirfs-brock.com/Design.html`
3. Cunningham, W., Beck, K.: A Laboratory For Teaching Object-Oriented Thinking. In: Proceedings of OOPSLA 1989 (October 1989)
4. `http://limitedwipsociety.org`
5. `http://www.codeweavers.net/support/index.php`

Tech Challenges in a Large-Scale Agile Project

Harald Søvik and Morten Forfang

Computas AS, Lysaker Torg 45, 1327 Lysaker, Norway
{hso,mfo}@computas.com
http://www.computas.com

Abstract. A five year, 25 man java project effort, that started with a waterfall-like methodology and that adopted Scrum after less than a year, has been concluded. We present three key technical challenges, briefly analyze their consequences and discuss the solutions we adopted. Firstly, we discuss how we modularized our architecture, module delineation principles, coupling and the trade-offs of abstraction. Then we discuss testing environments, their automation and relation to branches and the effect on customer involvement and feedback. Finally we discuss the benefits and disadvantages of representing domain knowledge declaratively. For all three challenges we discuss how the project's agility was affected.

Keywords: Java, scrum, agile, modularization, coupling, technical challenge, module bloat, dependency, applicaiton layer, pojo, ide, testing, branch, continuous integration, deploy, maven, database updates, domain expert, footprint, declarative knowledge, business logic, domain knowledge, process.

1 Introduction

A 5 year long Java and agile-project has recently come to a conclusion. It has been conducted between Computas (a Norwegian consultancy firm) and a major Norwegian governmental authority. As a rather large project (manning 20-30 developers throughout the project), it has faced a lot of challenges, but overall the project is recognized as a major success.

This experience reports focuses on three major technical challenges that arose during the project. We believe those challenges partially can be attributed to the SCRUM methodology. For each of them, we try to identify the consequence and the cause, and then follow up with any solutions we tried, and an analysis of whether the problem was successfully solved or not.

1.1 A Brief History

The project started out using a crossover variant of the waterfall methodology and long-term iterations, but turned towards agile after 8 months of development. The customer and domain experts needed to see, touch and feel the system being developed. A lot of them were previously not familiar with software development. Being able to see results of their decisions quickly made them more confident and eager.

A. Sillitti et al. (Eds.): XP 2010, LNBIP 48, pp. 353–361, 2010.
© Springer-Verlag Berlin Heidelberg 2010

To support parallel development, the project was organized into 4 different teams, whereas 3 were committing to the development branch, and one team working maintenance on the production branch. The teams were "self sufficient" in technical expertise - meaning that multiple programmers could be working simultaneously on the same module or layer of the system. The teams were also assigned a pool of domain experts suitable for the tasks they had chosen for the next iteration.

The project were divided into 4 overall domain-centric periods, each supporting a specific business target. All of these focused on similar goals:

- Enable self-service or more automated customer interaction
- Reduce the number of internal databases and managed systems
- Increase data quality
- Unify business processes to ensure quality

2   Coupling and Modularization

The dependency topology of a system and it's relation to evolvability is a current, active research field ([3]). It is predominantly argued that modularization, low coupling and high cohesion are characteristics that enhance salient non-functional characteristics of a system, like analyzability, integrity, changeability and testability ([4], [7]). In this section, we explore some of the trade-offs we have found between modularization and various forms of efficiency.

We use the terms *subsystem, cohesion, coupling* and *framework* as defined by [6] and *component* and *collaboration* as defined by [8].

2.1   Subsystems and Frameworks

The project consists of a series of core subsystems and legacy systems. In this article we focus on the *Mats subsystem*. This subsystem depends crucially on the *Framesolutions framework*. The *Framesolutions framework* is a fairly comprehensive set of customizable, proprietary components that many of our projects use. It at the same time provides core functionality on all application layers and it provides a fairly rigid set of programming patterns. The framework is centrally maintained separately from the project source code.

2.2   The Mats Subsystem

For the purposes of this article, the The *Mats subsystem* features four build-time modules; the *application server*, the *web server*, the *client* and a *common* module. The run-time and compile-time dependencies between these are illustrated in figure 1.

Technologically, the two first are realized as Java enterprise archives running on JBoss 4.2.3 servers, the *client* is a Java application and the *common* module is a jar file included in all the other modules.

Overall, this particular way of modularizing the *Mats subsystem* strikes a good balance between having increased complexity through many modules, decreased

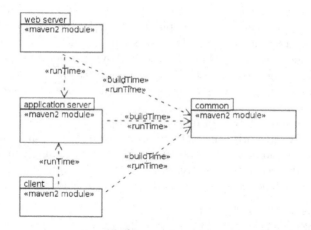

Fig. 1. The build time and runtime dependencies between important *Mats subsystem* modules

intra-module coupling and increased module cohesion. There are however a couple of major ill effects:

- The *common* module got bloated.
- New, distinct functional areas were not handled well enough as separate collaborations with proper dependency management.

Let's first briefly discuss the module bloat. On the surface of it, there are few reasons why one shouldn't put a piece of code or resource in the *common* module. It is always present and the developer doesn't have to think about possible reuse. As long as the entity in question is put in *common*, it can always be reused by some other module. This idea were thought to be a very good one in a large project, and were even more so thought of when we turned agile. We believed that an large and agile project should have a lot of supportive means to enhance reusability. When multiple teams were working on multiple tasks, it could be difficult to spot a candidate for reusability. But if the code was put in the very same module, we believed the programmers could hardly overlook the "reusabilityness". The idea were not very successful, and while reuse inside a specific sub-domain (read: team) sometimes has been possible, cross-domain (read: cross-team) reuse is virtually non-existent.

This leads to a bloated *common* module, lowers cohesion and heightens coupling. In runtime we increase the overall footprint since the *common* module is present with all the other modules. At build-time we increase the build time since the *common* module is bloated. Finally, each of the non-common modules become unnecessarily complex since there is much in the *common* module that is unwanted and unneeded by the module in question.

Now, let's move onto dependency management for new collaborations. Given some functionality you may choose to put this into one of the four mentioned modules, but you cannot choose to put it in a module governed by functional area. For example, if you are writing some web functionality from the *farm animal* domain, you can choose to put the code in the *web* or the *common* module, but there is no module that takes care of the *farm animal* domain. This leads to modules being characterized by having general purpose and very domain specific code side-by-side. Clearly this makes the modules lower their cohesion and calls for sustained developer discipline to avoid increasing intra-module coupling.

With the comprehensive, automatic test approach and environment in the Mats project, we categorize the tests according to test level and domain. Characterizing tests by domain alleviates the problem of discerning which functional area a particular piece of code belongs to. This doesn't improve module coupling, but it makes maintenance and refactoring easier. For example:

```
@Test(groups = {"unit", "husdyr"},
   dependsOnMethods = {"validererNyIndivid"},
   expectedExceptions = IllegalArgumentException.class)
   public void kanIkkeMerkesSammeDagenEllerTilbakeITid() {}
```

(from `Mats 4.0b-SNAPSHOT` depending on testng version 5.8)

Here "husdyr" (farm animal) is a category corresponding to a fairly large functional subdomain.

2.3   Application Layer Separation

From a developer's technical perspective we let the *Mats subsystem* (cf. section 2.2) be a single project. The Framesolutions framework and code pertaining to the Integration Platform is kept apart. Modern IDE's are getting quite good at providing instant and global symbol search and dependency tracking[1]. This means that all the previously mentioned modules appear as one seamless whole.

The *FrameSolution framework* (cf. section 2.1) provides two quite powerful mechanisms that makes the *Mats subsystem* (cf. section 2.2) module boundaries easier to handle.

There is the concept of a *FrameSolution Manager*. Such a manager serves as a "bridge" over a layer or between modules. The bridge may well cross physical hosts and application servers. An example invocation from Mats is

```
ImportMeldingManager.getInstance().
getSisteFoerstemottakerAdresser(importoer, foersteMottaker)
```

This code will look identical in all four *Mats subsystem* modules. For example, if this code is run on the web server, it will remote call a server stub on the application server. This code is easy for a developer to understand, quite condensed and not far from the ideal of a POJO method invocation. There is just this line needed, no annotation or other configuration.

There is the concept of a soft pointer that transparently deals with persistent objects that are not "owned", i.e. that the association between a class A and

---

[1] The Mats project is predominantly using IDEA IntelliJ version 8.

a class B is not such that CRUD operations on one is continued on the other. The soft pointer mechanism is together with a cache, implemented such that no matter where in a virtual machine an instance is soft referred to, it always points to the same, single persisted instance. This removes the burden of keeping track of multiple editions of the same object. It furthermore makes it possible to make intelligent, automated decisions w.r.t. persistent cascading and lazy loading.

Generally this particular configuration makes it very easy to create functionality covering the entire vertical stack from the GUI at the thick client or on the web through business logic and down to the persistence or integration service layer. The code looks surprisingly similar on all application layers. Developers are overall very happy with this arrangement.

One would perhaps think that this great freedom results in the inter-layer APIs to be in too great flux and that the entire subsystem architecture would over time loose necessary integrity. Due to the rigour of the *FrameSolution framework* (cf. section 2.1) that enforces quite strong patterns on all layers, this does in general not happen.

There are however still some major unintended effects:

- Just looking at the code in the IDE, it is not always clear on what layer (client, web server, application server) one is coding. Due to the powerful Framesolution abstraction features, the code would work, but not surprisingly, it often leads to highly resource demanding code.
- Since the entire *Mats subsystem* source is editable and available in the IDE, the build time on the individual developer host becomes intolerable. The IDE's automatic synchronization features also take an irritating amount of time.

These unintended effects were partially handled by using a hierarchical module structure, dividing all code into one of the *Mats subsystem* modules, cf. section 2.2. However, this was not a very effective layering, since a lot of code still resided in the common module.

Other mitigating actions were to introduce faster developer hardware (particularly SSDs) and optimizing the build procedure.

It remains a problem, and a fundamental trade-off, whether to let the developer use the powerful abstraction features of the *Framesolution* framework or write more module dependent, efficient, lower level code.

2.4   Summary

Overall we've found that developers are quite happy with the productivity boost they get from layer abstraction, having all the source in the IDE and the lack of bureaucracy when dealing with a small number of ever-present modules. We clearly could've introduced more modules, stronger barriers between them or different delineation principles. This could've bought us higher and better cohesion, and lower intra-module coupling. Chances are, we also would've introduced more overhead, increased inter-module coupling and increased demands on developer discipline.

3   Testing Environments

To support the idea of agile development with domain experts, several testing environments were accessible for the experts throughout the project. This was introduced as early as possible so that the experts could get comfortable with the system and the quirks of using a system that is under development.

We were working with two branches of the code (most of the time), and both of these had a range of environments associated with them. First, the development ("trunk") branch was the target of all changes bound for the next major release. Second, the maintenance branch was holding error fixes and small changes that could be deployed to production very often.

Each of these branches had three classes of testing environments: Continuous build [2], nightly build and manual, full-scale build. Thus, there were six different environments to maintain at all times. We did invest heavily in infrastructure and build automation for these environments.

3.1   Effect

Because of the wide variety of testing environments, the experts always had an appropriate environment to carry out their testing needs. At first, it proved a little difficult to realize how to employ this diversity, and it was frequently necessary to remind them of in which environment it would be advisable to test a new feature or a bug fix. After the first major release, most people got acquainted with the idea, and became very happy with the different environments. See Table 1 for the different applications.

Table 1. Different testing environments

	Continuous	Nightly	Manual
Development	Experimental features	New, stable features	Production ready features
Maintenance	Experimental bug fixes	Stable bug fixes	Regression tests

A key feature in maintaining all of these environments, was to have completely automated build- and deploy processes. It proved incredibly valuable - both for scheduled (nightly) builds, and whenever a new feature had to be tested immediately (continuous). To be able to automate the deploy process, it was close to necessary gather all build steps under a single command. This was successfully implemented with Maven. This helped assure similar builds on multiple platforms, i.e. different integration environments and development platforms.

3.2   Difficulties

Database structured updates proved to be difficult to automate, and were thus handled manually. It would have been possible to automate within the application, but the customer technicians discouraged such an approach. It was believed that an automated handling would weaken the exhibited control over database schema.

After spending a lot of time reimbursing the necessity of continuous testing, many of the domain experts got used to the idea of having a environment at hand all day and night. This notion was also backed by a stable production system. Thus, whenever a testing environment failed to deploy correctly at night, or a programming error lead to a critical failure of the application - the domain experts would quickly let us know that they were inhibited from doing their work efficiently. To counter this, the service monitoring tool used in production were also employed to testing environments - with email and even SMS alerts. The testing environments were subject to the same uptime requirements as production. Of course - there were no really dramatic consequences when a fault lead to unplanned downtime.

3.3   Conclusion

The biggest con of this approach was the impact on the development platform. Whereas nightly deployment worked fine, frequent deployments by developers or the continuous integration engine proved very time consuming. It is thus our conclusion that a more flexible and dynamic approach should be available for developers. This was partially implemented with hot code reloading tools, like Java hotspot and JRebel. These approaches were partially successful: Many changes were handled and deployed seamlessly, but changes to initialization code and structurally modeled data had to be handled otherwise.

Testing environments and infrastructure is at heart of an agile project. The ability to quickly recognize new or altered features, and give feedback to appropriate developers or domain experts, is a stepping stone in enabling agility.

4   Declaratively Represented Knowledge

A key concept in this project was Business Process Modeling: Separation between domain knowledge and implementation. From artificial intelligence, cognitive architecture work and knowledge modeling, the distinction between declarative and procedural knowledge has long been deemed important [1], [5]. This idea could be paraphrased as *separating what to do* from *how to do it*. It allows the domain programmers to work decoupled from the technical programmers. The processes can be modeled and mocked and remodeled, until the ideal workflow is reached.

A few vendors offers systems implemented this way, and Computas is perhaps the leading supplier in Norway. We believed that this technique would fit quite well in an agile project. It would be possible to change the behaviour of the system without altering the technical details, and visa versa: Altering the technical implementation without altering the business processes.

4.1   Effect

This approach presents challenges to the way a customer (and developers) manage software. Since the knowledge is decoupled from the program logic, it is possible to alter the behaviour of a running program.

Thus, whenever the developers decided to refactor the business logic, or the domain experts decided to alter the business processes, it would introduce no overhead for the other party. And this proved to be a correct assumption. Even though most of the business logic stayed the same once written, the business process often changed in subsequent iterations. This made the domain experts rater self sufficient in many questions, and made it possible to adapt to experiences in a quick fashion.

However, we underestimated the need of technical means to handle this distinction: It should not be necessary to rebuild and redeploy such a system when developing and testing processes. Nevertheless, developers often did so to "ensure correctness and consistency".

4.2   Difficulties

It might sound trivial, but postponing to figure out how to correctly reload process definitions at runtime reduced the development turnaround significantly. And not to mention the developers dissatisfaction of having to wait for changes to deploy before testing. Thus, it became clear that the application had to be designed for "hot knowledge reloading". This challenge was solved by implementing a re-initialization feature: Whenever process definitions or other domain defined data did change, the developer was able to reload the definitions and start using them right away. This feature is not used in production, but would theoretically allow process managers to alter a process in the middle of the day without scheduling downtime and employing technical personnel.

Also, our proprietary domain modeling language (although BPEL-compliant) were of course unsupported in any Integrated Development Environment (IDE). The language itself has a dedicated IDE which is well implemented and very functional for modeling purposes. But the functionality provided by our code IDE[9] were oblivious to such data representation, and provided no development support whatsoever. It hindsight, we should have realized the cost, and implemented a support plugin for our code IDE, so that it would treat changed to process code the same was it treated technical code. That is: provide support for syntax highlighting, autocompletion and code deployment.

4.3   Conclusion

Use of proprietary data formats can both be rewarding and expensive. One need to be aware of the necessary level of support, and accept the cost of maintaining such a level. Use of declarative knowledge representations is potentially a major catalysator when dealing with domain experts, but actually implementing the knowledge requires a high level of expertise. Also in this matter, one should be very careful with respect to the tools one choose to use for implementation and assist.

5   Summary

This experience report outlines three difficulties we experienced during this project. Although the details may appear minor, the impact of improvements was significant, because of the project size. We believe that it is incredibly important not to neglect those problems that were manageable in smaller projects, but may scale fast in large projects, and give the developers an arena where they can give an early warning of such challenges.

We would like to emphasize some key issues from this report:

- Abstraction and generalization should been driven by necessity and experience, not guesswork and intentions.
- Abstractions is not a substitute for decoupling and formally controlled module interfaces.
- Treat your testing environment like a small production environment. Define a Service Level Agreement for your domain experts and testers. Automate everything.
- Do not underestimate the accumulated overhead caused by small problems being ignored over a lengthy period of time.
- Do not underestimate the support that can be provided by modern day development tools.

References

1. Brachman, R., Levesque, H.: Knowledge Representation and Reasoning, 1st edn. Morgan Kaufmann, San Francisco (2004) ISBN 978-1558609327
2. Fowler, M.: Continuous Integration,
   http://www.martinfowler.com/articles/continuousIntegration.html
3. Breivold, H.: SOFTWARE ARCHITECTURE EVOLUTION AND SOFTWARE EVOLVABILITY, Malardalen University, Sweden (2009)
4. Breivold, H., et al.: ANALYZING SOFTWARE EVOLVABILITY. In: 32nd IEEE International Computer Software and Applications Conference (COMPSAC), Finland (2008)
5. Kendal, S., Creen, M.: An Introduction to Knowledge Engineering, 1st edn. Springer, Heidelberg (2006), ISBN 978-1846284755
6. Lethbridge, T., Laganiere, R.: Object-Oriented Software Engineering, 2nd edn. McGraw-Hill, New York (2005), ISBN 978-0073220345
7. Pressman, R.: Software Engineering: A Practitioner's Approach, 5th edn. McGraw-Hill, New York, ISBN 978-0073655789
8. Unified Modeling Language, version 2.x, http://www.uml.org
9. http://www.jetbrains.com/idea/

Energy Project Story: From Waterfall to Distributed Agile

Tomáš Tureček, Roman Šmiřák, Tomáš Malík, and Petr Boháček

Tieto, Výstavní 13, Ostrava, 70200, Czech Republic
{tomas.t.turecek,roman.smirak,tomas.malik,
petr.bohacek}@tieto.com

Abstract. Our team helps Tieto teams distributed over the entire world to set up effective way of working applying Agile, Lean, Kanban and Global sourcing principles. In May 2009 we have faced our biggest challenge. Energy sector product, 30 people in Norway, Sweden and Finland with waterfall way of working organized into regular 6 sub-applications wanted to achieve quite challenging targets. To grow to 70 people by setting up another teams in Czech Republic, to transfer 15 years legacy system knowledge and to be up and running with this all in 6 months while maintaining the production for the clients at full speed. Paper describes how we fought and won over the challenges by basing the service transfer on Agile.

Keywords: Agile, Lean, Global-sourcing, Distributed RUP, Coaching.

1 Introduction

In May 2009 we have faced our biggest challenge so far. We have got involved in project that is quite critical for Tieto business. Tieto Czech management has been also aware that if we manage to outsource it successfully then we get much bigger piece of energy business pie. This paper describes Ramp-up[1] of the offshore service into low cost country as well as all the changes we had to introduce into release project within certain constraints given by circumstances.

1.1 Our Team

We are small team of 8 consultants located in Tieto Czech global delivery centre. Our goal is to help out teams and their individual members to improve productivity and reduce work stress by using Agile, Lean [2], Global-sourcing and Kanban [9] principles. By this close cooperation with various people in whole customer-to-customer chain (as sales, management, development, testing, support and maintenance) we stay in touch with current problems, latest technologies and modern methodologies. We help and give support to Tieto teams for more than 4 years and during that time we have been involved in more than 50 distributed cases in basically all industries – Automotive, Financial services, Forest, Energy, ICT operations and others.

---

[1] Service ramp-up – set of activities that start up service in certain location with certain people.

A. Sillitti et al. (Eds.): XP 2010, LNBIP 48, pp. 362–371, 2010.

1.2 Energy Product and the Challenges

Product is intended for Scandinavian energy sector. It covers energy business from customer contract through administrating energy delivery and infrastructure to maintaining energy meters and invoicing. Product consists of 6 sub-applications called Product areas (PA) taking care of particular part of energy business processes – accounting, invoicing, contracting, metering, change of supplier and integration to other products in energy product portfolio.

Project had approximately 30 employees in Norway and 10 employees in Czech Republic organized into 6 PA teams closely cooperating together on the resulting product before Ramp-up to offshore. Goal of the Offshore ramp-up was to build integrated product teams formed by employees in Norway and 30 new employees in Czech Republic. Half of the Norwegian personnel was about to move to other projects after the Offshore ramp-up ends.

Main challenge was to hire and educate this big amount of specialists who should be responsible for development and testing of new features and error corrections in all product areas of 15 years old legacy system. The need was to have all this up and running in 6 months without affecting delivery of already planned release and compromising quality of the product. Time limit and goals were unchangeable by the circumstances that are not important for the paper.

2 Story

The story started in a bit unorthodox way. We met a project manager in a corridor that we had been associated with before. He had just a quick question. Of course, it turned out to be more than just a quick question, so we planned a follow up. He got nominated as a Ramp-up manager for Norwegian Energy product transfer to Czech Republic and he wanted to validate some of his ideas. After an hour we knew, thanks to our experience and intuition, that Czech delivery centre is headed for a failure, as the Offshore ramp-up plan contained several serious anti-patterns.

Since the project manager was open and we had gained his trust in the previous case, he acknowledged risks quickly and invited us to a dinner with the management of the case on the fly, which was planned for the same evening.

This **Informal meeting and introduction (pattern)** gave us opportunity to capture stakeholders' needs and promote our services in more relaxed environment than offices or sterile meeting rooms.

2.1 First Steps

Introduction went fine and we agreed to continue with discussions next day to come up with some next steps. Project had its own external global-sourcing consultant who had experienced transfer of one huge cell phone application development from Scandinavia to Russia before and he wanted to repeat the success with the same 3 main points as in his previous case:

- Manage Offshore ramp-up project separately from release project.
- Start with all training sessions first then focus on practice.
- Do not change process in the project during the ramp-up to offshore.

We learnt on many cases that these steps lead to everything else but new fully capable colleagues ready to work on release project. We would like to pinpoint here that **What works in one case does not necessarily works in other one (pattern)**.

We did not know project much and we always focus on **Learning constraints and details before we propose changes (pattern)** but to motivate leaders we presented couple of standard patterns that usually help to outsource and perform knowledge transfer as effective as possible. Patterns in fact said the complete opposite to suggestions of their expert.

– To **Merge Offshore ramp-up project with release project (pattern)**. No one else than seniors can educate and support newcomers in their learning. This definitely must be aligned with the release project plans.
– Let newcomers to work on real system features as soon as possible. We mean to base knowledge transfer on **Learning by doing (pattern)** [6], [5] known also as Shewhart's Plan-Do-Act-Check cycle (PDCA). Toyota production system [2], Kaizen [5] and countless of medical experiments clearly say that this is the most effective educational method that in fact goes hand in hand with the release project objectives – no extra work is done.
– To change the way of working from waterfall to iterative; we mean to introduce PDCA cycles also to release project. Iterations help us to get situation under control by introducing better visibility and clarity into project.

2.2 Kaizen Workshop – Getting to Know the Project

We invited key project people to one of the Agile training sessions that we provide for Tieto personnel. This is always great opportunity to explain Agile in context of trainees' context e.g. how Agile can boost Offshore ramp-up and solve project issues. Leaders got motivated to become one of our mentored cases therefore we organized **Kaizen workshop (pattern)**. Workshop is the opportunity for mentors to learn all possible project details to be able to come up with relevant proposals.

This is Kaizen workshop agenda we usually use:

– Interview key people from all areas (sales, executives, ramp-up and team roles)
  – Person's responsibilities, needs, fears and objectives – to get the context
  – Typical day activities – to learn operative and to identify anti-patterns
  – Top 5 issues and improvements – to **Involve closest people to the subject (pattern)** [2].
– Get the big picture from value-stream analysis [3] to be able to **Optimize whole in context (pattern)** [2], sub-optimization usually does not solve the issue.
– **Focus on root cause (pattern)** to not heal symptoms but sickness. We usually use Theory of Constraints' Current Reality Tree tool [4] to **Visualize all (pattern)** cause-effect chains leading to root causes.

As the project was based on waterfall it contained a lot of its weaknesses. The most important was huge waiting time periods resulting in really long feature lead time. We selected and prioritized practices carefully that we planned to implement into release project. Some of them are listed below:

- Iterative way of working (3 weeks Iterations).
- Base knowledge transfer on **Learning by doing (pattern)**.
- Organize newcomers into **Self-managed teams (pattern)** and **Cross-functional teams (pattern)**.

One of the project strengths was **Executive management support (pattern)**; executives approved the adoption roadmap and from that moment we can say we started with Agile implementation.

There was no time to stop, calm down and change release and Offshore ramp-up plans and to **Introduce the changes step by step (pattern)**. Newcomers were already hired, contracts were signed and new release project was about to start. To manage changes in 6 month deadline we had to put all into practice immediately. The circumstances forced us to follow **Big bang adoption (anti-pattern)**. We were aware (from our experience) of confusion that this anti-pattern causes among project people. If we change the process too much then no one knows exactly what to do and people tend to work the *old* way. Change and confusion lead usually to productivity drop as we can see on Fig. **1**.

Fig. 1. Illustrative figure shows productivity drop after the process change

Only heavy support and daily involvement from people skilled in this new way of working – **Mentoring (pattern)** – can keep the productivity on the same level and calm down the chaos. We offered our help and support to mitigate this risk.

2.3 Transition to Agile

The biggest pain in transition from Waterfall to Agile is usually the mindset. Agile way of working expects quite opposite approach from Taylor's worker-supervisor model [1]. As an example we can use the first Iteration planning and assessment that we went to facilitate to Norway. We expected to come up with concrete details together with release project people (so we did not prepare the solution upfront) but they expected more US army drill sergeant approach ordering exactly what to do and not a partner for a debate. We did not follow **Clarify expectations and reveal assumptions (pattern)** carefully and even if facilitation went pretty well these not filled hidden expectations harmed our short relationship for couple of next weeks when we were perceived more like *theoretical* guys.

We organized couple of sessions to **Train all the product personnel (pattern)** to **Synchronize vocabulary (pattern)** and to ensure that everyone understands new way of working. Since that time project carried on the track that we have set up for it more less smoothly. But we really focused on **Proactive issue identification (pattern)** by techniques described in section 2.5 that paid off many times later.

2.4   Organizing Release Project According to Patterns

Hi-level product organization remained the same – product consisted of 6 product areas – but one product area team is now organized according to **Team of teams (pattern)** as we can see on Fig. **2**. Each team (forming team of teams) has its own team leader playing **Boundary spanner (pattern)** role important for information synchronization. It does not mean that people do not communicate with each other, they do, but Boundary spanners ensure that no important information is lost and they represent **Single point of contact (pattern)** for important issues or ideas that needs to be spread over.

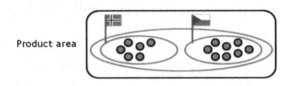

Product area

Fig. 2. Team of teams forming one product area

Product areas are to some extent independent on each other but they have agreed to use the same Iteration length – 3 weeks – to work in the same **Heart-beat (pattern)**. Product area builds need to be integrated periodically – **Continuous integration (pattern).** The same rhythm allows planning system integration tests within the same milestones.

As mentioned earlier Ramp-up to offshore was integrated into release project. It affected the project scope significantly as we can see in list below that describes content of typical Iterations:

- Iteration starts with joined Iteration planning Norwegian and Czech guys together in two meeting rooms connected by videoconference equipment[2].
- Scope contains features and error corrections prioritized also with respect to dependency on other product areas and respect to knowledge transfer.
- Iteration production time is organized according to **Learning by doing (pattern)**. Cycles start with brief information about business background to selected features and ECs followed by implementation with support from the seniors having explicitly allocated time for it. There was always travelling of senior guy to Czech Republic team or vice versa in our case according to **Ambassador (pattern)**.
- Iteration ends with Iteration objectives review and **Retrospective (pattern)** where team discusses (over videoconference) what went well and what should be improved. Team learns this way from its mistakes and applies corrective

---

[2] We have found the videoconference works surprisingly well after people, on the opposite side of videoconference, meet personally and spend some time together. Also BIG screen helps.

actions into very next Iteration. We have introduced MCIF self-check [7] as a regular point in retrospective meeting agenda. Self-check questions (carefully selected by us to cover Agile adoption roadmap) trigger team members to talk about current situation and the way of working. Self-check voting results gives us some soft data showing what principles have been successfully adopted.

Daily synchronization among Norwegian and Czech team within one PA is ensured by joint **Daily meetings (pattern)** over the phone and one computer with shared desktop. Since the teams track all their work items in Team Foundation Server they visualize their daily items in MS Excel view to TFS work items together with burn-down and workload report chart macros that we have created for them to **Automate repetitive work (pattern)**.

Teams use described tools more less the same way in all product area teams. But it was not this way all the time. As the way of working evolved tools did the same. We have experimented with many ways of doing these meetings from task board in form of sticky notes to task board on wiki page until we ended up with TFS Excel view as mentioned above. This evolution is in fact according to **Adapt tools to the way of working (pattern)**.

Product areas use couple of regular meetings to synchronize on information touching all PAs. Leaders from PAs contribute to each other Iteration scope priorities before Iteration planning to enable synergy on development and newcomers' education. Except these meetings they attend **Scrum of scrums meetings (pattern)** organized twice a week where they discuss issues and opportunities touching other PAs.

Teams use various tools for information sharing. Except TFS and macros generating charts we have introduced wiki. We originally started to use wiki only as a knowledge base. Some guidelines here and there and project people perceived it mostly as *another tool* they need to bother with. But after couple of months later we got to completely different situation. We created wiki template for Iteration planning and assessment and motivated all PA teams to get rid of SourceSafe MS Word based plans and create them on wiki instead. That boosted wiki usage and from that moment we saw that wiki was one of the most important collaboration tools that release project used. There is information from guidelines through functional and technical documentation to Iteration plans and meeting minutes from various meetings now. Templates to planning, meeting minutes, technical documentation and others contain links to guidelines and blogs so that people can instantly read the details to concrete topics.

2.5 Mentoring and Coaching Infrastructure

Since our team of mentors is located in Czech Republic we can easily support Czech part of the PA teams but it is really hard to do the same remotely with Norwegian teams. It is terribly difficult to explain new concepts over the phone. Face to face discussion in front of whiteboard is irreplaceable. Norwegians had no **Local mentor (pattern)** to support Norwegian part of teams at the beginning so Norwegian Ramp-up manager and Release manager took over the local mentor role.

To synchronize effectively we established two short meetings in a week to check Agile adoption status and agree on next steps till the next meeting. We established

Mentoring backlog (pattern) on wiki to keep track on improvements to be done together with actions points.

We also visited each other quite often. In 10 months we had more than 15 chances to see each other face to face either in Ostrava or in Norway. That heavy travelling helped a lot to build the relationship and to solve issues hanging in mentoring backlog.

3 Mentoring Lessons Learnt and Hints

Support to teams from mentors is crucial but we must resist temptation of **Mentors become leaders (anti-pattern)** – this exactly happened to us. We were in hurry because of constraints and pressure from customers and management to keep productivity on high level. To fulfill this objective we (mentors) overtook the initiative and started proactively solve all the possible issues. In one hand it enabled team to adopt practices and principles quickly but on the other hand the *release project became dependant on us mentors*. Considering this we failed to **Start up self-improvement framework (pattern)** in teams because most of team members got used to mentors walking around solving problem in behalf of them. This lesson is one that we learnt the hard way. In fact we still fight with the consequences.

Avoid **Big bang adoption (anti-pattern)** of changes if possible and **Introduce changes to project step by (pattern)** instead – we have paid this decision with heavy workload from the mentor side. 70 people project has consumed 3 FTEs[3] of mentoring work for more than 2 months. After that it went down slowly to current 1 FTE. This could be quite expensive business if you hire external consultants.

Also try to **Introduce process changes before Offshore ramp-up starts (pattern)**. It is easier to implement improvements into small co-located group. After the way of working is changed to acceptable state (and stabilized) it can be copied into new teams created by following offshore ramp-up.

Basic part of mentor's job is to see issues, predict problems and formulate risks earlier than others. This **Proactive issue identification (pattern)**[4] has paid off many times. We have spent a lot of time by visiting teams and individuals in important moments of the release project to keep ourselves up to date with the situation on the project.

Information from daily meetings, scrum of scrums, plannings, retrospectives and talks around coffee machine is irreplaceable. This helped us a lot to not get to into *ivory tower* and to come up all the time with relevant proposals. These visits are also great in sense that we can give feedback if there is any issue to team or person immediately after the meeting ends. It boosts grow and supports adoption of new principles and practices.

Visualize all (pattern) is not probably as appreciated as it should be. We have experienced the situation many times when hours of explanation led nowhere until the picture was drawn. Suddenly magic happened and people started to realize things.

---

[3] FTE – Full time equivalent, usually 1 FTE = 40h per week.
[4] We also call this approach *Smell the cheese* by famous book from Spencer Johnson [8].

In previous release we experienced teams constantly failing Iteration evaluation criteria. We saw that it is caused by constant over-committing. Teams failed to deliver half of promised scope with velocity 0.5 in compare to original optimistic estimates. Teams were under strong push from management to deliver more because scope was already promised to customer by fixed price & scope contract. Pressure led to many negative consequences like technical debt when cheap & dirty solution usually won or team frustration. People did not see the way how to fulfill overflowing Iteration scope so why should they even try?

We had a lot of talks but one figure (see Fig. 3) instantly changed the position of the management. They realized the pressure was not solving their problem.

Team can do only as much work as its velocity is. Pressure makes things worse. It results in no benefits but buggy and hard-to-maintain software at the output and de-motivated people as a *bonus*. In fact the only way to make teams more productive, according to our opinion, is to **remove obstacles continuously (pattern)** from their way of working, not to push.

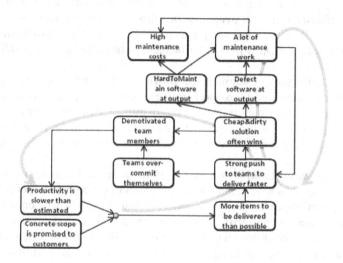

Fig. 3. Negative reinforcement loops, caused by management decisions, make situation worse

Ensure **local mentor (pattern)** for all locations where the project is situated – everyone needs help especially at the beginning of adoption. This local instant support can reduce confusion, frustration and keep productivity on high level. Mentors at different locations must act as one. See section 2.5 how we set up information channels.

Our mentoring backlog became huge in couple of last months. We did not follow **keep inventory low (pattern)** and it resulted in a lot of backlog items that we are forced to read through and prioritize twice a week now. It is pretty time consuming so we are now implementing Kanban [9] there to get rid of queues.

This is in fact more general pattern. We used to have a problem with one team not bringing into effect a single corrective action. They were taking always too many corrective actions to following Iteration. We advised them to select just one improvement and put that into one action. It is harder to postpone corrective action if there is only single one in the Iteration backlog. Long lists annoy people.

3.1 Summary of Mentioned Not Commonly Known (Anti) Patterns

- **Informal meeting and introduction (pattern)** – as mentioned in section 2.1, meeting at informal place helps to relax minds and build the relationship better than in office. We usually take our visits to beer or dinner to discuss informally all possible project, team and environment things.
- **What works in one case does not necessarily works in other one (pattern)** – well known problem of case studies. They cannot be copied and placed from one situation with its context into different one.
- **Learn constraints and details before we propose changes (pattern)** – to help the project we need first to learn as much as possible about the concrete situation in the project. There are many ways how to do it. We prefer to visit project place and interview key people as mentioned in **Kaizen workshop (pattern)** in section 2.2.
- **Merge Offshore ramp-up project with release project (pattern)** – see explanation in section 2.1. Pattern can be put more general way: All improvements shall be part of the release project plan. That includes outsourcing as well as all other investments.
- **Executive management support (pattern)** – as Standish group usually emphasizes in their chaos reports, support from executive management is crucial to any success, especially for improvements that are usually need investment first.
- **Mentoring (pattern)** – is a service offered by skilled people in all software development roles. Mentoring is based on coaching teams in time of introducing improvements.
- **Clarify expectations and reveal assumptions (pattern)** – it is common approach of effective non-blocking communication. The most essential is to get rid of prejudices, assumptions and expectations and try to listen to others with open mind.
- **Boundary spanner (pattern)** – also known from RUP as **Gatekeeper** is a role in distributed team that ensures the important information is propagated to all teams.
- **Heart-beat (pattern)** – important pattern for products in one portfolio. It enables product teams to synchronize on milestones and deliver software together as one product.
- **Ambassador (pattern)** – one of the most important patterns in case of building new remote teams. It comes from RUP and represents person from existing team coming to offshore team, staying there for some time and helping to build it. Ambassador boosts the knowledge transfer and team growth.

4 Final Words

Offshore ramp-up of the energy project ended after 6 months as planned and it was considered as a great success of project people, executive management and also us mentors. Teams in Czech Republic are productive, recently released product has fewer defects than before and all product people consider recent release time as less stressful. Ramp-up to offshore has ended but learning still continues because no matter what management goals are – some things need time; like growing knowledge and competences of newly created teams.

Story shows that even if the situation full of constraints and challenging targets looks desperate it can turn into success if we manage to motivate people and executives to follow patterns from software development and global-sourcing area.

There are still constraints that forbid the case to fully utilize Agile potential. The biggest pain now is the fixed price and scope contract generating a lot of issues for the release organization. The new release starts now and we are experimenting with couple of Agile contracts focusing on cooperation between customer and vendor instead of focusing to concrete result and budget.

References

1. Taylor, F.W.: The Principles of Scientific Management, 164p. Nabu Press (2010) ISBN 978-1141495429
2. Liker, J.: The Toyota Way, 1st edn., 330p. McGraw-Hill, New York (2003) ISBN 978-0071392310
3. Poppendieck, M., Poppendieck, T.: Lean Software Development: An Agile Toolkit, 240p. Addison-Wesley Professional, Reading (2003) ISBN 978-0321150783
4. Dettmer, W.H.: Goldratt's Theory of Constraints: A Systems Approach to Continuous Improvement. ASQ Quality Press (1997) ISBN: 978-0873893701
5. Imai, M.: Kaizen: The Key To Japan's Competitive Success, 260p. McGraw-Hill/Irwin (1986) ISBN 978-0075543329
6. Deming, E.W.: Out of the crisis, 1st edn. MIT Press, Cambridge (2000)
7. IBM MCIF Self-check, http://www.ibm.com/developerworks/rational/library/edge/08/may08/kroll_krebs/index.html (2008-02-24)
8. Johnson, S.: Who Moved My Cheese? In: An Amazing Way to Deal with Change in Your Work and in Your Life. P. Putnam's Sons (1999)
9. Japan Mgmt. Assoc.: Kanban Just-In-Time at Toyota: Management Begins at the Workplace, 211p. Productivity Press (1989) ISBN: 978-0915299485

Design and Development in the "Agile Room": Trialing Scrum at a Digital Agency

Katerina Tzanidou[1] and Jennifer Ferreira[2]

[1] Cimex Media Ltd., London, EC2A 4PJ, UK
katerina.tzanidou@cimex.com
[2] The Open University, Walton Hall, Milton Keynes, MK7 6AA, UK
j.ferreira@open.ac.uk

Abstract. Scrum was trialed at Cimex — a Digital Media Agency in the UK. Our insights centre in particular around the close interactions between the designers and developer working in the same room, and how the design roles were played out in the Scrum context. The lessons learned from this experience are now presented to our clients as a case study in order to make them more aware of the benefits of running an Agile project. Since this trial, we have adapted our current practice to include more immediate forms of communication. We now have hands-on experience integrating design with Scrum and can say that it was an enjoyable, bonding experience for the team.

Keywords: Designer, Developer, War room, Scrum, User Experience, Agile adoption, Agile integration.

1 Introduction

This report is based on the experiences of trialing Scrum at a Digital Media Agency in the UK, called Cimex Media Ltd. We decided to trial Scrum at our organisation for a number of reasons: Although our teams had borrowed parts of Agile methods before, from the organisation's point of view, it was an opportunity to get hands-on experience specifically with Scrum and to learn how Scrum would work with the existing organisational structures. One of the aims was to bring design and development closer, by seating the designers and the developer in the same room. The idea came from our experience working with a client who outsourced our Information Architect (IA) and asked that he would go and sit in the same room with their developer and designer at their premises. Talking to the IA about his experience at the client's premises prompted us to consider whether doing the same could also make our process easier and quicker. It was also clear that the IA enjoyed the experience. From the client's perspective an emergent solution, via feedback on actual working software was seen as a valuable way of overcoming the fact that requirements were not known up front. This made the project a good fit with our own motivations to try Scrum.

Since completing the trial we have incorporated some of the lessons learned into our current practice and can share our insights with other practitioners who

A. Sillitti et al. (Eds.): XP 2010, LNBIP 48, pp. 372–378, 2010.

have similar aims. Our insights centre in particular around the close interactions between the designers and developer working in the same room, and how different design roles were played out in the Scrum context. We have also concluded that while an Agile approach has allowed us to be more flexible towards our client requirements it does not suit all projects and all types of clients we deal with. Our public sector clients, for example, still prefer more traditional approaches and prefer detailed definitions and scope in advance.

2 Cimex and Agile

While we have separate teams at Cimex, such as Development, Design, User Experience, Content/SEO, Project Management and Producers we work collaboratively across teams and we apply User Centred Design (UCD) processes on all of our projects. As an organisation, Cimex goes back to 1994 and have been using very waterfall-based PRINCE 2 methodologies for several years. As our clients' needs change we have aimed to explore new methodologies ourselves. Katerina, as Head of User Experience (UX), spent a whole year bringing awareness of Agile methods to Cimex. It has been a challenge to get internal enthusiasm and commitment from all for such a big change. Maintaining trust internally, as well as with the client, was the biggest challenge we were faced with. This was after all a change to what people were familiar with and had been doing for a long time. It was difficult to get everyone internally to buy into the idea and overcome fears of the unknown. We had to explain that starting a project without detailed scoping documentation meant that we had to learn to work collaboratively, stay flexible and learn to trust our colleagues. We needed to build trust that what we agree in our brief meetings in the morning would be delivered by the end of play.

Teams at Cimex have borrowed from Agile methodologies in the past, although we had not adopted a coherent Agile method such as Scrum before. We started adding Agile aspects to our projects in 2008 and slowly each individual involved has become more familiar with Agile approaches. Those involved in other Agile projects had enjoyed the experience and were enthusiastic about taking more Agile practices on board.

3 Trialing Scrum

We had some specific goals in mind with this trial, which were also influenced by the type of project we had taken on:

- **Bringing design and development closer together.** Prompted by the IA's enthusiasm for working closely with developers, we wanted to enable the team to work closely and in the same working space. We believed that proximity of space would make a difference in how the team would engage and discuss, and we were hoping that this set-up would encourage more communication and more effective decision making. Traditionally, the team would tend to meet only when a meeting was set up by the project manager. However, we wanted them to feel free to ask each other immediate queries that came to mind while working.

– **Allowing a creative solution to emerge via frequent client input** The client was keen to be heavily involved in the project. They wanted to be able to give feedback and make changes on-the-fly in order to get the best possible results. By having the whole team working in an Agile way we hoped for more flexibility to make quick changes if needed.

– **Learning about the practical issues surrounding Scrum adoption at our organisation.** We wanted to explore other ways of adapting Agile, such as bringing the Agile team together in one room, having daily quick meetings and client involvement. We expected better outcomes, more transparency and engagement, as well as quick turnaround.

The project chosen for this trial was redesigning a client website. We had to keep a really tight reign on the resources we were using, as the client reduced their initial budget by 2/3 but still wanted a high impact website. The client was prepared to allow the creative solution to emerge and had agreed to be heavily involved. Scrum was seen as the ideal methodology to micromanage every aspect of the project with the client being closely involved. The team consisted of one software developer, two designers (a creative designer and an IA) and a project manager who was also the Scrum Master. The creative designer was responsible for the graphic design and the IA for producing wireframes. The developer was responsible for providing the back end code for the front-end designs. The team could work independently and they were not expected to integrate their work with other teams. This was their first experience with Scrum.

4   Life in the "Agile Room"

Figure 1 shows the team working environment. Management agreed that the team could be seated in a room that would normally be used as a meeting room or a usability lab. The team were seated at a large table, each at their own workstation. Colleagues would come and visit the team during the day and playfully ask: "Is this the Agile Room?" Or, "Are you the Agile team?" The project manager/Scrum Master was not seated in the same room, however he popped in at regular intervals during the day to answer questions and discuss project-related issues with the team. Basecamp[1] was used to share documents and log discussions with the client. The team reflected that in this room they were able to focus free from distractions.

Sprints lasted one week, including one to two client meetings per week where the website was demoed and further requirements were discussed. The team began each day with a short standup meeting, to discuss their progress and what

---

[1] http://basecamphq.com/

Fig. 1. The team in the "Agile Room"

they were going to work on during the day. As hoped, the team were talking and asking each other questions. The developer explained how valuable it was for him to be aware of the work of the designers. He could spot areas in the design that would cause problems for the implementation: "And that generally probably wouldn't have been spotted until all the wireframes had been signed-off, handed over and the designs would have been done." The team were making decisions together. For example, in a discussion about exploring alternatives to a drop-down list, one of the designers asked the developer directly whether her idea would be more difficult to implement. The developer could immediately give her an answer: "It would probably be just as easy." We counted the instances where the developer and the designers were talking to each other. On their first day together there were 27 instances where questions concerning client requirements were raised, 19 instances of talk about possible design solutions and 14 instances where the designers were directly asking the developer for feedback about either a design idea or client requirements. The team agreed this was more interaction than they normally have when sitting apart. The team had a very positive response to the outcomes of the trial. They all enjoyed the experience and indicated that they would like to work in a similar manner in the future.

5   Outcomes

Instant decision-making and making progress. When driven by tight deadlines we did not observe this kind of quick and efficient communication between team members when they were sitting apart. Small requests for clarifications often get lost along the way as team members are not easily motivated to get up and move around to talk to their colleagues. Instead, they are keen to get the work delivered and quite often only approach their colleagues once they have an issue they can not solve themselves. By placing the developer and designers together sped up the whole development effort and made it more effective. For example, while the IA was creating the wireframes she could ask the developer immediately about functionality constraints. In a similar manner, when the creative designer was working on the look and feel she would have quick access to the IA next to her and ask for clarifications. There were immediate responses to questions concerning design possibilities, but there were also immediate responses to questions about how long a design would take to implement in terms of code. In this way the team had the opportunity to resolve issues that would only have been identified further down the line when it would have had major implications. Before, the designers and developers communicated just prior to the client meeting — usually too late to address the technical problems in the design. Being together ensured everyone was negotiating the way forward together and making progress. The client requirements at the start were very vague and this would normally hamper progress on the project. However, the team asked each other "What do you remember from the client meeting?" "What did you understand the client wanting from the client meeting?" Allowing them to move forward by sharing their knowledge and opinions.

Understanding design roles. At Cimex we have several types of design that is carried out by different roles. For example, the IA designs the structure of the site, navigation and layout, whereas the creative designer is responsible for aspects such as the aesthetics of the site, the use of colours and the logo. Using Scrum inevitably means that the various design roles need to integrate and coordinate their work within the Sprints. *Design* at Cimex can not simply be added on to the Scrum methodology. We came up against questions such as how to time the tasks of the IA? For example, spending time working up the wireframes might delay the whole process unless the IA work starts earlier than either the creative design and development work. Another design issue was one of segmenting creative work into time-boxed Sprints. The creative designer commented on the pressure they felt to create a unique design within just one week. Traditionally, our projects would start with the requirements gathering phase. During this phase, we gather user insights and stakeholders' objectives, with IA work starting straight after. The IA would then create wireframes to demonstrate the structure of the site. Creative design would only start when all wireframes were created and signed off by the client. However, in this trial we started both wireframes and creative design simultaneously. This meant that creative design evolved more on-the-fly as the IA and creative designer were discussing and sketching out possible solutions.

6 Recommendations

During the course of trialing Scrum, we dealt with questions relating to the IA and creative design roles. In dealing with these questions we make some recommendations for projects dealing with more than one design role:

1. **Find the design guide.** A conscious decision about who leads the design direction should be made. Answering this question in turn requires a decision on where the dependencies are between the different kinds of design that need to be coordinated (in our case, IA and creative design). On this project, both the IA and creative design roles started working on designs at the same point in time. Vague requirements at the start of our project, combined with having no designs that were signed off by the client, meant that there was some uncertainty about who was taking the lead. Although our solution did emerge, to avoid the initial uncertainty, we now recommend that the IA is started prior to the other activities and given enough time to stay ahead. The IA provides a coherent structure to the overall user experience that the creative designer and developers can follow. All user requirements should therefore be reflected in the wireframes first, before they are addressed by the creative designer. How far the IA should work ahead in our case would depend on the overall number of wireframes affected by the user requirements.

   We questioned whether creative design and IA should be separated in the first place. Based on our experience we have concluded that whether IA and creative design are separated or not will depend on the particular project's needs. What is most important is that the IA should be in contact with the creative designer throughout the project to ensure that both roles are contributing to the overall user experience.

2. **Plan for evaluating designs and incorporating the results.** As time grew short, it became harder to avoid lowering the priority of design work. Assessment activities, such as user testing before launch, risked becoming a lower priority as the scoping changed throughout the Sprints and development aspects gained higher priority. We have made a point to include a Sprint for 'quick and dirty' user testing at least two weeks before launching. If a Sprint lasts two weeks then one week should be dedicated to user testing and one week dedicated to implementing changes based on the results. Careful planning of milestones before the start of the project and continuous assessment of the milestones throughout the project has proven effective in our subsequent Agile projects.

7   Agile at Cimex: Post-Trial

Since completing the trial we have adapted our current practice in terms of how we communicate within our teams. The set-up of our building is such that it does not allow all staff to work on the same floor, let alone nearby each other. One of our biggest projects now is run in an Agile-like manner, despite not having a dedicated room for the team. We have replaced the location proximity with communication tools that are used throughout the day. We encourage frequent communication between designers and developers by encouraging them to use Skype and instant messaging. We also hold daily face-to-face meetings with the whole team.

We continue to make use of Agile approaches on our projects and our Project Management team has used Agile methodologies on many or part of several projects now. We continue delivering functionality iteratively and incrementally, which enables us to be driven by our clients' priorities. Our first increments of useful functionality are often delivered within a short period of time following the start of the project. Rather than being dependent on finalising designs and detailed architectures, we are confident that requirements, architectures and designs can successfully emerge throughout the project.

Finally, we have found that new clients are motivated by our experience. We present our lessons learned from trialing Scrum to new clients as a case study in order to make them more aware of the flexibility an Agile project can provide.

Acknowledgments

We would like to thank all our colleagues at Cimex who worked on the Agile project reported in this paper and all those who continuously make an effort to try and explore new methodologies that allow us to evolve and learn more about our capabilities and new goals we can set.

Reinforcing the Learning of Agile Practices Using Coding *Dojos*

Mariana Bravo and Alfredo Goldman

CS - IME - University of São Paulo (USP)
{marivb,gold}@ime.usp.br

Abstract. Agile practices such as pair programming or test driven development are best learned when they are actually performed rather than read about. However, an unexperienced learner on his own might take a long time and might make mistakes that could be avoided if he had some help. In this work, we present an activity known as Coding *Dojo* as a technique to reinforce the learning of some Agile practices. We describe this method and present a study that evaluates its effect on learning.

Agile practices such as pair programming or test driven development cannot be learned by reading about them or being told how they work. That is because some Agile practices are not completely deterministic, but a subjective set of actions that can be taken and will have different effects depending on the context. For example, for continuous integration there may exist a compromise on when to commit the code when several small steps are being done.

However, simply trying a practice by oneself without outside help might not be the best way to learn an Agile practice. One might not see the benefits or effects that the practice has, might do it inappropriately or might even forget to do it altogether. So, a better idea would be for the student to receive feedback on how he is doing the practice, in such a way that will enable him to evolve more quickly.

One possible way to enable the learner to receive this feedback is with an activity known as Coding *Dojo*. A Coding *Dojo* is a meeting where a group of programmers gets together to learn, practice and share experiences on programming. This technique was first proposed in the end of 2004 and has since spread throughout many cities (codingdojo.org/cgi-bin/wiki.pl?CodingDojos). An experience report by Sato et al. [1] gives a full description of the principles and mechanics of a Coding *Dojo*, along with lessons learned from running Coding *Dojos* since July 2007.

The **goal** of a Coding *Dojo* session is usually to work on a specific and generally simple programming exercise. The group works on a solution to the exercise from scratch, using **test-driven development (TDD)**, **refactoring** and **pair-programming**. Some Coding *Dojos* also use **retrospectives** [2] as a way for the group to improve its practice of the sessions; and **frequent commits** as a way to document the evolution of the code written during a session.

A. Sillitti et al. (Eds.): XP 2010, LNBIP 48, pp. 379–380, 2010.

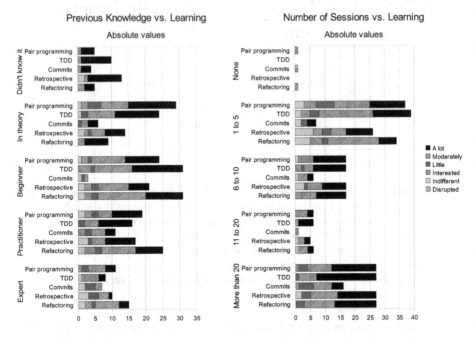

Fig. 1. The relationship between previous knowledge (left) and number of sessions (right) with learning, per practice, in number of responses

In order to investigate how the Coding *Dojo* sessions are perceived to help in the learning process, we conducted a survey[1] among Coding *Dojo* participants, mostly from Brazil. The survey was on-line and an e-mail was sent asking for collaboration on the main Coding *Dojo* lists. The survey received 91 answers.

In Figure 1 we see, for each practice, the relationship between the respondents' previous knowledge (left) and number of sessions he participated in (right) with his perception of learning in the Coding *Dojo*.

In summary, as far as participants' perception goes, the Coding *Dojo* is a very effective technique for learning Agile practices, independently of how much is already known about them. We may also notice a tendency that, in regard to previous knowledge, the less you know, the more you will learn; and in regard to number of sessions, the more you participate, the more you will learn.

References

1. Sato, D.T., Corbucci, H., Bravo, M.V.: Coding Dojo: An Environment for Learning and Sharing Agile Practices. In: AGILE 2008: Proceedings of the Agile 2008, pp. 459–464 (2008)
2. Derby, E., Larsen, D.: Agile Retrospectives: Making Good Teams Great. Pragmatic Bookshelf (2006)

---

[1] http://www.ime.usp.br/~marivb/DojoLearning/questionario_en.html

AnnoTestWeb/Run: Annotations Based Acceptance Testing

David Connolly[1], Frank Keenan[1], and Fergal Mc Caffery[2]

[1] Software Technology Research Centre
[2] Regulated Software Research Group,
Dundalk Institute of Technology, Dublin Road, Dundalk, Ireland
{david.connolly,fergal.mccaffery,frank.keenan}@dkit.ie

Abstract. Testing is frequently reported as a crucial stage in the software development process. With traditional approaches acceptance testing is the last stage of the process before release. Acceptance Test Driven Development (ATDD) promotes the role of an expert customer in defining tests and uses tool support to automate and execute these tests. This abstract outlines a tool, AnnoTestWeb/Run aimed at expert customers specifying acceptance tests with reuse of existing documentation.

1 Introduction

A large part of software development expenditure is attributed to *testing*. Traditionally, with plan-driven development, acceptance testing, the process of testing functional requirements with "data supplied by the customer" [1] occurs as the final stage of the development process long after the initial investigation has completed [2]. Many reports, however, highlight that costs can be reduced by detecting errors earlier in development [3]. Also supporting this, in many domains (e.g. medical device industry) software is developed in a regulatory environment with a tendency for extensive documentation. In contrast, agile approaches require constant customer collaboration throughout development, with customer provision of acceptance tests being an important part of this role. Often, it is recommended that tests be identified before implementation commences. In eXtreme Programming (XP) [4], for example, acceptance tests are defined as a part of the User Stories practice and, as such, are written before coding of the story begins. The practice of ATDD "allows software development to be driven by the requirements" [5]. A key advantage of ATDD in its wider context is that it leverages existing agile infrastructure including continuous integration and test-first development.

In many organisations business rules are documented in numerous formats. However, ATDD is currently not well supported with tools that enable reusing such existing documents, without rewrites, to create executable tests. A challenge therefore, is to support a suitably informed expert in performing the agile *customer role*, including easily creating tests from existing material. However, successful identification of accurate acceptance tests in this manner is not necessarily straightforward.

A. Sillitti et al. (Eds.): XP 2010, LNBIP 48, pp. 381–382, 2010.

2   AnnoTestWeb/Run Tool

AnnoTestWeb/Run is a browser based tool built using the Google Web Toolkit and CouchDB. Creation of tests involves using annotations that describe different elements of an acceptance test. A metadata system provides extra detail to annotations e.g. label, data types. It features a simplified interface and workflow partially because it is aimed at all members of agile teams, including non-developers.

Reporting of test results generated by program execution is also designed to occur in a simplified fashion through a Javascript Object Notation (JSON) API. This means that tests can execute in a wide variety of programming languages and environments. A library to speed up implementation of tests is also provided for Java and C#.

3   Conclusions and Future Work

The AnnoTestWeb/Run tool has been demonstrated to a domain expert and an agile team. Future work will involve empirical investigation of its use with both undergraduate and post-graduate students. A long running project with an agile team adopting the tool is also planned. These evaluations will examine the use of ATDD in an agile setting. Feedback from this work will also be used to inform changes to the tool and prepare for a future open source release.

Acknowledgments

This research is partially supported by Institutes of Technology, Technological Sector Research Programme, Strand 1 Fund and Science Foundation Ireland through the Stokes Lectureship Programme, grant number 07/SK/I1299.

References

1. Sommerville, I.: Software Engineering, 8th edn., pp. 80–81. Addison-Wesley, Reading (2007)
2. Pressman, R.S.: Software Engineering: A Practitioners Approach, European Adaption, 5th edn. McGraw-Hill, New York (2000)
3. Tassey, G.: The economic impacts of inadequate infrastructure for software testing. National Institute of Standards and Technology (NIST) (May 2002)
4. Beck, K., Andres, C.: Extreme Programming Explained: Embrace Change, 2nd edn. Addison Wesley, Boston (2005)
5. Park, S.S., Maurer, F.: The benefits and challenges of executable acceptance testing. In: APOS 2008: Proceedings of the 2008 international workshop on Scrutinizing agile practices or shoot-out at the agile corral, pp. 19–22. ACM, New York (2008)

Open Source and Agile Methods:
Two Worlds Closer than It Seems

Hugo Corbucci and Alfredo Goldman

CS - IME - Universidade de São Paulo (USP) - Brazil
{corbucci,gold}@ime.usp.br

Abstract. Agile methods and Free, Libre and Open Source Software communities have different approaches to produce high quality and successful software in different scenarios. This work presents two surveys, each one directed to one of the communities, aimed to identify communication issues encountered in each environment. The results provided point out to very different communities with common practices and behaviors but with very similar problems and view points to solve the issues encountered.

Keywords: agile methods, open source, distributed agile.

Free, Libre and Open Source Software (FLOSS) projects share several principles with the agile community. Eric Raymond quotes Linus Torvalds [1] about two specific development policies for the Linux Kernel: "Release early. Release often. And listen to your customers." and "Given a large enough beta-tester and co-developer base, almost every problem will be characterized quickly and the fix obvious to someone.". The first policy hints at an iterative and short development process with frequent feedback. The second points to many frequent tests. Both concerns are key elements to the agile manifesto [2]. Agile methods suggest constant face to face contact to mitigate communication issues while FLOSS is usually distributed and run by people that only meet through the Internet [3]. Could there be a way to improve development in distributed environments with changing requirements by using ideas from both?

Survey 1: To evaluate this possibility, we elaborated two surveys. The first one (www.ime.usp.br/~corbucci/floss-survey), aimed to the FLOSS community, collected data between 07/28 and 11/01/2009. The survey received 309 entries of which 7 were invalid and 122 were from people who never contributed to a FLOSS project. This shows that only about 60% of this community actually contributes with projects. The analysis was performed over the 180 answers left.

The answering public had 28 years of age averagely. The team sizes and role distribution matched the pattern identified in other FLOSS surveys [4]. The main communication channels within the team are mailing lists (27%) and Internet Relay Chat (IRC - 23%) and face to face (15%). Mailing lists were evaluated to be 44% effective against 52% for IRC channels and 49% for face to face. With the growing adoption of fast feedback channels over the Internet, mailing lists are showing signs of weakness comparing to higher bandwidth channels.

A. Sillitti et al. (Eds.): XP 2010, LNBIP 48, pp. 383–384, 2010.

Regarding user communication, mailing lists were the most used (32%) followed by websites (18%) and IRC, e-mails and issue trackers (11% each). About quality of communication, IRC scores 49% effectiveness against 44% for mailing lists, 37% for websites, 33% for issue trackers and 23% for e-mails.

The most useful tools to help the participants evolve their projects were automatic e-mail/message on build failure. Followed dynamic roadmap status from the issue tracking system and issue tracking management from repository commit logs. Several answers said that they already had messages on build failure so tools might not be the main issue.

Survey 2: Regarding the survey (`www.ime.usp.br/~corbucci/agile-survey`) aimed to the agile community, answers were collected from 10/01 to 12/01/2009. It received 195 valid answers. 14% of the participants had no experience in agile, 51% were involved in at most 2 agile projects and 23% were in more than 5. For the rest of the work, participants without agile experience will not be counted.

When it comes to team sizes, smaller teams are obviously preferred. 37% of teams have up to 5 people and 46% between 6 to 10. About 70% of those teams have face to face communication with their clients and evaluate the quality of such communication around 67%. In distributed environments, the results show that there is no consensus regarding the best communication channel within the team. However, there is a clearly less effective one – e-mails rated only 31% effectiveness. This can explain why 56% of the participants stated that "discovering what the clients want" is the biggest problem they face.

Regarding the useful tools to help agile practitioners, the results are very similar to the ones listed by FLOSS contributors. It is also no surprise that for the 35% of agilists who contribute to FLOSS projects, the problems encountered in their FLOSS environments and the tools to solve them are the same as in their agile environment. However, participants graded their FLOSS project to be only 56% agile so the similarity does not come from the projects being agile.

Conclusion: The results of the surveys indicate that the communities themselves are not that close to each other even if the mindset is quite similar. When it comes to the tools still missing, both communities share the same issues and hope to facilitate integration between developers and increase the frequency of feedback input. Both FLOSS and agile projects indicate better results by using fast feedback communication channels to communicate within the team.

References

1. Raymond, E.: The Cathedral & the Bazaar: Musings on Linux and Open Source by an Accidental Revolutionary (1999)
2. Beck, K., Cockburn, A., Cunningham, W., Fowler, M., Schwaber, K., et al.: Manifesto for Agile Software Development (2001), http://agilemanifesto.org
3. Dempsey, B., Weiss, D., Jones, P., Greenberg, J.: A quantitative profile of a community of open source Linux developers (1999)
4. International Institute of Infonomics - University of Maastricht: Free/Libre/Open Source Software: Survey and Study - Report, http://www.flossproject.org/report/

A Technique to Classify and Compare Agile Methods

João M. Fernandes and Mauro Almeida

Departamento de Informática / CCTC, Universidade do Minho, Braga, Portugal

Abstract. This manuscript describes a technique to perform comparisons on agile methods, based on a set of relevant features and attributes. This set includes attributes related to four SWEBOK Knowledge Areas (KAs) and to the Agile Manifesto principles. With this set of attributes, by analyzing the practices proposed by each method, we are able to assess (1) the coverage degree for the considered KAs and (2) the agility degree.

1   Introduction

This manuscript presents a technique to compare and classify agile methods, using as criteria a set of selected attributes. The proposed technique is exemplified by comparing two agile methods: XP and Scrum. The technique intends to be a contribution for the creation of a guide to help developers on the selection of the software development method (with a specific focus on agile methods) that best fits a given development context. The attributes chosen for this study were selected (1) to assess the coverage degree of each method to four SWEBOK KAs which are transversal to all development methods, and (2) to assess the agility degree for each method.

2   Proposed Technique

We have chosen to distil a set of important features inductively from several methods and compare each method agains it [1]. Regarding the attributes used in our technique, we selected four of the eleven knowledge areas (KAs) defined in the SWEBOK [2]: (1) Software Requirements, (2) Software Construction, (3) Software Testing, and (4) Software Engineering Management. With this subset of attributes, we intend to assess the coverage degree of each method with respect to the selected KAs. A fifth attribute, which relates the Agile Manifesto principles and the practices advocated by a given agile method, was selected to assess the agility degree of the methods.

To classify the existence of practices, advocated by the agile methods, that support the selected KAs, and to characterise the coverage of the principles of the Agile Manifesto by each method, there criteria were considered: (1) **NS – Not Satisfied** (the proposed practices/concepts of the method do not support the sub-attribute or principle); (2) **PS – Partially Satisfied** (the proposed practices/concepts support the sub-attribute or principle, but some of its aspects are not considered); (3) **FS – Fully Satisfied** (the proposed practices/concepts entirely support the sub-attribute or principle).

The challenge in quantifying the coverage of a given sub-attribute or principle, by a set of practices proposed by each analysed method, has lead to the choice of a qualitative

A. Sillitti et al. (Eds.): XP 2010, LNBIP 48, pp. 385–386, 2010.

classification system. Although simple, a qualitative classification system satisfies the objective of our technique.

Due to space limitations, we just consider the results for the Software Requirements attribute, but similar exercises are available for the other attributes. Concerning this attribute, each agile method was analysed against all the following sub-attributes: (1) Software Requirements Fundamentals, (2) Requirements Process, (3) Requirements Elicitation, (4) Requirements Analysis, and (5) Requirements Validation.

3   Comparing XP and Scrum

A summary of the classification of XP and Scrum under this attribute is presented in the next table.

Sub-attribute	XP	Aspects of XP	Scrum	Aspects of Scrum
Software Requirements Fundamentals	Partially Satisfied	– Definition of the concepts related to software requirements; – No distinction between different types of requirements.	Fully Satisfied	– Definition of software requirements related concepts; – Distinction among different types of requirements.
Requirements Process	Fully Satisfied	– Definition of a process to collect, specify, analyze and validate requirements, explicitly defining the actors and activities to be undertaken.	Fully Satisfied	– Pre-game phase; – Sprint planning meeting; – Definition of a process to collect, specify, analyse and validate requirements, explicitly identifying the actors and the activities to be undertaken.
Requirements Elicitation	Fully Satisfied	– On-site client; – User Stories.	Fully Satisfied	– Close interaction between the client and project team in early stages; – Product backlog; – Sprint backlog; – Possibility for any of the evolved entities to add a new element to the Product Backlog.
Requirements Analysis	Partially Satisfied	– Classification of requirements by setting priorities (business value criteria); – No techniques for detection and resolution of conflicts between requirements.	Partially Satisfied	– Classification of requirements by setting priorities (business value criteria); – No techniques for detection and resolution of conflicts between requirements.
Requirements Validation	Fully Satisfied	– Functional and acceptance tests written by the client.	Not Satisfied	

Based on this type of classification of the agile methods, a worksheet, available at http://www.di.uminho.pt/~jmf/AgMethComp.xls, allows the generation of a report that helps on the quantitative evaluation of the agile methods considered in a particular context. The user just needs to decide the weights to assign to the sub-attributes and principles that are part of the technique. With the results for all the methods under comparison, a decision can be made regarding the one to use.

References

1. Sol, H.G.: A feature analysis of information systems design methodologies: Methodological considerations. In: IFIP WG 8.1 Working Conference on Feature Analysis of Information Systems Design Methodologies, pp. 1–8 (1983)
2. Abran, A., Bourque, P., Dupuis, R., Moore, J.W. (eds.): Guide to the Software Engineering Body of Knowledge - SWEBOK. IEEE Press, Los Alamitos (2004)

What Language Does Agile Speak?

Rashina Hoda, James Noble, and Stuart Marshall

School of Engineering and Computer Science,
Victoria University of Wellington,
New Zealand
{rashina,kjx,stuart}@ecs.vuw.ac.nz
http://www.ecs.vuw.ac.nz

Abstract. Collaboration-intensive Agile practices are dependent on the development team understanding the customer's perspective and requirements. Through a Grounded Theory study of Agile teams in New Zealand and India, we discovered that a gap between the teams' *technical* language and the customers' *business* language poses a threat to effective team-customer collaboration. We describe this language gap and the 'Translator' role that emerges to bridge it.

Keywords: Agile Software Development, Customer Collaboration, Language Gap, Translator, Grounded Theory.

1   Introduction

Agile software development requires regular collaboration between development teams and their customers, in an effort to build software solutions that meet the customers' needs [1,4,5]. Collaboration-intensive Agile practices, such as release and iteration planning, user acceptance testing, and reviews; are unlikely to succeed unless development teams are able to effectively understand the customers' prespectives and requirements [3,7]. Through a Grounded Theory [2] study of 20 Agile practitioners across 12 different software organizations in New Zealand and India, we discovered this gap between the teams' *technical* language and the customers' *business* language threatens effective team-customer collaboration and found an informal *Translator* role that emerges to bridge this language gap.

2   The Language Gap

As a result our data analysis, we discovered that development teams and their customers use different languages when collaborating on Agile projects. While the development teams use a more *technical* language composed of technical terminology, their customers are used to a more *business* langauge composed of terminology from the customers' business domains. The language gap between development teams and their customers poses a threat to effective team-customer collaboration by limiting their understanding of each other's perspectives. Translation between the two languages was found to be necessary in order to maximize the effectiveness of collaboration-intensive Agile practices and led to the emergence of an informal *Translator* role.

A. Sillitti et al. (Eds.): XP 2010, LNBIP 48, pp. 387–388, 2010.

3   Translators — Bridging the Language Gap

The *Translator* is a development team member responsible for facilitating communication and collaboration between the team and their customers by translating between their respective languages. Initial analysis suggested that the role of the *Translator* was best suited to Business Analysts because of their perceived ability to act as a bridge between the two languages [4]. As our research progressed, we found that most members of mature Agile teams (fluent in use of Agile practices, for usually more than a year) were bilingual: all able to play the *Translator* role. Several participants believed that certain tools and techniques help in becoming a successful *Translator*:

Using a Dictionary. The *dictionary* was an online editable document (wiki) populated by the customers with business terms, their meaning, and their context of use. These business terms were translated directly into code by the team using the same variable names, providing one-to-one mapping between the customers' *business* terms and their *technical* implementation for a given project.

Using Story Cards. Story cards were used by customers to describe requirements in *business* language. The team can be assisted in translating these story cards into *technical* tasks by (a) assigning a coach to guide new teams on the use of story cards and (b) frequent release of software to ascertain the correctness of the translation through customer feedback.

Using Iterative Reasoning. Another key to becoming a *Translator* was found to be the power of questionning proposed technical solutions repeatedly till the abstract business reasoning behind the technical details was unraveled and were clearly aligned with their business drivers. *"Why do we need that database back up procedure? ...right down at the technical level [asking] the question why, why, why till...you'll eventually discover there's a good business reason for having it."* (Senior Agile Coach, NZ)

Promoting Cross-functionality. Interactions between members from diverse disciplines fosters understanding of the project from multiple perspectives [6]. As the team learns to understand their customer's perspective, they achieve greater levels of crossfunctionality and are able to translate between their respective languages.

References

1. Dybå, T., Dingsoyr, T.: Empirical Studies of Agile Software Development: A Systematic Review. J. Inf. Softw. Technol. 50(9-10), 833–859 (2008)
2. Glaser, B., Strauss, A.L.: The Discovery of Grounded Theory. Aldine, Chicago (1967)
3. Grisham, P.S., Perry, D.E.: Customer relationships and Extreme Programming. In: Proceedings of HSSE 2005. ACM, New York (2005)
4. Hoda, R., Noble, J., Marshall, S.: Organizing Self-Organizing Teams. In: Proceedings of ICSE 2010, Cape Town (to appear May 2010)
5. Highsmith, J., Fowler, M.: The Agile Manifesto. Soft. Dev. Magazine 9(8), 29–30 (2001)
6. Takeuchi, H., et al.: The new new product development game. Harvard Bus. Review (1986)
7. Misra, S.C., Kumar, V., Kumar, U.: Identifying some important success factors in adopting agile software development practices. J. Syst. Softw. 82(11), 1869–1890 (2009)

Combining Open Space Technology (OST) with XP through Scenarios for Enhanced Requirements Elicitation

Sandra Kelly, Frank Keenan, David Connolly, and Namgyal Damdul

Software Technology Research Centre,
Dundalk Institute of Technology, Dublin Rd, Dundalk, Ireland
{sandra.kelly,frank.keenan,david.connolly,
namgyal.damdul}@dkit.ie

Abstract. Numerous reports indicate that problems exist with the requirements phase of software development. Although agile approaches help, challenges that still exist involve supporting multiple diverse stakeholders including developers in understanding and representing a problem domain. This poster proposes the combination of Open Space Technology (OST) with eXtreme Programming (XP) through Scenarios to better facilitate all relevant stakeholders during requirements elicitation.

Keywords: Open Space, Scenarios, eXtreme Programming.

1 Introduction

Despite numerous techniques that exist for requirements development, there is an alarming failure rate attributed to the requirements phase in software development [1]. Agile approaches document requirements briefly to facilitate initial planning with further detail added later. eXtreme Programming (XP) employs user stories but despite widespread adoption reported problems include: involving appropriate stakeholders; conflicting requirements; and seeing beyond the current situation. Although the development team works closely with a customer representative, they often find it difficult to "understand the problem domain making it difficult to understand requirements" [2]. Face-to-face communication and interaction through Active Stakeholder Participation is strongly encouraged typically with a single representative present during development, however, supporting this representative is often difficult in complex situations involving multiple diverse stakeholders.

A potential solution is offered through OST which is recommended for complex situations involving a diverse participants and the need for a quick decision required [3]. However, in general an OST investigation can take time and produce substantial documentation. For use in an agile context it is necessary to streamline OST. In this work, OST is used by stakeholders, including developers, to discuss and agree a theme to focus progress. Concerns raised are explored by the stakeholders using simple tools such as flipcharts, paper and markers. Concerns can represent high level requirements which are eventually prioritized. Stakeholders subsequently develop

A. Sillitti et al. (Eds.): XP 2010, LNBIP 48, pp. 389–390, 2010.

pictorial and textual scenarios for the highest priority concern. From this more focused view user stories are then developed before the next 'concern' is considered. The OST session is conducted in a situation similar to a stand-up meeting.

2 Evaluation

A case study was conducted with 14 final year computing students, divided into two even groups, one followed XP and the other the OST/XP combination. During development each had access to a customer representative. Both teams were required to address the same problem, a "Student Registration" system, within an eight hour time frame spread across four separate sessions. Observations were recorded regularly and questionnaires were also used to collect data. The OST/XP group consistently referred to the artifacts during implementation. It appeared that the initial OST meeting did create an environment where viewpoints were easily exchanged, which initially appears to have helped the team to form a common understanding of the project. The XP group appeared to take a more plan-driven approach with a large initial design. The OST group seemed to be more focused on and better understand the whole problem. Observations indicated that scope creep was an issue for the XP group. Also, they initially expressed difficulty using XP "because it doesn't provide a clear path". Feedback indicated that overall the OST/XP group agreed that the combined approach was beneficial for: exploring requirements with the customer prior to writing stories; clarifying misunderstandings amongst the group; prioritizing requirements and writing user stories.

Despite extra time required initially, the OST/XP group did not appear to suffer in terms of productivity with at least as much functionality developed by the project end. Also, user stories and acceptance tests appeared to be of higher quality. This initial study, although limited, has provided positive feedback indicating that the OST/XP combination is helpful for exploring and clarifying requirements prior to writing user stories and that this can be achieved in an agile manner. This approach needs to be streamlined for effective use and future work will establish how this can be achieved.

References

1. Davis, C.J., Fuller, R.M., Tremblay, M.C., Berndt, D.J.: Communication Challenges in Requirements Elicitation and the Use of the Repertory Grid Technique. Journal of Computer Information Systems 46(5), 78 (2006)
2. Agile Requirements Modeling, http://www.agilemodeling.com/essays/agileRequirements.htm#Challenges
3. Owen, H.: Tales from Open Space. Abbot Publishing, Maryland (1995)

Balancing Scrum Project Management Process

Marion Lepmets[1] and Margus Nael[2]

[1] Institute of Cybernetics at Tallinn University of Technology
marion.lepmets@ttu.ee
[2] Tallinn University of Technology, Department of Computer Engineering
margus.nael@gmail.com

Abstract. We present a case of a previously plan-driven software development company going agile and requiring a balance between the two methods in its transition. As a result of our theoretical research, we provide a balanced project management process that has the agility of Scrum with the additional practices addressing the organizational context from plan-driven methods.

Keywords: Agile, Scrum, plan-driven methods, project management, CMMI, ISO/IEC 15504, PMBoK.

1 Introduction and Background

The goal of agile software development is to increase the ability to react and respond to changing business, customer and technological needs at all organizational levels (Abrahamsson et al. 2003). For a company in transition towards agile software development there is a need for practices and guidance for implementing and supporting an agile approach across the organization. This organizational context helps eliminate the suspicion about agility described by Boehm and Turner in (2004) that agility without discipline is the unencumbered enthusiasm of a startup company before it has to turn a profit. In our paper we will relate the Scrum project management practices with the already established practices of project management. As a result of our theoretical research, we suggest a balanced process of project management practices.

2 Balanced Process of Project Management

We modeled the Scrum process in industry to detailed project management practice level and grouped them with the plan-driven project management practices derived from CMMI, IS 15504, the PMBoK and project management literature. We then analyzed the plan-driven practices described in (Lepmets 2007) that didn't have corresponding Scrum practice for possible benefits of implementing them in the balanced process based on the relevant literature. Finally, we modeled a balanced process that has one new practice and two new artifacts that address the organizational level and should allow for better estimation and project performance.

A. Sillitti et al. (Eds.): XP 2010, LNBIP 48, pp. 391–392, 2010.

The new practice is called the release retrospective and stands for collecting and sharing information about the project after the release. This practice has an output of release retrospective report that is shared across the organization for everyone to learn from the failure and success factors of the completed project in order to improve the performance of the future projects.

The other artifact added to the balanced process is the progress status report that should enhance communication between project and organizational levels, allowing management to view the project progress attributes periodically against their estimations. The progress attributes described in the report are tasks, resources, costs, quality and schedule.

3 Conclusions

In our research, we constructed the balanced process of project management that would increase project performance and project estimation accuracy. We modeled the Scrum process in industry to detailed project management practice level and grouped them with the plan-driven project management practices derived from CMMI, IS 15504, the PMBoK and project management literature. We then analyzed the plan-driven practices that didn't have corresponding Scrum practice for possible benefits of implementing them in the balanced process based on the relevant literature. Finally, we modeled a balanced process that has one new practice and two new artifacts that address the organizational level and should allow for better estimation and project performance. With the progress status reports and release retrospective reports the estimation accuracy should increase. The estimation accuracy will be followed after implementation of the balanced process and compared to the earlier estimation results.

References

Abrahamsson, P., Warsta, J., Siponen, M.T., Ronkainen, J.: New Directions on Agile Methods: A Comparative Analysis. In: 25th IEEE International Conference on Software Engineering, Portland, Oregon, 244p. (2003)

Boehm, B., Turner, R.: Balancing Agility and Discipline - A Guide for the Perplexed, 266p. Pearson Education, Boston (2004)

CMMI for Development. CMU/SEI-2006-TR-008, ESC-TR-2006-008, Version 1.2, CMMI Product Team, Software Engineering Institute, 537p. (2006)

ISO/IEC 15504-5. ISO/IEC 15504-5 Information Technology - Process Assessment - Part 5: An Exemplar Process Assessment Model, 1st edn., ISO/IEC JTC1/SC7, 162p. (2006)

Lepmets, M.: Evaluation of Basic Project Management Activities - Study in Software Industry. Tampere University of Technology, Publication 699, Pori, Finland, 223p. (2007), http://dspace.cc.tut.fi/dpub/bitstream/handle/123456789/68/lepmets.pdf?

Project Management Body of Knowledge: A guide to Project Management Body of Knowledge, Project Management Institute, Pennsylvania, 209p. (2000)

TDD Effects:
Are We Measuring the Right Things?

Bruno Pedroso[1], Ricardo Jacobi[1], and Marcelo Pimenta[2]

[1] Universidade de Brasília, Brasília DF, Brasil
brunopedroso@gmail.com, rjacobi@cic.unb.br
[2] Universidade Federal do Rio Grande do Sul, RS, Brasil
mpimenta@inf.ufrgs.br

Abstract. Scientific studies about the impact of Test-Driven Development (TDD) start to appear since 2002, resulting in approximately 30 papers until now [6], [7], [3]. In general the two main evaluated hypothesis are the ones stated by Kent Beck[1]: that TDD produces code with less defects (external quality) and that it produces code that is simpler, less coupled and more cohesive (internal quality). Although studies may suggest good results in term of external quality, it does not conclude too much regarding internal attributes. Common difficulties, like controlling the experiments variables, are generally considered in the studies. But the few conclusions may be result of a bigger problem: we may have adopted wrong hypothesis or assumptions about the practice's benefits.

Keywords: test-driven development, agile software development, testing, design, programming.

1 TDD Does Not Influence Internal Quality Directly

The experiments observing the effects of TDD generally compare the results produced by two different teams (or the same team, two times) using different approaches. It is supposed that the used approach drives the code into specific characteristics that can be observed through code metrics.

The approach of TDD, however, guides the code in no specific direction at all. It helps the programmer assume the control of the evolving code by making its bad-smells [4] easier to observe, and making it safer to change the code. But it does not influence the developed solution directly.

The developers' experience with programming and their knowledge about the problem itself are more relevant factors that influence the final solution developed. This was one of the the conclusions of Müller and Höfer [8].

Let us suppose that two programmers with different experiences are using TDD strictly to develop a given problem. Suppose they both reach the same point, when code can be refactored in a way to make it less coupled, for example. At this point, one of the developers can make the refactoring while the other does not. The reason may be just because his experience does not allows him to see the problem, or because he explicitly decides that coupling is less important than performance. TDD doesn't influence this decision.

A. Sillitti et al. (Eds.): XP 2010, LNBIP 48, pp. 393–394, 2010.

The same programmer can intentionally develop two different solutions, with different characteristics and metrics, following TDD with 100% conformance. One could, as an exercise, develop the same problem two times with different algorithms in mind, and write, for example, a quick-sort and a bubble-sort.

It is even possible to refactor any TDD-produced code in any other functionally equivalent design, creating another TDD-produced code. So, if a TDD programmer produced a code with metrics X instead of Y, it can be just a matter of experience, aesthetic sense, or even luck.

Apparently, we may have made a too big assumption about the effect of TDD in internal quality of code. Maybe we should be observing intermediate results, like Huang and Holcombe [5] - that observe intermediate variables such as process conformance and testing effort -, to measure things such as planning, organization and estimates capacity of the programmer, or the ability to change or correct the design of a "ready" code. Canfora et al. [2], for example, observed the fact that TDD can be more predictable, but it is yet an initial observation that deserves more experimentation and validation.

The fact is that **we may be trying to validate a wrong hypothesis**. When Kent Beck affirmed that TDD generates more cohesive and less coupled code, it can be because he himself values these aspects and then evolved his TDD codes in this particular direction.

Maybe we should review our assumptions and hypothesis in order to derive what are the real benefits of the practice.

References

1. Beck, K.: Aim, fire. IEEE Softw. 18(5), 87–89 (2001)
2. Canfora, G., Cimitile, A., Garcia, F., Piattini, M., Visaggio, C.A.: Evaluating advantages of test driven development: a controlled experiment with professionals. In: ISESE 2006: Proceedings of the 2006 ACM/IEEE international symposium on Empirical software engineering, pp. 364–371. ACM, New York (2006)
3. Desai, C., Janzen, D., Savage, K.: A survey of evidence for test-driven development in academia. SIGCSE Bull. 40(2), 97–101 (2008)
4. Fowler, M.: Refactoring: Improving the Design of Existing Code. Addison Wesley, Reading (1999)
5. Huang, L., Holcombe, M.: Empirical investigation towards the effectiveness of test first programming. Inf. Softw. Technol. 51(1), 182–194 (2009)
6. Janzen, D., Saiedian, H.: Test-driven development: Concepts, taxonomy, and future direction. Computer 38(9), 43–50 (2005)
7. Jeffries, R., Melnik, G.: Guest editors' introduction: Tdd–the art of fearless programming. IEEE Software 24(3), 24–30 (2007)
8. Müller, M.M., Höfer, A.: The effect of experience on the test-driven development process. Empirical Softw. Engg. 12(6), 593–615 (2007)

Pair Programming: The Choice of a Partner

Laura Plonka

Research Centre in Computing, The Open University, Milton Keynes, UK
l.f.plonka@open.ac.uk

1 Introduction

Pair Programming (PP) is a software development practice in which two programmers are working together on one computer, sharing mouse and keyboard [4]. Knowledge transfer is reported to be one of the benefits of PP. A crucial condition in order to achieve knowledge transfer among the whole development team is that developers must swap partners. However, not all developers want to work with everyone else. Begel and Nagappan [1] reported that "finding a compatible partner is a difficult process". Therefore, we focus on the following question:

- *Which factors influence the choice of a pair programming partner in industrial settings?*

The current literature addressing this question is sparse. Begel *et al* [1], Choi [2] and Vanhanen *et al* [3] conducted surveys and identified PP problems, attributes of good pairing partners, for example flexibility and good communication, and factors that influence PP. These studies provide a good general overview of PP issues, but do not make a detailed analysis of the factors that influence the choice of partner. We used a different data gathering approach which enabled us to make such an analysis.

2 Data Gathering and Analysis

We conducted semi-structured interviews involving three different teams in different companies. Each development team consisted of 8-10 developers. The number of developers interviewed in each team varied from 6 to 7. All teams used agile software development processes. One company had just introduced agile software development and PP while the other two companies had been using agile approaches and PP for at least one year. The interviews were part of a larger data gathering process about PP and were conducted with pairs of developers who had worked together as a pair before. All interviews were transcribed and analysed using qualitative methods.

3 Results

We found four different categories of factors that influence the choice of a partner. The categories can be briefly summarised as follow:

A. Sillitti et al. (Eds.): XP 2010, LNBIP 48, pp. 395–396, 2010.

Workstation. Developer pairs are working on one computer. This implies that one developer is always working on an unfamiliar computer. This issue is unavoidable but nevertheless developers reported that working on an unfamiliar computer is especially challenging if computers are very customised. Customisation can include different IDE Plug-Ins, shortcuts, tools or different operating systems.

Organisational issues. Often developers have a special field of expertise and therefore they are working on a specific part of the software. This limits their choices for partners: some developers cannot find a suitable partner for a task or they only work with developers who have a similar field of expertise.

Working Habits/Programming style. Developers use different approaches to solving a development task. Some developers follow a very systematic approach with upfront planning while others work in a spontaneous "trial and error" mode. Furthermore, some developers prefer to use always certain programming practices for example the test-first approach. Developers stated that very different approaches can lead to continuous discussions about basic principles and that they prefer to work with someone with a similar approach.

Personal and skill differences. Some experienced developers are worried that a less skilful partner might slow down their progress. In general, experienced developers stated that they prefer to work with a partner with a similar "speed of thinking and typing". For the less skilful partner it is more important that the more skilful partner has the ability to explain intelligibly and is patient.

Our results provide detailed insights into factors that influence the choice of a partner and a confirmation of the factors reported by [1,2,3], as well as identifying new factors for example the category "workstation".

Acknowledgements

The author would like to thank the participating companies: disy Informationssysteme GmbH, FlowFact AG, and optivo GmbH.

References

1. Begel, A., Nagappan, N.: Pair programming: what's in it for me? In: ESEM 2008: Proceedings of the Second ACM-IEEE international symposium on Empirical software engineering and measurement, pp. 120–128. ACM, New York (2008)
2. Choi, K.: Team programming influencing factors: A field survey. Journal of International Technology and Management 18, 1–13 (2007)
3. Vanhanen, J., Lassenius, C., Mantyla, M.V.: Issues and tactics when adopting pair programming: A longitudinal case study. In: ICSEA 2007: Proceedings of the International Conference on Software Engineering Advances, p. 70. IEEE Computer Society, Los Alamitos (2007)
4. Williams, L., Kessler, R.: Pair programming illuminated. Addison-Wesley Longman Publishing Co., Inc., Boston (2002)

Agile Adoption Strategies in the Context of Agile in the Large: FLEXI Agile Adoption Industrial Inventory

Anna Rohunen[1], Pilar Rodriguez[1,2], Pasi Kuvaja[1], Lech Krzanik[1],
Jouni Markkula[1], and Burak Turhan[1]

[1] University of Oulu, Department of Information Processing Sciences,
P.O. Box 3000, 90014 University of Oulu, Finland
[2] Technical University of Madrid (UPM), E.U. Informatica,
Ctra. Valencia Km. 7, E-28031 Madrid, Spain
{Anna.Rohunen,Pilar.Rodriguez,Pasi.Kuvaja,Lech.Krzanik,
Jouni.Markkula,Burak.Turhan}@oulu.fi

Abstract. FLEXI Agile Adoption Industrial Inventory (FLEXI AAII) was intended to amass current knowledge and experiences about agile adoption strategies in large settings. It was conducted among industrial partners of FLEXI project (see acknowledgements) by reviewing project deliverables, publications and other relevant material. The ground for FLEXI AAII was based on an extensive literature analysis on existing agile adoption strategies. FLEXI AAII identified new approaches to manage the restrictions of adopting conventional agile methodologies, along with a comparison to reported approaches in the literature. These new approaches are: combining different agile adoption strategies and taking multidimensional nature of agility in the preliminary activities of agile adoption into account.

Keywords: Strategies in adoption of agile methodologies, agile in the large.

1 Objectives

The aim of FLEXI Agile Adoption Industrial Inventory (FLEXI AAII) was to amass and analyze current knowledge about strategies to adopt agile methods, especially in the context of agile in the large. The objective of it was also to identify new approaches for managing the restrictions of adopting conventional agile methods and for finding relevant future research issues.

2 Results

FLEXI AAII is based on a literature analysis on existing agile adoption frameworks and strategies. The main observations of FLEXI AAII were classified into three categories related to adoption of agile methods: 1) Strategy types, 2) Stages of strategies, and 3) Managing dependencies between different agile practices.

A. Sillitti et al. (Eds.): XP 2010, LNBIP 48, pp. 397–398, 2010.

It was discovered that in large settings agile adoption strategies are often incremental [1, 2, 3] and the continuous implementation of new agile practices is emphasized [1, 3]. In addition, both bottom-up and top-down strategies are needed in parallel [4]. Monitoring the response to changes and adjusting the adoption process accordingly were also discovered as prerequisites of a successful change process [3]. Furthermore, two rough stages of agile adoption were identified: 1) Preliminary activities (agility goals, means of agility, selection of agile practices, enabling factors and conditions), and 2) Introduction and implementation of agile practices [1, 2, 5]. Finally, in an incremental agile adoption process, dependencies between practices affect the order in which the practices will be adopted, and industrial partners highlight the role of key practices that enable quick feedback and adaptation (e.g. short iterations and retrospectives) [3].

3 Future Work

In FLEXI AAII, several starting points for potential future studies were identified: combining different agile adoption strategies, discovering preliminary activities in large settings from the viewpoint of multidimensional nature of agility (e.g. product and enterprise agility), and proper selection and use of key practices when adopting agile. Surveys and interviews among industrial partners are needed to obtain more detailed information in these areas.

Acknowledgments. This study has been carried out in ITEA2 project E06022 FLEXI, "Flexible global product development and integration: From idea to product in 6 months."

References

1. Sidky, A., Arthur, J.: A Disciplined Approach to Adopting Agile Practices: The Agile Adoption Framework. Innovations in Systems and Software Engineering 3(3), 203–216 (2007)
2. Sureshchandra, K., Shrinivasavadhani, J.: Adopting Agile in Distributed Development. In: Proceedings of the 2008 IEEE International Conference on Global Software Engineering, pp. 217–221 (2008)
3. Vilkki, K.: Juggling with the Paradoxes of Agile Transformation. Power Point presentation. In: XP (2008)
4. Vilkki, K.: Juggling with the Paradoxes of Agile Transformation or How to survive in a large scale agile transformation. An article in FLEXI Newsletter (February 2008)
5. Kettunen, P., Laanti, M.: Combining Agile Software Projects and Large-scale Organizational Agility. Software Process Improvement and Practice 13(2) (2008)

Educating 'RITA' with XP

Syed-Abdullah Sharifah-Lailee and Omar Mazni

Department of Computer Sciences, Faculty of Computer Sciences and Mathematics,
Universiti Teknologi MARA, Arau Campus, 02600 Arau, Malaysia
shlailee@perlis.uitm.edu.my, mazni@isiswa.uitm.edu.my

Abstract. The purpose of this paper is to discuss the importance of using XP activities to generate enthusiasm resulted from the positive affectivity of these activities. Quantitative method was used to collect empirical data and the statistical analysis was applied to infer the possibble conclusion on the relationship and the effect of applying XP activities. It can be concluded that selective XP activities do have the ability to improve the students' enthusiasm and performance.

Keywords: XP, enthusiasm, quality software.

1 Introduction

Educating Rita is a British comedy about a working class girl who wants to better herself by studying literature. Her assigned professor soon develops misgiving about her ability to adapt to academia based on her lack of education but her enthusiasm towards education soon overcome the initial difficulties between them. The play shows that with enough enthusiasm, it is possible to educate weak student. Therefore, it is the intention of this paper to discuss the elements in XP that increases enthusiasm amongst its users and consequently become a better tool for training weak students. This study is important because it revealed how the different elements in XP, when in used with each other, are synonym to the perspective of behaviourism and thus makes the teaching and learning process more enjoyable. This was achieved by incorporating social reinforces and focusing on the learners' appeal [1].

2 Methods and Result

The study was designed to investigate the effectiveness of using XP activities as teaching tools to train weak student-developers in two universities in Malaysia. We analysed 8 teams which composed of 28 students. 4 teams were students majoring in Quantitative Science, and the rest were students majoring in Artificial Intelligence. Even though these students must be taught formal approach to software development, the insufficient knowledge in programming amongst the students demand a more innovative approach for them to appreciate the fun of designing, creating and developing a web-based application project. Thus, the researchers resorted to introducing XP as an alternative approach to learning software engineering. The evaluators for

A. Sillitti et al. (Eds.): XP 2010, LNBIP 48, pp. 399–400, 2010.

these projects were lecturers who were not involved in the courses and the evaluations made were based on the quality of the projects delivered. To measure the students' state of enthusiasm, the positive affect scale of Positive and Negative Affect Schedule (PANAS) was used [2]. Positive affect was induced by introducing and requiring the XP activities to be used by the teams. The overall results from the study show an increase in the students' positive affectivity [2] and high quality software being delivered. This shows that activities which emphasize human potential and creativity such as XP activities do have influences in producing quality result. In this study, through the use of selected XP activities, instructional exercises [3] such as a) positive and corrective feedback, b) maintaining momentum and effective pacing and c) managing students during seatwork, do have the effect of alleviating weak students' emotion and performances. Feedback can increase or decrease defensiveness. XP activities demand constant communications with clients and thereby ensuring the most dynamic requirements to be met. Momentum in this study refers to situations and activities that exhibit certain pattern that is recognizable by the students. XP activities such as simple stories and pair program enable momentum to be generated early, because partial requirement can be understood and executed early in the development phase. Momentum is then maintained through continuous testing and integration of the project modules and thus modifies the ways weak students work. As a result, the students were more alert and committed towards their project. This is important in training and pushing weak students to achieve better performance. The instructional goals of seatwork [4] such as pair programming is to have students practice new skills, develop independent working skills, self check their work, and pace themselves through a set of task. By undertaking XP activities such as pair programming and planning games, students learn to use emotion to enhance the thinking process because specific skills such as paying attention, taking other persons perspective and thinking differently enable members to shift the thinking process which allow them to tackle complex problem.

Acknowledgments. The authors would like to thank all the lecturers, participants and clients for their support and cooperation in this study.

References

1. Molenda, M.: The Programmed Instruction Era: When Effectiveness Mattered. TechTrends 52, 52–58 (2008)
2. Sharifah-Lailee, S.-A., Mazni, O., Mohd-Nasir, A.H., Che-Latifah, I., Kamaruzaman, J.: Positive Affects Inducer on Software Quality. Computer and Information Science 2, 64–70 (2009)
3. Scheeler, M.C.: Generalizing Effective Teaching Skills: The Missing Link in Teacher Preparation. Journal of Behavioral Education 17, 145–159 (2008)
4. Riggio, R.E., Lee, J.: Emotional and interpersonal competencies and leader development. Human Resource and Management Review 17, 418–426 (2007)

A Multiple Case Study of Teamwork in Norwegian Software Development Organizations

Viktoria Gulliksen

Department of Informatics, University of Oslo, NO-0316 Oslo, Norway
viktoria.gulliksen@gmail.com

Keywords: Effective teamwork, collaborative leadership.

1 Introduction

The concept of autonomous and self-managing teams is recognized as one of the premises for succeeding with innovative projects, because it brings decision-making authority to the level of operational problems and uncertainties and, thus, increases the speed and accuracy of problem solving. Moreover, research suggests that teams with collaborative leadership outperform teams with less participatory forms of leadership. This strongly suggests a transition from traditional command-and-control management to collaborative leadership where leadership is shared both within teams and across teams. However, research on team performance indicates that the effects of autonomous work groups are highly situational dependent and that the effects of autonomous work-group practices depend on factors such as the nature of the workforce and the nature of the organization. Importantly, research also indicates that self-managing groups can be expected to be more successful in turbulent environments – the typical environments of software teams.

2 Objective and What to Achieve

The general topic is how to achieve effective teamwork and coordination across teams in national and global software development projects. My PhD work will focus on how to meet the challenges associated with introducing autonomous teams by providing direct answers to the complex questions about the "fit" of autonomous (and related forms of) workgroups in software development. What to achieve will be clearer when the first investigation of four companies that take part in the TeamIT research project, which also funds my PhD, has been carried out.

Two consultancy companies and two, partly global, companies that develop large, in-house software applications will be the hosts of my case studies. All companies work with agile methods, mainly Scrum. The study will be an embedded multiple case study with the units of analysis at the team level as well as at the organizational/departmental level If time allows, and if it can be integrated into the focus of my PhD, I may also include as a case aspects of teamwork in a global open source development project (http://www.ifi.uio.no/research/groups/gi/hisp.html).

A. Sillitti et al. (Eds.): XP 2010, LNBIP 48, pp. 401–402, 2010.

3 Research Questions, Theories and Research Method, and Data Collection and Analysis

The final research questions remains to be defined. Possible research questions are:

- How to meet the challenge in teamwork and how to make use of all the knowledge and skills in a team, and facilitate collaborative problem solving?
- How to establish and sustain shared leadership among the participants in the team, roles in the team and the general leadership in the company?
- How to achieve shared and overlapping competence to support flexibility in teamwork in a cost-effective way?

There are several relevant theories that can be used as a frame of reference for my case study, see the reference list.

The principal research method will be case studies in the four companies of the TeamIT project. Preferably, I will try to identify common problems and challenges in the companies as far as possible in order to compare the different cases with respect to the same research question, that is, I would like to conduct a multiple case study. Since the goal is to achieve actual improvement in the companies, the research method would also have aspects of action research. The selection of cases in this study will be pragmatic in that one of the intentions of the overall project, TeamIT, is to contribute to innovation of the software processes in the participating companies. The four companies can therefore be considered as a convenience sample of cases.

For data collection, I intend to follow the advice by Lethbridge et al., (Studying Software Engineers: Data Collection Techniques for Software Field Studies, *Empirical Software Engineering*, 10: 311-341, 2005). Data will be collected through interviews, observation and document analysis.

The interviews will be transcribed and coded. To simplify this process, some of the interviews will be (semi) structured. Data analysis will for the most part be based on Miles and Huberman (*Qualitative Data Analysis: An Expanded Sourcebook*, 2nd ed., Sage 1994), but will, among other things, depend on the kind of data I will collect, for example, what kind of documents that I find relevant and that I get access to.

References

1. Trist, E.: The evolution of socio-technical systems: a conceptual framework and an action research program. Ontario Quality of Working Life Centre, Ontario (1981)
2. Trist, E., Murray, H. (eds.): The Social Engagement of Social Science: A Tavistock Anthology. The Socio-Technical Systems Perspective, vol. II. University of Pennsylvania Press, Philadelphia (1997)
3. Guzzo, R.A., Dickson, M.W.: Teams in organizations: Recent research on performance and effectiveness. Annual Review of Psychology 47, 307–338 (1996)
4. Hoegl, M., Parboteeah, K.P.: Autonomy and teamwork in innovative projects. Human Resource Management 45(1), 67–79 (2006)
5. Langfred, C.W.: The paradox of self-management: Individual and group autonomy in work groups. Journal of Organizational Behavior 21(5), 563–585 (2000)

A Systematic Approach for Selection and Adoption of Agile Practices in Component-Based Projects

Iva Krasteva and Sylvia Ilieva

Sofia University St. Kliment Ohriski, 65 Akad. J. Boucher str.,
Sofia, Bulgaria
ivak@rila.bg, sylvia@acad.bg

1 Introduction

A lot of success stories of the adoption of agile development in continually growing number of software domains and projects have been published. However, every single adoption has unique challenges as well as general guidelines (e.g. [1]) which should be addressed when agile practices are introduced into a project. Depending on particular characteristics of the project, environment and people, certain considerations of the applicability of agile practices should be taken into account. In addition, the agile approach encourages adaptation and customization of the development method throughout the execution of the project, which makes the adoption process continuous and interactive activity.

Current PhD thesis seeks how to identify those practices that are the most applicable in given project situation and suggests a systematic way to introduce them into the development practice of a given organization. Case studies of the applicability of agile practices in the domain of component-based development are planned as a primary target for validation of the approach.

2 Description of the Study

The objective of this PhD thesis is the proposition of systematic approach for selection and introduction of agile practices that are the most appropriate for given project situation. Since the execution of such a general approach could involve huge volume of information and a lot of irrelevant data, we are targeting only projects in the field of component-based development including the development of both components and systems, based on components. The following questions formulate the two main directions of the research:

- How is the appropriateness of agile practices applicability analyzed?
- How is the new development method engineered systematically?

The appropriateness is assumed by considering both theoretical and empirical studies on agile practices applicability. A knowledge-base is designed to serve that purpose. It stores information for applicability of particular agile practice when given project situation is present. Factors that have been identified to characterize projects and have effect on agile practices adoption are selected for description of different project

A. Sillitti et al. (Eds.): XP 2010, LNBIP 48, pp. 403–404, 2010.

situations. The data is collected by systematic literature reviews as well as by conducting a survey on practices used in industrial component-based projects. Both qualitative and quantitative methods can be executed for data analysis. Through statistical methods, patterns for practices adoption in different project situations can be drown from a good number of empirical evidences.

The selected practices are introduced in the development process of the organization and a new method is created following a method engineering approach suggested by us. Method engineering provides theoretical foundation for method creation involving conceptualization, construction and adaptation of methods and tools [4].The approach is going to be exercised by different means so that greater number of project situations is studied. We plan to create simulation models as well as to try it in student projects. Depending on the availability, we hope to be able to execute it in real projects for development of components or component-based systems.

3   Current State

The work carried so far includes definition of the approach, which is built on Software Process Engineering Metamodel [5] and specifies a number of extensions to EPF Composer tool[1] to provide automated support for it. The organization of the knowledge-base is completed and is currently being fed up with data regarding theoretical and empirical applicability of agile practices in component-based projects. The results of the statistical analysis and execution of the approach are still to come.

References

1. Cockburn, A.: Agile Software Development: The Cooperative Game, 2nd edn. Addison-Wesley Professional, Reading (2006)
2. Brinkkemper, S.: Method engineering: engineering of information systems development. Information and Software Technology 38(7), 275–280 (1996)
3. Software process engineering metamodel. Version 2.0. formal/2008-04-01, OMG (2008)

---

[1] http://www.eclipse.org/epf/

Software Development: A Stakeholder Approach

Ken Power

Cisco Systems, Galway, Ireland & National University of Ireland, Galway
ken.power@gmail.com

The objective of this research is to develop a model that helps organizations understand the diversity of stakeholders that influence their product development efforts, provide a means of quantifying the nature of their stake, and understand how agile processes facilitate application of stakeholder theory in software development.

1 The Case

There is a body of knowledge that exists in Agile and Lean practices, organization patterns, and systems design that can help teams become more productive and understand better the context in which they are creating products. Separately, there is a body of knowledge in stakeholder theory that helps organizations understand the needs and influences of different stakeholder groups. A particular focus of my research is on the application of stakeholder concepts to software development, and specifically to geographically distributed product development organizations.

2 Theory

Stakeholder Theory is an area of strategic management that provides models for identifying and mapping stakeholders [1, 2], and for understanding who and what really counts in an organization. As far as I can tell, there is currently no formal use of Stakeholder Theory applied to software product development teams, and software development processes. Although the term stakeholder is often used in software development, it is predominantly limited to customers, end-users, or project sponsors. They do not focus on product development teams as a diverse group of stakeholders with diverse interests. Where there is deeper mention of stakeholders, they typically treat the development team or 'the customer' as a single stakeholder.

3 Research Questions

How can managers of an organization better identify and engage with the stakeholders that influence, and are influenced by, its product development efforts? Some stakeholders will naturally have a higher degree of relative importance, or *salience*, to the organization. There is a model based on attributes of power, legitimacy and urgency that helps managers understand and quantify the degree of salience a stakeholder possesses in terms of salience categories [3]. The category of salience of a

A. Sillitti et al. (Eds.): XP 2010, LNBIP 48, pp. 405–406, 2010.

stakeholder, or stakeholder group, from the perspective of the product development organization can change over time. Can this model help managers to understand what causes this transition, and to predict, and therefore effect or prevent, future transitions? How do agile practices facilitate identification of, and engagement with relevant stakeholder groups?

4 Methods and Selection Strategy

I will collect data through a series of interviews with stakeholders from across the product development organization. Surveys will be used to gather data from a wider community of product stakeholders. I will compare data from multiple products.

A large, geographically distributed organization will serve as the primary source for data collection. This organization has multiple business units, and multiple product development teams. I will also have access to stakeholders from other organizations so that I can compare data, and validate my research proposals from more than one source. I also plan to use workshops to gather data and exchange information with other practitioners and researchers.

5 Outline of Data Analysis Procedures

I have conducted pilot interviews and am in the process of analyzing the data and refining the research instruments. From the research data I have begun to map stakeholders in a product development organization to different stakeholder groups, and to specific salience categories. I have begun to understand the circumstances that cause stakeholders to transition from one category to another, and identify recommendations. This is helping me further refine my overall research questions.

References

[1] Freeman, R.E.: Strategic management: a stakeholder approach. Pitman, Boston (1984)
[2] Freeman, R.E., Harrison, J.S., Wicks, A.C.: Managing for stakeholders: survival, reputation, and success, New Haven, Conn. Yale University Press, London (2007)
[3] Mitchell, R.K., Agle, B.R., Wood, D.J.: Toward a Theory of Stakeholder Identification and Salience: Defining the principle of who and what really counts. Academy of Management Review 22(4), 853–886 (1997)

A Framework for Situated Evaluation of Methodology Usage in Agile Environments

Mali Senapathi

School of Computing and Mathematical Sciences, Auckland University of Technology,
Auckland, New Zealand
mali.senapathi@aut.ac.nz

1 Introduction

While certainly not the "silver bullet" to systems and software development problems, agile methodologies are definitely growing in popularity which is evident in the increasing number of success stories, experience reports and claims of their successful adoption. The majority of the published methodology research literature mainly deals with experimental studies of methodology use either in a single project or with the use of a specific practice such as pair programming with no consideration of the wider issues of systems development which innovations such as agile methods form part of. Research has continued to focus mainly on technical issues rather than on cultural and social aspects [2, 6], and the effect of all contextual and influential factors on usage has not been taken into consideration. Dyba & Dingsoyr [1] believe that the current state of theory and research is still clearly nascent, and highlight the need for exploratory qualitative studies that focuses on human and social factors.

2 Research Approach

The objective of this research is to 1) identify the factors that affect the perceptions of effective usage of agile methodologies, and 2) develop a framework for the situated evaluation of agile methodology usage in organizations by recognizing the significance of context through a thorough review of literature drawn mainly from two major disciplines: Information Systems and Software Engineering. It suggests that usage is at least partly dependent on the context in which it is used/applied, and therefore proposes to identify all the influential factors that affect the successful use of agile methods in authentic contexts of use, (i.e. 'situated evaluation').

The research aims to add value to our knowledge by carrying out evaluation studies of the effectiveness of agile development methodology usage in New Zealand (NZ) organizations to answer the following research questions: How do we define effective usage of Agile Methodology? , How can this be measured? And how can we find out if the use of a specific agile methodology to an IS project is being used in a manner which will be conducive to producing the potential benefits of 'effectiveness' and 'success'?

A. Sillitti et al. (Eds.): XP 2010, LNBIP 48, pp. 407–409, 2010.

3 Preliminary Study

Though anecdotal evidence of its popularity is rising, we do not have any information about the current state of practice of Agile Methodologies in New Zealand. Therefore, the objective of the preliminary study will be to gain an initial understanding of current agile practices and their benefits and challenges as perceived by a sample of early users of agile methodologies in New Zealand. It is intended to provide a broad view of Agile practices in the New Zealand Software Industry, focusing on categories such as size, type of development, popular agile method combinations, adaptations etc., The study will use a survey strategy to identify:

- the current adoption rate of agile usage in New Zealand and
- the factors affecting the adoption and use of Agile Methodologies in New Zealand organizations.

It will be influenced by theories such as diffusion of innovations [4] and IT innovation [3], and aims to empirically validate the factors that would affect Agile methodology usage and their effectiveness in organizations.

4 Research Design

For the preliminary study, it is planned to invite the registered members of the Agile Professionals Network (http://www.agileprofessionals.net) of New Zealand to participate. The data collected from the survey will be analyzed and is expected to inform the next phase of research, i.e. the design and development of the framework for situated evaluation of agile usage. The framework development will also be informed and guided by theoretical foundations and research findings from relevant literature, and intends to use an experiential approach. It is hoped that the identification of both situation specific and general factors will make a useful contribution to the development of grounded theory for effective usage of agile methodologies in organizations. The main differences between the proposed framework and other existing evaluation frameworks are, i) the importance of evaluating agile usage in combination of other development practices and resources in authentic contexts of use will be recognized, and ii) qualitative research based on interpretive and critical paradigms will be the preferred approach over scientific, experimental studies.

5 Research Methodology

Case study strategy using a flexible qualitative approach will be the preferred research method – this will be particularly applicable to novel situations where agile methods are used. Both data and methodological triangulation methods, where different techniques such as first degree (semi-structured interviews), second degree (indirect methods such as observations), and third degree (e.g., documentation) will be used for data collection [5]. The proposed unit of analysis for investigation is an IS project which has been using an agile methodology for a major portion of its development. The framework will be tested by applying it to three significantly different IS projects, each using a different agile method in three different development contexts. According to Runeson & Host [5], such projects can be treated as three units of analysis in an embedded case study where the context is the IS organization in general. The criteria for selection of the cases will be: 1) the project should be mainly intended for use by the organization that develops it; 2) the organization should have successfully implemented at least one previous agile project. The findings from the evaluation of agile usage effectiveness from the case studies will be evaluated, synthesized and conclusions will be derived keeping a clear chain of evidence.

References

1. Dyba, T., Dingsoyr, T.: What do we know about Agile Software Development? IEEE Software, 6–8 (September/October 2009)
2. Glass, R.L., Vessey, I., Rames, V.: Research in Software Engineering: an analysis of the literature. Information and Software Technology 44, 491–506 (2005)
3. Moore, G.C., Benbasat, I.: Development of an instrument to measure the perceptions of adopting an Information Technology innovation. Information Systems Research 2(3), 192–222
4. Rogers, E.M.: Diffusion of Innovations. Free Press, New York (2003)
5. Runeson, P., Höst, M.: Guidelines for conducting and reporting case study research in software engineering. Empirical Software Engineering 14(2), 131–164 (2009)
6. Segal, J., Grinyer, A., Sharp, H.: The type of evidence in produced by empirical software engineering. In: Inverardi, P., Jazayeri, M. (eds.) ICSE 2005. LNCS, vol. 4309. Springer, Heidelberg (2006)

Collaboration in an Agile World

Steven Fraser[1], Bjørn Alterhaug[2], David Anderson[3],
Diana Larsen[4], and Scott Page[5]

[1] Director, Cisco Research Center, USA
sdfraser@acm.org (panel impresario)
[2] Professor, Norwegian University of Science and Technology
bjornalterhaug@gmail.com
[3] President, David J. Anderson & Associates Management Consulting
for Knowledge Workers
dja@djandersonassociates.com
[4] Partner, FutureWorks Consulting and Chair, Agile Alliance, USA
dlarsen@futureworksconsulting.com
[5] Scott E. Page, Leonid Hurwicz Collegiate Professor of Complex Systems,
Political Science, and Economics (University of Michigan, Ann Arbor)
spage@umich.edu

Abstract. Collaboration, the art of working together, is an essential part of system development, often learned on the job rather than by academic training. Aspects of collaboration include: tangible and intangible "results" – the fruits of collaboration; community governance – the norms of ownership and usage; and modes of production – the processes for incubating and developing "results". This panel will bring together a diverse set of experts to share their opinions and strategies for collaboration.

Keywords: collaboration, governance, incubation, ownership, production.

1   Steven Fraser *(panel impresario)*

STEVEN FRASER is the Director of the Cisco Research Center in San Jose California (www.cisco.com/research) with responsibilities for developing university research collaborations and facilitating technology transfer between researchers and Cisco Business Units. Previously, Steven was a member of Qualcomm's Learning Center in San Diego, California enabling technical learning and development in software engineering best practices. Steven held a variety of technology roles at Bell-Northern Research and Nortel including Process Architect, Senior Manager (Global External Research), and Design Process Advisor. In 1994, he was a Visiting Scientist at the Software Engineering Institute (SEI) at Carnegie Mellon University (CMU) collaborating on the development of team-based domain analysis (software reuse) techniques. Fraser was the XP2006 General Chair, the Corporate Support Chair for OOPSLA'07 and OOPSLA'08, Tutorial Chair for both XP2008 and ICSE 2009 and co-Publicity Chair for XP2010. With a doctorate in Electrical Engineering from McGill University in Montréal, Fraser is a member of the ACM and a senior member of the IEEE.

A. Sillitti et al. (Eds.): XP 2010, LNBIP 48, pp. 410–415, 2010.

Aspects of collaboration in the context of software engineering have been described as topics of interest for almost forty years – beginning with the "The Psychology of Computer Programming" by Gerald Weinberg (1971), and "The Mythical Man-Month" by Fred Brooks (1975); – continuing through the 1980s with Tom DeMarco and Tim Lister's "Peopleware" (1987); into the 1990's with Eric S. Raymond's "The Cathedral and the Bazaar" (1999); and more recently with Kent Beck's "Extreme Programming Explained" (2000), Steven Weber's "The Success of Open Source" (2004), and Jean Tabaka's "Collaboration Explained" (2006).

Recently, there has been an emergence of a greater number of self-organizing collaborative teams from groups originally driven by "command and control" centric decision-making. We continue to learn how issues of scale and scope can be best addressed – in part by considering issues of governance which may place constraints on future usage and ownership of the fruits of collaboration (e.g., proprietary ownership, GNU General Public License).

Collaboration depends on inter and intra team communications, and a shared context determined by a common set of norms, beliefs, vocabulary, and goals. Trust and reputation are factors that build on a shared context.

While tools exist to foster a shared context for geographically distributed teams (e.g., tele-presence and web conferencing), it is still hard to match the fidelity of face-to-face interaction. However, even face-to-face teams can require catalysts such as "facilitation" to overcome challenges such as sustaining trust, avoiding groupthink (including false consensus), and a lack of requisite variety (diversity of opinion).

Tweets, blogs, social websites (e.g. Facebook), ultra portable networked digital cameras (both still and video), shared calendaring, location based services, and other emergent devices and services continue to combine in new ways to change the way we learn, communicate, play, work – and collaborate!

2 Bjørn Alterhaug

BJØRN ALTERHAUG is a Professor at the Department of Music, University of Trondheim (NTNU) teaching Bach harmony, arranging, jazz history, music and globalisation, and improvisation. He is a jazz musician and composer. Since 1999 Alterhaug has been leading a research project at NTNU titled *Interdisciplinary Perspectives on Improvisation*.

Alterhaug's use of the word improvisation is not limited only to music traditions; it comprises all kinds of human activity. Improvisation in the meaning of a private, therapeutic spontaneity-ideology, leading to self-indulgence and "love yourself"; is far from his understanding of the topic. Improvisation is rather to be understood as a humanistic project, based on dexterity, knowledge, reflection and solidarity, which can be a great resource in attempts for creating conditions for genuine dialogue in different contexts.

Alterhaug's composition activities have increased in breadth, and his compositions today range from pure treatments of Norwegian folk music to include modern chamber music as well. In 1975 he received the Norwegian Jazz Association's Buddy award, for his first album *Moments* he was awarded with "Spellemannsprisen". He has also been playing with international renowned jazz artists as: Lucky Thompson,

(1969) Ben Webster (1970), Pepper Adams, Bill Hardman / Junior Cook and James Moody (1979), Lee Konitz (1983 and 1985), Chet Baker (1983 and 1984), Harold Land (1986), Joe Henderson / Woody Shaw (1987).

Alterhaug: "To get the best out of music you need to play in your own manner and, of course, be extremely alert to everything that happens during the performance. In this way the individual and collective forces in a team will have the best possibilities to unfold, which leads to the best result through a collective, non-hierarchical approach".

Bjørn Alterhaug has through his double professional life had special opportunities to explore, in a wide range of contexts, processes of musical and verbal dialogues through his own personal experiences worldwide. Alterhaug is as a researcher and musician in a unique position to understand the phenomenology of such experiences and can therefore contribute to our understanding of these dynamics. This kind of knowledge is directly relevant for understanding communication and conditions for dialogue, negotiations and collaboration in a globalized world.

3 David Anderson

DAVID J. ANDERSON, leads a management consulting firm focused on improving performance of technology companies. He has been in software development for more than twenty-five years and has managed teams on agile software development projects at Sprint, Motorola, Microsoft and Corbis. David is credited with the first implementation of a kanban process for software development in 2005. David was a founder of the agile movement through his involvement in the creation of Feature Driven Development. He was also a founder of the APLN, a founding signatory of the Declaration of Interdependence, and a founding member of the Lean Software and Systems Consortium. He moderates several online communities for lean/agile development. He is the author of the book "Agile Management for Software Engineering - Applying the Theory of Constraints for Business Results". Most recently, David has been focused on creating a synergy of the CMMI model for organizational maturity with Agile and Lean methods through projects with Microsoft and the SEI. He is based in Seattle, Washington.

Let's pause for a moment and reflect on that word *advantage*. Within your organization, why would any one group or team require an *advantage* over another? Doesn't the organization have a set of common goals? And isn't the organization supposed to be collaborating to realize those goals? What can obtaining an *advantage* over another group possibly have to do with collaboration?

If you are beginning to think that there ought not to be a position of advantage in a truly collaborative organization, you're thinking along the right lines. Having an *advantage* and collaboration are incompatible. By implication then, information hiding is incompatible with collaboration. And negotiation ought to be unnecessary.

People can argue over the essence of agility or Lean Thinking, but for me optimizing a software development organization for high performance starts with building a high trust organization. High trust organizations are flat. They feature a high degree of empowerment and delegation. They encourage joint responsibility and mutual accountability. High trust organizations adapt dynamically to the needs of the organization regardless of reporting structure or formal organizational hierarchy. High trust organizations are social networks of highly collaborative knowledge workers.

High trust organizations are also lean. They expunge the overheads of low trust environments. High levels of trust and a flat structure mean that audits typical of hierarchies are eliminated and contracts are dispensed with. There is no concept of an internal market. In short, there is no negotiating. Negotiation is waste! The resultant contracts, their documentation, agreement, review and subsequent audit or enforcement are all considered as more waste! Subsequent negotiation for corrective action when required is yet more waste!

Negotiation is a symptom of an organization that has a lot of growth potential in its social capital. If you find yourself negotiating, you know there is room for improvement.

Transparency offers us the ability to turn negotiation in to collaborative problem solving. There is a simple question to be answered, "How best can we select job requests in order to maximize the value delivered through the supplier service?" Together your department and your value-chain partners can analyze and solve this problem. There is no negotiation. Negotiation is replaced by a puzzle of team optimization. Transparency, in this case, creates the opportunity for a collaboration game between consumer and supplier.

Naturally, there are a few snags. The work orders in a transparent system must be of a somewhat similar size. There must be a system of analysis that breaks work down in to types suitable for processing through a transparent system. If work items vary greatly in size, it leads to *need* negotiation. "If I give you two small ones, can you process them as if they were one regular item?" "How do I know they are two small ones?" Or, "We know this one is kind of big but it is really important, could you just squeeze it through?"

Soon you find yourself needing to estimate everything and to analyze the effort involved. Suddenly the problem to be solved revolves around trying to fit effort estimates against a calendar of available work hours. Since everyone knows that estimates are always wrong, and hence, the customer negotiator sharpens up her pencil and once again puts the squeeze on the supplier. I've recommended that organizations stop estimating simply because it opens the door for abusive relationships through negotiation. Now I'm going a step further and ask you to stop negotiating. As part of that plan you need to stop estimating. Play with the facts! Use the hard, objective data, transparently. The hard facts are historical throughput (number of work orders delivered), lead time, quality, and quantity of work-in-progress. Estimates are not bad. They simply open the door to negotiation, reduce trust and leave, hard to build, social capital on the table.

4 Diana Larsen

DIANA LARSEN is a senior consultant and partner at FutureWorks Consulting (www.futureworksconsulting.com) in Portland, Oregon. Diana consults with leaders and teams to create work processes where innovation, inspiration, and imagination flourish. With more than fifteen years of experience working with technical professionals, Diana brings focus to the human systems of organizations, teams and projects. She activates and strengthens her clients' proficiency in shaping an environment for productive teams and thriving in times of change. Diana co-authored "Agile Retrospectives: Making Good Teams Great!" and writes articles and occasional blog posts. Currently serving as chair of the Agile Alliance Board of Directors, she co-founded the Agile Open Northwest conference and the international Retrospective Facilitators Gathering.

XP/Agile teams and projects thrive in an atmosphere of high-bandwidth communication, frequent feedback, and effective collaboration. Many of the practices associated with Agile methods focus on creating an environment where collaboration can flourish – informative workspaces, sitting together, pairing, staying in close contact with the customer, big visible task boards and backlogs, planning meetings, daily meetings, reviews, retrospectives, and so forth. Self-organizing teams can't and don't happen without it. We continually seek to meet the gold standard of the most effective, most efficient interactions – two people working together face-to-face in front of a whiteboard.

Yet very often projects are planned with little attention to fostering collaboration. We assign people to teams (sometimes in far-flung places) without considering their skills, experience, capability, or even personal or electronic tools for collaborating. We ignore conditions that can inhibit collaboration like distance, time zones distribution, lack of travel budget, and cultural misunderstanding and do little to mitigate those risks. We look at easy to measure costs, such as wages, and ignore hard to measure costs like communication delays and hand-offs.

Managers often forget to consider collaboration skills when recruiting – instead relying solely on availability, technical skills, and domain knowledge. In order for an effective, productive team to form, the people involved need basic collaboration skills, such as: the ability to listen and respond to one another; the willingness to disclose one's status; what it means to trust, be trustworthy and make and meet commitments; giving and receiving interpersonal feedback; making decisions in a group; sharing leadership; and many more. One manager told me that he "hired for 'nice'" on his Agile team then ensured they had the collocated space, access to the customer, and tools and equipment to do the job. His project team ultimately exceeded all expectations for success, delivering greater functionality in a shorter time while returning more value than any other previous team in the history of his organization.

It pays to focus on fostering close collaboration among team members, between the team and its customers, and between the team and the organization.

5 Scott Page

SCOTT PAGE grew up in Yankee Springs, Michigan on Gun Lake, and pumped gas and dipped ice cream cones at Page's Resort. Following a modest high school basketball career, Page taught math at the University of Wisconsin-Madison, dressed as a box of Junior Mints for Madison's annual Halloween party, helped unionize the teaching assistants and failed to win an intramural basketball championship. Page earned his PhD in Managerial Economics and Decisions Sciences at the J.L. Kellogg Graduate School of Management at Northwestern University in 1993. Since 2008 Page is the Leonid Hurwicz Collegiate Professor of complex systems, political science, and economics at the University of Michigan and served as director of UM's Center for the Study of Complex Systems. He is also an external faculty member of the Santa Fe Institute.

Page studies the effects of diversity in complex systems. Earlier research focused on how in a world of perfect collaboration, diversity groups should outperform groups of high performing individuals. He's currently interest in how we foster collaboration yet maintain diversity. His work provides mathematical foundations for the power of collaboration. He's currently puzzling over the differences between collaboration in uncertain environments and collaboration on complex problems. At least, that's what he does when he's out walking his dogs.

Author Index